The United States and Asia

ASIA IN WORLD POLITICS
Series Editor: Samuel S. Kim

The United States and Asia

Regional Dynamics and Twenty-First-Century Relations

Robert G. Sutter

ROWMAN & LITTLEFIELD
Lanham • Boulder • New York • London

Published by Rowman & Littlefield
A wholly owned subsidary of The Rowman & Littlefield Publishing Group, Inc.
4501 Forbes Boulevard, Suite 200, Lanham, Maryland 20706
www.rowman.com

Unit A, Whitacre Mews, 26-34 Stannary Street, London SE11 4AB,
United Kingdom

British Library Cataloguing in Publication Information Available

Library of Congress Cataloging-in-Publication Data
Sutter, Robert G., author.The United States and Asia : regional dynamics and twenty-first-
century relations / Robert G. Sutter.
pages cm. — (Asia in world politics)
Includes bibliographical references and index.
ISBN 978-1-4422-2632-6 (cloth : alk. paper) — ISBN 978-1-4422-2633-3 (pbk. : alk.
paper) — ISBN 978-1-4422-2634-0 (electronic)
1. United States—Foreign relations—Asia. 2. Asia—Foreign relations—United States. 3.
United States—Foreign relations—21st century. I. Title.
DS33.4.U6S86 2015
327.7305—dc23
2015014723

∞ ™ The paper used in this publication meets the minimum requirements of American
National Standard for Information Sciences Permanence of Paper for Printed Library
Materials, ANSI/NISO Z39.48-1992.

Printed in the United States of America

Contents

v

Acronyms

ADIZ	air defense identification zone
ADMM+	ASEAN Defense Ministers Plus Forum
AIIB	Asian Infrastructure Investment Bank
ANSF	Afghan National Security Forces
APEC	Asia-Pacific Economic Cooperation
ARF	ASEAN Regional Forum
ASB	air-sea battle
ASEAN	Association of Southeast Asian Nations
BJP	Bharatiya Janata Party
BMD	ballistic missile defense
BOJ	Bank of Japan
BSA	Bilateral Security Agreement
CIS	Commonwealth of Independent States
CSIS	Center for Strategic and International Studies
CST	Collective Security Treaty
CSTO	Collective Security Treaty Organization
CTR	Cooperative Threat Reduction
DMZ	Demilitarized Zone
DOD	Department of Defense
DPJ	Democratic Party of Japan

DPP	Democratic Progressive Party
EAI	Enterprise for ASEAN Initiative
EAS	East Asia Summit
EDCA	Enhanced Defense Cooperation Agreement
ESF	Economic Support Fund
FATA	Federally Administered Tribal Areas
FDI	foreign direct investment
FRF	Futenma Replacement Facility
FTAAP	Free Trade Area of the Asia-Pacific
GATT	General Agreement on Tariffs and Trade
GDP	gross domestic product
GNP	gross national product
GSP	generalized system of preferences
HIG	Hizb-e-Islami Gulbuddin
IAEA	International Atomic Energy Agency
IISS	International Institute for Strategic Studies
IMF	International Monetary Fund
IMU	Islamic Movement of Uzbekistan
IR	international relations
ISAF	International Security Assistance Force
IT	information technology
KMT	Kuomintang
LDP	Liberal Democratic Party
LeT	Lashkar-e-Taiba
LNG	liquefied natural gas
MCAS	Marine Corps Air Station
MFN	most favored nation
NLD	National League for Democracy
NOTAM	notice to airmen
NPT	Nuclear Nonproliferation Treaty
NSG	National Security Guard
NSG	Nuclear Suppliers Group

NSR	New Silk Road
NSSP	Next Steps in Strategic Partnership
NTR	normal trade relations
OECD	Organisation for Economic Co-operation and Development
OFW	overseas Filipino workers
OPIC	Overseas Private Investment Cooperation
PFP	Partnership for Peace
PIF	Pacific Islands Forum
PLA	People's Liberation Army
PNTR	permanent normal trade relations
PPP	purchasing power parity
PRC	People's Republic of China
PSI	Proliferation Security Initiative
QST	Quetta Shura Taliban
RCEP	Regional Comprehensive Economic Partnership
ROC	Republic of China
ROK	Republic of Korea
SAARC	South Asian Association for Regional Cooperation
SACO	Special Action Committee on Okinawa
SBY	Susilo Bambang Yudhoyono
SCO	Shanghai Cooperation Organization
SDF	Self-Defense Forces
SIGAR	special inspector general for Afghanistan reconstruction
SOFA	Status of Forces Agreement
TAC	Treaty of Amity and Cooperation
TEPCO	Tokyo Electric Power Company
TIFA	trade and investment framework agreement
TPA	trade promotion authority
TPP	Trans-Pacific Partnership
TRA	Taiwan Relations Act
TTP	Tehrik-e-Taliban Pakistan

UAV	unmanned aerial vehicle
UMNO	United Malays National Organization
UNCLOS	United Nations Convention on the Law of the Sea
USAID	U.S. Agency for International Development
USCC	U.S. China Economic and Security Review Commission
USMC	U.S. Marine Corps
USTR	U.S. trade representative
VCP	Vietnamese Communist Party
WMD	weapons of mass destruction
WTO	World Trade Organization

Chapter One

Introduction

It's hard to exaggerate Asia's importance for the United States and American foreign relations after the Cold War. The region is by far the most economically dynamic in the world and of fundamental importance in American trade, investment, and international economic exchanges. Of all world powers, only China, with remarkable growth in economic and military power, is in a position to become a so-called peer competitor[1] of the United States, with the potential to seriously challenge and overtake American leadership in regional and international affairs in the twenty-first century. The long-standing and deep American official and unofficial engagement with eastern Asia and the western Pacific over the centuries of U.S. history is reflected most recently in initiatives of the government of President Barack Obama under the rubric of an American "rebalance" policy, explained in detail in chapter 4 of this book. The comprehensive policy shows a broad scope of important and well-founded American interests stretching from India in the west to northern Japan and extending south and east to include all of eastern Asia, Australia, New Zealand, and the Pacific Islands. The rebalance policy notably does not include enhanced American interests in Afghanistan, Pakistan, and Central Asian countries, which for a time after the terrorist attack on America and the start of the U.S.-led war against the terrorist-harboring Taliban regime in Afghanistan in 2001 were at the center of American foreign policy priorities. The importance of relations with these countries is now in decline, along with the American withdrawal of military forces from the Afghanistan conflict.

Given repeated changes in the broad expanse of Asia and the underlying dynamics in American foreign relations, uncertainty characterizes U.S. leadership in the region in the twenty-first century. Security issues abound and challenge American interests in regional stability, free use of global commons, antiterrorism, opposition to the proliferation of weapons of mass destruction (WMD), and a balance of power favorable to the United States. Though Osama bin Laden is dead and the strident emphasis on the war on terrorism is past, the struggle against terrorists continues. In late 2011, U.S.-led allied forces left Iraq, and in 2014 it was announced that U.S. forces were leaving Afghanistan. But American air forces and ground force advisers returned to Iraq in late 2014 to support efforts to counter the extremist Islamic State militants wreaking havoc across a broad swath of Iraq and neighboring Syria. In late 2014, stability in Afghanistan seemed tenuous, depending on the Kabul government, with ambiguous American backing, facing a resurgent Taliban in a contest with important implications for neighboring countries.

North Korea seems constrained and deterred from egregious aggression by U.S.-led military readiness, international sanctions, and pressure from China. But the fact remains that its nuclear weapons and related missile-delivery programs advance while the stability of the regime appears undermined by life-or-death struggles for power.

The serious challenges to American interests posed by a rising China are more likely than any other set of factors to continue to preoccupy American leaders and U.S. relations in Asia for many years to come. Tensions associated with the so-called Taiwan issue have subsided, though China sustains impressive military buildups intended to intimidate Taiwan and deter American involvement. The corresponding U.S. military preparations to discourage and defend against a Chinese attack on Taiwan have underscored for two decades the growing security dilemma between the two major powers of the region. The political situation in Taiwan remains volatile and could result in the choosing of a president in Taiwan's January 2016 election at odds with recent efforts by the Taiwan government to ease tensions with China.

Chinese assertiveness over sovereignty and security issues in the disputed East and South China Seas has developed in tandem with growing Chinese military, coast guard, economic, and diplomatic capabilities and influence. Some regional governments try to finesse the disputes and implicitly accommodate China's demands. A few are prepared to directly confront and challenge China. Those that do, notably U.S. allies Japan and the Philippines, are subjected to Chinese security, economic, and political pressures well beyond prevailing international norms.

Some American and foreign scholars have made the case that China is merely responding to assertiveness by Japan, the Philippines, and other claimants and that China is not particularly assertive as it pursues its claims.[2] Unfortunately, such arguments have a hard time presenting as reasonable China's reaction to a perceived Japanese infraction in September 2012 regarding Japanese-controlled but Chinese-claimed islands in the East China Sea that are known as the Senkaku Islands in Japan and the Diaoyu Islands in

China. In addition to demonstrations of force, political threats, and economic coercion, Beijing mobilized its seven top leaders and its enormous propaganda and organizational enterprise to foster mass anti-Japanese demonstrations in 120 Chinese cities. The result was predictable widespread illegal destruction and looting of Japanese businesses. Veteran China watchers had not seen such an officially encouraged outpouring directed at a foreign country since the mass demonstrations against the Soviet Union during the Cultural Revolution, and even those demonstrations were not nearly as widespread as the anti-Japanese actions in 2012. The main point of comparison seems to be the mass demonstrations against the United States during the darkest days of the Cold War at the start of the armed conflict with America in Korea in the early period of the People's Republic of China (PRC). At bottom, in September 2012 Beijing showed new assertiveness by employing its widespread control and state power to engage in reprisals far beyond international norms in order to intimidate Japan and any other country that might support Tokyo or challenge China's territorial claims.[3]

The United States endeavors to walk a middle line that supports U.S. allies, avoids taking sides in territorial disputes, and seeks to foster calm while working against unilateral actions by China and others that exacerbate regional tensions. The impasse between China and Japan, Asia's leading powers, poses a danger of great power conflict, with some Asian leaders and international commentators drawing comparisons with Europe just prior to the start of World War I.[4] Despite U.S. and other efforts, there is no clear path toward easing tensions in the foreseeable future.

Adding to regional doubt and angst over security issues is uncertainty over American capabilities and resolve. The United States has a history of sometimes intense involvement and sometimes unwelcomed intrusion into Asian security matters and sometimes pronounced disengagement and withdrawal. The U.S. military pullbacks from Iraq and Afghanistan have been accompanied by Obama administration pledges to "rebalance" U.S. security and other foreign policy concerns with a greater emphasis on the broad Asia-Pacific region. Those initiatives are in doubt amid American foreign policy debates reflecting war weariness and reluctance to resort to American military force to deal with international crises raging from the civil war in Syria, the Russian annexation of Ukraine's Crimea, and revived sectarian violence threatening the government of Iraq. The protracted recovery from the major economic recession of 2009–2010 and acute partisan divisions leading to repeated policy gridlock in Washington add to the mix of factors contributing to the perceived international decline of America.

The struggle to regain momentum in the recovery from the global recession adds to economic problems without clear solutions for the United States in Asia. U.S. interest in sustaining and reinforcing a liberal international order characterized by free trade, investment, and financial interchange is increasingly challenged by the success and growing influence of more state-directed economic policies and practices, notably by China. China's role as a trader, a site for foreign investment, and an increasingly important foreign investor continues to grow in regional and world affairs. Unlike the United States, China has a great deal of money that could be used to the benefit of its neighbors, and the neighboring governments see their interests well served by interchange with Chinese counterparts in finding possible ways that such resources could be used in accord with China's "win-win" formula pledging mutual benefit in foreign affairs. China's location and advancing infrastructure connecting China to its neighbors are major positive attributes supporting closer Chinese economic and other relations with neighboring states.

Of course much of the trade is dependent on foreign investment and access to markets in developed countries, the United States in particular. The United States sustains the very large trade deficit, especially with China, that supports the export-oriented economies of the region. Asian leaders are watchful for signs of American protectionism. The Obama government's rebalance policy features strong emphasis on ever-greater American commitment to openness and free trade. A serious problem comes because China's commitment to free trade and other economic interchange seems more selective and narrow. Beijing is prone to go well beyond international norms in retaliating against others over trade and other issues. Its cybertheft of trade and economic information and property is enormous. Its currency manipulation and other neomercantilist practices disadvantage neighboring economies, along with the United States.[5] China has also pursued extraordinary pressure on Japan for the sake of territorial claims, thereby risking very serious negative consequences for regional economic growth.

While the United States gains regional approval as it endeavors to calm recent tensions, play the role of stabilizer, and sustain free trade and economic interchange,[6] the fact remains that America has no good way to thwart what President Obama has called China's "gaming" of the existing liberal international economic order for its own narrow interests.[7] In effect, America watches China exploit the existing order where the United States and others sustain free exchanges and China uses state-directed means for the benefit of Chinese industries. Confronting China's unfair economic practices risks state-directed retaliation well beyond international norms.

President Obama has endeavored to deal with this problem partly through a free trade arrangement, the Trans-Pacific Partnership (TPP), which now involves twelve Asian-Pacific countries and requires entrants, presumably including China at some point, to commit to practices in line with much higher standards of free economic interchange than now seen in China. Beijing has strongly opposed the TPP in the past, favoring a much less demanding regional economic grouping, the Regional Comprehensive Economic Partnership (RCEP), that excludes the United States and forecasts little change in existing Chinese trade and international economic practices. At the Asia-Pacific Economic Cooperation (APEC) leaders' meeting held in Beijing in November 2014, China pushed for a broader Free Trade Area of the Asia-Pacific (FTAAP) that presumably could include the twenty-one members of the APEC group. The initiative met with American wariness as it was seen to undermine the U.S.-backed TPP with its requirements for higher standards of free economic interchange.[8] The outlook for the United States and the TPP is clouded and contingent on several other variables, notably President Obama's success in receiving so-called trade promotion authority (TPA) from a wary and partisan U.S. Congress. Without the special legislative treatment for trade bills allowed under TPA, any U.S. agreement to the TPP would be unlikely to pass Congress. Other countries are well aware of this American contingency and are reluctant to follow Obama administration urgings to join the free trade arrangement until the U.S. negotiators have TPA in hand.

Diplomatic and political issues complicating and adding to uncertainty about U.S. leadership in Asia include the difficulty Obama administration leaders have had in sustaining priority for their rebalance in the Asia-Pacific because of other major preoccupations at home and abroad. President Obama canceled scheduled participation at important annual meetings with Asian-Pacific leaders in October 2013 on account of the stalemate with Congress over a U.S. government shutdown and allowing the United States to take on additional national government debt. Secretary of State John Kerry does the needful in the Asia-Pacific, but he clearly gives priority to issues in the Middle East and Europe centered on Syria, Russia, Iran, and the Israeli-Palestinian split. Former Secretary of Defense Robert Gates and other observers bemoan decisions of the Obama government regarding limiting involvement in Southwest Asia,[9] but the president's policies seem in line with public opinion. Critics in Congress are generally careful in calling for greater U.S. involvement in conflicts that could lead to casualties and other serious costs. Meanwhile, U.S. interest in promoting human rights, democracy, and better governance have achieved only mixed results in Asia. Notably, Indonesia has become democratic, and Myanmar has turned toward more openness and political pluralism, but human rights and governance likely will decline in Afghanistan, Thailand's democracy remains unstable, and Chinese authoritarianism remains formidable.

SEARCHING FOR AN ENDURING FRAMEWORK AMID CONTINUED FLUX IN ASIA

In the post–Cold War period, there have been numerous assessments by officials and policy leaders endeavoring to provide stable frameworks for guiding and understanding the emerging order in Asia and relations with the

United States. Unfortunately, they have not diminished pervasive uncertainty regarding American leadership and the evolving situation in Asia. The reason is that the course of developments has shown the assessments to be incomplete, flawed, and repeatedly overtaken by unanticipated events. The failure to establish a stable framework of order in Asia in the post–Cold War period rests heavily on the failure to establish an enduring framework in U.S. relations with China. This book shows that American relations with Asia are much more than U.S. relations with China, but the latter relations are by far America's most important in Asia and are arguably the most important relations in the contemporary world. As explained in more detail in chapter 5, U.S. relations with China have zigged and zagged after the Cold War, confounding reliable assessment.

Major shifts between the United States and China in this period started with the end of the Soviet Union and the Cold War, which had a profound impact on the United States and all the governments in Asia. Notably, it freed them from the constraints on their actions in world affairs imposed by the need for discipline in playing their roles in the East-West and Sino-Soviet competition for influence in Asian and broader world affairs. In particular, the end of the USSR destroyed the strategic framework for the Sino-American cooperation initiated by U.S. president Richard Nixon and Chinese chairman Mao Zedong. It coincided with China's bloody crackdown on dissent at Beijing's Tiananmen Square and in other Chinese cities in 1989, unleashing broad-ranging opposition by the American public and elites to positive interchange with the Chinese government. The sometimes dramatic crises associated with the twists and turns in relations since that time have seen policy makers, strategists, and specialists in both the United States and China endeavor to establish new and firmer bases for cooperative relations, or at least to establish better understanding of the different elements in the relationship, how they fit together, and what they mean for the future. The frameworks that resulted often proved useful in comprehending relations and motivating policy at particular times, but they also often proved to be misleading, flawed, or ephemeral, achieving mediocre results.[10]

A surprising and acute military crisis in the Taiwan Strait in 1995 and 1996 saw a dangerous escalation of military tension, eventually involving a face-off between two U.S. aircraft carrier battle groups confronting Chinese military forces carrying out ballistic missile tests and other military exercises designed to intimidate Taiwan. Against this background, the Bill Clinton administration sought to avoid future confrontation and worked hard to positively engage theretofore alienated China. Both sides eventually agreed to emphasize common ground and play down differences in pursuing a "strategic partnership" guiding their relations. But crises over the U.S. bombing of the Chinese embassy in Belgrade in 1999 and strident domestic opposition in the United States scuttled the incipient partnership.

The George W. Bush administration came into office in 2001 openly critical of the Clinton China policy and wary of a cooperative partnership with China. Forecasts focused on serious trouble ahead. Those projections were proven wrong; they overlooked strong imperatives on the Chinese side as well as on the side of the Bush administration to avoid confrontation and ease tensions. Pragmatic cooperation in following years saw prevailing assessments switch to the positive. It was commonly asserted that the United States and China had become "friends" and "comrades,"[11] soft-pedaling profound differences like the ongoing buildup of Chinese forces focused on fighting American forces in a Taiwan contingency and the vigorous American response preparing to fight Chinese forces under such an eventuality. Meanwhile, U.S. calls on China to behave as a "responsible power" raised an optimistic vision of close Sino-American relations sustaining international order and norms that proved to be unrealistic.[12]

President Barack Obama tried to build on Bush's legacy with China with an accommodating posture and strong emphasis on cooperation during his first year in office. He endeavored to get the Chinese to cooperate and contribute more in support of the challenged international order and norms. At this juncture, some prominent nongovernment specialists on the American side argued for establishing a G-2 framework, where Beijing and Washington would work together closely in shaping and guiding international developments. The proposed framework failed. China viewed such American plans with suspicion, seeing U.S. efforts as intended to slow China's growing power by burdening Beijing with greater international commitments.[13]

Meanwhile, Obama's strong positive attention to and accommodation toward China reportedly were seen in China as signs of American weakness and apparently added to reasons for China to pressure the United States more over long-standing and recent differences. Specialists and scholars on both sides switched from the positive to the negative, forecasting serious trouble ahead. When the Obama government in 2011 publicly recast its Asian policy along lines of the "rebalance" that broadened American interests in advancing relations throughout the Asia-Pacific region in ways that competed with China, the Chinese reaction was harsh; specialist and scholarly opinion emphasized a tattered structure of Sino-American dialogues endeavoring to cover an increasingly acrimonious relationship.[14]

A series of tests in the relationship were provided in 2012. Growing Chinese-U.S. divergence and competition in Asia headed the list of issues that challenged and tested the abilities of Chinese and American leaders to manage their differences. They exacerbated the obvious security dilemma in this sensitive region, featuring China's rising power and America's reaction, shown notably in the two sides' respective military buildups.

The Republican presidential primaries saw often hyperbolic attacks on Chinese economic and security policies. Governor Mitt Romney emerged from the pack as the party's nominee, supporting tough trade and security measures to protect U.S. interests against China. President Obama joined the fray with harsh rhetoric not seen in his presidential campaign in 2008. Calling China an "adversary," he highlighted his administration's stronger engagement with countries in the Asia-Pacific region as a means to compete with China in security, economic, and other terms. [15]

Chinese media and officials condemned the so-called China bashing seen in the American presidential and congressional election campaigns. Chinese leaders remained firm in deflecting American pressure on the value of China's currency and broader trade practices and strongly rebuffed U.S. efforts to gain China's cooperation in dealing with some sensitive international issues, notably the conflict in Syria. China continued to give priority to nurturing close ties with the new North Korean leadership despite the latter's continued provocations. [16]

China resorted to extraordinary demonstrations of state power, short of direct use of military force, in response to perceived challenges by U.S. allies, the Philippines and Japan, regarding disputed territory in the South and East China Seas. Chinese commentary accused the United States of encouraging neighboring countries to be more assertive in challenging China's claims as part of alleged American efforts to contain China under the rubric of the Obama government's rebalance in the Asia-Pacific region. Top Chinese leaders also highlighted the RCEP and other regional trade arrangements that excluded the United States in order to undermine U.S.-led efforts to advance U.S. interests through the trans-Pacific trade pact. [17]

At the start of the year, prominent specialists Kenneth Lieberthal and Wang Jisi saw pervasive and deeply rooted distrust between the two governments. [18] By the end of the year, leading scholar David Shambaugh joined other commentators in concluding that the overall U.S.-China relationship had become "more strained, fraught and distrustful." Intergovernmental meetings meant to forge cooperation had become more pro forma and increasingly acrimonious, he said; the two sides wrangled over trade and investment issues, technology espionage and cyberhacking, global governance challenges like climate change and Syria, nuclear challenges like Iran and North Korea, and their security postures and competition for influence in the Asia-Pacific. [19]

It was against this background that commentators, specialists, and scholars have emphasized since late 2012 growing security competition along the lines of what is called the "Great Divergence." This framework for understanding regional dynamics maintains that security friction is growing among Asian powers, including the United States, even as their growing economic interchange is drawing them closer because of ever-stronger economic interdependence and mutual benefit. [20] Security differences have been portrayed in sometimes graphically dangerous terms, with Chinese assertiveness against major U.S. ally Japan over disputed islands in the East China Sea possibly leading to a direct Sino-American military confrontation that could escalate to nuclear war.[21] The Great Divergence framework portrayed economic ties as a positive glue that brings the United States and China as well as other powers together in mutually agreeable ways. While there is a good deal of validity in the framework for understanding the Asia-Pacific region's reaction to China's rise and related issues, closer examination showed its application to U.S.-China relations and the broader region is incomplete and flawed.

For example, the twists and turns in U.S.-China relations since the end of the Cold War highlighted above demonstrate that the danger of U.S.-China military confrontation appeared much worse during various crises over Taiwan from 1995 to 2008. And yet the two powers found ways to manage the tensions even as they beefed up forces to fight one another in a Taiwan contingency. There is little evidence today that the Chinese military is willing or even able to confront U.S. forces in Japan and the Western Pacific over the disputed Senkaku/Diaoyu Islands in the East China Sea. Thus far, Chinese assertiveness against Japan and against U.S. ally the Philippines in the South China Sea has been carefully controlled in order to avoid direct military-to-military confrontation with the United States.

Meanwhile, the Great Divergence framework gives an impression that economic ties are strong positives in the relationship. The 2012 presidential campaign and President Obama's strong emphasis on economic competition with China as part of his overall rebalancing policy in the Asia-Pacific region undermine that perspective. Economics are no longer the positive force of convergence that they proved to be in previous years, even though the interdependence they foster does help to curb Sino-American confrontation and conflict. The Obama administration seems in line with mainstream American opinion in its stronger opposition to a variety of Chinese economic practices seen as disadvantaging the United States.[22]

CONFLICTED SCHOLARSHIP COMPLICATES ASSESSMENT AND FORECASTING

Political scientists specializing in the field of international relations (IR) take pride in the rigor of their assessments, especially when compared to policy analysts often compelled by circumstances to use incomplete data and more loosely defined analytical tools to assess important developments requiring policy decisions. Nevertheless, the IR scholars have proven to be very conflicted and unable to discern an agreed-upon way to analyze America and its future relations in Asia. Their recommendations are often at odds, offering an overall contradictory and confusing mix of suggestions for future policy and practice.

The end of the Cold War saw a number of specialists of the "realist" school of thought in international relations argue that Asia was ripe for rivalry. As time went on, the main challenge to the U.S. position as the leading power was seen as China with its rapidly rising economy, ever-stronger military capabilities, and ambitious leadership. America's decline in the face of China's ascendance was sometimes depicted in stark terms, with books and articles premised on an actual or forecast "power shift" in the Asia-Pacific from U.S. leadership to Chinese leadership. The scholarship warned that power shifts in which a rising power challenges a dominant but declining power often result in confrontation and war.

In his book *A Contest for Supremacy: China, America, and the Struggle for Mastery in Asia* published in 2011, international relations scholar Aaron Friedberg viewed China's challenge in realist terms and urged the United States to strengthen and prepare for protracted resistance to China's advances. Australian scholar Hugh White took a very different tack in assessing the power shift he saw underway between rising China and the declining United States. He argued that the United States and the region would be much better off if the United States took the opportunity soon to work constructively with China in shaping a regional order where the United States would pull back in deference to China's advances. Other scholars using realist theory and sensitive to a power shift in Asia include Denny Roy, who generally agrees that China's rising power forecasts serious trouble ahead.[23] On the other hand, Andrew Nathan and Andrew Scobell have used realist thinking to show China as constrained and not yet at a point where it is prepared to seriously challenge U.S. leadership.[24]

The latter line of argument is in line with the assessment in this book, which shows strong American leadership continuing while rising China remains conflicted and encumbered as it deals with its neighbors and the United States. The assessment shows that U.S. interests are better served with a strategy of engagement with China and the entire region along with strong American competition with China for influence and in support of American interests in the face of Chinese challenges. It finds the Obama government's wide-ranging and evolving rebalance policy generally well suited to the complicated, multifaceted, and changing environment in Asia.

Though American realists tend to dominate the debate among international relations specialists about the United States and Asia, American and international scholars of the liberal school of thought in international relations theory have grounds for seeing developments in accord with their point of view. As noted in the discussion of the so-called Great Divergence above, U.S.-Chinese and other relationships are characterized by ever-greater degrees of economic interdependence.[25] While vigilant regarding changing circumstances that could have an impact on their security, sovereignty, and other important interests, most government leaders of Asia and the United States also clearly recognize the importance of economic development, the linchpin of their political legitimacy. Thus they endeavor to use the liberal international economic order in ways that benefit them and their countries, and in so doing they subscribe in various ways and to varying degrees to aspects of liberalism in international relations theory.

Asian-Pacific leaders also show support for aspects of the international relations school of thought known as constructivism. Such support is manifest in their ongoing efforts to build regional and international organizations as communities that support norms as effective means to manage interstate tensions and differences and to promote greater interstate cooperation.[26] Domestically, most Asian-Pacific governments also foster a strong identity for their nations as independent actors in regional and global affairs representing the interests and qualities of the peoples of their respective countries. Supporting such an identity is an important element in their continued political legitimacy. Identity is among the important dimensions in world politics emphasized by American and international IR scholars of the constructivist school of thought.[27]

Over a decade ago, international relations scholar David Kang challenged the predominant realist assessments of post–Cold War Asia's future.[28] He judged that IR theories are weak in assessing Asian developments because they are grounded in the history of modern Europe. He argued in a subsequent book that post–Cold War Asia had not followed the path toward balancing, confrontation, and conflict predicted by many prominent realists; the reason seemed to lie in the prolonged stability of the China-centered regional order prevalent during China's Ming (1368–1644) and Qing (1644–1912) dynasties and its relevance to the contemporary relationships among China, Korea, Vietnam, and Japan in particular. Chinese foreign relations during the Ming and Qing occurred within a formal framework known as the "tribute system," where China's superiority was duly recognized by the neighboring states in return for legitimacy and order provided by China along with various trade and other tangible benefits.

Coincidental with Kang's important analysis, Chinese officials, commentators, and scholars conveyed a view of historical Chinese dynasties as benevolent and peaceful as they dominated eastern Asia. The image of a historically peaceful China was used repeatedly to reassure contemporary Asia that as China rose in power and prominence, it would follow what China called the path of "peace and development," seeking win-win cooperation of mutual benefit to China and its neighbors. The image served to underline China's message to its neighbors that China has never been dominating or hegemonic.[29]

Historians and other specialists had long debated the actual peaceful practices of Chinese dynasties and their importance for contemporary behavior. The leader of American historians of China during the Cold War, John Fairbank of Harvard University, had a clear-eyed view of the ruthless use of force and intimidation by Chinese rulers against real or imagined adversaries. Fairbank was inclined to see the past model of the tribute system as having importance in contemporary Chinese views of a desired regional order. In a 1968 compendium, Fairbank laid out his views about the importance of the past order for modern China. Fairbank's close colleague, Benjamin Schwartz, an intellectual historian with a large following in this formative period of Chinese studies in the United States, used his conclusion to the volume to offer a rigorous and systematic rebuttal of his colleague and others who would see China's past tribute system as relevant to the People's Republic of China. In his view, the protracted, violent, and costly Chinese revolution thoroughly destroyed the old order. The coming of the West had an enormous impact on China and its neighbors. Nationalism, industrialization, and Western thinking and ideologies permanently changed China and most other Asian countries. [30]

Writing forty years later, prominent Columbia University political scientist Samuel Kim agreed with Kang that IR theories represent "Europe's past" and are thus less relevant for Asia's present. But he also agreed with Schwartz that the China-centered order of the Chinese imperial period had been destroyed and would not be restored. He averred that the fluid order we have seen in post–Cold War Asia will endure and that any Asian order we see today represents at best a work in progress. [31]

Overall, the complicated situation in IR scholarship dealing with the United States and the recent regional dynamics in Asia highlighted above favors the judgment of Amitav Acharya, David Shambaugh, and others in arguing in favor of an eclectic approach, using the frameworks of realism, liberalism, and constructivism, as appropriate, in order to ensure comprehensive treatment of relevant determinants and developments. [32] This volume endeavors to follow such a pragmatic path in using theory to analyze and explain behavior where deemed useful in the book's analysis.

Meanwhile, the complexities and perceived shortcomings in assessing Asian dynamics and the United States discussed above lead this author to employ throughout the book the type of contextual analysis used by U.S. government and other policy and intelligence analysts. The author's intention is to offer a comprehensive assessment of the various determinants seen in the context of Asian and U.S. decision making in order to provide a realistic view of why and how government officials and others influential in decisions relevant to the United States and the evolving Asian order have made their choices and a realistic view of the implications of those decisions. Those determinants take into account the changing interplay of power, interests, development, identity, norms, and values present in different countries and regions. As seen in the chapters to follow, the context and determinants for decisions in the unsettled Afghanistan-Pakistan region and in North Korea are very different from much of the rest of the Asia-Pacific region. And the context and determinants for decisions in a great power like China are very different from those in the many smaller states around China's periphery.

This book discerns five general sets of determinants laid out in the next section that overall influence regional dynamics, but their influence in specific areas and countries varies according to contextual circumstances salient in that area or country.

THE PURPOSE AND SCOPE OF THIS BOOK

Given the repeated change and pervasive uncertainty characterizing Asia and relations with the United States in the post–Cold War period, this book

- Provides a cogent overview of the historical context and an assessment of enduring patterns of U.S. relations (government and nongovernment) with Asia[33] as a whole and with different parts of Asia in particular.
- Provides a balanced analysis of post–Cold War dynamics in Asia, which involve issues of security, economics, national identity, and regional institution building. These issues are examined from the perspective of international relations theories to show how a complicated mix of realist, liberal, and constructivist tendencies is manifest in the regional order. More uniformly, a contextual approach is used throughout the book that takes into account the changing interplay of power, interests, norms and values, and identity.
- Provides an analysis on how well or poorly the recent Obama government's emphasis on "rebalancing" with the broader Asia-Pacific region has fit with regional dynamics. The analysis assesses in the process how the United States has reacted to Asia's rising power and importance, how the United States has maintained a leading position as a regional power having better relations with the region than China or any other possible contender for leadership, and how the United States on balance sustains better relations with the region than regional powers currently have with one another.
- Asia is defined as East Asia, Southeast Asia, and the "Pacific," notably Australia, South Asia (including Afghanistan), and Central Asia (including Russia).

With the Barack Obama government's emphasis on a policy of rebalance in Asia, the United States is in the midst of a new round of discussions and debate about how to position the United States in the changing security, economic, and political dynamics in Asia.[34] This book shows how such discussions and debate have occurred in the past and how they have continued fairly steadily since the end of the Cold War.

Post–Cold War dynamics in Asia are seen in this volume as determined by five sets of factors:

1. the changing power relationships among Asia's leading countries (e.g., the rise of China and India, change in Japan, rising or reviving middle powers—South Korea, Indonesia, Australia);
2. the growing impact of economic globalization and related international information interchange;
3. the ebb and flow of tensions in the Korean Peninsula and southwestern Asia, and the broader U.S.-backed efforts against terrorism and the proliferation of weapons of mass destruction
4. the rise of Asian multilateralism; and
5. the changing extent of U.S. engagement with and withdrawal from involvement in Asian matters.

International relations theory will be used to assist in explaining the above five sets of factors. The analysis will show that factors 1, 3, and 5 deal with security issues, including nontraditional security, that will be explained in part using realist perspectives. The assessment in this book shows the author's tendency to favor a realist perspective. And the book's focus on recent enhanced competition between the United States and China inclines the analysis toward realism in assessing such power politics. At the same time, factors 2 and 4 (and to a degree factors 1 and 5) deal with economic issues that will be explained in part using liberal perspectives. Factor 1 contains issues of national identity conflicts and territorial disputes; those issues, along with regional cooperation seen in factor 4, will be explained in part using the perspective of constructivists.

With a focus on developments after the Cold War, this study will review and assess U.S. relations with the important nations and multilateral groups of Asia, providing overall judgments on U.S. effectiveness in promoting regional stability and economic development and advancing liberal values amid the changing regional dynamics noted above.

The chapters cover the following issues:

1. Introduction. After discussing uncertainty and flux in assessments and practice of U.S.-Asian relations after the Cold War, this chapter provides the purpose and scope of the study. It introduces issues regarding security, economic, identity, and regional multilateral groupings and the five sets of factors noted above that are seen to determine the

state of play in contemporary Asian dynamics and relations with the United States.

2. Evolution of U.S. engagement with Asia. This chapter assesses developments until the end of the Cold War. It discerns important and enduring American interests and patterns of behavior at both government and nongovernment levels.

3. Post–Cold War Asia and the United States. This chapter explains at greater length the evolving post–Cold War security, economic, and political dynamics of Asia and the varied American approaches and responses from the George H. W. Bush administration to the Barack Obama government.

4. Obama government rebalancing policies. This chapter reviews the purpose, scope, and evolution of the policies and relations, their strengths and weaknesses, and regional reactions.

5. U.S.-China relations. This chapter assesses the status and outlook of these relations. In general terms, it and the following chapters, 6 through 10, assess the priorities, policies, and relations of the concerned Asian government or governments and the priorities, policies, and relations of the United States regarding those governments. In this way, the study shows the success and shortcomings of U.S. relations with these countries and regions in Asia.

6. U.S. relations with the Koreas. This chapter examines U.S. relations involving North Korea and South Korea.

7. U.S. relations with Japan. This chapter considers American, Japanese, and other determinants of the changing course of U.S. relations with this key ally.

8. U.S. relations with Southeast Asia and the Pacific. The scope of this chapter will include bilateral and multilateral American diplomacy with the countries of the Association of Southeast Asian Nations (ASEAN), along with treatment of Australia, New Zealand, and the Pacific Islands.

9. U.S. relations with South Asia. The scope of this chapter will focus heavily on U.S. relations with India, Pakistan, and Afghanistan.

10. U.S. relations with Central Asia, Mongolia, and Russia in Asia. Each of these sets of relationships will be considered in turn.

11. The future of U.S.-Asian relations. This chapter provides the main findings of the study in order to present an overall assessment of how well or poorly U.S. policies and behavior fit with the regional dynamics of Asia. Seeing weak evidence of a power shift and predicting that American leadership in Asia will endure, it highlights the main uncertainties prevalent in U.S. policies and relations with the region and offers recommendations.

NOTES

1. Thomas Szayna et al., *The Emergence of Peer Competitors: A Framework of Analysis* (Santa Monica, CA: RAND Corporation, 2001), 7–8.

2. Alistair Iain Johnston, "How New and Assertive Is China's New Assertiveness?," *International Security* 37, no. 4 (Spring 2013): 7–48.

3. Robert Sutter, *U.S.-Chinese Relations: Perilous Past, Pragmatic Present*, 2nd ed. (Lanham, MD: Rowman & Littlefield, 2013), 172.

4. Mira Rapp-Hooper, "Rhyme and Reason: Why 2014 Doesn't Have to Be 1914," *The Diplomat*, January 2, 2014, http://thediplomat.com/2014/01/rhyme-and-reason-why-2014-doesnt-have-to-be-1914.

5. Wayne Morrison, *China-U.S. Trade Issues*, Report RL33536 (Washington, DC: Library of Congress, Congressional Research Service, December 16, 2013).

6. Michael Green and Nicholas Szechenyi, *Power and Order in Asia: A Survey of Regional Expectations* (Washington, DC: CSIS, July 2014), http://csis.org/files/publication/140605_Green_PowerandOrder_WEB.pdf.

7. Doug Palmer and Matt Spetalnick, "Obama Hits China on Trade," Reuters, October 7, 2011, http://www.reuters.com/article/2011/10/07/us-usa-china-idUSN1E7950FF20111007.

8. Michael Martina, "Xi Urges Faster APEC Talks on China-Backed Free Trade Area," Reuters, November 11, 2014, http://www.reuters.com/assets/print?aid=USKCN0IV045201 41111.

9. "Gates Stands by Memoir as 'Honest Account," Associated Press, January 14, 2014, http://www.huffingtonpost.com/2014/01/12/robert-gates-memoir_n_4585245.html.

10. Reviews of post–Cold War U.S.-Chinese relations include David Michael Lampton, *Same Bed, Different Dreams: Managing U.S.-China Relations, 1989–2000* (Berkeley: University of California Press, 2001); Sutter, *U.S.-Chinese Relations*; David Shambaugh, ed., *Tangled Titans: The United States and China* (Lanham, MD: Rowman & Littlefield, 2012); Michael Swaine, *America's Challenge: Engaging a Rising China in the Twenty-First Century* (Washington, DC: Carnegie Endowment for International Peace, 2011).

11. Victor Cha, "Winning Asia: Washington's Untold Success Story," *Foreign Affairs*, November–December 2007, http://www.foreignaffairs.com/articles/58454/victor-d-cha/winning-asia.

12. Robert Zoellick, "Whither China: From Membership to Responsibility," Speech, September 21, 2005, http://2001-2009.state.gov/s/d/former/zoellick/rem/53682.htm.

13. Elizabeth Economy and Adam Segal, "The G-2 Mirage," *Foreign Affairs*, May–June 2009, http://www.foreignaffairs.com/articles/64996/elizabeth-c-economy-and-adam-segal/the-g-2-mirage.

14. See, among others, Robert Sutter, Michael Brown, and Timothy Adamson, *Balancing Acts: The U.S. Rebalance and Asia-Pacific Stability* (Washington, DC: Elliott School of International Affairs, George Washington University, 2013).

15. Don Keyser, "President Obama's Re-election: Outlook for U.S.-China Relations in the Second Term" (China Policy Institute, Nottingham University, UK, November 7, 2012).

16. Sutter, Brown, and Adamson, *Balancing Acts*, 39.

17. Bonnie Glaser, "US-China Relations," *Comparative Connections* 14, no. 3 (January 2013), http://www.csis.org/pacfor.

18. Kenneth Lieberthal and Wang Jisi, *Addressing U.S.-China Strategic Distrust* (Washington, DC: Brookings Institution, March 2012).

19. David Shambaugh, "The Rocky Road Ahead in U.S.-China Relations," *China-U.S. Focus*, October 23, 2012, http://www.chinausfocus.com/foreign-policy/the-rocky-road-ahead-in-u-s-china-relations.

20. Evan Feigenbaum and Robert Manning, "A Tale of Two Asias," *Foreign Policy*, October 20, 2012, http://www.foreignpolicy.com/articles/2012/10/30/a_tale_of_two_asias.

21. Avery Goldstein, "First Things First," *International Security* 37, no. 4 (Spring 2013): 49–89.

22. Richard Wike, "Americans and Chinese Grow More Wary of Each Other," Pew Research Center, June 13, 2013, http://www.pewresearch.org/fact-tank/2013/06/05/americans-and-chinese-grow-more-wary-of-each-other.

23. Aaron Friedberg, *A Contest for Supremacy: China, America, and the Struggle for Mastery in Asia* (New York: Norton, 2011); Hugh White, *The China Choice* (Collingwood, Australia: Black Inc., 2012); Denny Roy, *Return of the Dragon: Rising China and Regional Security* (New York: Columbia University Press, 2013).

24. Andrew Nathan and Andrew Scobell, *China's Search for Security* (New York: Columbia University Press, 2012).

25. Kishore Mahbubani, *The Great Convergence: Asia, the West, and the Logic of One World* (New York: Public Affairs, 2013); Ming Wan, "Economic Interdependence and Economic Cooperation," in *Asian Security Order: Normative and Institutional Features*, ed. Muttiah Alagappa, 280–310 (Stanford, CA: Stanford University Press, 2003).

26. Amitav Acharya, "Power Shift or Paradigm Shift? China's Rise and Asia's Emerging Security Order," *International Studies Quarterly* 58, no. 1 (March 2014): 158–73; Evelyn Goh, *The Struggle for Order: Hegemony, Hierarchy and Transition in Post–Cold War East Asia* (Oxford: Oxford University Press, 2013).

27. Amitav Acharya, *The Making of Southeast Asia* (Ithaca, NY: Cornell University Press, 2013); Goh, *The Struggle for Order*; Gilbert Rozman, *East Asian National Identities: Common Roots and Chinese Exceptionalism* (Stanford, CA: Stanford University Press, 2012); see also Alistair Iain Johnston, "Is China a Status Quo Power?," *International Security* 27, no. 4 (Spring 2003): 5–56.

28. David Kang, "Getting Asia Wrong: The Need for New Analytical Frameworks," *International Security* 27, no. 4 (Spring 2003): 57–85.

29. Zoe Murphy, "Zheng He: Symbol of China's 'Peaceful Rise,'" BBC News Asia-Pacific, July 28, 2010, http://www.bbc.com/news/world-asia-pacific-10767321.

30. John K. Fairbank, ed., *The Chinese World Order: Traditional China's Foreign Relations* (Cambridge, MA: Harvard University Press, 1968).

31. Samuel Kim, "The Evolving Asian System," in *International Relations of Asia*, ed. David Shambaugh and Michael Yahuda, 50–53 (Lanham, MD: Rowman & Littlefield, 2008).

32. Amitav Acharya, "Thinking Theoretically about Asian IR," in Shambaugh and Yahuda, *International Relations of Asia*, 77–80; Roy, *Return of the Dragon*, 7.

33. As seen from the following chapters, the scope of "Asia" in this book ranges from Afghanistan in the west to Japan in the east and from Russian Asia in the north to New Zealand in the south.

34. The discussion in this book of the American rebalance policy and practice relies heavily on American scholarship, but the assessment also benefited from non-American perspectives. See Hugo Meijer, ed., *Origins and Evolution of the US Rebalance toward Asia: Diplomatic, Military and Economic Dimensions* (London: Palgrave Macmillan, 2014); Elena Atanassova Cornelius and Frans-Paul van der Putten, eds., *Changing Security Dynamics in East Asia: A Post U.S. Regional Order in the Making* (London: Palgrave Macmillan, 2014).

Chapter Two

Historical Lessons and the Evolution of U.S. Relations with the Asia-Pacific

The United States has a long record of active interaction with Asia-Pacific countries. The purpose of this chapter is to identify and explain lessons from this record that are relevant for the objective of this book—discerning the weaknesses, strengths, and outlook of contemporary U.S. relations in the Asia-Pacific region. The lessons are identified and explained in summary form in the next section of this chapter. Following that is a chronological narrative of major developments of U.S. relations with the Asia-Pacific that explains those lessons in more detail and provides background information for readers unfamiliar with the context of contemporary U.S. relations with the Asia-Pacific.

LESSONS OF HISTORY

The record of American relations with the Asia-Pacific region surveyed in this chapter reveals several findings of relevance to contemporary U.S. relations with the region.

U.S. Interests: Economics, Values, and Strategy

Historically, American relations with Asia were grounded in advancing trade and economic interests and promoting religious and other American values. The U.S. Navy sometimes preceded U.S. diplomats in opening official relations with Asian governments in the nineteenth century, but the navy's mission focused heavily on fostering and protecting American commercial, missionary, and related interests.

Northeast Asia, especially China and Japan, was the focus of U.S. interest and has remained the top priority of the United States in Asia. The acquisition of the Philippines in the late nineteenth century gave the United States a modest stake in Southeast Asia. The United States generally cooperated with British, French, and other European colonial powers in Southeast Asia and in South Asia. Central Asia was the preserve of tsarist Russia and later the Soviet Union.[1]

U.S. Reluctance to Lead: Major Costs and Risks of Leadership

The United States came late to leadership in the Asia-Pacific. After World War I, the United States was in its third decade as the world's largest economy. It was a major world power and one of two leading powers in East Asia (Japan was the other). Nevertheless, the United States was reluctant to undertake the risks, costs, and obligations of leadership. It avoided involvement with the League of Nations. The United States used inexpensive diplomatic efforts to curb Japanese expansion in East Asia following World War I and the collapse of Russia and the weakening of Britain, France, and other European powers. These failed by the early 1930s. The United States remained very reluctant to confront Japanese expansion.[2]

The surprise Japanese attack on Pearl Harbor abruptly changed American international calculations and put the United States in the leading role in the armed conflict to destroy Japan's war machine and to create a new order in Asia and the Pacific. The scope of U.S. interests spread widely to include Northeast and Southeast Asia, Australia and New Zealand, and many Pacific Island countries. South Asia was still ruled by U.S. ally Great Britain, and Stalin's Soviet Union controlled Central Asia.[3]

American leaders had ambitions for a post–World War II order in the Asia-Pacific region that featured a strong and united China friendly to the United States and newly independent countries in Southeast and South Asia. The ambitions ran aground on realities of Chinese division and weakness, the refusal of European colonial powers to withdraw from Southeast Asia, and emerging Cold War competition with the Soviet Union and its allies and associates. Reflecting a reluctance to bear the continued costs of strategic leadership in the Asia-Pacific, the U.S. government rapidly demobilized its military forces in the region after World War II, apart from occupation forces in Japan.[4]

Repeated Challenges to U.S. Leadership in the Asia-Pacific

U.S. calculations of military withdrawal, continued peace, and other American interests in Asia were fundamentally challenged by the emerging Cold War. The Soviet Union and its ally the People's Republic of China

(PRC) backed a North Korean assault on South Korea in June 1950. This aggression followed the failure of U.S. policy in China. The PRC was a communist government hostile to the United States; it aligned with Stalin's Soviet Union in a pact directed at the United States in February 1950. The situation posed major problems for the United States. The war in Korea saw three years of U.S. combat against mainly Chinese forces in Korea that resulted in over thirty thousand American dead. The experience reinforced in blood the United States' determination over the next two decades to take the lead, pay the costs, and run the risks in building and maintaining strategic, economic, and political bulwarks to "contain" the spread of Chinese- and Soviet-backed communist expansion in the Asia-Pacific. [5]

American leadership in Asia was repeatedly and seriously challenged. U.S.-backed French forces failed in Indochina in 1954 in the face of Chinese-backed Vietnamese communists. The United States moved in to become more directly involved as the main backer of the noncommunist regime in South Vietnam, leading by the 1960s to the commitment of hundreds of thousands of U.S. troops to the war there against Vietnamese communist forces that were supported by the Soviet Union and China. China militarily confronted Chiang Kai-shek and U.S. forces in the Taiwan Strait twice in the 1950s; it developed a nuclear bomb by 1964 and widely promoted "wars of national liberation" against U.S.-supported governments in Southeast Asia and elsewhere. [6]

The nadir of American influence in the Asia-Pacific region and the most serious challenge to U.S. leadership in Asia since Pearl Harbor came with the collapse of U.S.-backed governments in Cambodia and South Vietnam in 1975. These defeats for the United States—despite enormous U.S. costs, including fifty thousand dead—came amid a major American economic set-back on account of the oil shocks and energy crisis of the time, and weak and divided U.S. governments following the resignation of President Richard Nixon and his pardon by President Gerald Ford. Anxiety among U.S.-supported governments in Northeast and Southeast Asia saw those governments maneuver internationally and take measures at home in order to compensate for the obvious decline in U.S. power. The United States and China also cooperated together to deal with the rise of Soviet power in the Western Pacific, Southeast Asia, and South Asia; they anticipated a continued decline in U.S. regional power and influence in the Asia-Pacific region as Soviet dominance grew. [7]

Faulty Forecasts of U.S. Decline in the Asia-Pacific

Forecasts of U.S. decline in the Asia-Pacific proved incorrect. American economic and military power at home and abroad, including in the Asia-Pacific region, rose markedly during the early 1980s. American resolve backed by strong allies in Europe and Japan prompted the new Soviet leadership of Mikhail Gorbachev to seek to ease tensions and reduce military competition and confrontation.

Nonetheless, a new challenge to U.S. leadership emerged in this period. For over ten years, a wide range of respected specialists and commentators argued that the United States could not keep pace with Asia's rapidly rising great power, Japan. Japan was seen as so competitive in Asian and world markets that it was widely asserted that Japan was emerging as Asia's dominant power and the United States was gradually falling to second place in Asian-Pacific affairs. Such predictions lasted well into the first years of the post–Cold War period. They did not cease until Japan experienced several years of economic stagnation and deflation, and U.S. economic and military power rose to new prominence in the 1990s.[8]

Current Challenges in Light of the Past

Current challenges to U.S. leadership in Asia that are reviewed in the introduction and elsewhere in this book are serious. However, they have not reached the level of the challenges faced by the United States in the Asia-Pacific at the start of the Cold War, during the Vietnam War, and after the U.S. defeat in Indochina in 1975. They may be more serious than the challenges that the U.S. encountered in the face of Japan's rise in the late 1980s. Most notably, unlike in those past instances, the United States today sustains clear military leadership. And although regional and global economic power has become diffused in interdependent relationships fostered by globalization, the globally influential American economy undergirds an ability to exert continued strong U.S. leadership in Asian and world affairs. Meanwhile, no individual power or collection of powers has shown willingness or ability to undertake even a fraction of the risks and costs borne by the United States in providing common security, economic, and other benefits deemed essential by the vast majority of Asian-Pacific governments.

Past assumptions of U.S. decline in the face of rising powers and challenges tended to exaggerate American weaknesses without assessing U.S. strengths, and they tended to exaggerate the strengths of the rising powers and challenges to U.S. leadership without assessing their weaknesses and limitations. Credible assessments dealing with contemporary U.S. difficulties in the Asia-Pacific would appear to call for better balance in considering both contemporary U.S. weaknesses and strengths, as well as similar balance in assessing the power and influence of rising powers and other regional challenges to U.S. leadership in the Asia-Pacific, before offering projections and recommendations. That is one intention of this study.

EVOLUTION OF U.S. RELATIONS WITH THE ASIA-PACIFIC REGION

Looked at broadly, current American policy represents the culmination of a long-standing pursuit of three sets of objectives toward Asia and the Pacific. First, the United States remains concerned with maintaining a balance of power in Asia favorable to American interests and opposed to efforts at domination of the region by hostile powers.[9] Second, U.S. economic interests in the region grow through involvement in economic development and expanded American trade and investment. Third, American culture and values prompt efforts to foster democracy, human rights, and other culturally progressive trends in Asia, along with other parts of the world. The priority given to each of these goals has changed over time. U.S. leaders have varied in their ability to set priorities and organize American objectives as part of a well-integrated national approach to the Asia-Pacific.[10]

ROOTS OF AMERICAN FOREIGN POLICY IN THE ASIA-PACIFIC

The roots of American foreign policy in the Asia-Pacific extend to the formative experiences of the late eighteenth and the nineteenth centuries. At that time, the United States endeavored to be seen as a nation interested in peaceful and friendly dealings with the world. U.S. relations focused primarily on commercial and cultural affairs. American interaction with the Asia-Pacific, like U.S. relations with other parts of the world, was characterized by informal activities such as trade, missionary endeavors, and tourism. Military and diplomatic considerations played only a minor role and were almost always subordinate to commerce and shipping. Economic activities in turn were often secondary to cultural relations. American trade with Asia never amounted to more than a few percent of total American trade, whereas thousands of Americans went to Asia as missionaries and in other nongovernment and noncommercial capacities to bring American civilization to Asia. American missionary, educational, and related initiatives were timely in that Japan, China, and Korea were in the midst of the process of modernization— a process that benefited from the presence of American missionaries, educators, scientists, engineers, and travelers who offered Asian elites and others needed advice and information. Thus, in the first phase in their encounter, which ended with the nineteenth century, America and the Asia-Pacific met at three levels—strategic, economic, and cultural—but the cultural dimension was clearly the most significant.

U.S. relations with China were the most active and important of American relations with the Asia-Pacific during this period. Beginning in the late eighteenth century, new American freedom from British rule brought

American loss of access to previous British-controlled trade partners. This new situation prompted an American search for new trading opportunities in China. Though actual American trade with China remained relatively small, the China market often loomed large in the American political and business imagination. Meanwhile, U.S. officials in the latter part of the nineteenth century and the early part of the twentieth century sometimes sought to channel American investment in ways that would preserve American commercial opportunities in China in the face of foreign powers seeking exclusive privileges and spheres of influence.[11]

Americans also were in the vanguard of Protestant missionaries sent to China in the nineteenth century. U.S. missionaries came in groups and as individuals, set to work initially in China's so-called treaty ports, and eventually grew to many hundreds working throughout China to spread the Gospel and to carry out relief, education, medical, and other works of benefit to Chinese people. Part of a well-organized network of church groups that reached deep into the United States for prayers and material support, American missionaries explained Chinese conditions to interested Americans, fostering a sense of a special bond between the United States and China. The missionaries also served as advisers to U.S. officials dealing with China and sometimes became official American representatives in China. Their core interest remained unobstructed access to Chinese people for purposes of evangelization and good works carried out by the American missionaries and their foreign and Chinese colleagues.[12]

Though commercial and missionary interests remained at the center of U.S. interests in China well into the twentieth century, a related strategic interest also had deep roots. In 1835, several years before the first U.S. treaty with China in 1844, the United States organized the Asiatic Squadron. This U.S. Navy group began in 1842 to maintain a regular presence along the China coast. It later was called the Asiatic Fleet. Initially two or three vessels, it grew to thirty-one vessels by 1860, before forces were recalled on account of the American Civil War. It varied in size after the Civil War but was sufficiently strong to easily destroy the Spanish forces in Manila harbor during the Spanish-American War in 1898. It protected American lives and commerce in China and throughout maritime East and South Asia and reinforced American diplomacy in the region.[13]

Strong American interest in commercial and missionary access to China seemed to contrast with only episodic American diplomatic interest in China. The U.S. government occasionally gave high-level attention to the appointment of envoys or the reception of Chinese delegations. Caleb Cushing, Anson Burlingame, and some other nineteenth-century U.S. envoys to China were well connected politically. Some U.S. envoys endeavored to use their actions in China to influence broader American policy or to advance their own political or other ambitions. U.S. envoys sometimes came from the missionary community in China. On the other hand, the post of U.S. minister in China often was vacant, with an interim official placed in charge in an acting capacity. Generally speaking, whenever nineteenth-century U.S. envoys pushed for more assertive U.S. policies that involved the chance of significant expenditure of American resources or political risk, Washington decision makers reflected the realities of limited U.S. government interests in China and responded unenthusiastically. This broad pattern continued into the twentieth century, though U.S. officials from time to time took the lead in low-risk political and diplomatic efforts in support of U.S. interests in unimpeded commercial and other access to China. [14]

China's unexpected defeat by Japan in the Sino-Japanese War of 1894–1895 led European powers to join Japan in seeking exclusive spheres of influence and commercial and territorial rights in China. Alarmed that American interests in free commercial access to China would be jeopardized, U.S. officials formulated a response that led to the so-called Open Door notes of 1899 and 1900. The 1899 notes sought the powers' agreement that even if they established special spheres in China, they would not discriminate against foreign trade or interfere with customs collection. They underlined U.S. interests in preserving equal commercial access to China and the preservation of the integrity of the Chinese Customs Service, a crucial source of revenue for the struggling Chinese government. Though generally unenthusiastic about the U.S. initiative, most concerned powers offered evasive and qualified responses, but all in effect endorsed the principles in the so-called Open Door notes. As the United States and other foreign powers dispatched troops to crush the Boxer Uprising and lift the siege of foreign legations in Beijing, the United States in July 1900 sent a second round of Open Door notes that expressed concern for preserving Chinese sovereignty. The foreign powers went along with the notes. [15]

U.S. policy makers repeatedly referred to the U.S. Open Door policy following the issuing of the Open Door notes. The William H. Taft administration in 1910 interpreted the policy as extending beyond equal trade opportunity to include equal opportunity for investment in China. The Wilson administration in 1915 reacted to the Japanese Twenty-One Demands against China by refusing to recognize such infringements on the Open Door policy. The related principles concerning U.S. support for the territorial integrity of China were featured prominently in the Nine Power Treaty of the Washington Conference in the Warren Harding administration in 1922 and in the nonrecognition of Japanese aggression in Manchuria during the Hoover administration in 1932. The Harry Truman administration sought Soviet Union leader Joseph Stalin's promise that the Open Door policy would be observed in the Soviet-influenced areas of Manchuria following the Soviet military defeat of Japanese forces there in 1945. In general, American political leaders dealing with China throughout the twentieth century tended to refer to the

Open Door policy in positive terms, as a U.S. attempt to prevent China from being carved up into commercially impenetrable foreign colonies. Chinese interpretations often emphasized that Americans were more concerned about maintaining their own commercial access and were prepared to do little in practice in supporting Chinese sovereignty.

Not surprisingly, the Americans with an interest in China tended to emphasize the positive features of U.S. policy and behavior. Thus the United States was seen to have behaved benignly toward China, especially when compared with the European powers and Japan, which repeatedly coerced and attacked China militarily. The U.S. government repeatedly voiced its support of China's territorial and national integrity. Through missionary and other activities, including education activities that eventually brought tens of thousands of Chinese students for higher education to the United States by the 1940s, Americans also showed strong sympathy and support for the broader welfare of the Chinese people.[16]

U.S. officials, opinion leaders, and commentators tended to ignore or soft-pedal negative features of U.S. relations with China. Most notable was the so-called exclusion movement that grossly discriminated against and often violently persecuted Chinese immigrants to the United States. The movement took hold in American politics beginning in the 1870s and lasted for almost a hundred years. At first centered in western states with some significant concentrations of Chinese workers, the exclusion movement reflected widespread American prejudice against and fear of Chinese workers amid sometimes difficult economic times in the United States. American elites and common people took legal and illegal actions, including riots and the murder of hundreds of Chinese in the United States, to stop Chinese immigration and drive away those Chinese already in the United States. Various state governments and the national government passed an array of laws and U.S. courts made a variety of decisions that singled out Chinese immigrants for negative treatment and curbed the legal rights of Chinese residents and Chinese citizens of the United States. The movement eventually broadened to include all Asians. The National Origins Act of 1924 barred all new Asian immigration. U.S. mistreatment of Chinese people in the United States became a major issue for the Chinese government, which complained repeatedly against unjust U.S. actions, but with little effect. It was the target of a Chinese anti-American boycott in 1905.[17]

GROWING STRATEGIC INTERESTS AND ECONOMIC POWER

U.S. strategic interests in Asia-Pacific changed markedly at the end of the nineteenth century. The United States fought a war in the Philippines, started a naval expansion program, and acquired Pacific Island possessions. The

United States developed as a major power in the Pacific and, by extension, in nearby Asia as well. Simultaneously, American trade and investment in Asia grew. The United States exported industrial products and invested capital in railways and mines in East Asia, as well as elsewhere in the world. The period between the Spanish-American War and World War I was a time of transformation in U.S. policy. By 1914, the United States had one of the largest navies in the world and naval bases in the Caribbean and the Pacific; the Panama Canal had just been opened. As the world's largest economy for over two decades and its leading industrial producer, the United States had become a major exporter of manufactured goods, especially to Asia and Latin America.[18]

The American experience in Asia had become as much military and economic as cultural. Thousands of American soldiers and sailors experienced warfare in the Philippines. Thousands served during the Boxer Uprising in China at the turn of the century. Hundreds of marines were stationed in China to safeguard Peking's access to the sea. The American military began considering the possibility of war with Japan, which was also developing and expanding its military power in the Asia-Pacific region. The United States did not contemplate a war with Japan in the immediate future, but it became concerned with maintaining some sort of balance of power in the region, a task it could not leave to other powers alone.[19]

Economically, too, there was strong competition between American and Japanese cotton textiles imported into Manchuria. The United States affirmed its interest in an economic "Open Door" as official policy in part in order to prevent Japan from establishing dominance over the China market. At the same time, economic ties between the United States and Japan grew. Japan shipped 30 percent of its exports to America. Japan obtained hundreds of millions of dollars of U.S. loans as it fought a war against Russia in 1905 and managed its expanding empire on the Asian continent.[20]

The cultural dimension of U.S. policy and relations with the Asia-Pacific also remained strong. The Progressive movement reinforced the American sense of mission. The reformist impulse found an outlet in Asia, particularly China, which was trying to transform itself into a modern state. Many reformers in China were open to the Progressive emphasis on education; they were coming to the view that educational reform must precede other changes. In their efforts to chart a new political order for China following the collapse of the Manchu dynasty in 1911, some Chinese reformers also eagerly turned to the U.S. Constitution for a model. Japanese reformers, on their part, drew inspiration from American capitalism, and Japanese radicals from American socialism. Thus the sense of cultural connections grew. But missing was a sense of order among the various aspects of America's relations with the Asia-Pacific. Balance-of-power politics, trade, and reform movements continued without a clear sense of priority or interrelationships.[21]

President Woodrow Wilson provided more coherence for U.S. foreign policy in the Asia-Pacific and elsewhere in the world. He set out a comprehensive definition of international affairs in which military, economic, and cultural aspects were integrated in order to establish a more progressive world order. International peace would be maintained by a system of collective security, economic interdependence, and cultural change in order to promote democracy and human rights everywhere. To carry out such a foreign policy, the United States would play a military role in cooperation with other nations. U.S. resources would be available to open up markets of the world; to help other countries through loans, investment, and technology transfer; and to collaborate with other advanced nations in the development of dependent areas. U.S. universalistic values and reformist ideals would be used to transform world conditions. Of course, Wilson's conception was not just an agenda of selfless ideals; it meshed international and national affairs in ways that promoted American interests. [22]

For Asia and the Pacific, Wilson's approach called for an end to the naval race with Japan and to the latter's attempted domination of China and sought a new security arrangement on the basis of cooperation with Japan, Great Britain, and other powers. U.S. policy challenged Japan's and other nations' monopolistic economic enclaves in China and called for outside powers to attempt anew the doctrine of the Open Door. The United States promoted democratization in Asia, as well as elsewhere, and supported reformist movements in China and Japan. [23]

For a time, the Wilsonian agenda put an end to the wartime antagonism between the United States and Japan. There was a "collective security" in the Pacific on the basis of naval disarmament agreements and other accords, such as those at the Washington Conference of 1921–1922. American goods, capital, and technology flowed into China and Japan. Japan shifted its China policy away from military to economic interests. During the decade of the 1920s, the Americanization of Japan was promoted through the spread of American movies, consumer goods, and, even more important, political, economic, and social values.

In contrast, the 1930s were a time of the coming to power of leaders in Japan who were oriented toward military strength. Military expenditures grew much faster than the economy. To justify and support such increases, the military undertook aggressive acts in China and prepared for war against the Soviet Union, the United States, and Great Britain. In order to pay for such expenditures, Japan sought to establish control over resources and markets of the Asian continent and the European colonies in Southeast Asia. [24]

Japan undertook these ultimately destructive policies as part of a misguided effort to establish an autarkic region, an area of economic self-sufficiency in Asia that would, it was thought, enrich the country as well as contribute to financing its military force. The Great Depression and world economic crisis added impetus to Japan's effort and helped to undermine the Wilsonian system of global interdependence. Rather than relying on close economic relations with the United States and an open door in China, the Japanese decided to reduce their dependency on the West and monopolize markets and resources in Asia. The Japanese never quite gave up their fascination with, and even dependence on, America's material and popular culture, but Japanese leaders during the 1930s were determined to reduce the influence of the ideals of democracy, individualism, and human rights. To counter these influences, Japanese leaders focused on the absence of racial equality seen in the practice of U.S. policy at home and abroad. Japanese military leaders in the 1930s repeatedly asserted that their determination to get Westerners out of their region was Asia's answer to American (and Western) racial injustice. [25]

WORLD WAR II, U.S. LEADERSHIP, AND THE COLD WAR

The Americans' initial isolationist reaction to Japanese militarism and Nazi Germany's expansionism gave way to a new vision authored by President Franklin D. Roosevelt. Over time, he formulated what some refer to as a new Wilsonianism to bring the world out of the turmoil and chaos of the 1930s. Roosevelt's vision shared with the original Wilsonianism a commitment to an integrated world order—militarily, economically, and culturally. The United States would be more willing to augment its armed forces and to be involved in different parts of the world in order to maintain a balance of power. It would also cooperate more closely with a few other powers to police the world order. This was still selective security with a few carefully chosen partners, but with a greater readiness to use force. The past stress on the open door and interdependence remained, but the government, not just the private sector, would be ready to help other countries undertake economic change. At the same time, worldwide bodies, such as the International Monetary Fund (IMF) and the World Bank, would be established to monitor and to ensure a more open international economic system. Roosevelt's "four freedoms" speech in January 1941 contained principles that were Wilsonian—such as human rights and self-determination—but it also mentioned new values such as social justice and racial equality, values of particular importance to Asians. [26]

Roosevelt's vision defined a new phase of American relations with the Asia-Pacific. After defeating Japan, the United States and its allies (including China and other Asian countries and people resisting Japanese aggression) would reestablish regional order on the basis of this definition. As codified at the Cairo, Yalta, and Potsdam Conferences, as well as through various other meetings, the new regional arrangement would be based on close cooperation among victorious nations, particularly America, China, Great Britain, and the Soviet Union. Japan would be disarmed and democratized. Korea would be unified and eventually become independent, and the European colonies in Southeast Asia would be ultimately granted independence, but in the meantime placed under a trusteeship scheme under the aegis of the United Nations. Economic liaisons would be fostered throughout the Asia-Pacific region.[27]

Plans were one thing and realities something else. As noted earlier, the Japanese attack on Pearl Harbor thrust the United States into a leadership position in China, the Asia-Pacific, and global affairs generally. Heading the Allied coalition that would eventually defeat the Axis powers, U.S. leaders focused on fighting the massive worldwide conflict and dealing with issues that would determine the postwar international order. In this context, the complicated conditions in China, notably the bitter rivalry between Chiang Kai-shek's Nationalist forces and the communist forces under the direction of Mao Zedong, received secondary attention. As a result, American officials tended to follow paths of least resistance as they reinforced existing proclivities to back Chiang Kai-shek's Nationalists, who enjoyed broad political support in the United States. They avoided the difficult U.S. policy reevaluation that would have been required for American leaders to position the United States in a more balanced posture in order to deal constructively with the Chinese communists as well as the Chinese Nationalists. The drift and bias in U.S. policy, strengthened by interventions of U.S. presidential envoy and ambassador to China Patrick Hurley, foreshadowed the American failure in China once the communists defeated the Nationalists on mainland China in 1949 and moved in early 1950 to align with the Soviet Union against the United States in the Cold War.[28]

Neither the government of Mao Zedong nor the Truman administration sought or foresaw a U.S.-China war in early 1950. The Americans were surprised when North Korean forces, with the support of Soviet and Chinese leaders, launched an all-out military attack against South Korean forces in June 1950. The Chinese communist leaders and their Korean and Soviet communist allies apparently calculated that the better-armed North Koreans would attain victory quickly without provoking a major or effective U.S. military response. Thus it was their turn to be surprised when the United States quickly intervened militarily in the Korean War and also sent the U.S. Seventh Fleet to prevent the anticipated Chinese communist attack on Taiwan. U.S. forces and their South Korean allies halted the North Korean advance and carried out an amphibious landing at Inchon in September 1950 that effectively cut off North Korean armies in the South, leading to their destruction.

The string of miscalculations continued. With UN sanction, U.S. and South Korea forces proceeded into North Korea. The Chinese communists warned and prepared to resist them, but American leaders thought the warnings were a bluff. By November, hundreds of thousands of Chinese communist forces were driving the U.S. and South Korean forces south in full retreat. Eventually, the Americans and their allies were able to sustain a line of combat roughly in the middle of the peninsula, as the two armies faced off for over two more years of combat, casualties, and destruction. [29]

The complications of the postwar situation in Asia and the start of the Cold War severely undermined Roosevelt's idealistic vision for the Asia-Pacific after World War II. Principles of economic interdependence, human rights, and democracy remained, but these were now subordinated to an overall strategic conception in which military confrontation between the United States and the Soviet Union became the overriding framework of American policy. Asia became part of a global anti-Soviet coalition. American troops and bases were maintained in Japan, Korea, the Philippines, and eventually Taiwan and elsewhere. Japan was encouraged to rearm. Defense alliances were established with these countries, as well as Australia and New Zealand. The communist People's Republic of China, the U.S. foe in the bloody Korean War and the main adversary in Asia, was ostracized, denied recognition, and excluded from trade. [30]

The military-strategic considerations of the Cold War provided the key to Asian international affairs and American relations with the Asia-Pacific for at least two decades, the 1950s and the 1960s. Accounting for more than half of the world's income and industrial production at the end of World War II, the United States put forth billions of dollars and tens of thousands of lives to uphold the "containment" arrangement in the Asia-Pacific. It fought two wars for the same purpose. It seems clear that the origins and consequences of the Korean and the Vietnam wars were part of the same picture, reflecting the primacy of strategic considerations in America's approach to Asia. What is subject to more debate is the notion that had the vision of Franklin Roosevelt retained a stronger influence in postwar American policy, there might have been a greater readiness to come to grips with the profound social and cultural changes taking place in China, Korea, Vietnam, and elsewhere and to deal with them in an integrated fashion, not simply in the framework of a global balance of power.

But that was not to be. In the interests of Cold War competition and the doctrine of containment, the United States for a time reversed Roosevelt's vision and supported the West European powers that tried to sustain colonies in Southeast Asia. The United States followed through with its commitment to provide the Philippines with independence and to contribute to the economic rehabilitation of the country. But U.S. opposition to the communist-led Hukbalahap and American demands for U.S. military installations saw the U.S. government align with conservative political forces in the Philippines. These actions seemed to underscore that U.S. policy was less interested in free democracy and broad economic development than in sustaining stability and preventing the spread of communism.[31]

One consequence of America's Cold War strategy in the Asia-Pacific was Japanese economic growth and its spread to nearby noncommunist Asian states. American officials thought an economically healthy Japan would be the best guarantee against its falling under Soviet or Chinese influence. Washington helped Japan's reentry into the international economic arena through membership in organizations such as the General Agreement on Tariffs and Trade (GATT), the predecessor to the World Trade Organization (WTO), and the IMF. The United States even tolerated significant trade between Japan and the PRC, which, if small in comparison with Japanese trade with the United States or Southeast Asia, steadily grew in importance for China because of the latter's increasing alienation from the Soviet Union. Viewed from the perspective of intense U.S.-Japanese economic rivalry in the 1980s, it was remarkable that America was supportive of Japanese economic interests—Japan appeared to give little in return. In part, this was because the 1950s and 1960s were periods of high American growth, and until at least the late 1960s, the United States seemed able to afford to engage in a costly war in Southeast Asia and to remain calm even as Japan and European nations expanded their trade and industrial production and came to challenge American economic supremacy.[32]

NIXON'S OPENING TO CHINA AND STRATEGIC SHIFT IN THE ASIA-PACIFIC

The U.S.-PRC rapprochement, the U.S.-Soviet détente in nuclear arms, and the oil shocks of the 1970s shook the foundations of the Cold War system in the Asia-Pacific. The United States incorporated mainland China into the Asia-Pacific security system and turned to Asian countries to contribute much more to their own defense as the United States withdrew over six hundred thousand U.S. forces from the region under terms of the "Nixon Doctrine" of President Richard Nixon. American leaders now expected Japan as well as European countries to do more to help stabilize international economic conditions. Given a period of negative growth and double-digit inflation, the United States was no longer seen as the dominant international economic leader. It was more concerned with safeguarding more narrow national interests. With Japan and other allies, significant gaps developed between the security and economic aspects of U.S. relations. Trade disputes grew, Americans criticized Japan for taking advantage of American military protection, and U.S. officials asked whether Japan should contribute more to regional security. Japanese leaders remained unwilling to devote more than 1 percent of GNP to defense. Japan's 1976 "general guidelines for defense policy" reiterated the nation's commitment to a small-scale military force for purely defensive purposes. To some American officials, China began to seem a more promising ally.[33]

Following the collapse of American-supported regimes in South Vietnam and Cambodia in 1975, U.S. policy in Asia was in considerable disarray. Indeed, authority was challenged from several quarters in the United States. The Watergate scandal and ensuing resignation of President Nixon in 1974, followed by the takeover of South Vietnam by Vietnamese communist forces the following year, left American credibility badly damaged and its policies (especially toward Asia) uncertain in the eyes of both friends and adversaries. There was particular concern in the U.S. government just after the fall of Saigon that North Korea might think the time was opportune to strike militarily against South Korea.

Within the United States, there was rising concern over issues of morality regarding both the ends and the means of foreign policy. America had become involved in a policy of détente—the idea that there were good as well as bad communists confused many people. Higher standards were demanded and additional constraints imposed upon the presidency. A newly assertive Congress passed the War Powers Resolution over a presidential veto, thereby imposing new constraints on the president's freedom to use military force. Congress also passed laws requiring countries that received U.S. economic and military assistance to meet certain minimum (if vague) human rights standards domestically, and later the administration was required to publish an annual report on human rights conditions in all countries. Congress enacted numerous "legislative vetoes," requiring the president to provide Congress with notice of proposed arms deliveries and allowing it to block such actions.[34]

U.S. POLICY DURING THE CARTER AND REAGAN ADMINISTRATIONS

President Carter came to office holding many of the beliefs of the critics of the Vietnam War and of the Nixon-Kissinger emphasis on realism and balance-of-power policies. The president seemed determined to shift the emphasis of U.S. policy from power toward morality and to give less attention to seeking specific short-term advantages over the Soviet Union. He had several genuine accomplishments: the Panama Canal Treaty, the Camp David Accords between Egypt and Israel, and the establishment of full diplomatic relations with China. Yet the Carter administration was ultimately overwhelmed by a combination of events over which it had little control, combined with its own divisions and vacillation. Among the key events were the

Iranian Revolution and the ensuing hostage crisis, the second oil shock, and growing and internationally expanding Soviet strategic military power.[35]

The Soviet Union became more assertive in several parts of the world. Notably, Moscow intervened militarily in Afghanistan at the end of 1979 to shore up the communist regime, which had seized power in a coup in 1978 but was threatened by internal conflicts and the growing strength of anticommunist tribesmen. The different approaches of Secretary of State Cyrus Vance and National Security Adviser Zbigniew Brzezinski in dealing with the Soviet Union were never clearly resolved by Carter until Soviet aggressiveness and Vance's resignation in the wake of a failed hostage rescue attempt in 1980 made the issue moot. Carter's public vacillation on such issues as developing the neutron bomb and his startling statement that he had learned more about the USSR as a result of the invasion of Afghanistan than he had ever known previously convinced many Americans that he was naive, inept, and indecisive. Despite his emphasis in the late 1970s on rebuilding American military power, there was a widespread American and foreign view that the U.S. position vis-à-vis the Soviet Union was deteriorating.

In the Asia-Pacific, Carter initially benefited from the lack of serious challenges faced by the United States after the fall of South Vietnam. Nonetheless, his administration from the outset faced a problem in the Asia-Pacific because of the 1975 public statement by then governor Carter that the United States should withdraw its ground troops from South Korea over the next several years. Carter had been critical of the Republic of Korea (ROK) for its suppression of human rights, and the "Koreagate" scandal involving alleged South Korean gifts of money to U.S. members of Congress in an attempt to secure continued American support of South Korea's military security had generated widespread criticism of Seoul. While President Carter insisted that U.S. air force units would remain in Korea and the U.S.-ROK Security Treaty would still be valid, South Koreans of all political persuasions were fearful that withdrawing American troops would remove a key factor deterring North Korea. The Japanese government, as well as most Asian nations friendly with the United States, was also worried about what was seen as further American retreat from Asia and as another example of American unilateralism on an issue of vital interest to many Asian countries. Even China, though publicly calling for the removal of U.S. troops from Korea, was widely reported to have told U.S. officials that it understood the need for the continued presence of American ground troops in South Korea.[36]

Several factors led President Carter to reverse his position and agree early in 1979 to keep U.S. ground troops in South Korea. For one thing, there were few domestic political pressures pushing him to follow through on his promise. Moreover, opponents of the move pressed for a major intelligence study of the North Korean military forces, which in 1978 concluded that North

Korean forces were much larger, better equipped, and more offensively oriented than previously thought, providing the justification Carter needed to shift his position.

President Carter also was unsuccessful in efforts to normalize relations with Vietnam. The efforts ran across strong opposition in the United States. Other obstacles included Vietnamese demands seen as excessive by Carter administration leaders and the U.S. administration's competing interest in pursuing closer strategic ties with China against the expanding Soviet Union and its associates in Asian and world affairs, notably Vietnam. Vietnam in late 1978 was strongly backed by the Soviet Union as it toppled the Chinese-backed Khmer Rouge regime in neighboring Cambodia. This set the stage for China to confront and attack Vietnam along the Sino-Vietnamese border in early 1979. The convergence of these developments prompted Carter administration negotiators to halt normalization talks with Hanoi.[37]

The Carter administration devoted considerable effort to complete the formal structure of U.S.-China normalization, begun during the Nixon administration, by establishing full diplomatic relations with the PRC and breaking all official ties with the Republic of China (ROC) on Taiwan. In relations with China, President Carter and National Security Adviser Brzezinski followed the pattern of secret diplomacy used successfully by President Nixon and National Security Adviser Henry Kissinger in early interactions with that country. Thus there was very little consultation with Congress, key U.S. allies, or the Taiwan government regarding the conditions and timing of the 1978 normalization agreement. In contrast to general American congressional, media, and popular support for the surprise Nixon opening to China, President Carter and his aides notably were less successful in winning U.S. domestic support for their initiatives. Many in Congress were satisfied with the stasis that developed in U.S.-PRC-ROC relations in the mid-1970s and were unconvinced that the United States had a strategic or other need to pay the price of breaking a U.S. defense treaty and other official ties with a loyal government in Taiwan for the sake of formalizing already existing relations with the PRC. Bipartisan majorities in Congress resisted the president's initiatives and passed laws, notably the Taiwan Relations Act (TRA), that tied the hands of the administration on Taiwan and other issues.[38]

The Taiwan Relations Act was passed by Congress in March 1979 and signed by President Carter on April 10, 1979. The initial draft of the legislation was proposed by the Carter administration to govern American relations with Taiwan once official U.S. ties were ended in 1979. Congress rewrote the legislation, notably adding or strengthening provisions on U.S. arms sales, opposition to threats and use of force, economic relations, human rights, and congressional oversight. Treating Taiwan as a separate entity that would continue to receive U.S. military and other support, the law appeared to

contradict the American stance in the U.S.-PRC communiqué of 1978 establishing official U.S.-PRC relations. Subsequently, Chinese and Taiwan officials and their supporters in the United States competed to incline U.S. policy
toward the commitments in the U.S.-PRC communiqué or the commitments
in the TRA. U.S. policy usually supported both, though it sometimes seemed
more supportive of one set of commitments than the other.[39]

President Carter's Asia policy played a significant role in the 1980 U.S.
presidential campaign. Ronald Reagan attacked Carter's emphasis on human
rights, which he argued was applied more strongly against U.S. allies than
was appropriate. He castigated Carter's admission that the Soviet invasion of
Afghanistan in late 1979 had taught him much about Soviet intentions and
behavior as an indication of Carter's naïveté. Reagan also attacked Carter's
policy toward Taiwan. Asserting for a time that he would restore official
relations with Taipei, Reagan later backed away from this stance but still
claimed he would base his policy on the Taiwan Relations Act.

After the 1980 election, continued rancor appeared likely between President Reagan, who took a hard-line foreign policy stance, and Congress,
which was divided between the House of Representatives controlled by the
Democratic Party and the Senate controlled by the Republican Party. Over
time, however, there emerged a growing spirit of bipartisanship in U.S. policy toward the Asia-Pacific region in the 1980s. In part this had to do with the
fact that the administration's actions were seldom as strong as its rhetoric
might have suggested. Democrats also came to see a need for the stronger
U.S. defense and foreign policy that the Reagan administration advocated in
the face of continued Soviet expansion. The Reagan administration and
Democratic leaders also were willing to consult and compromise on key
issues.[40]

On sensitive matters regarding the authoritarian regime in South Korea,
President Reagan, shortly after he took office, invited South Korean president Chun Doo Hwan to the United States and gave him strong public backing. There apparently was at least an implicit agreement that President Chun
would not execute and would release prominent opposition leader and later
democratically elected president of South Korea Kim Dae Jung and allow
him to leave the country, which Chun did. President Reagan thus could point
to an early success for quiet diplomacy, and Seoul felt that it had a firm
friend in the White House.[41]

The administration also formed policy and practices toward Japan in a
calm and generally supportive manner. Instead of publicly criticizing Japan
for not spending enough on defense in relation to GNP, the focus was placed
upon the appropriate roles and missions Japanese forces should undertake in
conjunction with U.S. forces. Tokyo in 1981 accepted the primary responsibility for its own air defense and agreed to develop the capacity to help
defend sea lanes to one thousand miles to the east and south of Japan. Japan's

steady though small increases in defense spending were regarded by the U.S. administration with satisfaction. Congressional criticism of Japan on such "burden sharing" matters continued but had no major effect on American policy.[42]

It took longer for the Reagan administration to come to a consensus on China policy. President Reagan's pro-Taiwan rhetoric in the 1980 campaign and in the initial period of the administration saw China respond strongly. The Chinese government put heavy pressure on the Reagan administration. It threatened serious deterioration in relations over various issues, especially continuing U.S. arms sales to Taiwan. Viewing close China-U.S. relations as a key element in American strategy against the Soviet Union, Secretary of State Alexander Haig led those in the Reagan administration who favored maintaining close China-U.S. relations and opposed U.S. arms sales to Taiwan that might provoke China. For a year and a half, Haig and his supporters were successful in leading U.S. efforts to accommodate PRC concerns over Taiwan, especially regarding U.S. arms sales to the ROC, in the interest of fostering closer U.S.-China cooperation against the Soviet Union. The United States ultimately signed the August 17, 1982, communiqué with China. In the communiqué, the United States agreed gradually to diminish arms sales, and China agreed that it would seek peaceful reunification of Taiwan with the mainland. Subsequent developments showed that the vague agreement was subject to varying interpretations. President Reagan registered private reservations about this arrangement, and his administration also took steps to reassure Taiwan's leader of continued U.S. support.[43]

Amid continued strong Chinese pressure tactics on a wide range of U.S.-China disputes, American policy shifted with Haig's resignation in 1982 and the appointment of George Shultz as secretary of state. Reagan administration officials who were at odds with Haig's emphasis on the need for a solicitous American approach to China came to the fore. They were led by Paul Wolfowitz, who was chosen by Shultz as assistant secretary of state for East Asian affairs; Richard Armitage, the senior Defense Department officer managing relations with China and East Asia; and the senior National Security Council staff aide on Asian affairs and later assistant secretary of state for East Asian affairs, Gaston Sigur. While officers who had backed Haig's pro-China slant were transferred from authority over China policy, the new U.S. leadership contingent with responsibility for Asian affairs shifted American policy toward a less solicitous and accommodating stance toward China while giving much higher priority to U.S. relations with Japan. There was less emphasis on China's strategic importance to the United States in American competition with the Soviet Union, and there was less concern among U.S. policy makers about China's possibly downgrading relations over Taiwan and other disputes.

This position seemed more in line with the preferences of many in the U.S. Congress, who had resisted efforts to cut back ties with Taiwan for the sake of strengthening American alignment with China against the Soviet Union. The U.S. military buildup and the close U.S.-Japanese security relationship seemed to reduce China's strategic importance in the United States. The administration established a general consensus in the U.S. government and with Congress for the first time since the controversy over the Carter administration's secret move to normalize diplomatic relations with China. By the mid-1980s, there was general agreement that the role of the PRC in U.S. policy calculations was less important than in the previous fifteen years. U.S. officials felt less compelled to make additional sacrifices regarding Taiwan for the sake of ensuring close relations with the PRC.

The more moderate foreign policy of the Soviet Union in the Asia-Pacific following the coming to power of Mikhail Gorbachev in 1985 reinforced stability in the balance of power in the region. At a minimum, Moscow seemed interested by the latter 1980s in easing tensions around its periphery, thereby gaining at least a temporary "breathing space" in which to revive the ailing Soviet economy. At the same time, Gorbachev highlighted political and economic initiatives designed to increase Soviet influence abroad. Gorbachev had more difficulty expanding Soviet influence in Asia than in Europe, and he appeared to view an opening to China as a key link in efforts to improve Soviet influence in the region. Soviet leaders followed through on their repeated pledges to ease military tensions with China by addressing substantive Chinese security concerns. Beijing summarized these concerns as the so-called three obstacles to improved Sino-Soviet relations posed by the Soviet military occupation of Afghanistan, the Soviet military presence along China's northern border, and Soviet support for Vietnam's military occupation of Cambodia.[44]

U.S. ECONOMIC WEAKNESS AND THE RISE OF JAPAN

While a more stable security situation for American interests in the Asia-Pacific developed in the 1980s, a growing set of economic challenges emerged. These challenges seemed fundamentally to undermine important U.S. interests and the leading U.S. position in the region. Overall, East Asian countries advanced rapidly in economic development in the 1980s. They doubled their percentage of world output—from 10 to 20 percent—in ten years. Their combined export trade expanded similarly, leading to huge surpluses with the United States ($27 billion in 1981, $105 billion in 1987). The decade saw American trade with East Asian countries surpass that with European countries. As the Asian economies grew, Asian investment began to enter the United States in order to finance part of its deficits. America and East Asia became economically more interdependent than ever. [45]

In retrospect, it seems ironic that just as resilient American power and obvious Soviet decline appeared to put to rest the widely perceived threat to American leadership seen posed by rising Soviet power, American strategists, specialists, and commentators focused on growing American economic interdependence with Asia in the 1980s as marking a steady decline of U.S. influence and leadership in Asia. During the Cold War, America's ability to counter Soviet power and to promote economic growth and political stability abroad depended heavily on U.S. economic strength and American willingness to make economic sacrifices in order to achieve military and political goals. Such U.S. costs included a large military budget, substantial foreign aid programs, and the free flow of exports from other countries to the U.S. market. By the 1980s, America's economic position was seen by many experts and pundits to be so seriously weakened that America's long-term ability to sustain its leading role in the world, and the Asia-Pacific in particular, was cast in doubt.

Among the salient reasons for the perceived U.S. economic decline was economic progress abroad, especially in East Asia. The Asian economies headed by Japan added competitive pressures on the American economy not seen since before World War II, when foreign trade had a much smaller impact on the U.S. economy. At home, American educational standards were widely reported to have declined, as had product quality, and businesses were seen to be giving increasing priority to short-term profits and financial mergers. Investment levels were inadequate for a more competitive international environment, as were low U.S. savings rates. Federal budget deficits rose, as did the U.S. dollar, and with it the U.S. trade deficit, greatly increasing pressures for protectionism. [46]

The trend toward U.S. economic and trade protectionism grew for important reasons. The first was economic. In 1971, the United States had its first trade deficit since World War II. Trade deficits continued, increasing in size through most of the 1970s and the early 1980s, averaging about $25 billion in 1979–1981. But a surplus in services meant that the United States had a current account surplus and was earning and paying its way in the world, except briefly in 1977 and 1978.

From 1980 there was a dramatic rise in the trade account deficit, which in 1986 amounted to $153 billion. This was due mainly to a sharp rise in imports from $245 billion in 1981 to $370 billion in 1986, while American exports declined from $234 billion in 1981 to $217 billion in 1986. The deficit in the trade balance with Asia, mainly East Asia, increased from $21.8 billion in 1981 to $95.7 billion in 1987. The total deficit for 1987 rose further to $159 billion, despite the fall in the value of the U.S. dollar that year. Exports rose to $253 billion, but imports continued to increase to $412 billion. These trade deficits made the United States a debtor nation for the first time since World War I. It soon became the world's largest debtor nation.[47]

Seeming American economic weakness and decline came as Japan rose to great power prominence in Asian and world affairs. The 1980s witnessed a sweeping change in the relative power of the United States and Japan. This change went well beyond the implications of the bilateral trade deficit, which remained around $50 billion annually even after the major drop in the value of the U.S. dollar in relation to the Japanese yen in the latter 1980s. As the persisting U.S. trade and budget deficits of the early 1980s led to a series of decisions in the mid-1980s that called for a major realignment of the value of the American and Japanese currencies, the immediate result was to greatly strengthen Japan's ability to purchase American goods and to invest in the United States. By the end of the decade, as the United States had reversed its previous position as the world's largest creditor and had become the world's largest debtor, Japan, with its stronger currency, was the largest international creditor.[48]

Americans found it hard to compete with Japan in Asia and were seemingly unable to preserve market share even in the U.S. home market. Japan's growing investments in the United States led to complaints from some American constituencies. Moreover, Japanese industry seemed well positioned to use its economic power to invest in the range of high-technology products where U.S. manufacturers still had the lead. American ability to compete under these circumstances was seen as hampered by heavy personal, government, and business debt, a low savings rate, and other factors.

Based on its economic power and seemingly unstoppable competitiveness, Japan was able steadily to expand its role in the World Bank, the IMF, and such regional organizations as the Asian Development Bank. Investment and trade flows made Japan by far the dominant economic actor in Asia. U.S. leadership seemed to be in steady decline as Japan used its burgeoning investment and trade links to expand political influence in the Asia-Pacific region. While countries in Northeast and Southeast Asia were the main targets of Japanese economic networks of influence, countries in South Asia and the new republics in Central Asia, among others, actively sought Japanese aid and investment, while the United States seemed to have less to offer.[49]

NOTES

1. Akira Iriye, *Across the Pacific: An Inner History of American–East Asian Relations* (New York: Harcourt, Brace & World, 1967); Warren Cohen, ed., *Pacific Passage: The Study of American–East Asian Relations on the Eve of the 21st Century* (New York: Columbia University Press, 1996).

2. Akira Iriye, *After Imperialism: The Search for a New Order in the Far East, 1921–1931* (Cambridge, MA: Harvard University Press, 1965).

3. Ronald Spector, *Eagle against the Sun: The American War with Japan* (New York: Free Press, 1985).

4. John L. Gaddis, *The United States and the Origins of the Cold War, 1941–1947* (New York: Columbia University Press, 1972).

5. Robert M. Blum, *Drawing the Line: The Origins of the American Containment Policy in East Asia* (New York: Norton, 1982).

6. Akira Iriye, *The Cold War in Asia: A Historical Introduction* (Englewood Cliffs, NJ: Prentice Hall, 1974).

7. Robert S. Ross, *Negotiating Cooperation: The United States and China, 1969–1989* (Stanford, CA: Stanford University Press, 1995).

8. James Fallows, "Containing Japan," *Atlantic Monthly* 263 (May 1989): 40–53; George R. Packard, "The Coming U.S.-Japan Crisis," *Foreign Affairs* 66 (Winter 1987–1988).

9. Sometimes the United States has seemed to avow an interest in strategic dominance in the region. During the George W. Bush administration, the U.S. Defense Department's Quadrennial Defense Review of 2006 said, "It [the United States] will also seek to ensure that no foreign power can dictate the terms of regional or global security. It [the United States] will attempt to dissuade any military competitor from developing disruptive or other capabilities that could enable regional hegemony or hostile action against the United States or other friendly countries, and it will seek to deter aggression or coercion. Should deterrence fail, the United States would deny any hostile power its strategic and operational objectives." These stated objectives seemed generally consistent with the United States seeking a favorable balance of power in the Asia-Pacific, though they also seemed more assertive than past U.S. positions. U.S. Department of Defense, *Quadrennial Defense Review Report*, February 6, 2006, 30, http://www.defenselink.mil (accessed August 27, 2007).

10. For sources in addition to those noted for the following historical assessment, see Robert Sutter, *East Asia and the Pacific: Challenges for U.S. Policy* (Boulder, CO: Westview Press, 1992), 15–27.

11. Warren I. Cohen, *America's Response to China: A History of Sino-American Relations* (New York: Columbia University Press, 2010).

12. John K. Fairbank and Suzanne W. Barnett, eds., *Christianity in China* (Cambridge, MA: Harvard University Press, 1985).

13. Michael Schaller, *The United States and China: Into the Twenty-First Century* (New York: Oxford University Press, 2002), 28.

14. Cohen, *America's Response to China*.

15. Michael H. Hunt, *The Making of a Special Relationship: The United States and China to 1914* (New York: Columbia University Press, 1983).

16. Cohen, *America's Response to China*. Schaller, *The United States and China*.

17. Schaller, *The United States and China*, 18–24.

18. For a review of this period, see Michael Hunt, *The American Ascendance: How the United States Gained and Wielded Global Dominance* (Chapel Hill: University of North Carolina Press, 2007), 55–78.

19. Robert Sutter, *East Asia and the Pacific: Challenges for U.S. Policy* (Boulder, CO: Westview Press, 1992), 16.

20. Ibid.

21. Whitney Griswold, *The Far Eastern Policy of the United States* (New York: Harcourt, Brace, 1938).

22. Joseph Nye, *Presidential Leadership and the Creation of the American Era* (Princeton, NJ: Princeton University Press, 2013), 31–35.

23. Sutter, *East Asia and the Pacific*, 17.

24. Ibid.

25. Ibid., 18.

26. Nye, *Presidential Leadership*, 35–40; Hunt, *The American Ascendance*, 100–14.

27. Sutter, *East Asia and the Pacific*, 19.

28. Tang Tsou, *America's Failure in China* (Chicago: University of Chicago Press, 1963).

29. Robert Sutter, *U.S.-Chinese Relations: Perilous Past, Pragmatic Present*, 2nd ed. (Lanham, MD: Rowman & Littlefield, 2013), 55–56.

30. Sutter, *East Asia and the Pacific*, 19.

31. Ibid.

32. Ibid., 19–20.

33. Surveys for this period include Michael Yahuda, *The International Politics of the Asia-Pacific: Change and Continuity in Asian International Relations since World War II* (New York: Routledge, 2004), 62–84, and Alice Lyman Miller and Richard Wich, *Becoming Asia* (Stanford, CA: Stanford University Press, 2011), 161–93.

34. James M. Lindsay, *Congress and the Politics of U.S. Foreign Policy* (Baltimore, MD: Johns Hopkins University Press, 1994).

35. Surveys for this period include Robert Scalapino, Seizaburo Sato, Jusuf Wanandi, and Sung-Joo Han, eds., *Asia and the Major Powers: Domestic Politics and Foreign Policy* (Berkeley: University of California Press, 1988). See, in particular, William Barnds's chapter, "Trends in US Politics and Their Implications for America's Asian Policy." See also, Yahuda, *The International Politics*, 107–12; Miller and Wich, *Becoming Asia*, 170–90.

36. Sutter, *East Asia and the Pacific*, 21–22.

37. Ibid., 22.

38. Sutter, *U.S.-Chinese Relations*, 78–79.

39. Ibid., 79–80.

40. Sutter, *East Asia and the Pacific*, 23.

41. Ibid.

42. Sutter, *East Asia and the Pacific*, 24.

43. Developments in this paragraph and the next two paragraphs are reviewed in Sutter, *U.S.-Chinese Relations*, 70–83.

44. Miller and Wich, *Becoming Asia*, 194–202.

45. Surveys on these topics include Richard Cronin, *Japan, the United States, and Prospects for the Asia-Pacific Century* (Singapore: Institute for Southeast Asian Studies, 1992), and Takashi Inoguchi, *Japan's International Relations* (London: Pinter, 1991).

46. Sutter, *East Asia and the Pacific*, 24.

47. Ibid., 25.

48. Sutter, *The United States and East Asia*, 24–25.

49. Robert Sutter, *The United States in Asia* (Lanham, MD: Rowman & Littlefield, 2009), 22.

Chapter Three

Post–Cold War Developments

POST–COLD WAR AMERICAN PRIORITIES

The 1980s saw the crumbling and collapse of communism in Eastern Europe and soon after in the Soviet Union, a major thaw in U.S.-Soviet relations, and progress toward democracy and political reform in the Soviet Union and Soviet bloc states and many other nations previously influenced by communism. The revolutionary changes reinforced American interest in pursuing closer interaction with reforming Asian countries. These developments made cultural elements and values more important considerations in the making of American foreign policy. Those elements had remained strong in U.S. policy toward the Asia-Pacific even as overall U.S. influence in the region was seen to decline, notably in the face of economic problems and Japan's remarkable rise in regional influence at that time.[1]

Democratization movements in China, South Korea, the Philippines, Taiwan, Burma (Myanmar), and elsewhere in the region during the 1970s and 1980s were all inspired at least in some part by the American example. The 1989 student uprising in Beijing would not have been as massive or at least initially as successful without the knowledge that Americans were watching the event on television. The revolutionary innovations in information and communications technology, much of them products of American engineering, were weaving countries of the world closer together into a global network, and the sense of instantaneous communication was nowhere more pronounced than in the hitherto closed societies of Asia. Even in a more open society like Japan, there were forces tending further to Americanize people's lifestyles.

American society, too, was coming under increasing Asia-Pacific influences. The landmark immigration act of 1965 finally established color-blind

U.S. immigration practices. When combined with various measures to reset-
tle refugees, this development brought an influx of people from the Asia-
Pacific region to the United States. Asians came to account for 2.4 percent of
the U.S. population by the early 1990s. In the largest American state, California, the ratio was much higher, and there was an expectation that Asians
might soon amount to one-third of the state's population. Immigrants from
Vietnam, Korea, China, Taiwan, India, the Philippines, Thailand, Pakistan,
Afghanistan, and other Asia-Pacific countries were much more visible in
American society than before. American people became accustomed to va-
rieties of Asian food, clothing, and religious practices. There were also hundreds of thousands of temporary visitors from Asia as tourists and students.
In 1988 close to three million Japanese tourists came to America, and over
two hundred thousand additional Japanese resided in the United States study-
ing and working. The numbers of Korean and Chinese students in the United
States were larger than the number of Japanese students.

The American reaction to the Chinese government's crackdown on the
Tiananmen Square demonstrations in June 1989 underscored the influence of
culture and values in American foreign policy at the time. The Tiananmen
massacre sharply changed American views about China. Instead of pursuing
policies of political and economic reform, the leaders in Beijing were now
widely seen as following policies antithetical to American values and as
therefore unworthy of American support. Rapidly changing U.S.-Soviet relations also meant that there was no longer a realpolitik or national security
rationale of sufficient weight to offset the new revulsion with Beijing's leaders and their repressive policies.

Other parts of the world, meanwhile, saw political, economic, and security changes that attracted wide and generally positive attention from
American people, media, interest groups, and legislators. Russia, some new
republics of the former Soviet Union in Asia, and former Soviet bloc states
like Mongolia were increasingly following policies of reform in their government structures and economies that seemed to be based on values of individual freedom, political democracy, and economic free enterprise that were
well regarded in the United States. As a result, these American interest
groups, media, and policy advocates tended at times to push U.S. government decision makers to be more forthcoming in negotiations and interaction
with them involving arms control, trade, foreign assistance, and other matters.

The importance of this shift in domestic U.S. opinion regarding China
and the former Soviet Union and Soviet bloc countries appeared to be of
greater significance than it might have been in the past in determining the
course of U.S. foreign policy. Since the start of the Cold War, the executive
branch had been able to argue, on many occasions quite persuasively, that
such domestic U.S. concerns with common values should not be permitted to

override or seriously complicate realpolitik U.S. interests in the protracted struggle and rivalry with the USSR. Now that it was widely seen that the Cold War was ending and the threat from Moscow was ended or greatly reduced, the ability of the executive branch to control the course of U.S. foreign policy appeared somewhat weakened. The U.S. administration could no longer argue that the dangers of Cold War contention and confrontation required a tightly controlled foreign policy.

Indeed, following the end of the Cold War, Americans were deeply divided over foreign policy, and contending policy perspectives were not easily bridged to develop coherent policy toward the Asia-Pacific or other important areas. Because security issues and opposition to Soviet expansion no longer drove U.S. foreign policy, economic interests, democratization abroad, and human rights gained greater prominence. Various pressure groups and other institutions interested in these and other subjects also enhanced influence in policy making. Historically, such fluidity and competition among priorities were more often than not the norm. Woodrow Wilson and Franklin Roosevelt both set forth comprehensive concepts of a well-integrated U.S. foreign policy, but neither framework lasted long.[2] The requirements of the Cold War were much more effective in establishing rigor and order in U.S. foreign policy priorities, but that era now was over.

In particular, the post–Cold War period saw substantial changes in the way foreign policy was made in the United States. In general, there was a shift away from the elitism of the past and toward much greater pluralism. This increased the opportunity for input by nongovernmental or lobby groups with particular interests in foreign policy.

The elitist model of foreign policy making included the following characteristics[3]:

- Domination of the process by the executive branch, particularly by the White House, the State Department, and the Pentagon.
- Presidential consultation with a bipartisan leadership in Congress and mobilization through them of broad congressional support for the administration's foreign policy.
- Parallel consultations with a relatively small group of elites outside government, some of whom were specialists on the particular issue under consideration and others of whom had a more general interest in foreign policy as a whole.
- Mobilization of public support through the major newspapers and television programs, other media outlets, and civic organizations.

Gradually, however, this process was transformed in much more pluralistic directions to take on quite different characteristics:

- A much greater range of agencies within the executive branch involved in foreign policy, with the rise of the economic agencies (Commerce Department, Treasury Department, and U.S. Trade Representative [USTR] Office) of particular importance.
- A seeming reallocation of power within government, away from the executive branch and toward Congress.
- Much greater participation by nongovernmental organizations and lobbying groups, which attempt to shape foreign policy to conform to their interests.
- Much less consensus within Congress, and within the broader public, over foreign policy.

In the 1990s, there was consensus that foreign policy should not be expensive. The fate of the international affairs budget in the U.S. Congress after the Cold War in the 1990s indicated that Americans wanted foreign policy both to cost less and to give more benefit. Unfortunately, there was little agreement on how to accomplish these objectives. Few Americans were aware that foreign policy spending accounted for less than 1 percent of the federal budget. There appeared to be different tendencies or schools of thought regarding post–Cold War foreign policy. These approaches seemed to divide into three schools, though they were not necessarily exclusive. In particular, a U.S. leader demonstrated aspects of one tendency at some times and aspects of another tendency at other times. An understanding of what these schools stood for underscores how difficult it was to gauge the direction of U.S. policy toward the Asia-Pacific or other key areas of international concern.[4]

One school was particularly prominent in the first half of the 1990s when troubled U.S. economic conditions and large U.S. government budget deficits added to a sense of relative decline in U.S. power and its implications for U.S. ability to protect its interests. It called for the United States to work harder to preserve important interests while adjusting to limited resources and reduced influence. Advocates of this position expected continued international instability and limited U.S. ability to respond. They observed that there was no international framework to shape policy; that U.S. policy must use a complex mix of international, regional, and bilateral efforts to achieve policy goals; and that security, economic, and cultural-political issues would compete for priority in policy making. They argued that in this uncertain environment, pressing domestic problems would take precedence over attention to international affairs and restrict financial resources available for foreign policy, defense, and international security. They also believed that policy making would remain difficult because the executive branch might remain under the control of one political party and Congress under the control of the other party.

This school—reflected in the commentary of such leaders as former president George H. W. Bush, Henry Kissinger, and others—argued that these circumstances required the United States to work closely with traditional allies and associates. Regarding the Asia-Pacific, it contended that it was consistent with U.S. goals to preserve long-standing good relations with Japan and other friends and allies in the Asia-Pacific whose security policies and political-cultural orientations complemented American interests. It urged caution in policy toward other regional powers: Russia, China, and India. All three countries were preoccupied with internal political-development issues and did not appear to want regional instability. All sought closer economic and political relations with the West and with other advancing economies. Washington would be well advised, they said, to work closely with these governments wherever there were common interests. In considering U.S. assets available to influence regional trends, they called on the United States to go slowly in reducing its regional military presence. The economic savings of cutbacks would be small; the political costs could be high insofar as most countries in the Asia-Pacific encouraged the United States to remain active in the region to offset the growing power of Japan and China.

A second school was also particularly prominent during the troubled American economic conditions of the early 1990s. It argued for major cutbacks in U.S. international activity, including military involvement, and a renewed focus on solving such domestic problems as crime, drug use, economic competitiveness, educational standards, homelessness, poverty, decaying cities, and transportation infrastructure. Variations of this view were seen in the writings of William Hyland, Patrick Buchanan, and other well-known commentators and in the political statements of independent presidential candidate Ross Perot and some segments of U.S. labor organizations. Often called an "America first" or "neo-isolationist" school, it contended that the United States had become overextended in world affairs and was being taken advantage of in the current world security-economic system. It called for sweeping cuts in spending for international activities, favoring a U.S. pullback from foreign bases and major cuts in foreign assistance and foreign technical-information programs. It was skeptical of the utility of international financial institutions and the United Nations and of international efforts to promote free trade through the World Trade Organization (WTO). It advocated termination of international economic talks that help to perpetuate a liberal world trading system that in practice increased U.S. economic dependence and injured some American workers and industries. Some favored trade measures that were seen as protectionist by American trading partners.

A third position became much more prominent as American economic conditions improved and government spending resumed increases amid record budget surpluses in the mid- and later 1990s. It argued that U.S. policy needed to promote American interests in international political, military, and

economic affairs more actively and to use U.S. influence to pressure countries that did not conform to U.S.-backed norms of an appropriate world
order. Supporters of this position wanted the United States to maintain military forces with worldwide capabilities, to lead strongly in world affairs, and
to minimize compromises and accommodations.

This school of thought was present in American politics throughout the
twentieth century, especially since World War II. However, for several reasons it was stronger in the middle and late 1990s than at any time since the
1960s. During the Reagan administration, after a prolonged period of intro-
spection and doubt following the Vietnam War, oil shocks, and the Iran
hostage crisis, the American public became more optimistic about the future
of the United States. This trend was reinforced by the end of the Cold War, a
landmark victory for the U.S.-backed system of collective security and for
U.S. political and economic values. The outcome of the 1991 Persian Gulf
War with Iraq further inspired confidence in U.S. military doctrine, equipment, and performance and in America's international leadership ability. The
improved economic conditions of the U.S. government later in the 1990s
reinforced this trend.

Those who supported this view acknowledged that America faced many
serious international and domestic challenges, but they were optimistic that
the United States could succeed in a competitive world economy. They also
insisted that the United States was better positioned than any other country to
exert leadership in the realm of ideas and values, political concepts, lifestyle,
popular culture, and international organizations. They perceived a global
power vacuum, caused notably by the collapse of the Soviet Empire and the
demise of communism, which allowed the United States to exert influence.
They argued that Russia, China, and India would remain preoccupied with
domestic problems. They acknowledged that Japan and Germany were economically powerful but also uncertain regarding how to use their power; they
lacked American cultural attractiveness and influence.

In the middle and late 1990s, advocates of this third tendency were most
vocal in pressing for a strong policy in support of democracy and human
rights. They argued for a more active foreign policy, which led some targeted
countries to view U.S. policy as interference in other countries' internal
affairs. They opposed economic or trading policies of other countries seen as
inequitable or predatory. They pressed for a strong policy against proliferation of weapons of mass destruction. Members of this school also argued
variously for sanctions against countries that practiced coercive birth control,
seriously polluted the environment, or harbored terrorists and promoted the
illegal drug trade. They believed the United States should be more assertive
in promoting humanitarian relief and in recognizing the legitimacy of people's right to self-determination. Republican leaders in Congress following
the victory of the Republican Party in the 1994 congressional elections in-

cluded Speaker of the House Newt Gingrich and were seen to push this more assertive U.S. role in world affairs.

The shifts and evolution of U.S. policy and developments in U.S.-Asian relations in the post–Cold War period are examined in chapters 5 through 10 dealing in detail with U.S. relations with specific countries and regions. To demonstrate here the flux in American policy toward the region in the post–Cold War period, highlighted in the following section is an examination of the twists and turns in the most important American relationship in the region, the U.S.-China relationship.

The uncertainty and fluidity in the Sino-American relationship at this time underlined the shifts and flux in American relations with the entire region. The sometimes abrupt changes in U.S.-China relations were driven in part by continued American debate on how to deal with major differences with a Chinese state growing in power and influence in ways that challenged U.S. security, economic, and political interests. For their part, Chinese leaders maneuvered between policies designed to assert Chinese interests and challenge the United States where America impeded Chinese objectives and policies that pragmatically sought stability in Sino-American relations. Major developments included the creation of a massive security dilemma caused by China's impressive military buildup of coercive power to secure its sovereignty and security interests in Taiwan and in other disputed territory along China's rim and by vigilant U.S. military measures to counter and offset the Chinese advances. Trade and other economic relations moved from being the main common ground between the two countries to become a source of increasing acrimony and friction despite ever-growing Sino-American economic interdependence. Whatever trust had been built between U.S.-Chinese leaders in the previous two decades was shattered with the Tiananmen crackdown and many years of virulent American attacks against Chinese leaders' policies and practices seen as illegitimate and beyond the pale of accepted world norms. American actions seemed to support regime change in China—undermining the core Communist Party determination to sustain one-party rule.

U.S. ASIA-PACIFIC POLICY IN FLUX: THE EXAMPLE OF U.S. CHINA POLICY AFTER THE COLD WAR

The broad scope of contending interests and schools of thought in American policy toward the Asia-Pacific region in the post–Cold War period is well illustrated in the tortuous course of U.S. policy toward China.[5] Unexpected mass demonstrations centered in Beijing's Tiananmen Square and other Chinese cities in spring 1989 represented the most serious challenge to China's post-Mao leadership. Chinese leader Deng Xiaoping was decisive in resolving Chinese leadership differences in favor of hard-liners who wanted a violent crackdown on the demonstrators and a broader suppression of political dissent that began with the bloody attack on Tiananmen Square on June 4, 1989. Reform-minded leaders were purged and punished.

Anticipating shock and disapproval at the Tiananmen crackdown from the United States and the West, Deng nonetheless argued that such unfavorable reactions would have few prolonged negative consequences for China. The Chinese leader failed to anticipate the breadth and depth of American disapproval, which would profoundly influence U.S. policy into the twenty-first century. The influence was compounded by the unanticipated and dramatic collapse of communist regimes in the Soviet bloc and other areas, leading to the demise of the Soviet Union by the early 1990s. These developments undermined the perceived need for the United States to cooperate pragmatically with China despite its brutal dictatorship on account of a U.S. strategic need for international support against the Soviet Union. Meanwhile, Taiwan's authoritarian government was moving steadily at this time to promote democratic policies and practices, marking a sharp contrast to the harsh political authoritarianism in mainland China and greatly enhancing Taiwan's popularity and support in the United States.

Taken together, these circumstances generally placed the initiative in U.S.-China relations with American leaders. Chinese leaders at first focused on maintaining internal stability as they maneuvered to sustain workable economic relations with the United States while rebuffing major U.S. initiatives that infringed on Chinese internal political control or territorial and sovereignty issues involving Taiwan and Tibet. As the Chinese government presided over strong economic growth beginning in 1993, enjoying the U.S. and other international attention that came with it, Chinese leaders reflected more confidence as they dealt with American pressures for change. However, they generally eschewed direct confrontation that would endanger the critically important economic relations with the United States unless China was provoked by U.S., Taiwan, or other actions.

Effective U.S. policy toward China proved elusive in the midst of contentious American domestic debate over China policy during the 1990s. That debate was not stilled until the September 11, 2001, terrorist attack on America muffled for a time continued American concerns over China amid an overwhelming American concern to deal with the immediate, serious, and broad consequences of the global war on terrorism.

President George H. W. Bush, with strong personal conviction in the importance of cooperative U.S. relations with China, strove to preserve cooperative ties despite widespread American outrage and pressure for retribution and sanctions against Chinese leaders. President Bush was the U.S. chief executive most experienced in dealing with China. He had served as the head of the American Liaison Office in China in the mid-1970s. Bush took the lead in his own administration (1989–1993) in dealing with severe problems in China-U.S. relations caused by the Tiananmen crackdown and the decline in American strategic interest in China as a result of the collapse of the Soviet bloc. He resorted to secret diplomacy to maintain constructive communication with senior Chinese leaders, but the latter remained fairly rigid and were unable or unwilling to make many gestures to help Bush justify a continued moderate U.S. stance toward China amid wide-ranging American skepticism and hostility in the U.S. Congress, media, and interest groups. While his administration officials said all high-level official contact with China would be cut off as a result of the Tiananmen crackdown, President Bush sent his national security adviser and the deputy secretary of state on secret missions to Beijing in July and December 1989. When the missions became known in December 1989, the congressional and media reaction was bitterly critical of the administration's perceived duplicity.[6]

Bush eventually became frustrated with the Chinese leadership's intransigence and took a tough stance on trade and other issues, though he made special efforts to ensure that the United States continued most-favored-nation (MFN) tariff status for China despite opposition by a majority of the U.S. Congress and much of the American media. Reflecting more positive American views of the Republic of China (ROC) government on Taiwan, the Bush administration upgraded U.S. interchange with the ROC by sending a cabinet-level official to Taipei in 1992, the first such visit since official relations were ended in 1979. He also seemed to abandon the limits on U.S. arms sales set in accord with the August 1982 U.S. communiqué with China by agreeing in 1992 to a sale of 150 advanced F-16 jet fighters to Taiwan worth over $5 billion.[7]

Presidential candidate Bill Clinton used sharp attacks against Chinese government behavior, notably the Tiananmen crackdown, and President Bush's moderate approach to China to win support in the 1992 election. The presidential candidate's attacks, though probably reflecting sincere anger and concern over Chinese behavior, also reflected a tendency in the U.S. China debate in the 1990s to use China issues, particularly criticism of China and U.S. policy toward China, for partisan and other ulterior purposes. For candidate Clinton and his aides, using China issues to discredit the record of the Republican candidate, George H. W. Bush, proved to be an effective way to take votes from the incumbent. Once he won the election and was in office, President Clinton showed little interest in China policy, leaving the responsibility to subordinates.[8]

In particular, in 1993, Assistant Secretary of State for East Asia Affairs Winston Lord played the lead administration role in working with congressional leaders, notably Senate Majority Leader George Mitchell and a House of Representatives leader on China and human rights issues, Representative Nancy Pelosi, among others, to establish the human rights conditions the

Clinton administration would require before renewing most-favored-nation tariff status for China. The terms he worked out were widely welcomed in the United States at the time. However, Chinese government leaders were determined not to give in on several of the U.S. demands, and they appeared to calculate that American business interests in a burgeoning Chinese economy would be sufficient to prevent the United States from taking the drastic step of cutting MFN tariff treatment for China and risking the likely retaliation of the PRC against growing American trade interests. In the event, American business pressures did push Clinton to intervene in May 1994 to reverse existing policy and allow for unimpeded U.S. renewal of MFN status for China.

Pro-Taiwan interests in the United States, backed by American public relations firms in the pay of entities and organizations in Taiwan, took advantage of congressional elections in 1995 giving control of Congress to pro-Taiwan Republican leaders. They pushed for greater U.S. support for Taiwan, notably a visit by ROC president Lee Teng-hui to his alma mater, Cornell University. Under heavy domestic political pressure, President Clinton intervened again and allowed Taiwan's president to visit the United States.

A resulting military confrontation with China in the Taiwan Strait eventually involving two U.S. aircraft carrier battle groups saw the Clinton administration move to a much more coherent engagement policy toward China that received consistent and high-level attention from the president and his key aides and was marked by two U.S.-China summit meetings in 1997 and 1998. Progress included U.S.-China agreement on China's entry into the World Trade Organization and U.S. agreement to provide permanent normal trade status for China. However, the new approach failed to still the vigorous American debate against forward movement in U.S. relations with China on a wide range of strategic, economic, political, and other issues.

As in the case of Clinton's attacks on George H. W. Bush, many of the attacks on Clinton's engagement policy with China after 1996 were not so much focused on China and China issues for their own sake as on partisan or other concerns. Most notably, as congressional Republican leaders sought to impeach President Clinton and tarnish the reputation of his administration, they endeavored to dredge up a wide range of charges regarding illegal Chinese fund-raising, Chinese espionage, and wide Chinese deviations from international norms regarding human rights, nuclear weapons and ballistic missile proliferation, and other questions. They used these charges to discredit President Clinton's moderate engagement policy toward China and, in so doing, cast serious doubt on the moral integrity and competence of the president and his aides.[9]

The Clinton policy of engagement with China also came under attack from organized labor interests within the Democratic Party, some of which used the attacks on the administration's China policy as a means to get the administration to pay more attention to broader labor interests within the Democratic Party. In a roughly similar fashion, social conservatives in the Republican Party used sharp attacks against the continuation of U.S. most-favored-nation tariff status for China (a stance often supported by congressional Republican leaders) because of that country's coercive birth control policies; they did this in part as a means to embarrass and pressure Republican leaders to pay more attention to the various issues on the agenda of the social conservatives.

During the 1990s, congressional criticism of China and moderation in U.S. policy toward China was easy to do and generally had benefits for those doing the criticism. The criticism generated positive coverage from American media strongly critical of China. It generated positive support and perhaps some fund-raising and electioneering support for the congressional critics by the many interest groups in the United States that focused criticism on Chinese policies and practices at that time. The Chinese government, anxious to keep the economic relationship with the United States on an even keel, was disinclined to punish such congressional critics or take substantive action against them. More likely were Chinese invitations to such critical congressional members for all-expenses-paid trips to China in order to persuade them to change their views by seeing actual conditions in China. Finally, President Clinton, like President George H. W. Bush, often was not in a position to risk other legislative goals by punishing members critical of his China policy. In short, from a congressional perspective and a broader perspective in American politics, sharp congressional criticism of China in the 1990s became, in congressional parlance, a "free ride," with many benefits for those doing the criticizing and few perceived drawbacks.

As President Clinton and his White House staff took more control over China policy after the face-off with Chinese forces in the Taiwan Strait in 1996, they emphasized—like George H. W. Bush—a moderate policy of engagement, seeking change in offensive Chinese government practices through a gradual process involving closer Chinese integration with the world economic and political order. The U.S.-China relationship improved but also encountered significant setbacks and resistance. The president's more activist and positive policy of engagement with China saw such high points as the China-U.S. summits in 1997 and 1998, the Sino-U.S. agreement on China's entry into the WTO in 1999, and passage of U.S. legislation in 2000 granting China permanent normal trade relations status. Low points in the relationship during this time included strong congressional opposition to the president's stance against Taiwan independence in 1998, the May 1999 bombing of the Chinese embassy in Belgrade and Chinese demonstrators trashing U.S. diplomatic properties in China, strident congressional criticism in the so-called Cox Committee report of May 1999 charging administration officials with gross malfeasance in guarding U.S. secrets and weaponry from Chinese spies, and partisan congressional investigations of Clinton adminis-tration political fund-raising that highlighted illegal contributions from sources connected to the Chinese regime and the alleged impact they had on the administration's more moderate approach to the PRC.

Lee Teng-hui added to Taiwan Strait tension and worried American poli-cy makers when he asserted in July 1999 that Taiwan was a state separate from China and that China and Taiwan had "special state-to-state relations." Chinese leaders saw this as a step toward Taiwan independence and reacted with strong rhetoric, the intrusion of military probes into ROC-controlled airspace over the Taiwan Strait, and the cutting off of cross-strait communi-cation links.

TWENTY-FIRST-CENTURY DEVELOPMENTS

The initial toughness that the George W. Bush administration adopted toward China subsided with the September 11, 2001, terrorist attack on America and later developments. There followed several years of generally cooperative relations where the George W. Bush administration and Chinese counterparts dealt with differences in a burgeoning array of official dialogues and worked together to deal with such sensitive issues as North Korea's nuclear weapons program and efforts by Taiwan's president to promote greater separation and independence of Taiwan from China. The Taiwan issue declined in impor-tance as Taiwan president Ma Ying-jeou took power in May 2008 and car-ried out a policy of accommodation and reassurance toward China that was welcomed by both the PRC and U.S. governments.

The Barack Obama government strove in vain to preserve the overall positive momentum in U.S.-Chinese relations seen in the latter Bush years. Relations deteriorated over trade and related economic policies and a range of other issues, notably reaching a low point during the prolonged U.S. presidential primaries and election campaign in 2012, which featured often harsh attacks on China. China became more assertive in support of its inter-ests at odds with the United States, notably claims to disputed territory along its rim, especially in the East and South China Seas. For its part, the Obama government focused on a new approach known as the "pivot" to and later as the "rebalance" in the broad Asia-Pacific region that had military, economic, and diplomatic dimensions at odds with Chinese interests. Amid widely pub-licized assessments of deep mutual suspicion and mistrust among Sino-American leaders, U.S.-China relations became overtly competitive as both powers sought greater influence and power in Asia. Overall, the develop-ments challenged but did not reverse the continued strong pragmatic interest on both sides to seek cooperation where possible and to avoid conflict and confrontation.

RELATIONS DURING THE GEORGE W. BUSH ADMINISTRATION

George W. Bush became president in 2001 with a policy more critical of China than the policy of his predecessor had been. Seeking to sustain economic relations with China, the new president was wary of China's strategic intentions and took steps to deter China from using military force against Taiwan. Relations deteriorated when on April 1, 2001, a Chinese jet fighter crashed with a U.S. reconnaissance plane, the EP-3, in international waters off the China coast. The jet was destroyed and the pilot killed. The EP-3 was seriously damaged but managed to make an emergency landing on China's Hainan Island. The U.S. crew was held for eleven days and the U.S. plane much longer by Chinese authorities. Weeks of negotiations produced compromises that allowed the crew and plane to return to the United States, but neither side accepted responsibility for the incident.

Many specialists predicted continued deterioration of relations, but both governments worked to resolve issues and to establish a businesslike rapport that emphasized positive aspects of the relationship and played down differences. The terrorist attack on America on September 11, 2001, diverted U.S. attention away from China as a potential strategic threat. Preoccupied with leadership transition and other issues in China, Chinese leaders worked hard to moderate previous harsh rhetoric and pressure tactics in order to consolidate relations with the United States.

Some specialists were encouraged by the surprising improvement in U.S.-China relations during the administration of President George W. Bush. They tended to emphasize greater Chinese leadership confidence and maturity as the cause for the turnabout in relations, arguing that such confidence and maturity prompted the Chinese government to deal more moderately and with restraint regarding some of the seeming challenges posed by the new U.S. administration and its policies regarding Taiwan, weapons proliferation, and ballistic missile defense and the overall greater U.S. assertiveness and national security power in Asian and world affairs. Another group of specialists was less convinced that U.S.-China relations were destined to converge substantially over Asian and world affairs. These specialists emphasized the importance of what they saw as the Bush administration moving fairly rapidly from an initial toughness toward China to a stance of accommodation and compromise. The shift toward a moderate U.S. stance prompted Chinese leaders to pursue greater moderation in turn in their overall approach to Asian and world affairs. A third view involved specialists, including this writer, who gave more weight to the Bush administration's firm and effective

policies toward China, which were seen to have curbed assertive and potentially disruptive Chinese tendencies and to have made it in China's interests
to avoid confrontation, seek better U.S. ties, and avoid challenges to U.S.
interests in Asian and world affairs. This view held that it was more China
than the United States that took the lead in seeking better ties in 2001 and
that greater U.S.-China cooperation in Asian affairs depended not so much
on Chinese confidence and maturity as on effective U.S. use of power and
influence to keep assertive and disruptive Chinese tendencies in check and to
prevail upon China to limit emphasis on differences with the United States. [10]

All three schools of thought judged that the improvement in U.S.-China
relations reinforced generally moderate Chinese tendencies in Asian and
world affairs, but their differences over the causes of the U.S.-China thaw
had implications for assessing future Chinese policy and behavior. In the first
instance, the key variable seemed to be Chinese confidence and maturity,
which presumably would continue to grow along with Chinese development
and moderation, suggesting a continued moderate Chinese approach for the
next several years if not longer. The latter two views depended heavily on the
United States, with the first view arguing that continued U.S. moderation and
accommodation of Chinese interests was required, as a firmer U.S. stance
presumably could lead to a more assertive and aggressive Chinese stance in
the region. The second of the latter two views indicated that much depended
on continued U.S. resolve, power, and effectiveness in dealing with China.
Weakness or extremism in the U.S. stance could reverse the prevailing trend
of Chinese moderation in the region and lead to a more assertive and disruptive approach.

In any event, the course of U.S.-China relations was smoother than at any
time since the normalization of U.S.-China relations. U.S. preoccupation
with the wars in Afghanistan and Iraq and the broader war on global terrorism meant that U.S. strategic attention to China as a threat remained a secondary consideration for American policy makers. Chinese leaders for their part
continued to deal with the broad problem of trying to sustain a one-party
authoritarian political regime amid a vibrant economy and rapid social
change. In this context, the two powers, despite a wide range of continuing
differences spanning from Taiwan and Tibet to trade issues and human
rights, managed to see their interests best served by generally emphasizing
the positive. In particular, they found new common ground in dealing with
the crisis caused by North Korea's nuclear weapons program beginning in
2002, and the Chinese appreciated Bush's warning in December 2003 to
Taiwan's leader Chen Shui-bian to avoid steps toward independence for
Taiwan that could lead to conflict in the Taiwan Strait.

Looking back, it appears that patterns of Bush administration policy and
behavior toward China began to change significantly in 2003. American
officials sometimes continued to speak in terms of "shaping" Chinese poli-

cies and behavior through tough deterrence along with moderate engagement. However, the thrust of U.S. policy and behavior increasingly focused on positive engagement. China also received increasingly high priority in U.S. policy in Asia and the world.[11]

The determinants of the U.S. approach now appeared to center on the Bush administration's growing preoccupations with the war in Iraq, the mixed record in other areas in the war on terror and broader complications in the Middle East, and broad international and growing domestic disapproval of Bush administration policies. The North Korean nuclear program emerged as a major problem in 2003, and the U.S. government came to rely heavily on China to help manage the issue in ways that avoided major negative fallout for the interests of the U.S. government. Although Asian policy did not figure prominently in the 2004 presidential campaign, Senator John Kerry, the Democratic candidate, used a televised presidential debate to challenge President Bush's handling of North Korea's nuclear weapons development. President Bush countered by emphasizing his reliance on China in order to manage the issue in accord with U.S. interests.[12]

The Bush administration's determination to avoid trouble with China at a time of major foreign policy troubles elsewhere saw the president and senior U.S. leaders strongly pressure Taiwan's government to stop initiating policies seen as provocative by China and that could be possible causes of confrontation and war in U.S.-China relations.[13] The strong rhetorical emphasis on democracy promotion in the Bush administration's second term notably avoided serious pressures against China's authoritarian system.

The U.S. government's emphasis on positive engagement with China did not hide the many continuing U.S.-China differences or American efforts to plan for contingencies in case a rising China turned aggressive or otherwise disrupted U.S. interests. The United States endeavored to use growing interdependence, engagement, and dialogues with China to foster webs of relationships that would tie down or constrain possible Chinese policies and actions deemed negative to U.S. interests.[14]

On the whole, the Chinese administration of President Hu Jintao welcomed and supported the new directions in U.S. China policy. The Chinese leaders endeavored to build on the positives and play down the negatives in relations with the United States. This approach fit well with the Chinese leadership's broader priorities of strengthening national development and Communist Party legitimacy that were said to require China to use carefully the "strategic opportunity" of prevailing international circumstances seen as generally advantageous to Chinese interests. As in the case of U.S. policy toward China, Chinese engagement with the United States did not hide Chinese contingency plans against suspected U.S. encirclement, pressure, and containment and the Chinese use of engagement and interdependence as a type of Gulliver strategy to constrain and tie down possible U.S. policies and actions deemed negative to Chinese interests. [15]

As China expanded its military power along with economic and diplomatic relations in Asian and world affairs at a time of U.S. preoccupation with the war in Iraq and other foreign policy problems, debate emerged inside and outside the U.S. government about the implications of China's rise for U.S. interests. Within the Bush administration, there emerged three viewpoints or schools of thought, though U.S. officials frequently were eclectic, holding views of the implications of China's rise from various perspectives. [16]

On one side were U.S. officials who judged that China's rise in Asia was designed by the Chinese leadership to dominate Asia and in the process to undermine American leadership in the region. A more moderate view of China's rise in Asia came from U.S. officials who judged that China's focus in the region was to improve China's position in Asia mainly in order to sustain regional stability, promote China's development, reassure neighbors and prevent balancing against China, and isolate Taiwan. Officials of this school of thought judged that China's intentions were not focused on isolating and weakening the United States in Asia. Nevertheless, the Chinese policies and behavior, even though not targeted against the United States, contrasted with perceived inattentive and maladroit U.S. policies and practices. The result was that China's rise was having an indirect but substantial negative impact on U.S. leadership in Asia.

A third school of thought was identified with U.S. Deputy Secretary of State Robert Zoellick, who by 2005 publicly articulated a strong argument for greater American cooperation with China over Asian and other issues as China rose in regional and international prominence. This viewpoint held that the United States had much to gain from working directly and cooperatively with China in order to encourage the PRC to use its rising influence in "responsible" ways in accord with broad U.S. interests in Asian and world affairs. This viewpoint seemed to take account of the fact that the Bush administration was already working closely with China in the six-party talks to deal with North Korea's nuclear weapons development and that U.S. and Chinese collaboration or consultations continued on such sensitive topics as the war on terror, Afghanistan, Pakistan, Iran, Sudan, Myanmar, and even Taiwan as well as bilateral economic, security, and other issues. Thus, this school of thought put less emphasis than the other two on competition with China and more emphasis on cooperation with China in order to preserve and enhance U.S. leadership and interests in Asia as China rises.

Bush administration policy came to embrace the third point of view. Senior U.S. leaders reviewed in greater depth the implications of China's rise and the strengths and weaknesses of the United States in Asia. The review showed that U.S. standing as Asia's leading power was basically sound. American military deployments and cooperation throughout the Asia-Pacific region were robust. American economic importance in the region was growing, not declining. Overall, it was clear that no other power or coalition of powers was even remotely able or willing to undertake the costs, risks, and commitments of the United States in sustaining regional stability and development essential for the core interests of the vast majority of regional governments. Thus China's rise—while increasingly important—posed less substantial and significant challenge for U.S. interests than many of the published commentaries and specialists' assessments might have led one to believe.

On this basis, the U.S. administration increasingly emphasized positive engagement and a growing number of dialogues with China, encouraging China to act responsibly and building ever-growing webs of relationships and interdependence. This pattern fit well with Chinese priorities regarding national development in a period of advantageous international conditions while building interdependencies and relationships that constrained possible negative U.S. policies and behaviors.

The Republicans lost control of the U.S. House of Representatives and the U.S. Senate in the 2006 election, and the Bush administration faced greater criticism of its foreign policies, including policies toward China, from congressional Democrats backed by the American media. Congressional critics focused special attention on economic problems including the large trade deficit with China and a resulting loss of American jobs. Against this backdrop, Treasury Secretary Henry Paulson was appointed to lead a new Strategic Economic Dialogue with Chinese counterparts. They met twice a year in an effort to manage differences and ease tensions, especially over salient trade and related economic problems.

The positive stasis in U.S.-China relations that emerged in the latter years of the George W. Bush administration generally met the near-term priorities of the U.S. and Chinese governments. Converging U.S. and Chinese engagement policies tried to broaden common ground while they dealt with differences through engagement policies and dialogues designed to constrain each other's possible disruptive or negative moves.

Neither the Chinese leadership nor the U.S. administration sought trouble with the other. Both were preoccupied with other issues. Heading the list of preoccupations for both governments was dealing with the massive negative consequences of the international economic crisis and deep recession begun in 2008. Other preoccupations of the outgoing Bush administration included Iraq, Afghanistan, Pakistan, Iran, broader Middle East issues, North Korea, and other foreign policy problems, which came on top of serious adverse economic developments.

The global economic decline added to Chinese leaders' preoccupations in dealing with the results of the October 2007 Seventeenth Chinese Communist Party Congress and the Eleventh National People's Congress in March

2008. Those meetings and subsequent developments showed a collective leadership, with Hu Jintao first among equals but not dominant, that continued to debate appropriate ways to meet a wide variety of pressing economic, social, political, and other issues at home and abroad. The leaders sought, with only mixed results, lines of policy and action that avoided major cost and risk to China's ruling party leadership while endeavoring to promote Chinese development and the stability of one-party rule. There remained uncertainty about the major leadership transition expected at the Eighteenth Congress in 2012—a serious matter in an authoritarian political system like China's.[17]

The U.S. and Chinese administrations worked hard to use multiple formal dialogues, high-level meetings and communications, and official rhetoric emphasizing the positive in their relationship in order to offset and manage negative implications from the many differences and issues that continued to complicate U.S.-China relations. Neither leadership publicly emphasized the major differences over key policy issues regarding economic, military, and political questions. Notably, growing trade and economic disputes came with continued military buildups along China's rim that worsened an ongoing security dilemma between the two powers in the Asia-Pacific region.

RELATIONS DURING THE BARACK OBAMA ADMINISTRATION

As a presidential candidate in 2008, Barack Obama was unusual in recent U.S. presidential politics in not making a significant issue of his predecessor's China policy. Like President Bush, the new president showed a measured and deliberative course with China involving pursuing constructive contacts, preserving and protecting American interests, and dealing effectively with challenges posed by rising Chinese influence and power.[18]

A major theme in President Obama's initial foreign policy was to seek the cooperation of other world powers, notably China, to deal with salient international concerns such as the global economic crisis and recession, climate change, nuclear weapons proliferation, and terrorism. He and his team made vigorous efforts to build common ground with China on these and related issues. China's leaders offered limited cooperation, disappointing the Obama government.[19]

More worrisome, Chinese actions and assertions in 2009 and 2010 directly challenged the policies and practices of the United States:

- Chinese government patrol boats confronted U.S. surveillance ships in the South China Sea.
- China challenged U.S. and South Korean military exercises against North Korea in the Yellow Sea.

- Chinese treatment of U.S. arms sales to Taiwan and President Obama's meeting with the Dalai Lama in 2010 was harsher than in the recent past.
- Chinese officials threatened to stop investing in U.S. government securities and to move away from using the U.S. dollar in international transactions.
- The Chinese government for a time responded very harshly to American government interventions in 2010 urging collective efforts to manage rising tensions in the South China Sea and affirming the U.S.-Japan security treaty during Sino-Japanese disputes over East China Sea islands. [20]

The Obama government reacted calmly and firmly to what Secretary of State Hillary Clinton called these "tests" or manifestations of a new assertiveness by China. It also found that prominent Chinese assertiveness and truculence with the United States and neighboring Asian countries over maritime, security, and other issues seriously damaged China's efforts to portray a benign image in Asia. Asian governments became more active in working closely with the United States and in encouraging an active U.S. presence in the Asia-Pacific. Their interest in closer ties with the United States meshed well with the Obama government's broad effort under the rubric of the U.S. rebalance to Asia in order to "reengage" with the countries of the Asia-Pacific, ranging from India to the Pacific Islands. The overall effect was a decline in China's position in the Asia-Pacific and a rise in the position of the United States. [21]

Meanwhile, the Obama government made clear to the Chinese government and the world that the United States was prepared to undertake military measures needed to deal with the buildup of Chinese forces targeting Americans and American interests in the Asia-Pacific. U.S. officials also helped to move China to curb North Korea's repeated provocations by warning privately as well as publicly that the United States viewed North Korea's nuclear weapons development as not just a regional issue and a concern for global proliferation but a direct threat to the United States. [22]

The period leading up to the January 18–20, 2011, visit of President Hu Jintao to Washington saw actions from China designed to ease recent tensions and set a smoother course for U.S.-China relations. The harsh Chinese rhetoric criticizing American policies and practices subsided; the Chinese put aside their objections to high-level military exchanges, and Secretary of Defense Robert Gates reestablished businesslike ties at the top levels of the Chinese military during a visit to Beijing in early January 2011; China used its influence to get North Korea to stop its provocations against South Korea and to seek negotiations over nuclear weapons issues; China avoided undercutting international sanctions to press Iran to give up its nuclear weapons program; China allowed the value of its currency to appreciate in line with U.S. interests; and Chinese officials were more cooperative over climate change issues at an international meeting in Cancun than they were a year earlier. [23]

The successful U.S.-China summit helped to sustain positive momentum in U.S.-China relations, even though many differences continued between the two countries. In particular, President Obama made clear during 2011 and 2012 that he would pursue closer engagement with China as part of his administration's overall new emphasis on American rebalance with the Asia-Pacific. Obama administration leaders from the president on down articulated the outlines of a new emphasis on American reengagement with the Asia-Pacific that promised more competition with China for influence in the region while averring strong U.S. interest in greater engagement with China. The effort culminated with the president's visit to the Asia-Pacific region in November 2011 where he articulated his vision of enhanced American security, economic interchange, and diplomatic engagement. In January 2012, the president joined his civilian and military chiefs in announcing a new U.S. military strategy for the years ahead. [24]

2012: A YEAR OF TESTS AND CHALLENGES AMID RESILIENT U.S.-CHINA ENGAGEMENT [25]

In 2012, the world saw unprecedented demonstrations of Chinese power short of using military force in advancing Chinese claims to disputed territories in the South and East China Seas. The demonstrations, which continued into 2013 and 2014, were directed against U.S. allies Japan and the Philippines. The measures were accompanied by official Chinese commentary accusing the United States of having fostered the territorial disputes and of using them to advance U.S. influence in the Asian region to the detriment of China. The Chinese demonstrations of power went well beyond established international norms and resulted in extralegal measures and, in some cases, widespread violence and property destruction. They placed China's neighbors and concerned powers, notably the United States, on guard. They compelled the neighbors and the United States not only to consider methods of dealing effectively with Chinese pressures, but also to consider more carefully the wide range of differences they have with China that might set off highly disruptive and assertive actions by the now second-ranking and rapidly growing power in world politics. The implications for regional order clearly took a negative turn in 2012.

The year was also one of leadership transition in China and a presidential election in the United States. At the Eighteenth Congress of China's Communist Party in November, President Hu Jintao passed party and military leadership positions to Xi Jinping, who was named president during the National People's Congress meeting in March 2013. President Barack Obama ended a long and acrimonious presidential campaign, defeating Republican nominee Mitt Romney in the U.S. elections of November 2012.

Growing divergence and competition in Asia headed the list of issues in 2012 that challenged and tested the abilities of American and Chinese leaders to manage their differences, avoid confrontation, and pursue positive engagement. Senior U.S. and Chinese leaders stayed in close contact with one another in an avowed effort to search for what China called a "new type of great power relationship" that would avoid conflict and manage tensions as China's rising power and expanding interests rubbed against American interests, policies, and practices. Nevertheless, competition for influence along China's rim and in the broader Asia-Pacific region exacerbated an obvious security dilemma in this sensitive region featuring China's rising power and America's reaction, shown notably in the two sides' respective military buildups. These problems and Sino-American differences on a wide range of international issues and domestic pressures on both sides led to what leading specialists on both sides characterized as pervasive and deeply rooted distrust between the two governments.[26]

The Republican presidential primaries saw sharp and often hyperbolic attacks on Chinese economic and security policies. Governor Romney became the party's nominee, supporting tough trade and security measures to protect U.S. interests against China. President Obama joined the fray with harsh rhetoric not seen in his presidential campaign in 2008. In the third presidential debate on October 22, the president publicly referred to China for the first time as "an adversary," though the president added that it is a "potential partner in the international community if it follows the rules." Highlighting his administration's reengagement with countries in the Asia-Pacific region as a means to compete with China in security, economic, and other terms, the president went on to emphasize, "We believe China can be a partner, but we're also sending a very clear signal that America is a Pacific power, that we are going to have a presence there. . . . And we're organizing trade relations with countries other than China so that China starts feeling more pressure about meeting basic international standards."[27]

The Obama government's rebalance policy toward the Asia-Pacific region indeed underlined a stronger American determination to compete more broadly for influence in the region.[28] The security aspects of the so-called pivot to Asia received high-level attention by the president, secretary of defense, and secretary of state. They explained in speeches throughout the Asia-Pacific region and in the release of a defense planning document in January 2012 the purpose and scope of U.S. redeployment of forces from the Middle East and other areas to the Asia-Pacific region and the determination of American leaders to sustain and advance U.S. security relations and power despite anticipated cuts in overall U.S. defense spending. Actual advances in

U.S. force deployments remained modest, though the scope, tempo, and intensity of U.S. military interactions with the region continued to grow.

American diplomatic activism in support of its interests was registered with an impressive advance in senior U.S. leaders headed by President Obama traveling to the region and participating actively in bilateral relations and existing and newly emerging regional groupings involving the United States. Problems having an impact on U.S. interests in regional stability, freedom of navigation, and relations with allies and partners saw the American leaders take an active role in discussing ways to manage and hopefully ease tensions over sensitive sovereignty and security concerns in disputed maritime territories along China's rim.

As President Obama indicated in his remarks in the October 2012 presidential debate, the United States also was more active in competing in support of its economic interests as part of the reengagement with Asia. A highlight of U.S. interest was the proposed Trans-Pacific Partnership (TPP) free trade agreement involving the United States and countries on both sides of the Pacific in an arrangement seen moving American interests forward in regional and international trade liberalization. The proposed agreement was viewed as competing with groupings favored by China that required less trade liberalization and that excluded the United States.

Chinese media and officials condemned the so-called China bashing seen in the American presidential election campaigns. Chinese leaders remained firm in deflecting American pressure on the value of China's currency and broader trade practices and strongly rebuffed U.S. efforts to get China's cooperation in dealing with certain sensitive international issues, notably the conflict in Syria. China continued to nurture close ties with the new North Korean leadership despite the latter's repeated provocations and U.S. calls for greater pressure on Pyongyang. Chinese commentary accused the United States of fostering neighboring countries to be more assertive in challenging China's territorial claims as part of alleged American efforts to contain China under the rubric of the Obama government's reengagement with the Asia-Pacific region. Top Chinese leaders countered American-supported efforts at dealing with the disputed claims; they also highlighted regional trade arrangements that excluded the United States in order to undermine American-led efforts to advance U.S. interests through a trans-Pacific trade pact.[29]

COOPERATION AND MODERATION

On the other side of the ledger in 2012–2014 were Sino-American developments and circumstances supporting continued pragmatism on both sides in seeking to manage escalating competition and other differences without major incident. Despite the serious differences noted above, the overall trend of resilient and positive U.S.-China engagement continued.

Among instruments serving to moderate Sino-American frictions were the wide range of Chinese-American official exchanges. A major departure showing the strong commitment of both the Barack Obama and Xi Jinping leaderships to carefully manage differences in sustaining stable relations came with the June 2013 informal summit between the two leaders at an estate in California. There followed a November 2014 summit in Beijing. Meanwhile, an array of ninety bilateral dialogues continued and made significant progress in several areas. An important dialogue initiated in 2011 reportedly at China's request involved U.S.-China relations in the Asia-Pacific region. The dialogues also provided mechanisms for dealing with contentious issues and advancing common ground between the two countries.[30] The on-again, off-again pattern of exchanges between the military leaders of both countries—the weakest link in the array of dialogues between the two countries—was on again with improved exchanges in 2012–2014.

The so-called Taiwan issue—historically the leading cause of friction between the United States and China—remained on a recent trajectory of easing tensions. Taiwan's election in 2012 and the victory of incumbent president Ma validated the continued moderate approach to cross-strait relations, foreshadowing closer engagement along lines welcomed by both Beijing and Washington.[31] Local Taiwan elections in November 2014 saw a resurgence of the opposition Democratic Progressive Party (DPP) and a decline of the ruling Nationalist (Kuomintang) Party. The DPP is viewed very suspiciously by Beijing. If it were to win the January 2016 Taiwan presidential elections, cross-strait relations could become more tense.[32]

Despite pervasive Sino-U.S. distrust, there were also episodes in 2012 demonstrating notable cooperation and seeming trust building between the two powers. An instance of close and successful cooperation over highly sensitive issues involving sovereignty and strong national sentiment was the Sino-American handling of the case of Chen Guangcheng. The prominent Chinese civil rights activist in April 2012 escaped house arrest and fled from his home province to Beijing, where he eventually took refuge in the U.S. embassy. After several days of talks between U.S. officials working with Chen on one side and Chinese officials on the other, a deal was reached to safeguard Chen and his family and to provide Chen with medical treatment. Chen subsequently changed his mind and sought to go to the United States with his family. He appealed for American support, notably in a highly publicized phone conversation directed to a U.S. congressional committee hearing. Intensive renewed U.S.-Chinese talks concurrent with the annual Security and Economic Dialogue between top American and Chinese department leaders then underway in Beijing resulted in a second deal where Chen and his family were allowed to leave for the United States on May 19, 2012.[33]

Meanwhile, the Obama government endeavored after mid-2012 to stress its interest in sustaining broader and deeper American engagement with the Asia-Pacific region on the one hand, while on the other hand playing down the emphasis seen in 2011 and early 2012 on American security and military moves that added directly to the growing security dilemma with China. President Obama's trip to Southeast Asia and meetings with regional leaders at summits with Southeast Asian and Asian-Pacific leaders in November 2012 received extraordinary U.S. government publicity. U.S. National Security Adviser Thomas Donilon stressed sustained engagement in nonsecurity as well as security areas and played down American competition with China. Concurrently, the secretary of defense and the secretary of state similarly emphasized the broad and multifaceted reasons for strong and sustained American engagement with Asia and played down competition with China.[34]

Specialists on both the American and Chinese sides seemed to agree that effectively managing differences through a process of constructive engagement remained in the overall interests of both countries—a trend reinforced by the Sino-American presidential meeting in California in June 2013 and in Beijing in November 2014.[35] American specialists noted that there were three general reasons for this judgment:

- Both administrations benefit from positive engagement in various areas. Such engagement supports their mutual interests in stability in the Asia-Pacific, a peaceful Korean Peninsula, and a peaceful settlement of the Taiwan issue; U.S. and Chinese leaders recognize the need to cooperate to foster global peace and prosperity, to advance world environmental conditions, and to deal with climate change and nonproliferation.
- Both administrations see that the two powers have become so interdependent that emphasizing the negatives in their relationship will hurt the other side but also will hurt them. Such interdependence is particularly strong in Sino-American economic relations.
- Both leaderships are preoccupied with a long list of urgent domestic and foreign priorities; in this situation, one of the last things they would seek is a serious confrontation in relations with one another.

Prominent Chinese specialists underscored the futility of conflict and the need for cooperation in a somewhat different way. They averred that the U.S.-China relationship was becoming increasingly important to both sides and that three "realities" compelled the two governments to seek ways to manage their differences while trying to broaden common ground:

- Each country is too big to be dominated by the other.

- Each country has too unique a political and social structure to allow for transformation by the other.
- Each country has become too interdependent with the other to allow conflicts to disrupt their relationship.

NOTES

1. Sources for this section come from Robert Sutter, *U.S. Policy toward China: An Introduction to the Role of Interest Groups* (Lanham, MD: Rowman & Littlefield, 1998), 10–17.

2. Joseph Nye, *Presidential Leadership and the Creation of the American Era* (Princeton, NJ: Princeton University Press, 2013), 31–40.

3. Harry Harding, *Public Engagement in American Foreign Policy* (New York: American Assembly, Columbia University, February 23–25, 1995), 8–9.

4. Charlotte Preece and Robert Sutter, *Foreign Policy Debate in America*, Report 91-833F (Washington, DC: Library of Congress, Congressional Research Service, November 27, 1991).

5. Surveys include David M. Lampton, *Same Bed, Different Dreams: Managing U.S.-China Relations, 1989–2000* (Berkeley: University of California, 2001); Jean Garrison, *Making China Policy: From Nixon to G. W. Bush* (Boulder, CO: Lynne Rienner, 2005); Robert Seuttinger, *Beyond Tiananmen: The Politics of U.S.-China Relations, 1989–2000* (Washington, DC: Brookings Institution, 2003); David Shambaugh, ed., *Tangled Titans: The United States and China* (Lanham, MD: Rowman & Littlefield, 2013); Michael Swaine, *America's Challenge: Engaging a Rising China in the Twenty-First Century* (Washington, DC: Carnegie Endowment for International Peace, 2011); and Jeffrey Bader, *Obama and China's Rise* (Washington, DC: Brookings Institution, 2012). The account in this section is taken from Robert Sutter, *Historical Dictionary of United States–China Relations* (Lanham, MD: Scarecrow Press, 2006), lxv–lxxv, and from Robert Sutter, *U.S.-Chinese Relations: Perilous Past, Pragmatic Present*, 2nd ed. (Lanham, MD: Rowman & Littlefield, 2013), 95–182.

6. Michael Schaller, *The United States and China: Into the Twenty-First Century* (New York: Oxford University Press, 2002), 204–5.

7. Sutter, *U.S. Policy toward China*, 26–44.

8. James Mann, *About Face* (New York: Knopf, 1999), 274–78.

9. For this and the next two paragraphs, see Sutter, *Historical Dictionary of United States–China Relations*, lxix–lxx.

10. Sutter, *U.S.-Chinese Relations*, 125–26.

11. Ibid., 128.

12. "Bush, Kerry Square Off in 1st Debate," *Japan Today*, October 1, 2004, http://www.japantoday.com/jp/news/313422/all (accessed March 21, 2008).

13. Robert Sutter, "The Taiwan Problem in the Second George W. Bush Administration: U.S. Officials' Views and Their Implications for US Policy," *Journal of Contemporary China* 15, no. 48 (August 2006): 417–42.

14. Secretary of State Condoleezza Rice, remarks at Sophia University, Tokyo, Japan, March 19, 2005, http://www.state.gov/secretary/rm/2005/43655.htm (accessed March 21, 2008); Evan Medeiros, "Strategic Hedging and the Future of Asia-Pacific Stability," *Washington Quarterly* 29, no. 1 (2005–2006): 145–67.

15. Rosemary Foot, "Chinese Strategies in a U.S.-Hegemonic Global Order: Accommodating and Hedging," *International Affairs* 82, no. 1 (2006): 77–94; Wang Jisi, "China's Search for Stability with America," *Foreign Affairs* 84, no. 5 (September–October 2005): 39–48; Yong Deng and Thomas Moore, "China Views Globalization: Toward a New Great-Power Politics," *Washington Quarterly* 27, no. 3 (Summer 2004): 117–36.

16. Sutter, *U.S.-Chinese Relations*, 129–30.

17. Kerry Dumbaugh, *China's 17th Party Congress, October 15–21, 2007*, Congressional Research Service Memorandum, October 23, 2007; David Shambaugh, "China's 17th Party Congress: Maintaining Delicate Balances," *Brookings Northeast Asia Commentary*, November 2007, http://www.brookings.edu (accessed November 11, 2007).

18. For an overview of the Obama government's approach to China, see notably Bader, *Obama and China's Rise.*

19. Martin Indyk, Kenneth Lieberthal, and Michael O'Hanlon, *Bending History: Barack Obama's Foreign Policy* (Washington, DC: Brookings Institution, 2012), 24–69.

20. Bonnie Glaser and Brittany Billingsley, "Friction and Cooperation Co-exist Uneasily," *Comparative Connections* 13, no. 2 (September 2011): 27–40; Minxin Pei, "China's Bumpy Ride Ahead," *The Diplomat*, February 16, 2011, http://www.the-diplomat.com; Robert Sutter, *Positive Equilibrium in U.S.-China Relations: Durable or Not?* (Baltimore: University of Maryland School of Law, 2010).

21. Bader, *Obama and China's Rise*, 69–129; "Interview of Hillary Clinton with Greg Sheridan of the *Australian*," November 8, 2010, http://www.state.gov.

22. Elisabeth Bumiller, "U.S. Will Counter Chinese Arms Buildup," *New York Times*, January 8, 2011, http://www.nytimes.com; David Sanger, "Superpower and Upstart: Sometimes It Ends Well," *New York Times*, January 22, 2011, http://www.nytimes.com.

23. Sanger, "Superpower and Upstart"; "Beyond the US-China Summit," *Foreign Policy Research Institute*, February 4, 2011, http://www.fpri.org.

24. Bonnie Glaser and Brittany Billingsley, "Strains Increase and Leadership Transitions," *Comparative Connections* 14, no. 3 (January 2012): 29–40; *Pivot to the Pacific? The Obama Administration's "Rebalancing" toward Asia*, Report 42448 (Washington, DC: Library of Congress, Congressional Research Service, March 28, 2012).

25. Reviewed in Sutter, *U.S.-Chinese Relations*, 166–69.

26. Kenneth Lieberthal and Wang Jisi, *Addressing U.S.-China Strategic Distrust* (Washington, DC: Brookings Institution, March 2012).

27. Don Keyser, "President Obama's Re-election: Outlook for U.S.-China Relations in the Second Term," November 7, 2012 (China Policy Institute, Nottingham University, UK), http://blogs.nottingham.ac.uk/chinapolicyinstitute/2012/11/07/present-obamas-re-election-outlook-for-u-s-china-relations-in-the-second-term.

28. Robert Ross, "The Problem with the Pivot," *Foreign Affairs* 91, no. 6 (November–December 2012): 70–83; Shawn Brimley and Ely Ratner, "Smart Shift," *Foreign Affairs* 92, no. 1 (January–February 2013): 177–81.

29. Ralph Cossa and Brad Glosserman, "Regional Overview," *Comparative Connections* 14, no. 3 (January 2013): 1–12; Bonnie Glaser and Brittany Billingsley, "US-China Relations: Strains Increase amid Leadership Transitions," *Comparative Connections* 14, no. 3 (January 2013): 29–40.

30. Daljit Singh, "US-China Dialogue Process: Prospects and Implications," *East Asia Forum*, November 2, 2012, http://www.eastasiaforum.org.

31. Richard Bush, *Unchartered Strait* (Washington, DC: Brookings Institution, 2013), 213–50.

32. Aries Poon, Jenny Hsu, and Fanny Liu, "Taiwan Election Results Likely to Complicate Relations with China," *Wall Street Journal*, December 1, 2014, http://www.wsj.com/articles/taiwan-election-results-set-to-complicate-relations-with-china-1417366150.

33. Bonnie Glaser and Brittany Billingsley, "Xi Visit Steadies Ties; Dissident Creates Tension," *Comparative Connections* 14, no. 1 (May 2012): 29–30; Bonnie Glaser and Brittany Billingsley, "Creating a New Type of Great Power Relations," *Comparative Connections* 14, no. 2 (September 2012): 29.

34. Donilon's speech and the officials' media briefing were released on November 15, 2012, at http://www.whitehouse.gov/the-press-office.

35. Consultations in Washington, DC, involving groups of visiting Chinese specialists assessing U.S.-China relations after the U.S. elections and groups of concerned American specialists, November 8, 15, and 16, 2012; consultations with leading Communist Party and other foreign policy specialists in Beijing, May 2013; consultations with six Chinese government and academic specialists on U.S.-China relations, Washington, DC, December 4–5, 2014.

Chapter Four

The U.S. Rebalance to the Asia-Pacific

The Barack Obama administration has endeavored to secure American interests amid the current complexity of Asian dynamics by following an evolving and multifaceted structure in the rebalance policy that provides the current framework for U.S. policy toward the Asia-Pacific. The initiatives in the new policy that became prominent in 2011 have been in line with the interests of most Asian-Pacific governments, though China has objected, sometimes strongly. The initiatives reinforce long-standing U.S. priorities in Northeast Asia involving China, Japan, and Korea while increasing the American priority toward the broad expanse of the Asia-Pacific ranging from India to Japan to New Zealand and the Pacific Islands. The United States has adjusted the emphasis of the policy. At first (2011–2012) it focused on strategic initiatives, which were particularly controversial in China. It shifted in late 2012 to greater emphasis on economic and diplomatic initiatives, though security dimensions have continued to develop. President Obama has been viewed as sometimes less than resolute in pursuing the policy, though his visits to the region in April and November 2014 seemed to reinforce his determination to pursue the rebalance.

In sum, the policy represents a work in progress. Administration officials are sometimes frank in acknowledging that the recent U.S. initiatives are largely extensions of long-standing trends in U.S. policy and practice; they build on and call greater attention to the positive advancements of American interests in the region by the George W. Bush and earlier administrations.[1]

Security aspects of the rebalance include the following:

- The Obama government avows priority attention to the Asia-Pacific region following U.S. military pullbacks from Iraq and Afghanistan. The Asia-Pacific's economic and strategic importance is said to warrant heightened U.S. policy attention even as America withdraws from Southwest Asia and appears reluctant to intervene militarily in other world conflicts.

- The Obama government pledges to sustain close alliance relationships and maintain force levels and military capabilities in the Asia-Pacific region despite substantial cutbacks in overall U.S. defense spending. If needed, funding for the Asia-Pacific security presence is said to come at the expense of other U.S. military priorities.
- U.S. officials promote more widely dispersed U.S. forces and basing/ deployment arrangements, which indicates the rising importance of Southeast Asia, the Indian Ocean, and the western Pacific in tandem with strong continuing support for long-standing American priorities, notably those in Northeast Asia. Thus far, the advances involve developing arrangements in Australia, the Philippines, and Singapore, among others.
- The dispersal of U.S. forces and a developing U.S. air-sea battle concept are viewed as means to counter growing "area denial" efforts in the Asia-Pacific region, mainly by China.

Economic aspects of the rebalance involve strong emphasis on the U.S. pursuit of free trade and other open economic interchange. President Obama and his economic officers stress that American jobs depend on freer access to Asian-Pacific markets. Against the backdrop of stalled World Trade Organization (WTO) talks on international liberalization, the United States has devoted extraordinary attention to the multilateral Trans-Pacific Partnership (TPP) arrangement involving twelve Asian and Pacific countries in order to promote freer market access for American goods and services. The TPP is seen to pose a challenge to China, and if successful it may bring about a change in Chinese neomercantilist policies and practices that grossly disadvantage American sales to China and competition with China in international markets.

Political and diplomatic aspects of the rebalance are manifest in significantly enhanced and flexible U.S. activism and engagement both bilaterally and multilaterally in pursuing American interests in regional security and stability, free and open economic exchange, and political relations and values involving the rule of law, human rights, and accountable governance. The Obama government has markedly advanced U.S. relations with the Association of Southeast Asian Nations (ASEAN) and with the various regional groups convened by ASEAN. The U.S. engagement shows sensitivity to the interests of so-called third parties, notably China's neighbors, when pursuing bilateral U.S. relations with China. The U.S. rebalance demonstrates how the United States adapts to and works constructively with various regional multilateral groupings, endeavoring overall to build a regional order supported by the rule of law, good governance, and other accepted norms.

While the rebalance forecasts enhanced U.S. competition with China and American challenges to China's area denial security strategy and its neomercantilist economic policies and practices, it also strongly emphasizes enhanced American engagement with China. Thus the greater U.S. engagement with Asia seen in the rebalance *includes* greater U.S. engagement with China. The best recent examples of such enhanced engagement were the summits between the Chinese and U.S. presidents in California in June 2013 and in Beijing in November 2014. The greater Sino-American engagement is designed to reassure not only China but also China's neighbors that U.S. efforts to compete for influence and to dissuade China from taking assertive and disruptive policies toward its neighbors are done in ways that do not result in major friction or confrontation with China, which would be at odds with the interests of almost all of China's neighbors. In effect, the rebalance involves a delicate "balancing act" of American resolve and reassurance toward China that thus far has worked reasonably well but faces major challenges, most recently in China's continued advancement of control over contested areas in the East and South China Seas through coercive means but short of direct use of military force. Other serious challenges for U.S. policy come from domestic American interests that have been disadvantaged by growing U.S.-China economic interdependence. These Americans see China as an economic threat to America. They steer the United States toward trade protectionism, which seriously complicates Obama government efforts to win congressional support for the TPP and other trade liberalization efforts.

As the rebalance is complexly multifaceted, it is better understood from varied perspectives in international relations theory. Realists rightly see the application of various aspects of state power in order to advance the influence of the United States in an important area of the world. And they see these U.S. efforts as being made in competition with China, with many viewing the rebalance policy as a manifestation of a struggle for supremacy between the current leading power, the United States, and the main rising power, China.[2] At the same time, key elements of the policy relate to promoting free trade and investment, the rule of law, and human rights and democracy. These can be understood as manifestations consistent with the liberal school of thought of international relations. And the recently strong American resolve to deepen cooperation with ASEAN and related Asian multilateral organizations shows adherence to a concern for community building and regional identity associated with the constructivist school of international relations theory.

THE OBAMA REBALANCING POLICIES, REGIONAL
REACTIONS, STRENGTHS, AND WEAKNESSES

Origins and Evolution

The historical context of the Obama administration's rebalancing policies is the deep American engagement with the Asia-Pacific region going back two centuries. In his first official visit to the region in June 2013, U.S. Secretary of Defense Chuck Hagel underlined America's long-standing commitment to the Asia-Pacific, including "precious sacrifices" made by him, members of his family, and millions of Americans who have served in the region in war and peace since the start of World War II.[3]

As examined in chapter 2, the strong U.S. connection with the Asia-Pacific has deep roots in American society. Throughout the more than two hundred years of American interaction with the region, U.S. nongovernmental actors—including businesses, religious groups, educational organizations, foundations, and the media—have been very important in establishing and maintaining close American relations in the region. Asia's recent economic growth has enhanced the interest of U.S. businesses, academics, journalists, and others. These nongovernmental connections have created elaborate webs of strong, positive U.S.-Asian relations.

Adding to the strengths of American ties with the region is immigration from the Asia-Pacific region to the United States. The United States is a country of immigrants, but for more than one hundred years in the late nineteenth and much of the twentieth centuries, the United States adopted discriminatory, racist policies regarding immigration from Asia. This dark period came to an end with civil rights legislation in the mid-1960s that established color-blind immigration standards. Millions of Asia-Pacific people subsequently came to the United States. Over the past half century, many Asian immigrants have flourished in the American education and free enterprise systems, becoming leading figures in the United States while sustaining close ties with their home countries. In sum, the United States is integrated with the Asia-Pacific region at multiple levels. No other developed country, with the possible exception of Canada, has these strong societal connections with the Asia-Pacific region.

The Obama policies also built on the strengths of the Clinton and George W. Bush governments' active engagement in the Asia-Pacific. The Clinton administration, for example, announced a "New Pacific Community Initiative" in 1993, elevating the importance of the Asia-Pacific Economic Cooperation (APEC), a forum for promoting trade and good economic relations in the region. In 1995, President Clinton announced the normalization of relations with Vietnam.[4]

President Clinton endeavored both to engage and deter China. He promised to welcome China's president to Washington and to energize negotiations leading to China's accession to the World Trade Organization. The Chinese leader visited Washington in 1998, and, through U.S. auspices, China joined the WTO in 2001. President Clinton also sent two aircraft carrier battle groups to the Taiwan area to deter China when it took provocative military actions prior to a Taiwan presidential election in 1996.

Harvard University professor Joseph Nye, a leading Clinton administration strategist, argued that the Clinton administration sought to "integrate" China into the WTO and other world bodies while "hedging" through closer American security cooperation with Japan and other means. He equated the Clinton policy with President Ronald Reagan's "trust but verify" approach in arms control negotiations with the Soviet Union.[5]

Similarly, the Bush administration strengthened U.S. ties with allies and friendly countries in the Asia-Pacific region. It signed a pledge to promote bilateral cooperation with Indonesia in 2001, and it designated the Philippines and Thailand as major non-NATO allies in 2003. It signed free trade agreements with Singapore in 2003, Australia in 2004, and South Korea on 2007, and it brought the United States into the negotiations for the multilateral free trade area, the Trans-Pacific Partnership, in 2008. In a major breakthrough, it signed a ten-year defense cooperation agreement with India in 2005, establishing a new "global partnership" and a strategic rapprochement with India.[6] Despite widespread regional criticism of President Bush's often unilateral foreign policy actions and controversial military involvement in Southwest Asia, a 2008 survey by the Chicago Council on Global Affairs highlighted the strength of the United States' "soft power" in Asia. As cited above, this soft power has been developed and nurtured as a result of two centuries of U.S. cultural, diplomatic, military, and economic interaction with the Asia-Pacific region.[7]

Meanwhile, the Bush administration seemed successful in pursuing a stronger relationship with Beijing. As noted in chapter 3, the Bush government put aside its early claim that China was a "strategic competitor" and the hard feelings resulting from the April 2001 crash between a U.S. surveillance plane and a Chinese jet fighter. The Bush administration became preoccupied with al-Qaeda and counterterrorism along with the wars in Afghanistan and Iraq. Echoing the efforts of President Clinton, the Bush government became explicit in its aspiration to integrate China into the international system. It hoped to achieve this by encouraging Beijing to take on a more active and "responsible" approach to international affairs. Along these lines, administration leaders encouraged China to become a leading actor in the international system. As the decade unfolded, China's leaders saw their interests best served by a moderate approach that played down differences with the preoccupied U.S. government.

As in the Clinton years, the Bush government carefully "hedged" against rising Chinese military power directed against U.S. interests, notably in Taiwan and around China's rim. The extensive American web of military relationships in the region and resulting capabilities were evident in repeated and sometimes remarkably large-scale military exercises. In June 2006, the United States conducted its largest Pacific Ocean exercise since the Vietnam War. This exercise involved 22,000 personnel, 280 aircraft (including B-2 and B-52 bombers), and 30 ships (including three U.S. aircraft carrier battle groups operating together in the Pacific Ocean for the first time in ten years).[8] Another notable exercise occurred in 2007 in the Bay of Bengal along the sea line of communication leading to the Strait of Malacca, which is very sensitive to China.[9] This exercise saw two U.S. aircraft carrier battle groups join with an Indian aircraft carrier battle group and warships from Japan and Australia. At the end of the Bush administration, the United States had good and improving relations with many key countries in the Asia-Pacific region.

In sum, the story of the Obama administration's rebalance toward Asia is not a story of U.S. disengagement and then reengagement in Asia; instead, it is a matter of emphasis and priority. The Obama administration has built on an elaborate foundation of U.S.-Asia relations that was already in place.

OBAMA ADMINISTRATION INITIATIVES

As noted in chapter 3, during the 2008 presidential campaign, candidate Obama avoided the common and politically expedient practice of criticizing China on security, economic, and other grounds. Following his inauguration, President Obama sought to sustain and enhance the positive direction in U.S.-China relations that had developed in the later years of the Bush administration. During a visit to China in his first year in office, President Obama aimed to establish even closer ties with Beijing. The results were mixed and somewhat disappointing from the Obama administration's perspective, setting the stage for the president's greater emphasis on other Asia-Pacific countries as the rebalance policy emerged later in his first term.

Meanwhile, U.S. "hedging" against China's growing military power and episodes of Chinese assertiveness involving territorial claims in nearby seas continued. In 2009–2010, Beijing asserted a more aggressive regional foreign policy that was seemingly at odds with China's "peaceful rise" strategy. This strategy, established in the 1990s, had emphasized Chinese modernization and sought to downplay fears of Chinese regional hegemonic ambitions. Evidence of greater assertiveness in 2009–2010 involved the harassment of U.S. Navy ship *Impeccable* by Chinese ships in international waters off China's coast in 2009, Beijing's vociferous warning to foreign powers not to interfere in China's sovereignty disputes at the ASEAN Regional Forum (ARF) in 2010, and China's angry reproach of Japan in 2010 for detaining a Chinese captain who had rammed a Japanese fishing boat in disputed waters. [10]

Foreshadowing the recent American military buildup in the Asia-Pacific region, the U.S. Navy carried out a remarkable demonstration of naval power in mid-2010 when three ballistic missile submarines reconfigured for cruise missile attack surfaced simultaneously in Diego Garcia (Indian Ocean), Busan (South Korea), and Subic Bay (the Philippines). The implications of such submarine capabilities for China seemed severe as Chinese military forces were viewed as unable to detect U.S. subs that could approach close to China's shores with massive firepower for possible surprise attack. [11]

Although there has been considerable continuity in U.S. policy toward the Asia-Pacific region, the rebalance nonetheless represents a significant shift in U.S. policy. For one thing, the Obama administration has explicitly identified the broad Asia-Pacific region, from India to New Zealand and the Pacific Islands to northern Japan and the Korean Peninsula, as a geostrategic priority for the United States. The Obama administration has given the region a remarkable degree of high-level attention, including multiple presidential and cabinet-level visits. The administration's diplomatic engagement has included bilateral engagement with key countries as well as a much higher level of engagement with regional multilateral institutions. The administration's policy has also included new security and economic initiatives.

As noted earlier, the Obama administration's rebalance toward the Asia-Pacific region has evolved over time and thus far has gone through two distinct phases. When the new policy was first rolled out in 2011–2012, much of the emphasis was initially placed on military initiatives in the region. China disapproved of these actions. Beijing took steps to demonstrate its power in maritime territorial disputes with U.S. allies—the Philippines and Japan. Chinese commentators claimed that the disputes with the Philippines and Japan were caused in part by stronger U.S. support for these allies under the rubric of the new U.S. policy. Senior U.S. officials, notably Director of National Intelligence James Clapper, saw the strong Chinese actions in the disputes with the Philippines and Japan as being motivated in part as a response to the new U.S. emphasis on the Asia-Pacific region. [12]

Against this background, the Obama administration adjusted its approach in late 2012, playing down the significance of U.S. military initiatives, emphasizing Washington's economic and diplomatic efforts, and calling for closer U.S. engagement with China. In particular, U.S. Secretary of Defense Leon Panetta's speech at the Shangri-La Dialogue in July 2012 signaled the administration's awareness of rising concern in the Asia-Pacific region of the ramifications of an increased U.S. military presence in the region as part of the rebalance. Downplaying the importance of the rebalance's military initiatives, Panetta argued that "the vast majority of America's rebalance comes in non-military areas like trade and development." His argument helped to reduce a source of tension in U.S.-China relations. [13]

President Obama and China's new president Xi Jinping's informal summit in California on June 7–8, 2013, provided an opportunity for the two presidents to focus on this important great power relationship, which had drifted somewhat in 2012 due to the presidential election in the United States and the leadership transition in China. The summit was successful in meeting its limited aims. There was no public expectation that this meeting would produce any major, formal agreements or even a joint communiqué. It appears that both presidents succeeded at the summit in conveying their concerns: for the United States, cyberespionage and theft of U.S. intellectual property, North Korea, and keeping the peace with respect to island disputes in the East and South China Seas; for China, its domestic priorities, especially economic challenges and reforms; protecting China's sovereignty (Taiwan, island/maritime claims), and North Korea. Some of the bilateral issues raised at the summit were discussed in more detail by cabinet-level officials at the Strategic and Economic Dialogue, held in Washington, D.C., in July 2013 and later high-level meetings.

While the summit succeeded in facilitating the management of U.S.-China relations at the very top levels, it still remains to be seen if the summit has represented a turning point in a relationship that has many growing tensions. In particular, the United States and China's simultaneous hedging strategies against one another have been in evidence throughout the past two decades and have contributed to significant mutual distrust between the two countries. [14]

In July 2013, U.S. ambassador to the United Nations Susan Rice replaced Tom Donilon as the president's national security adviser. Though the president himself is a driving force behind the rebalance policy, Donilon played an important role in developing and implementing the new approach to Asia. Rice is not an Asia specialist, and circumstances in subsequent months saw the Asia-Pacific policy appear to drift.

A period of significant stress in the global geopolitical environment and in the wake of a series of U.S. policy setbacks and mistakes ignited criticism of the viability of the U.S. rebalance policy. Notably, tensions in Ukraine reestablished a schism in Russia's relations with the United States and the European Union (EU) not seen since the Cold War. Ongoing instability in the Middle East and Southwestern Asia, a U.S. government shutdown in October 2013 resulting in a postponement of President Obama's widely touted trip to key Asian countries and important regional annual meetings, and deep spending cuts to the U.S. defense budget also diverted Washington's attention. To compound these problems, President Obama and his senior associates seemed reactive to developments in the Asia-Pacific region and other world areas. Notably, they had a hard time coming up with a clear plan to dissuade China from its increasing probes and coercive measures to advance Chinese territorial claims to disputed maritime regions at the expense of U.S. allies Japan and the Philippines and other regional claimants.[15]

Beginning at the turn of 2013–2014, U.S. administration leaders adopted a more publicly critical stance against Chinese coercive tactics in the East and South China Seas that were seen as well beyond the bounds of international norms. The president in April 2014 followed earlier visits to Asia by Secretary Hagel and Secretary Kerry to reassure U.S. allies and friends of American support in the face of Chinese "provocations." He thereby put to rest at least for a time considerable angst in the region and in the United States as to whether or not the Obama rebalance and related U.S. strength and resolve are enduring and effective in the face of incremental Chinese expansionism at the expense of their neighbors. President Obama underscored commitment to the rebalance with over a week of high-level diplomacy with Asian-Pacific leaders in China, Myanmar, and Australia in November 2014.[16]

STRATEGIC RATIONALE FOR THE REBALANCE

Although commentators in China and some observers elsewhere have suggested that the rebalance has been designed to contain China, this appears to be a simplistic (and, in the case of China, partially contrived) reading of the new policy. As seen in chapter 3, U.S. policy makers are certainly focused on economic, strategic, and political competition with China, but the rebalance has been driven by a much broader set of strategic, economic, and political considerations. Following more than a decade of war in Afghanistan and Iraq, the Obama administration has been trying to place more emphasis on Northeast, Southeast, and South Asia—parts of the world that will be of growing strategic and economic importance in the first half of the twenty-first century. In geostrategic terms, the rebalance is seen as the Obama administration's grand strategy for U.S. foreign policy. Domestically, it is notable that Republicans have been mainly supportive or silent on the administration's Asia initiatives, though some have argued for greater American resolve in pursuing those initiatives.

The new U.S. policy is also based on the need—widely felt throughout most of the Asia-Pacific region—for strategic reassurance in the face of a rising and increasingly assertive China. It is generally accepted among U.S. scholars that China's assertive actions in 2009–2010 influenced the United States and the region to look for ways to hedge against China's growing power. As American scholar David Shambaugh notes, "although the Obama administration began planning the reorientation as soon as it entered office in

2009, with an eye toward winding down the wars in Iraq and Afghanistan, it was the 2009–10 'year of assertiveness' by China that triggered many Asian states to grow sharply concerned about Beijing and therefore ask Washington to increase its presence and attention to the region. Thus, to the extent China is an element of focus in the pivot strategy (and it is), Beijing's own assertive behavior is the cause."[17] The rebalance is also driven by a desire to reassure U.S. allies, friends, and other countries in the region that the United States has not been exhausted after a decade of war, that it has not been weakened by economic and political problems at home, and that it is not going to disengage from Asia-Pacific affairs.[18]

The fundamental goals of the new U.S. policy are to broaden areas of cooperation beneficial to the United States with regional states and institutions; to strengthen relations with American allies and partners, including great powers such as China and India as well as important regional powers such as Indonesia; and to develop regional norms and rules compatible with the international security, economic, and political order long supported by the United States.

ELEMENTS OF THE REBALANCE

Although much attention has been focused on the military aspects of the U.S. rebalance to Asia—the most visible and perhaps the most controversial aspects of the policy—it is important to recognize that the rebalance is multidimensional. It contains three main sets of initiatives: security elements, economic elements, and diplomatic elements.

SECURITY ELEMENTS

- The rebalance demonstrates that the Obama administration is giving priority attention to the Asia-Pacific region following U.S. pullbacks from Iraq and Afghanistan.
- The military elements of the new policy signal the administration's determination to maintain force levels and military capabilities in the Asia-Pacific region despite substantial cutbacks in overall U.S. defense spending.
- The administration's military steps will generate more widely dispersed U.S. forces and basing/deployment arrangements. This reflects the rising importance of Southeast Asia, South Asia, and the Indian Ocean, along with the long-standing U.S. emphasis on Northeast Asia.
- The dispersal of U.S. forces and the development of the new air-sea battle concept are designed to counter growing "anti-access/area denial" efforts

in the Asia-Pacific region, mainly by China in the Taiwan area and along the Chinese maritime rim (but also by Iran in and around the Gulf).

New deployments and agreements. The U.S. rebalance involves new, significant military connections with Australia, Singapore, and the Philippines. In Australia, beginning in April 2012, a company-size rotation of 200 to 250 marines was rotated to an existing Australian military facility at Darwin for approximately six months at a time. The size of the rotation will gradually expand—over the course of years—into a force of approximately 2,500 Marine Corps personnel (a full Marine Air-Ground Task Force). The United States and Australia have agreed to plans for greater access by U.S. military aircraft to the Royal Australian Air Force facilities. Moreover, the two militaries are also said to be discussing greater U.S. Navy access to Australia's Indian Ocean naval bases. Secretary Hagel said in June 2013 that the two navies reached agreement to deploy an Australian warship in a U.S. carrier strike group in the Western Pacific. In Singapore, the first of four U.S. littoral combat ships is based at the city-state's naval facility. The Philippines and the United States are discussing new military cooperation options, including the rotation of surveillance aircraft in the Philippines, rotating U.S. troops more frequently into the country, and staging more frequent joint exercises. They signed an Enhanced Defense Cooperation Agreement in 2014.[19]

The U.S. Department of Defense (DOD) has designed a strategy for the broad Asia-Pacific/Indo-Pacific region that takes advantage of American forces freed from the wars in Iraq and Afghanistan and better integrates U.S. capabilities with those of allies and partners. As noted above, Secretary Hagel and other U.S. leaders have pledged that anticipated reductions in defense spending will not come at the expense of the Asia-Pacific. U.S. Deputy Secretary of Defense Ashton Carter gave a speech at the Center for Strategic and International Studies on April 8, 2013, in which he insisted that "[the Department of Defense has] the resources to accomplish the rebalance. The rebalance will continue and in fact gain momentum. The U.S. defense rebalance to the Pacific is not in jeopardy."[20] President Obama and U.S. military leaders released the DOD's January 2012 "Strategic Guidance," which pledged to minimize cuts in the size of the navy, with reductions focused instead on army and marine ground forces. With the exception of the Korean Peninsula, the Asia-Pacific region is seen largely as a naval theater of operations. The decision to focus U.S. defense cuts on non-naval forces reflects a shift in priorities that is unusual in defense planning.

The U.S. Department of Defense is complementing these changes with shifts in military-technological priorities in the U.S. defense posture aimed at responding to potential future challenges. A number of initiatives are relevant to assessments of potential challenges in Asia in general and from China in particular. The Department of Defense has endorsed the continued deployment of eleven aircraft carriers and reemphasized efforts to improve capabilities to defeat anti-access/area denial strategies, which are known to be a focus for China's military.

Specific steps announced by U.S. leaders include the following:

- Shifting military capacities—especially naval and air capabilities involving surface ships, including eventually aircraft carriers; intelligence and surveillance capabilities; and unmanned aerial vehicles—from the Afghanistan conflict and other theaters of operation to the Asia-Pacific.
- The United States plans to deploy 60 percent of U.S. naval capabilities in the broad Asia-Pacific/Indo-Pacific region, instead of 50 percent as in the past. This will involve a net increase of one carrier, seven destroyers, ten littoral combat ships, and two submarines.
- U.S. defense officials recently highlighted military advances relevant to the region, including the successful launch of a remotely piloted aircraft from an aircraft carrier and the planned deployment in 2014 of a directed energy weapon (a solid-state laser) aboard ships for ship-defense purposes.
- The U.S. Air Force has already allocated 60 percent of its overseas-based forces to the Asia-Pacific region. Other advances include lethal and surveillance unmanned aerial vehicles (UAVs), new fighters and bombers, and reconnaissance, cyber, and space capabilities. The air force is also focusing 60 percent of its space and cyber-capabilities on the Asia-Pacific region.
- The U.S. Army's Twenty-Fifth Infantry Division and the First and Third Marine Expeditionary Forces are returning to their home stations in the Pacific theater as a result of the drawdowns in Iraq and Afghanistan.[21]

U.S. plans call for a broader and more flexible distribution of forces in the Asia-Pacific region. This accelerates changes underway since the Bush administration to make the U.S. defense posture in Asia "more broadly distributed," particularly by strengthening the U.S. military presence in the southern part of the western Pacific. The guiding premise appears to be that it is more advantageous for the United States, and a better reflection of the way in which states in the region view their interests, to strengthen the U.S. military presence in the increasingly vital southern part of the region.

The shift in focus toward the south will be carried out by what officials describe as a more flexible approach to deployments in the region. Going forward, U.S. deployments will be smaller, more agile, expeditionary, self-sustaining, and self-contained. In contrast to a reliance on large permanent bases in Japan and South Korea, U.S. forces in the south will carry out operations mainly through rotational deployments of military units to different parts of the region. Measures to sustain the U.S. presence include a substantially expanded array of naval access agreements; expanded training exercises with other countries; and other, diverse means of engagement with foreign militaries. The new approach seeks to avoid large expenditures on permanent new bases.

A corollary effort under the rebalance is strengthening the independent security capacities of key "partner states" through more flexible security assistance mechanisms and through cooperative counterterrorism, counter-drug, and counterinsurgency operations. The White House and the Department of Defense have stressed their desire to increase training and joint exercises with allies and new military partners in order to "ensure collective capability and capacity for securing common interests."[22]

As part of this move, the United States is reinvigorating its formal U.S. alliances—particularly with Australia, Japan, the Philippines, and South Korea—as well as its relationship with Singapore. Secretary Hagel highlighted all of these relationships during his first visit to the region in June 2013. Simultaneously, the Obama administration is expanding the Bush administration's push to diversify the range of U.S. partners to include India, New Zealand, Vietnam, and Indonesia. For many years, India has participated with the United States in a variety of sophisticated military exercises. After trying for some time to get beyond the break in their alliance relationship in the 1980s, New Zealand and the United States have reinvigorated their military ties with close collaboration and defense dialogues over areas of mutual concern. Vietnam has signed agreements with the United States dealing with defense cooperation over maritime security and other issues; the two countries have also held joint military exercises. Indonesia and the United States have formalized defense assistance arrangements, and they have conducted a large number of military and security exercises through the U.S.-Indonesian Comprehensive Partnership that was established in 2010.[23]

New operational plans. Among the strategic initiatives that the U.S. Department of Defense has been developing with the Asia-Pacific in mind is a new air-sea battle (ASB) concept that is intended to increase the joint operating effectiveness of U.S. Navy and Air Force units, particularly in operations for countering anti-access strategies. Development of the ASB was announced in the Obama administration's 2010 Quadrennial Defense Review. Although authoritative information about the ASB is limited, it appears that the new approach will emphasize attacks on the sensors and weapons an adversary would need for a successful area-denial strategy.[24] U.S. military officials have said the ASB will "break the kill chain" by disrupting an adversary's command, control, communications, computers, intelligence, surveillance, and reconnaissance systems; by destroying weapon launchers (including aircraft, ships, and missile sites); and by defeating any weapons an adversary launches. This approach is based on the idea that, to attack U.S. forces, an adversary must complete a complicated sequence of actions: locating U.S. forces, targeting those forces, launching weapons, and directing those weapons effectively. Each of these steps is vulnerable to interdiction or disruption. Because each step must work in order to carry out a successful strike, U.S. forces can focus on the weakest links of the chain. Many observers believe that the ASB is focused to a large degree, if not principally, on countering Chinese and Iranian anti-access/area denial efforts.[25]

MILITARY COOPERATION WITH CHINA

As noted in chapter 3, the Obama administration initially had high hopes for closer engagement with China. Those expectations were dampened by China's reluctance to join with the United States in dealing with salient international problems and by China's challenging and assertive behavior, especially over maritime and territorial disputes. The U.S. rebalance was in part a response to China's rising assertiveness with respect to its neighbors as well as an effort to deepen engagement with Beijing to keep the U.S.-China relationship from becoming confrontational.

U.S. military commanders have been in the lead in seeking greater engagement with their Chinese counterparts. Chairman of the Joint Chiefs of Staff Martin Dempsey underlined this priority in a successful visit to China in April 2013. U.S. military commanders and civilian officials recognize that U.S. military rebalancing could lead to frictions with China that could, in turn, disrupt regional stability. As a result, the U.S. Department of Defense is increasingly looking to engage its Chinese counterpart on issues of defense. In an address to a Chinese military academy in September 2012, U.S. Secretary of Defense Leon Panetta outlined his belief that Washington's increased engagement as part of the rebalance can promote regional stability and deepen Sino-U.S. ties. Central to this ambition is a more integrated U.S.-China military relationship: "Our rebalance to the Asia-Pacific region is not an attempt to contain China. It is an attempt to engage China and expand its role in the Asia-Pacific. It's about creating a new model in the relationship of our two Pacific powers. It's about renewing and revitalizing our role in a part of the world that is rapidly becoming more critical to our economic, diplomatic, and security interests. And as I've made clear, essential to all of these goals—essential to these goals is a constructive military-to-military relationship with China."[26]

It is not clear exactly why Chinese military leaders, long suspicious of interchanges with the United States, have recently adopted the more positive approach to military-to-military dialogue seen during General Dempsey's 2013 visit. Some observers connect the change with the U.S.-China summit held in California in June 2013. The run-up to that meeting featured some moderation in China's approach to differences with the United States. Active military exchanges continued in 2014.

ECONOMIC ELEMENTS

- The U.S. rebalance includes an array of economic initiatives. This reflects the recognition in the United States that Asia is and will continue to be a vital economic region for decades to come. Close American economic interaction and integration with Asia's growing economies and its burgeoning economic multilateral groupings will be essential for the health of the U.S. economy.
- Much of the public discussion has focused on the Trans-Pacific Partnership (TPP), a set of multilateral negotiations that now involves twelve countries, including Japan, Canada, and Mexico.[27]
- The United States is also in the process of increasing its foreign aid to the Asia-Pacific region by 7 percent. This is another element of Washington's effort to strengthen its multidimensional economic ties with the region.

Asia's Importance and U.S. Initiatives

Projections indicate that the greater Asia-Pacific region (including India) is rising in importance in the global economy and world trade. The region has been actively pursuing greater economic integration at a pace exceeding that of other parts of the globe. The annual flow of U.S. investment into East Asia increased from $22.5 billion in 2009 to $41.4 billion in 2011. U.S. exports to the Asia-Pacific totaled more than $320 billion in 2012, after growing nearly 8 percent since 2008.

The Obama administration has increased the U.S. focus on economic and trade relations in the Asia-Pacific. The region plays a crucial role in the President's National Export Initiative: four of the ten emerging export markets targeted in the 2011 National Export Strategy—China, India, Indonesia, and Vietnam—are part of the Asia-Pacific region. In addition, heightened U.S. economic engagement—for instance, through the TPP—demonstrates that the United States wants to remain a major force in the region's economic and geopolitical integration.

Elements of the Obama administration's trade policy in the region are broadly consistent with and build on policies of the Clinton and Bush administrations. Both of these administrations supported the granting of normal trade relations (NTR) and membership in the World Trade Organization to China, Taiwan, Hong Kong, and Vietnam. In addition, President Clinton elevated the importance of the Asia-Pacific Economic Cooperation forum in 1993 and initiated free trade negotiations with Singapore that eventually were concluded under the Bush administration. President Bush concluded a similar agreement with Australia, initiated ultimately unsuccessful FTA negotiations with Malaysia and Thailand, signed an FTA with South Korea, and announced the intent to enter into talks with the existing TPP. The Obama administration's decision to pursue the South Korea–U.S. FTA (which was successful, after some negotiated modifications) and the TPP show that there is a great deal of continuity in U.S. trade policy in Asia.

The United States also worries about the impact that maritime territorial disputes and infringements on freedom of navigation will have on the vast and internationally important commerce that crosses the Indian Ocean and the western Pacific Ocean. These are areas where the U.S. Navy has played a leading role in enforcing stability for decades. [28]

China's Responses [29]

Regional governments face a choice that will likely determine how well or poorly future regional economic integration supports U.S. interests. American involvement in the TPP negotiations supports a path of regional economic integration consistent with a U.S.-style free trade agreement (a binding, comprehensive agreement that liberalizes trade and investment to parties to the agreement). The U.S. approach stands in contrast to efforts supported by China. Beijing's approach involves agreements that are narrower in scope, open to certain Asian countries while often excluding the United States, and more lax in requiring free trade in services as well as goods, free investment, market access, and protection of intellectual property rights.

For years, China has favored regional economic and other groups that focus on Asian participants and simultaneously exclude the United States. The China-fostered Shanghai Cooperation Organization (SCO) includes China, Russia, and four Central Asia governments as members and several regional observer states. The SCO repeatedly makes statements and adopts policies that oppose U.S. goals in the region.

In eastern Asia, China has favored groups centered on the ten ASEAN countries plus China, Japan, and South Korea—known as ASEAN+3. China unsuccessfully opposed the opening of the East Asia Summit (EAS) in 2005 to include India, Australia, and New Zealand, and the opening of the group to U.S. membership. With the support of Japan and ASEAN members such as Singapore and Indonesia, President Obama joined the group and has participated in annual group leaders' summits he has attended. The U.S. government views the group as a key element in American regional interaction.

A new stage of Sino-American competition over Asian regional economic groups emerged over the past two years with China backing a new regional body known as the Regional Comprehensive Economic Partnership (RCEP). The RCEP excludes the United States while including all ASEAN+3 states as well as India, Australia, and New Zealand. Chinese and other commentators see the RCEP competing with the more demanding standards of the TPP favored by the United States. China has also expressed concern about the Obama administration's recent initiative to start free trade talks with the European Union along with its TPP negotiations; the talks could lead to agreements that will establish international economic standards that China is reluctant to meet. A highlight of the China-hosted APEC leaders' meetings in November 2014 was Beijing's proposed Free Trade Area of the Asia-Pacific, which allowed U.S. participation but was widely seen as designed to overshadow and undermine the U.S.-backed TPP.[30]

The United States and China are very far apart on the critical issue of intellectual property rights protection. The Obama administration has repeatedly and strongly criticized Chinese use of cybertechnology to steal valuable intellectual property from more developed countries. China has agreed to talks with the United States on this issue, but the chasm is wide.

Prospects

It will be a challenge for the Obama administration to carry out two major multilateral FTA negotiations concurrently (with Asia-Pacific and European partners) and achieve a successful outcome that can garner congressional approval. A key requirement is the administration's obtaining trade promotion authority (TPA) from Congress. Without TPA and its provision for restricted congressional consideration of trade agreements, U.S. conclusion of the TPP and other trade accords is seen as unlikely. Meanwhile, the RCEP's standards will be easier for Asian countries to meet. A report by the Center for Strategic and International Studies (CSIS) noted that the RCEP "anticipates the bare minimum of trade liberalization." The report said, "[The RCEP's] numerous flexibility caveats ensure that no member has to adopt trade policies with which it disagrees, and it protects sensitive industries from exposure to enhanced competition. This condition made it possible to attract less-developed countries to the grouping and ensure wider membership." As a result, its creation presents a challenge to the United States' ambition to foster economic cooperation that meets its own standards. The potential for competition between the United States and China over regional economic policy is therefore set to continue and perhaps intensify.[31] What is certain is that the United States and China are likely to compete, not just economically but in regional economic diplomacy.

DIPLOMATIC ELEMENTS

* The rebalance entails a significant enhancement of U.S. diplomatic activism in the region. The Obama administration has been engaged at the presidential and cabinet levels, its engagement has been intense and sus-

tained, and its efforts have entailed a range of bilateral and multilateral efforts. U.S. goals include regional security and stability, free and open economic exchange, and political relations and values involving human rights, accountable governance, and rule of law.

- Insufficient U.S. engagement would run the risk that Asia-Pacific states and regional groups would fail to create and sustain norms consistent with the inclusive, transparent, and liberal international order long fostered by the United States that emphasizes collective security, free trade, and open societies.
- Misaligned U.S. engagement would run the risk of regional states, most of which closely watch American involvement in the region, viewing U.S. policy as focused excessively on competition with China and deterrence of Chinese assertiveness and expansion, or focused excessively on accommodation with China at the expense of other regional states and their interests. The ability of the United States to strike the right balance in relations with China has implications that extend far beyond the U.S.-China relationship.

Bilateral and Multilateral Initiatives

The strong record of Obama administration diplomacy in the Asia-Pacific region has involved strengthening U.S. alliances; building deeper relationships with partners such as Singapore, Indonesia, and India; deepening engagement with Asia-Pacific multilateral institutions; and managing the U.S.-China relationship.

Secretary of State Clinton made far more visits to countries in East Asia and the Pacific than her three predecessors. U.S. diplomatic activism was most evident in intensified efforts to expand and upgrade U.S. participation in multilateral Asian and Asia-Pacific institutions. The latter include the ASEAN Regional Forum, a regular security dialogue among twenty-seven nations, and the East Asia Summit involving eighteen Asia-Pacific states. As noted earlier, China has made concerted efforts to develop regional groupings in ways that excluded the United States.

The Obama administration attaches great importance to regional institutions and arrangements in the Asia-Pacific region. The administration sees regional institutions as opportunities for the United States to shape the security and economic development of the region.[32] Through the rebalance and the focus on multilateral regional institutions, the administration seeks to advance America's role in discussions over a broad range of issues, from maritime security and nonproliferation to the liberalization of trade and investment across the region. Moreover, leaders in the region, particularly in Southeast Asia, generally prefer that U.S. engagement in the Asia-Pacific be anchored in a strong U.S. commitment to the region's multilateral institutions. In this important respect, the new U.S. approach is very much in line with the preferences of every regional power—except China.[33]

Starting with its 2009 decision to sign the Treaty of Amity and Cooperation (TAC) with ASEAN, the Obama administration has pursued a range of policies that have deepened U.S. participation in regional organizations, a process that led to President Obama's attendance at the annual EAS in 2011, 2012, and 2014. The United States has also sought regional cooperation on nuclear nonproliferation and disaster preparedness through its engagement in security-related multilateral institutions, as well as regional agreements on trade facilitation initiatives through APEC and the TPP. The Obama administration has sought Economic Support Fund (ESF) monies for assistance to ASEAN for the strengthening of the organization's secretariat, as well as education, disaster preparedness, transnational crime, and anticorruption programs in the region. The administration has also sought funding for disaster preparedness programs under the ASEAN Regional Forum.

The annual gathering of regional defense officials at the International Institute for Strategic Studies (IISS) Shangri-La Dialogue in Singapore has become a favored venue for U.S. defense secretaries to explain U.S. policies and initiatives. Secretary Hagel used the June 2013 meeting to highlight the strong, continuing U.S. commitment to regional security. He noted the Obama administration's strong support for ASEAN and ASEAN-led regional groups. Secretary Hagel called attention to U.S. plans to host a meeting of the ASEAN defense ministers in Hawaii in 2014, and to U.S. support for the ASEAN Defense Ministers Plus grouping that includes the United States in a variety of security-related discussions. The secretary summarized the U.S. commitment by saying, "Our relationships with ASEAN nations are critical." Hagel followed through with his ASEAN commitments and returned to Singapore and the Shangri-La Dialogue in 2014 with an address underlining the Obama government's recently vocal objections to Chinese coercive and intimidating tactics in pursuit of greater control of disputed territories in the East and South China Seas at the expense of China's neighbors.[34]

U.S. Engagement with China

At the same time, the Obama administration has continued to engage Beijing at the highest levels. In the first months of his second term, President Obama sent the secretaries of treasury and state to China, along with the chairman of the Joint Chiefs of Staff and the national security adviser. Beijing has welcomed these initiatives and the continuation of more than ninety formal dialogues with the United States, including the annual Strategic and Economic Dialogue chaired by the U.S. treasury and state secretaries and their Chinese counterparts. As noted earlier, military-to-military exchanges also have improved. Chinese officials and nonofficial commentators were more inclined to emphasize the positive following the announcement in spring 2013 of the presidential summit in California in June and in the lead-up to the U.S.-China summit in Beijing in November 2014.

REGIONAL RESPONSES TO THE REBALANCE

China has reacted at two levels to the Obama administration's rebalancing of U.S.-Asia relations. At the official level, Chinese government representative and official media have leveled measured criticism at the U.S. rebalance, especially the military aspects of the new policy. Official sources have also criticized U.S. diplomatic activism that has been seen in Beijing as U.S. support for American allies and associates that have maritime and territorial disputes with China. In China's burgeoning nonofficial media, criticism of the rebalance and the United States has been more intense and even vociferous. Some commentators have alleged that the United States is engaged in a conspiracy to develop a Cold War–style "containment" of China. [35]

The run-up to the June 2013 summit between President Obama and President Xi coincided with the start of greater moderation in official Chinese assessments. China's ambassador in Washington stated in May that the Obama administration over the past year had been making "a serious effort" in explaining to China why the rebalance should not be seen as directed against China. He said "we have to wait and see what will happen in reality," adding in regard to the TPP that "it's too early to come to the conclusion that the TPP is against any particular country." [36] Veteran Chinese foreign policy officials told visiting Americans in late May 2013 that there were "no fundamental, structural, or irreconcilable differences" between the two countries. [37] As noted earlier, Chinese military commanders also have recognized the shift in U.S. policy away from military initiatives and with less of a focus on China. While still wary of U.S. intentions, Chinese officials have been more positive toward U.S.-China military engagement than at any time during the Obama administration. [38]

In late 2013 and 2014, as the Obama government became openly critical of provocative and coercive Chinese tactics to advance territorial claims at neighbors' expense, Chinese officials registered strong opposition. The back-and-forth critiques marking Secretary of Defense Hagel's 2014 visit to China were emblematic of the major divisions between the two nations. Thus far, President Obama and President Xi have not engaged in direct accusations against one another, preserving interest in cooperative efforts to create a new relationship, seen notably in their summit meeting in Beijing in November 2014. [39]

Almost every other regional power in Northeast, Southeast, and South Asia holds to two positions. First, most regional powers have been publicly or privately pleased to see the stronger U.S. commitment to the Asia-Pacific region. Second, regional powers are also keen to avoid having to choose between the United States and China. They very much want to have good relationships with both countries.

Many regional governments have therefore not made strong public statements in support of the U.S. rebalance. Avoiding any public sign of leaning one way or the other, they have been "straddling the fence" in an effort to balance their relations with the United States and China. The Philippines, Japan, South Korea, and Singapore have been exceptions to the generally muted official reactions in the region; their support for a higher level of U.S. security and diplomatic involvement in the region has been quite explicit. It is not a coincidence that the Philippines, Japan, and South Korea are embroiled in territorial and security disputes. The Philippines and Japan have been engaged in protracted, intense arguments and maneuvers with China over maritime territorial disputes, with China in both cases exerting extraordinary coercive diplomatic, economic, and military power. A recent survey by the Pew Center illustrated the high degree of concern among Asia-Pacific states currently engaged in territorial and maritime disputes with China over the development of these disputes.[40] A small and vulnerable city-state, Singapore has done more than some U.S. allies to embrace close strategic cooperation with what it sees as the stabilizing influence of the United States.

Australia and New Zealand also have warmly welcomed the new U.S. policy, although both have taken pains to avoid upsetting China and their important economic ties with Beijing. Many other key countries in the region—including India, Vietnam, and Myanmar—have taken significant steps to improve relations with the United States in recent years. Although governments in these countries have been careful to preserve their close economic ties with China and to avoid offending the region's rising power, they have found it strategically reassuring to position themselves a few steps closer to the world's preeminent superpower.

In the face of a rising and increasingly assertive China, many countries in the Asia-Pacific region have drawn on classic balance-of-power thinking and "rebalanced" their own positions closer to the nonthreatening great power. At the same time, a number of important states including Indonesia, Thailand (a formal U.S. treaty ally), and Malaysia have been "straddling the fence," avoiding clear signs of tilting toward the United States or China.

Prompted in part by Chinese assertiveness, the many countries that have explicitly supported or quietly embraced the U.S. rebalance to the Asia-Pacific have probably been motivated more by concerns over China than by the intrinsic appeal of U.S. policies. Rising concerns about China's power and China's policies have influenced strategic calculations throughout much of the Asia-Pacific region. Although many Chinese commentators accuse the United States of having a stealthy containment strategy, it might be more accurate to say that China, by resorting to assertive practices on territorial disputes and other matters, is engaging in self-containing behavior.

Competition between the United States and China in Asia influences and in turn is influenced by the policy priorities of the Asia-Pacific countries. Those priorities focus on economic development and sustaining national sovereignty and independence. The former attracts the governments to both China and the United States; the latter inclines the governments to be wary of China while seeking closer U.S. ties.

Seeking development, most governments give high priority to export-oriented growth and to working effectively with the region's burgeoning trade. This trade is highly interdependent, placing a premium on sustaining regional stability and cooperative relations with major foreign investors and trading partners. Thus China, the region's and the world's largest trader, sees over half of its trade controlled by foreign invested enterprises in China, with about 35 percent of Chinese trade made up of so-called processing trade, where commodities are made from components from several countries and cross several borders before a finished product is completed (often in China but with only a minority of value added in China). Such trade depends heavily on foreign investment in China on the one hand and on exports out of Asia, notably to the United States and the European Union, on the other.

Because of concerns with sovereignty and national independence, most Asia-Pacific governments remain wary of their neighbors and of other powers that might challenge their sovereignty and independence. Apart from the U.S. alliance system in the Asia-Pacific, there are few allied relationships in this region. The strategic distrust that one sees today between China and the United States and between China and Japan quietly pervades regional relationships despite efforts to build regional cooperative organizations. The regional governments are willing to work reasonably well together on efforts seeking cooperative economic relations, but they use regional groupings like those in ASEAN and affiliated bodies in order to control their neighbors and preserve and strengthen their sovereignty and independence, a marked contrast with the European Union and other international groups where nations compromise sovereignty and independence for the broader regional good.

Against this background, regional governments tend to maneuver and engage in contingency plans in order to preserve their interests in the face of new challenges posed most recently by China's rise. On the one hand, they seek cooperative relations with China and mutually beneficial development. On the other hand, they worry about China's ambitions and possible dominance. In general, the governments no longer see a danger of U.S. dominance, while many see the United States and closer relations with it as a useful hedge against possible domineering behavior by China.[41]

NORTHEAST ASIAN RESPONSES

China

China's official response to the new U.S. policy has been largely measured and restrained. Nonetheless, repeated but considered criticism has been directed at the military elements of the rebalance. Beijing has urged the United States to "discard the Cold War mentality" in light of U.S. alliance building and more integrated military partnerships, which, it argues, threaten regional stability. In a thinly veiled rebuke of U.S. policy, China's April 2013 defense white paper stated that "some country has strengthened its Asia-Pacific military alliances, expanded its military presence in the region, and frequently makes the situation there tenser." Unofficial reactions in China have offered harsher criticism against an increased U.S. presence in the region. Chinese scholar Wu Xinbo asserted that President Obama's policies had left "a legacy of growing mutual suspicion and rising competition." He noted Chinese perceptions of the rebalance as a direct challenge to China's rise and a changing balance of power in global affairs that will ultimately favor China.[42]

In the heated sovereignty disputes in the East and South China Seas, Beijing has accused the United States of sensationalizing divisive issues and fomenting regional conflicts with the goal of hindering China's rise. Increasing Chinese nationalist sentiment and growing Chinese maritime capabilities have led to calls for a more confrontational approach to China's sovereignty disputes, reflected in what American scholar Bonnie Glaser described as "evidence of a top leadership decision to escalate China's coercive diplomacy" in nearby seas. China's leaders have repeatedly advised Washington to desist from interfering in the disputes and to urge its partners to avoid overtly provocative displays of hostility.[43] They welcomed President Obama's message at the East Asia Summit in November 2012, which appeared calibrated to avoid emboldening U.S. allies who are party to the disputes. However, Washington's ongoing interests in freedom of navigation and international maritime law continue to be challenged by China's rapidly expanding civilian maritime forces that, replete with nationalist vigor, have harassed foreign ships in international waters and heightened the possibility of armed escalation between China and its neighbors. The escalation of sharp U.S. criticism of Chinese coercive tactics characterized U.S.-China discourse over the sensitive territorial issues in 2014.[44]

China has also resisted Washington's efforts to promote regional integration even as Beijing's official rhetoric welcomed the prospect of initiatives aimed at promoting regional stability. For example, increased U.S. attention to ASEAN has not been censured publicly, but Beijing's visible attempts to divide the organization as ASEAN has sought to address regional sovereignty disputes have reflected its ongoing preference for dealing with sovereignty questions in a bilateral setting, where it can exert more of its significant power to achieve its ambitions. Similarly, China's official response to the launching of the TPP was one of caution, emphasizing its "open attitude towards all cooperative initiatives conducive to the economic integration and common prosperity in the Asia-Pacific," although nonofficial commentary accused the United States of promoting an economic enterprise that deliberately excluded China. As noted earlier, Beijing reacted by promoting the RCEP, which, as noted above, will not be bound by the strict provisions likely to govern the TPP, thereby providing a direct challenge to U.S. attempts to establish a rules-based economic order in Asia.

Looking ahead, China and the United States will have a hard time sustaining the more moderate stance toward U.S. policy seen in the months preceding the June 2013 and November 2014 summits. China remains unconvinced and deeply skeptical of the rebalance, although Beijing has been somewhat eased by Washington's attempts to provide reassurances over U.S. intentions and its emphasis on the diplomatic, rather than the military, elements of the new policy. However, China's growing nationalist societal undercurrents— whose views may be shared by China's new leaders and are increasingly influential in Beijing—are pushing for a more robust Chinese response to both the U.S. rebalance and to regional affairs. The nationalists also react negatively to public criticism from U.S. leaders. As the Chinese Communist Party wrestles with its long-term legitimacy, it may see a need to cater to these factions at some cost to its international reputation, even as it struggles to ensure the economic growth on which China's prosperity depends. This is a complex balancing act, with an uncertain future.

Japan

The Japanese government and mainstream foreign policy community have generally welcomed the rebalance, greeting the U.S. intention to maintain and even enhance its military presence in Asia in the context of a rising China. In April 2013, Japan's prime minister Shinzo Abe avowed that "the very existence of the Japan-U.S. alliance is a stabilizing factor, which contributes to peace and stability of the region," amid heightened tensions in the East China Sea over Japan's island dispute with China. A bone of contention remains the U.S. commitment to Japan over the disputed Senkaku/Diaoyu Islands. Washington continues to pledge neutrality over the disputed territorial claims, although the U.S. Congress, President Obama, and senior administration officials have affirmed that the scope of the U.S.-Japan security treaty covers the islands, thereby clouding the debate further.[45]

Japanese officials also worry that U.S. domestic fiscal problems and preoccupations elsewhere will prevent Washington from fully implementing the rebalancing strategy and that, as a global power, the United States could once again focus its attention on regions such as the Middle East and the Ukraine. Accordingly, Tokyo holds that Washington will expect greater contributions from Asia-Pacific allies like Japan to promote common security interests. In response to this expectation, the Abe government has begun to increase defense expenditures after a decade-long spending freeze and to push for a reinterpretation of the constitution to enable Japan to exercise the right of collective self-defense. Since the rebalance entails enhancing U.S. military activities in Southeast Asia and Australia and developing Guam as a military hub, Tokyo defense planners understand that Japan must assume greater responsibility for maritime security in the East China Sea. They are also considering ways that Japan can facilitate capacity building in the security realm of friendly Southeast Asian countries so that they can better resist Chinese assertiveness.

President Obama's visit to Japan in April 2014 helped to reassure Japan of U.S. support and energized defense cooperation and collaboration in support of common interests in Southeast Asia and elsewhere in the region. China endeavored to demonize Japanese prime minister Abe as he traveled to all ten ASEAN countries and other states in the region seeking greater cooperation. During the Obama visit to Tokyo, the United States indicated that it embraced the Japanese efforts and would work jointly with Japan in creating synergy beneficial to the Japanese-American alliance.[46]

Insofar as the U.S. rebalancing encompasses nonmilitary dimensions such as foreign economic policy, Japan views the American embrace of the TPP as both a strategic opportunity and a difficult challenge. Japan formally entered the TPP negotiations in March 2013, with Prime Minister Abe declaring that "the TPP is turning the Pacific Ocean into an inland sea and a huge economic zone." For the Japanese government, the TPP will provide helpful external pressure to overcome domestic resistance to internal reforms necessary to revitalize Japan's economy. However, if the TPP negotiations are not handled well, the Japanese government could face a debilitating domestic political backlash, with damage to its agricultural sector set to be substantial.

South Korea

The U.S. alliance with South Korea has been a constant feature of American foreign policy in Asia since the Korean War, illustrating the long-standing U.S. commitment to stability in the Asia-Pacific. While South Korea's relations with Washington have often fluctuated, the economic and military modernization of China and Beijing's support and protection of Pyongyang as it carried out provocations including attacks on South Korea have seen Seoul move closer to the United States in recent years.

South Korea has therefore welcomed the U.S. rebalancing, which reassures Seoul that the United States' commitment to regional stability is enduring. In May 2013, South Korean president Park Geun Hye argued that "the Korea-U.S. alliance . . . could reinforce President Obama's strategy of rebalancing toward the Asia-Pacific."[47] The rebalance builds on renewed ties under President Obama beginning with the "Joint Vision for the Alliance" signed in 2009, which outlined closer military and economic relations and precipitated the conclusion of the U.S.–South Korea Free Trade Agreement, which entered into force in March 2012.

Saber rattling by the North Korean regime in recent years has helped legitimate the Obama administration's rebalancing policy and reinforced U.S.–South Korea ties. President Obama has tried to reassure South Korean leaders that the United States is fully prepared and capable of defending America and its allies with the full range of capabilities available. Washington has demonstrated its commitment to Northeast Asian security in the face of threats from Pyongyang with increased military exercises, part of a joint show of force with Seoul. North Korea's actions have also undermined Chinese accusations that the rebalance is aimed entirely at China. However, reduced troop levels on the Korean Peninsula in recent years, as part of U.S. plans to redistribute its force posture across the Asia-Pacific, and concerns over U.S. fiscal constraints have raised concerns in Seoul over the long-term viability of U.S. security commitments. President Obama endeavored with some success to calm these concerns and reassure South Korea of U.S. resolve during his visit to the country in April 2014.[48]

Ongoing friction between South Korea and Washington's other key ally, Japan, has frustrated U.S. efforts to forge a coherent security policy in Northeast Asia. The two countries continue to clash over the disputed Dodko/Takeshima Islands in the Sea of Japan, while rising nationalism over historical issues in both countries threatens trilateral cooperation with the United States. The U.S.-ROK 123 Agreement, dealing with South Korea's desire to reprocess its nuclear waste, has also put the U.S. and South Korean governments at odds.

Taiwan

Chinese and American leaders have agreed with Taiwan president Ma Yingjeou's reversal beginning in 2008 of Taipei's past intense competition with China in favor of policy reassuring to Beijing. In their view, the past six years of stability and growing exchanges across the Taiwan Strait stand in favorable contrast with repeated crises in the previous decade. Today, Taiwan remains an exception to the turmoil along China's eastern rim in the Korean Peninsula and the East and South China Seas. Neither Beijing nor Washington nor Taipei sees their interests served by new tensions in cross-strait relations.

Against this background, the U.S. rebalance has rarely made explicit reference to Taiwan. President Ma told former U.S. national security adviser James Jones in June 2012 that "Taiwan not only welcomes this [rebalancing] development, but also desires to further strengthen its interaction with the United States on the economic, trade, security and cultural fronts." But Taiwan has not strongly associated with the rebalance. In a November 2014 interview with Japanese media, President Ma made a brief reference in support of the U.S. rebalance but added that a more nuanced American approach is needed because of China's economic importance to its neighbors, including Taiwan.[49] Meanwhile, because Taiwan has the same claims as China to disputed territories in the East and South China Seas, it has adopted sometimes confrontational policies toward Japan and South China Sea disputants that exacerbate tensions and work against U.S. efforts to calm regional tensions.[50]

SOUTHEAST ASIA, SOUTH ASIA, AND PACIFIC RESPONSES

Australia and New Zealand

The reactions of Australia and New Zealand are typical of many Asia-Pacific countries that are intent to strike a balance between relations with commercially vital China and the strategically important United States. China is Australia's largest trading partner, accounting for a large proportion of its iron, coal, and base metals exports.[51] In 2013, China became New Zealand's largest export market for the first time. At the same time, the United States remains a key security partner for both countries, providing a counterweight to rapidly growing Chinese power. As a result, Australia and New Zealand have publicly welcomed the increased U.S. focus in the Asia-Pacific and pledged their support for it—most notably through the new rotational deployment of U.S. marines to Darwin, Australia. Australian member of Parliament and former prime minister Kevin Rudd stated in early 2013 that "the Obama Administration's renewed focus on the strategic significance of Asia has been entirely appropriate," reflecting increasing regional concerns over China's strategic intentions.[52]

In keeping with efforts to maintain positive relations with Beijing, the Australian government has been careful to frame the significance of a more integrated U.S.-Australia military partnership. Australia's May 2013 defense white paper explicitly stated that Australia "does not approach China as an adversary" and that Australia's "policy is aimed at encouraging China's peaceful rise and ensuring that strategic competition in the region does not lead to conflict." In 2012, then prime minister Julia Gillard outlined plans to reduce the country's defense budget by AUS$5.4 billion (about $5.2 billion), easing rising fears in Beijing over Australia's strategic intentions. However, the move raised concerns in Washington and among Australia's defense industry of the country's ongoing ability to support the U.S. rebalancing strategy. Meanwhile, following the ousting, in June 2013, of Prime Minister Gillard by longtime rival Kevin Rudd, the Australian general election, in September 2013, pit Rudd against the leader of the Liberal Party, Tony Abbott. Abbott won. Both Abbott and Rudd were widely seen to be inclined to align Australia's foreign policy closer to the United States.[53]

A public rapprochement between the United States and New Zealand in September 2012 led Washington to grant Wellington's ships access to U.S. bases for the first time in twenty-six years, building on improved relations beginning with New Zealand troop deployments in U.S.-led military operations in Afghanistan starting in 2001. China's leaders appear to be untroubled by a more integrated military relationship between New Zealand and the United States given the diminutive stature of Wellington's forces.

The Philippines

The government of the Philippines has publicly welcomed the U.S. rebalance in light of the perceived threat from China and its ongoing island disputes with that country in the South China Sea. As President Benigno Aquino said early in his administration, the United States and the Philippines have a "shared history [and] shared values, and that's why America is just one of two that we have strategic partnerships with [alongside Japan]." Following increased Chinese assertiveness in the South China Sea, especially since 2012, the Philippines has sought to "internationalize" its sovereignty disputes in a bid to counter coercive pressure from Beijing. This has involved thus far unsuccessful efforts to get ASEAN to take a position against Chinese expansion. The Philippines has invited the United States to stand up for its interests in maritime security and international law, and Washington has generally supported Manila. President Obama was eloquent in remarks during his visit in April 2014 asserting that America "stands with" the Philippines. President Aquino seemed satisfied with the visit, and the United States and the Philippines were busy determining a variety of next steps to advance defense cooperation now that a ten-year Enhanced Defense Cooperation Agreement has been concluded allowing rotating American forces to be in the country at Philippine military facilities.[54]

The Philippines has paid a price for its public opposition to Chinese claims and intimidation. Beijing has followed through with threats that bilateral ties, including the trade relationship, will surely be affected as Manila continues to challenge Chinese interests. Bilateral trade between China and the Philippines reached $30 billion in 2011, making it a key economic partner. However, in response to escalating maritime tensions, Beijing placed travel suspensions and trade barriers on Filipino exports, hitting the Philippines' fragile economy. With an increasingly nationalistic public urging the country to stand up to China, Manila appears ready to accept financial and diplomatic losses in a likely protracted dispute with China over claims in the South China Sea.

Vietnam

Since the normalization of diplomatic relations between the United States and Vietnam in July 1995, the two countries have significantly expanded ties in trade and military cooperation. Bilateral trade has increased tenfold since the normalization of trade relations in 2001, with Washington now serving as Vietnam's largest trading partner. Military cooperation has grown substantially, with joint exercises and information sharing increasingly common. Growing Chinese assertiveness in the South China Sea in recent years has concerned both Vietnam and the United States, with Hanoi "internationalizing" its sovereignty disputes with China by appealing to U.S. interests in freedom of navigation and maritime security. Against this background, U.S. Secretary of State Clinton stated in July 2010 that "the Obama Administration is prepared to take the U.S.-Vietnam relationship to the next level . . . as part of a strategy aimed at enhancing American engagement in the Asia Pacific."[55]

Nevertheless, China remains a key export market for Vietnam and is essential to its economic development. Moreover, China's military power and its proximity to Vietnam mean that Hanoi has to maintain relations with both powers simultaneously, despite privately encouraging American regional participation in view of China's growing presence. As Vietnam's minister of defense General Phung Quang Thanh stated in June 2012, "Vietnam would like to have fine relations with . . . the major powers of the world. [But] we all know that China is a close neighboring country of Vietnam. China is a comprehensive and a strategic partnership [*sic*] of Vietnam."[56] Moreover, Vietnam's authoritarian communist government continues to be wary of U.S. efforts to campaign for human rights. Conservative elements within Vietnam have criticized renewed U.S.-Vietnamese defense cooperation. Washington is keen to negotiate with Vietnam to permit its warships access to Vietnamese ports as part of a strategy to more widely distribute its Asia-Pacific force posture, but thus far Hanoi has resisted. In May and June 2014, a major Chinese-Vietnamese confrontation took place over a large Chinese oil rig deployed and operating near South China Sea islands controlled by China but claimed by Vietnam. Large-scale anti-Chinese rioting saw violence directed at Chinese people and the destruction of Chinese property in Vietnam. In response to Vietnamese requests at this time, the United States said it was willing to sell weapons to Vietnam.[57]

Singapore

Singapore has long welcomed a U.S. presence in the Asia-Pacific as a hedge to local regional powers, particularly so in light of China's recent economic and military modernization. Accordingly, it has publicly embraced the increased U.S. emphasis on the region. As Singapore's prime minister Lee Hsien Loong stated, "We fundamentally think it's good that America is interested in Asia and in the Asia-Pacific region and that their presence since the Second World War has been a tremendous benign influence. It's generated peace, stability, predictability and enabled all the countries to prosper."[58] Singapore has so far played a key role in the Obama administration's execution of the military aspect of the rebalance: Singapore welcomed the first of four littoral combat ships to its ports in April 2013 as part of Washington's ambition for a more robust naval presence in the Asia-Pacific.

Singapore's success in becoming a global trade and financial hub has been built on a commitment to economic liberalism and foreign policy pragmatism, so it is not surprising that Singapore has been a key proponent of the Trans-Pacific Partnership. Still, Singapore is careful to balance its relations with the United States with those of other partners, most notably China. As its proportion of trade with the United States has declined and economic integration with China and Asia has developed, this has become even more important. In any case, Singapore has traditionally remained neutral and alliance free, emphasizing its primary desire for regional stability to promote economic success.

Thailand

Thailand is a long-standing U.S. treaty ally. It annually hosts a large-scale U.S.-Thai military exercise, including participants from other Asian states, called Cobra Gold. The 2013 exercise involved three U.S. warships and thirteen thousand participants, including contingents from Japan, South Korea, Indonesia, Singapore, and Malaysia. The Bush administration elevated Thailand's status to that of a major non-NATO ally. The Obama administration has announced a joint vision statement with Thailand, and President Obama visited Bangkok in 2012. Under U.S. law, the Thai military coup in 2014 required the curbing of U.S. defense ties with Thailand.

At the same time, Thailand fosters close ties with China. Bangkok for a time was designated as ASEAN's liaison with China. The two countries have strong economic ties, and Thailand is central to China's efforts to build roads, railways, power lines, and other means to integrate mainland Southeast Asia with China's growing economy. Thailand came to rely on China for its security following the U.S. retreat from mainland Southeast Asia in 1975.

At bottom, Thailand welcomes closer ties with the United States, but not if they come at the expense of its strong relations with China. The U.S. rebalance has led this U.S. ally to straddle the fence, avoiding a tilt to one side or the other.

Indonesia

The Obama administration has continued the strong efforts by the Bush administration to foster closer ties with Southeast Asia's largest country and the world's largest Muslim country. The U.S. rebalance has reinforced U.S. security and economic assistance in recent years, which has been welcomed by Jakarta. President Obama is personally popular in the country, given his years living there as a youth.

At the same time, Jakarta has developed closer relations with China in recent years, following decades of conflict. In 1965, Indonesia experienced a leftist assassination of army generals and a countercoup by General Suharto and army allies. Mass killings throughout the country destroyed the China-backed Indonesian Communist Party, theretofore the world's largest nonruling Communist Party. Communists and ethnic Chinese were the main targets of the assaults. In the end, with over half a million people killed and many thousands imprisoned, General Suharto emerged as Indonesia's leader and as deeply suspicious of China. The Suharto regime eventually normalized relations with China in the early 1990s and subsequently collapsed as a result of the 1998 Asian economic crisis.

The more recent, democratic rulers of Indonesia have seen their interests best served by closer economic, political, and even some military ties with China. They see little to gain in tilting closer to the United States, even with the rebalance, preferring to straddle the fence and stay on good terms with both the United States and China. From time to time, Indonesian officials have voiced concern over recent Chinese assertiveness in advancing claims in the South China Sea.

Myanmar

Heavily influenced by Beijing's policies in the past, Myanmar's authoritarian regime had icy relations with the United States for decades. However, since U.S. Secretary of State Clinton's momentous visit to Myanmar in November 2011, U.S.-Myanmar ties have developed remarkably, as the country has opened itself up to foreign investment and started on a path to democracy, culminating in May 2013 in Myanmar president Thein Sein's historic visit to Washington, D.C. Thein Sein has stated his "commitment to continue cooperation to strengthen our bilateral relations in the years to come," although he has not gone as far as explicitly embracing the Obama administration's rebalancing policy. Even so, the public reconciliation between the United States and Myanmar has been a notable success for the Obama administration.

Myanmar's rapprochement with the United States has concerned and surprised China. In May 2011, only months before the U.S. rebalance was launched, Myanmar signed a "Comprehensive Strategic Partnership" with China. However, decades of Chinese influence in Myanmar's affairs had seen anti-Chinese sentiment slowly build as Myanmar began to perceive itself as a pawn in Beijing's calculations. Myanmar remains strategically significant for China, with key oil, gas, and natural resources flowing from the country to China. China's *Global Times* accused Washington of "undermining the [Chinese] wall in Myanmar," illustrating China's frustrations.[59] Against the above background, Beijing has sought to reengage Myanmar, for example, by successfully mediating in talks between the Burmese government and regional separatists.

Myanmar's reform process is still in flux. The government has continued to be criticized by American human rights groups. Its intimate relationship with China has existed for decades, meaning that it is unlikely to turn entirely toward the United States and away from China. Even so, it appears that Myanmar's leaders have recalibrated their strategic position and taken several steps closer to the United States.[60]

India

India generally welcomed Washington's renewed focus on Asia following the announced rebalance. However, in common with many of China's neighbors, Delhi has been cautious to publicly embrace the new initiative. Privately, Indian officials are understood to have encouraged greater U.S. commitment to the Asia-Pacific in the context of growing Chinese assertiveness in the region. Nevertheless, they remain wary of provoking Beijing, particularly in light of the widening Sino-India gap in defense capabilities and the two countries' ongoing border disputes. China is also India's largest trading partner and an engine for growth. Moreover, India's historical aversion to alliance building has led its political establishment to avoid entering into any comprehensive strategic partnership thus far, despite U.S. Secretary of Defense Leon Panetta's description of India as a "linchpin" of the rebalance.[61]

At the same time, Delhi's stance is subject to modification. Unambiguous Chinese assertiveness on the India-China border or in neighboring countries could lead Delhi to align itself more closely with the United States, building on a decade of improved ties. Indian officials remain sensitive to domestic political charges of bowing to American interests. However, the continuing distrust of China and the potential emergence of a China-centric Asia as a growing threat could push India to play a more prominent role in supporting the U.S. rebalance.

DEBATE OVER STRENGTHS AND WEAKNESSES OF THE REBALANCE

There has been some debate in U.S., Asian, and other international scholarly and analytic circles, the news media, Congress, and various interest groups regarding the Obama administration's rebalancing initiatives. Most of the debate has involved specialists who criticize or support the policies for various reasons. Thus far, the debate appears to have resulted in little change in U.S. policy, though some of the issues presented appear to have been taken into account by the Obama administration as it adjusts its approach.

The Danger of Backlash from China

Some U.S. foreign policy specialists and their Chinese counterparts worry that the rebalance will prompt China to react negatively, leading to a downward spiral in relations and greater confrontation with a danger of conflict, including possibly military conflict. A few experts argue that Washington has exaggerated recent Chinese assertiveness and reacted in strong ways that are likely to prompt even stronger Chinese measures. They warn of a U.S.-China "action-reaction" dynamic that could destabilize the Asia-Pacific region.[62]

Other specialists disagree.[63] They argue that American firmness is needed in the face of China's assertiveness regarding territorial disputes, its employment of coercive measures in foreign affairs, its use of military power, and its allegedly egregious cyberespionage and theft of intellectual property.

The danger of a downward spiral in relations was at least temporarily reduced with the moderation in Chinese views in the run-up to the presidential summit in June 2013. The danger appeared to rise again as China's unrelenting and provocative assertiveness over maritime claims met with increasingly strong criticism from American leaders in 2014.

The Rebalance Is Unaffordable and Unsustainable

Some analysts argue that the rebalance is unrealistic because plans to restructure U.S. military deployments in Asia will run up against unavoidable budget constraints. As many governments in Asia monitor Washington's ability to sustain its costly military structure in the region, a critical issue in the debate over the Obama rebalancing initiatives is whether long-term procurement trends will support a level of investment spending in new weapons systems and other requirements sufficient to back planned naval and other force levels in the Pacific and elsewhere. For example, there is considerable concern that long-term navy budgets will not sustain a navy of 313 ships, as called for in recent plans; the U.S. Navy now has about 280 ships. The recently superseded sequestration process entailed significant and precipitous reductions in military end-strength and operational and training funds, as well as delays in investments. The cuts in spending are particularly disruptive to defense planning. Even if future cuts are more rationally allocated, additional reductions might well entail further decline in the size of U.S. military forces.

Meanwhile, it remains uncertain whether the choices reflected in the Obama administration's initiatives will, in themselves, be fully sufficient to reconcile global commitments and resources. Even without further cuts in the size of the navy, for instance, a critical issue raised by analysts, politicians, and interest groups is whether planned force levels are sufficient to sustain projected commitments both to the Asia-Pacific theater and to the Middle East/Persian Gulf, particularly if regional crises require a surge of force into either region. Very similar kinds of capabilities may be required in each region, potentially including capabilities in assets such as long-range precision strikes as well as intelligence, surveillance, and reconnaissance systems.

The Obama administration continues to assert that it can maintain planned deployments in the Asia-Pacific. When President Obama addressed the Australian Parliament in November 2011, he was adamant in stating that "reductions in U.S. defense spending will not—I repeat, not—come at the expense of the Asia Pacific." In his June 2013 address at the IISS regional security conference in Singapore, Secretary of Defense Hagel was equally adamant about the prospects for the rebalance: "I can assure you that . . . the United States will continue to implement the rebalance and prioritize our posture, activities and investments in Asia-Pacific. We are already taking many tangible actions in support of that commitment."[64]

Significantly, the rebalance—and a strong U.S. defense posture—enjoys bipartisan support in the U.S. Congress, which is not the case in many other domestic and foreign policy areas. Such backing also supports the scenario for successful implementation of the military elements of the rebalance. However, a rising chorus in Congress seeks more funding in support of defense to ensure that America can maintain its regional commitments.[65]

President Obama's Commitment to Asia Is Thin

Some analysts in the United States, Asia, and elsewhere abroad have suggested that President Obama and his close associates are not particularly committed to the Asia-Pacific. For one thing, the rebalance is said to have been a tactical not a strategic change; it has been a useful political tool to show the American people and international audiences strong evidence of American international resolve at a time of retreat from Iraq and Afghanistan. The president and his aides may have judged that initiatives like the rebalance were desirable, but budget realities and more pressing concerns at home and abroad are said to be sapping and will continue to undermine the administration's commitment to the stated goals of the government's rebalancing policy. The president's failure to attend important annual meetings in Asia in October 2013, on account of more pressing priorities at home, was seen as evidence supporting the judgment that President Obama's personal commitment to the new Asian policy is thin.

Moreover, the administration's lack of expertise on Asian issues in its upper ranks looms large in the judgments of American skeptics. Well into the president's second term, the administration still has no high-level officials with a strong background on Asia or a deep commitment to the region. Secretary of State Kerry has devoted much of his first year in office to pressing issues in the Middle East and reassuring allies in Europe. In an April 2013 trip to Seoul, Secretary Kerry perhaps unwisely mentioned that this was his first visit to Korea (even though he had been a member of the Senate Foreign Relations Committee for over two decades).[66] Chairman of the Joint Chiefs of Staff Martin Dempsey took his first official trip to China in April 2013. Expertise on Asia in the U.S. Congress suffered setbacks with the departure of Richard Lugar and James Webb from the Senate Foreign Relations Committee.

To skeptics, U.S. domestic funding constraints and other pressing issues at home and abroad are likely to crowd out Asian issues on the president's agenda, especially since he is not surrounded by high-level energetic advocates of strong, sustained U.S. engagement with Asia.

The Obama administration counters such charges by pointing to its impressive, multiyear track record of engagement in the Asia-Pacific region and its diligent implementation of the multidimensional rebalance. President Obama insisted in his November 2011 address to the Australian Parliament: "The United States is a Pacific power, and we are here to stay." The president reiterated this position when he returned to Australia in November 2014.[67]

NOTES

1. Mark E. Manyin, Stephen Daggett, Ben Dolven, Susan V. Lawrence, Michael F. Martin, Ronald O'Rourke, and Bruce Vaughn, *Pivot to the Pacific? The Obama Administration's "Rebalancing" toward Asia*, Report 42448 (Washington, DC: Library of Congress, Congressional Research Service, March 28, 2012); Philip Saunders, *The Rebalance to Asia: U.S.-China Relations and Regional Security* (Washington, DC: National Defense University, Institute for National Security Studies, 2012); Robert Sutter, Michael Brown, and Timothy Adamson, *Balancing Acts: The U.S. Rebalance and Asia Pacific Stability* (Washington, DC: George Washington University, Elliott School of International Affairs, 2013); Timothy Adamson, Michael Brown, and Robert Sutter, *Rebooting the U.S. Rebalance to Asia* (Washington, DC: George Washington University, Elliott School of International Affairs, 2014). For a book-length compendium on the rebalance, see Hugo Meijer, ed., *Origins and Evolution of the US Rebalance toward Asia: Diplomatic, Military and Economic Dimensions* (London: Palgrave Macmillan, 2015). For an overview of recent U.S. relations with allies and partners in Asia, see Ashley Tellis, Abraham Denmark, and Greg Chaffin, eds., *Strategic Asia 2014–2015: U.S. Alliances*

and Partnerships at the Center of Global Power (Seattle, WA: National Bureau of Asian Research, 2014). For an in-depth assessment foreseeing gradual American decline in Asia, see Xenia Dormandy with Rory Kinane, *Asia-Pacific Security: A Changing Role for the United States* (London: Chatham House, Royal Institute of International Affairs, April 2014).

2. Aaron Friedberg, *A Contest for Supremacy: China, America and the Struggle for Mastery in Asia* (New York: Norton, 2011).

3. U.S. Department of Defense, "Remarks by Secretary Hagel at the IISS Asia Security Summit," news transcript, Shangri-La Hotel, Singapore, June 1, 2013, http://www.defense.gov/transcripts/transcript.aspx?transcriptid=5251.

4. Department of State, Office of the Historian, *History of the Department of State during the Clinton Presidency, 1993–2001*, section 14, "East Asia and the Pacific," January 2009, http://2001-2009.state.gov/r/pa/ho/pubs/8530.htm.

5. Joseph Nye, "Our Pacific Predicament," *American Interest* 8, no. 4 (March–April 2013), http://www.the-american-interest.com/2013/02/12/our-pacific-predicament.

6. Sutter, Brown, and Adamson, *Balancing Acts*, 5–6.

7. Christopher Whitney and David Shambaugh, *Soft Power in Asia: Results of a 2008 Multinational Survey of Public Opinion* (Chicago: Chicago Council on Global Affairs, 2008).

8. U.S. Department of Defense, "Exercise Valiant Shield Kicks Off," http://www.defense.gov/home/photoessays/2006-06/p20060619a1.html (accessed December 12, 2014).

9. U.S. Navy, "Exercise Malabar 07-2 Kicks Off," September 7, 2007, http://www.navy.mil/submit/display.asp?story_id=31691.

10. Thomas Christensen, "The Advantages of an Assertive China: Responding to Beijing's Abrasive Foreign Policy," *Foreign Affairs* 90, no. 2 (March–April 2011): 54–57.

11. Mark Thompson, "U.S. Missiles Deployed Near China Send a Message," *Time*, July 8, 2010, http://content.time.com/time/nation/article/0,8599,2002378,00.html.

12. Sutter, Brown, and Adamson, *Balancing Acts*, 7.

13. U.S. Department of Defense, "Secretary of Defense Speech," Shangri-La Dialogue, Singapore, June 2, 2012, http://www.defense.gov/speeches/speech.aspx?speechid=1681.

14. Kenneth Lieberthal and Wang Jisi, *Addressing U.S.-China Strategic Distrust* (Washington, DC: Brookings Institution, March 2012).

15. Adamson, Brown, and Sutter, *Rebooting the U.S. Rebalance*, 1.

16. Scott Snyder, "Obama's Rebalance to Asia in His Own Words: Where Does It Stand?," *PacNet*, no. 82 (November 24, 2014), http://csis.org/files/publication/Pac1482_0.pdf.

17. David Shambaugh, "Assessing the U.S. Pivot to Asia," *Strategic Studies Quarterly* 7, no. 2 (Summer 2013): 18.

18. Sutter, Brown, and Adamson, *Balancing Acts*, 9.

19. For a detailed analysis of the security, as well as other elements of the U.S. Asia-Pacific rebalance, see Manyin et al., *Pivot to the Pacific?*, and Saunders, *The Rebalance to Asia*.

20. Ashton Carter, "The U.S. Defense Rebalance to Asia," Speech at the Center for Strategic and International Studies, Washington, DC, April 8, 2013, http://www.defense.gov/Speeches/Speech.aspx?SpeechID=1765.

21. Sutter, Brown, and Adamson, *Balancing Acts*, 12.

22. U.S. Department of Defense, *Sustaining U.S. Global Leadership: Priorities for the 21st Century Defense*, January 2012, 2, http://www.defense.gov/news/defense_strategic_guidance.pdf.

23. Sutter, Brown, and Adamson, *Balancing Acts*, 14.

24. The U.S. Department of Defense's January 2012 white paper detailed the U.S. military's heightened focus on deterring "potential" adversaries through power projection in areas where its "access and freedom to operate are challenged." This appears to be a reference to China's increased anti-access/area denial capabilities, which the ASB concept may help to counter. U.S. Department of Defense, *Sustaining U.S. Global Leadership: Priorities for the 21st Century Defense*, January 2012, 2.

25. For a more detailed analysis of the air-sea battle concept, see Jonathan Greenert and Mark Welsh, "Breaking the Kill Chain," *Foreign Policy*, May 16, 2013, http://foreignpolicy.com/2013/05/17/breaking-the-kill-chain.

26. Leon Panetta, Speech to the PLA Engineering Academy of Armed Forces, September 19, 2012, cited in Sutter, Brown, and Adamson, *Balancing Acts*, 13.

27. Brock Williams, *Trans-Pacific Partnership (TPP) Countries: Comparative Trade and Economic Analysis*, Report R42344 (Washington, DC: Library of Congress, Congressional Research Service, June 10, 2013).

28. Sutter, Brown, and Adamson, *Balancing Acts*, 14.

29. Susan Lawrence, *U.S.-China Relations: Overview of Policy Issues*, Report R41108 (Washington, DC: Library of Congress, Congressional Research Service, August 1, 2013), 18–20.

30. Joe McDonald and Youkyung Lee, "Asia-Pacific Leaders Endorse Working toward China-Backed Free Trade Pact," Associated Press, November 11, 2014, http://www.usnews.com/news/business/articles/2014/11/11/china-wins-support-for-asia-pacific-trade-proposal.

31. Murray Hiebert and Liam Hanlon, *ASEAN and Partners Launch Regional Comprehensive Economic Partnership* (Washington, DC: Center for Strategic and International Studies, December 7, 2012).

32. In November 2011, U.S. Secretary of State Hillary Clinton stated, in an article titled "America's Pacific Century," that the United States' ambition, as part of the rebalance, is to establish a framework for stability in the Asia-Pacific similar to that which the United States helped to construct in Europe. Alliance building and the strengthening of regional institutions is therefore absolutely fundamental to the rebalance and, in Washington's eyes, the stability of the international order. As Clinton argues, the United States' "challenge is to build a web of partnerships and institutions across the Pacific that is as durable and as consistent with American values as the web we have built across the Atlantic." Hillary Clinton, "America's Pacific Century," *Foreign Policy*, no. 189 (November 2011): 56–63.

33. In particular, China has vehemently opposed efforts by the United States to use ASEAN as a forum for the resolution of sovereignty debates in the South China Sea. At the ASEAN Foreign Ministers Meeting in July 2012, and again at the East Asia Summit the following November, Beijing was reported to exert pressure on host Cambodia—a longtime recipient of significant Chinese aid—to keep territorial and maritime disputes off the agenda. Beijing continues to insist that its sovereignty disputes be resolved bilaterally, where it believes it can exert greater leverage over fellow claimants, making incremental gains. According to a report by the Center for Strategic and International Studies, the reputations of both Cambodia and China "took a beating as a result." Ralph Cossa and Brad Glosserman, "Regional Overview: US Rebalances as Others Squabble," *Comparative Connections* 14, no. 2 (September 2012): 2, http://www.csis.org/pacfor.

34. U.S. Department of Defense, "Secretary of Defense Speech IISS Shangri-La Dialogue," May 31, 2014, http://www.defense.gov/Speeches/Speech.aspx?SpeechID=1857.

35. Criticism from China's unofficial sources has generally asserted that the rebalance has negatively contributed to a decline in mutual trust, not only between the United States and China, but between the United States and the Asia-Pacific region. Even traditionally moderate Chinese scholars such as Wang Jisi and Wu Xinbo have at times bemoaned the impact of the rebalance on Sino-U.S. relations. Wu argued, for example, in an article in late 2012, that the rebalance has "created a legacy of mutual suspicion and rising competition." Wu Xinbo, "Beijing's Wish List: A Wiser China Policy in President Obama's Second Term" (Washington, DC: Brookings Institution, December 2012).

36. "Beijing's Brand Ambassador: A Conversation with Cui Tiankai," *Foreign Affairs* 92, no. 4 (2013): 10–17.

37. Remarks by senior Chinese foreign policy officials, International Symposium on China's Development Strategy and China-U.S. Relations, China Center for Contemporary World Studies, Beijing, May 28, 2013 (attended by Robert Sutter).

38. Yao Yunzhu, "Boost for Sino-U.S. Military Ties," *China Daily*, June 17, 2013, 6.

39. "China-Southeast Asia Relations," *Comparative Connections* 16, no. 1 (May 2014): 67; "Xi and Obama in Beijing Summit," BBC News, November 12, 2014, http://www.bbc.com/news/world-middle-east-30015677.

40. Richard Wike and Bruce Stokes, "Who Is Up, Who Is Down: Global Views of China and the U.S.," Pew Research Center, Global Attitudes Project, July 2013.

41. Sutter, Brown, and Adamson, *Balancing Acts*, 18.

42. Wu Xinbo, "Beijing's Wish List."

43. To an outsider, the value attributed by China to its sovereignty claims often appears to outweigh the practical benefits of sovereign ownership of these territories, such as the tiny, contested Senkaku/Diaoyu Islands and the disputed islands in the South China Sea. But the importance Beijing and the Chinese people attribute to issues of sovereignty is rooted in history. According to Michael Swaine, a leading China expert, "the intensity of the Chinese response to sovereignty-related challenges or issues is reinforced by the emotional association of these issues with the violations of China's sovereignty that occurred during China's 'Century of Humiliation' at the hands of foreigners (extending from the mid-19th to the mid-20th centuries)." Repeated violations of China's sovereignty by foreign countries during this period have contributed to a collective determination in China to defend its sovereignty even at significant cost. Michael Swaine, "China's Maritime Disputes in the East and South China Seas" (testimony to the U.S.-China Economic and Security Review Commission, April 4, 2013), http://origin.www.uscc.gov/sites/default/files/transcripts/USCC%20Hearing%20Tran script%20-%20April%204%202013.pdf.

44. "US-China Relations," *Comparative Connections* 16, no. 1 (May 2014): 29–31.

45. Japanese officials have welcomed the rebalance in part because of China's assertive policies on its rim, in particular, China's actions in defending its sovereignty claims in the East and South China Seas. Japanese prime minister Shinzo Abe was quite explicit when stating, in late 2012, that, "with the increasing severity of the security environment in East Asia, the importance of the Japan-US alliance is increasing." Shinzo Abe, "Comments at the East Asia Summit," Phnom Penh, Cambodia, November 20, 2012, cited in Sutter, Brown, and Adamson, *Balancing Acts*, 20.

46. "Japan-US Relations," *Comparative Connections* 16, no. 1 (May 2014): 21–22.

47. President Park Geun Hye, Republic of Korea, "Speech to Joint Session of U.S. Congress," May 8, 2013, http://seoul.usembassy.gov/p_pv_050813a.html.

48. "US-Korea Relations," *Comparative Connections* 16, no. 1 (May 2014): 45.

49. Debbie Wu, "Taiwan President Wants a More Nuanced U.S. Approach to China," *NIKKEI Asian Review*, November 13, 2014, http://Asia.NIKKEI.com.

50. Alexander Chieh-Cheng Huang, "Taiwan in an Asian 'Game of Thrones,'" *Asia Policy* 15 (January 2013): 18–20.

51. As a report by the Center for Strategic and International Studies notes, a fairly vigorous debate has emerged in Australia over the logic of deepening the country's alliance with the United States as it becomes further intertwined with—if not partially reliant on—China economically. In general, the country saw the moves to accommodate the U.S. rebalance as a positive move intended to stabilize the South Pacific. Nevertheless, former leader of the opposition Malcolm Turnbull reflected Australian concerns when he stated, shortly after the announcement of the U.S. marine deployment to Darwin, that "an Australian government needs to be careful not to allow a doe-eyed fascination with the leader of the free world to distract from the reality that our national interest is truly—and not just rhetorically—to maintain both an ally in Washington and a good friend in Beijing, which is after all our most important trading partner." Such a move has been typical of regional responses, which have sought to balance their countries' relations with the United States and China. Graeme Dobell, "Australia-East Asia/U.S. Relations: Rebooting the Alliance," *Comparative Connections* 14, no. 2 (September 2012).

52. Kevin Rudd, "Beyond the Pivot: A New Road Map for U.S.-Chinese Relations," *Foreign Affairs* 92, no. 2 (March–April 2013): 9.

53. Sutter, Brown, and Adamson, *Balancing Acts*, 22.

54. "US-Southeast Asia Relations," *Comparative Connections* 16, no. 1 (May 2014): 54–56.

55. U.S. Department of State, "Secretary of State Hillary Rodham Clinton Remarks with Vietnam Deputy Prime Minister and Foreign Minister Pham Gia Khiem," Hanoi, Vietnam, July 22, 2010, http://www.state.gov/secretary/20092013clinton/rm/2010/07/145034.htm.

56. U.S. Department of Defense, "Joint Press Briefing with Secretary Panetta and Vietnamese Minister of Defense Gen. Phung Quang Thanh from Hanoi, Vietnam," Hanoi, Vietnam, June 4, 2012, http://www.defense.gov/transcripts/transcript.aspx?transcriptid=5052.

57. Joshua Kurlantzik, "Selling Vietnam Lethal Weapons: The Right Move?," *National Interest*, October 8, 2014, http://nationalinterest.org/blog/the-buzz/selling-vietnam-lethal-weapons-the-right-move-11430.

58. "Singapore Prime Minister Lee Hsien-Loong on CNN," February 6, 2012, http://www.youtube.com/watch?v=5-LmLTy9AUo.

59. According to the article, the United States, "by loosening its economic sanctions on Myanmar and increasing assistance . . . is pressuring the Myanmar government to reform its current political system, speed up the process of democratization, and grant the opposition party more freedom and rights." Zhou Fangyin, "Short-Term Success Won't Prove Enough to Achieve US Aims in Asia-Pacific," *Global Times*, February 6, 2013.

60. "US-Southeast Asia Relations," 57–58.

61. U.S. Department of Defense, "Panetta Says U.S.-India Relations Must Deepen, Grow for Peace," New Delhi, India, June 6, 2012, http://www.defense.gov/news/newsarticle.aspx?id=116636.

62. Most prominent among this view is Robert Ross, professor of political science at Boston College. Ross argues that China's more assertive actions between 2009 and 2010 were a symptom of the leadership's deep insecurities—Beijing moved to support a more hostile stance in foreign affairs in order to entrench Communist Party legitimacy by appeasing an increasingly nationalist public through "symbolic gestures of force." As a result, the United States has misread Beijing's ambitions. For Ross, the new U.S. policy unnecessarily compounds Beijing's insecurities and will only feed China's aggressiveness, undermine regional stability, and decrease the possibility of cooperation between Beijing and Washington." Ross argues that increasing U.S. military presence in the Asia-Pacific can only destabilize the U.S.-China relationship by undermining Chinese confidence in U.S. intentions. Robert Ross, "The Problem with the Pivot," *Foreign Affairs* 91, no. 6 (November–December 2012): 70–82.

63. Shawn Brimley and Ely Ratner, "Smart Shift: A Response to 'The Problem with the Pivot,'" *Foreign Affairs*, January–February 2013, http://www.foreignaffairs.com/articles/138720/shawn-brimley-and-ely-ratner/smart-shift.

64. The Obama administration has been forced to defend the viability of the rebalance to both national and international media and scholarly analysis. In particular, Chinese analysis has often argued—shaped by its own perceptions of American decline and Chinese rise—that the United States will find it difficult to implement such an overarching strategy in the face of ongoing economic problems. For example, Chinese scholar Zhou Fangyin argued that "whether the United States will achieve [its goals as part of the rebalance] depends on the long-term strength of competition between the two countries. If the United States cannot solve its own problems, its strategy will not be sustainable." Zhou Fangyin, "Short-Term Success Won't Prove Enough to Achieve US Aims in Asia-Pacific," *Global Times*, February 6, 2013. Following the sequestration in March 2013, these suspicions have only intensified.

65. Christopher Cavas and John Bennett, "Interview: Rep. Randy Forbes," *Defense News*, May 11, 2014, http://www.defensenews.com/article/20140311/DEFREG02/303110019/Interview-Rep-Randy-Forbes.

66. Moreover, in his confirmation hearing at the U.S. Congress, Kerry appeared hesitant to offer his full backing to the rebalance: "I'm not convinced that increased military ramp-up is critical yet. I'm not convinced of that. . . . We have a lot more bases out there than any other nation in the world, including China today. We have a lot more forces out there than any other nation in the world, including China today. And we've just augmented the president's announcement in Australia with additional Marines. You know, the Chinese take a look at that and say, 'What's the United States doing? They trying to circle us? What's going on?' And so, you know, every action has its reaction." John Kerry, Confirmation Hearing to the U.S. Senate, Washington, DC, January 24, 2013.

67. The White House, "Remarks by President Obama to the Australian Parliament," Canberra, Australia, November 17, 2011, http://www.whitehouse.gov/the-press-office/2011/11/17/remarks-president-obama-australian-parliament; Scott Snyder, "Obama's Rebalance in Asia in His Own Words."

Chapter Five

Status and Outlook of U.S. Relations with China

The discussion in chapter 3 assesses the evolution of Sino-American relations since the Cold War in order to illustrate the complicated and fluid Asia-Pacific regional dynamics, including the role of the United States, during this period. The Obama government's rebalance policy examined in detail in chapter 4 shows the framework being used by the United States to advance American interests in the Asia-Pacific in the years ahead. Chapters 5 through 10 examine relevant developments in U.S. relations with specific countries or regions. In general, each chapter follows a pattern of assessing the success and shortcomings of U.S. relations with countries and regions in Asia by explaining how well or poorly Asian country and regional developments and priorities mesh with American behavior and priorities.

Since the background of Sino-American relations was already covered in chapter 3, this chapter focuses on the mixed and uncertain status and outlook of the U.S.-China relationship. The two powers converge and show strong interdependence on such key issues as mutual trade and investment; tourism, student, and other interactions of the citizens of both countries; and sustaining a stable regional and international order favorable to both countries. At the same time, they differ strongly on their respective treatments of maritime territorial disputes in East Asia; international initiatives seeking to change regimes grossly exploiting or brutally suppressing their people, flouting accepted norms regarding nonproliferation of weapons of mass destruction, or fostering terrorists; and what should be done to remedy the large and growing mutual security dilemma along China's rim posed by buildups in Chinese and U.S. military forces targeted at each other.

The complex American relationship with China has many features that may best be assessed using different perspectives from international relations theory. Deepening strategic competition and a massive security dilemma between China and the United States in the Asia-Pacific region underline forces and phenomena that seem best understood through a realist lens. At the same time, American stress on open trade and investment, related social and political liberalism, and deepening Chinese engagement with the existing world order seem best assessed through a liberal perspective in international relations theory. In addition, a fundamental reason why U.S. efforts to engage and change China's policies and practices have occurred on the U.S. side and have been resisted on the Chinese side has to do with a profound gap between the national identity in China and that in the United States, a topic well explained by constructivist international relations theory.

The fragile but enduring positive engagement seen in U.S. relations with China in recent years appears likely to continue, but serious uncertainties remain. As noted earlier, Sino-American leaders have important pragmatic reasons to continue positive engagement and avoid confrontation and conflict. Looking ahead, it's hard to envisage how the Obama government would see its interests well served with a more assertive U.S. stance leading to a major confrontation with China. Indeed, the U.S. government at times has adjusted its rebalance and related initiatives in the Asia-Pacific in ways that reduce public emphasis on military strengthening sensitive to China and to those many Asian-Pacific governments seeking to avoid the disruption that would be associated with serious Sino-American differences. It reached out to President Xi Jinping and the new Chinese leadership in holding the California summit and seeking greater engagement through senior-level interchange in cabinet-level visits and structured dialogues. Its criticism of Chinese economic practices adverse to American interests remains measured. It has responded firmly when Chinese actions over disputed territory along its maritime rim escalate tensions and endanger stability, underlining America's commitments to regional stability and the status quo. Its posture on the preeminent issue of Taiwan has been supportive of Taiwan president Ma Ying-jeou's reassurance of and greater alignment with China.

CHINA'S TOUGHER STANCE IN THE ASIA-PACIFIC

Less certainty prevails regarding China's calculus, especially given the continued assertive and incremental advances China has made recently in pursuing its claims at the expense of its neighbors. Repeated episodes of Chinese assertiveness and expansion over territorial and other disputes involving U.S. allies and interests in recent years are supported by seemingly growing public and elite opinion in China arguing for stronger initiatives to change aspects of the regional order seen adversely in China.[1]

China's tough stand on maritime territorial disputes evident in the 2012 confrontations with the Philippines in the South China Sea and with Japan in the East China Sea has endured through China's leadership transition and now marks an important shift in China's foreign policy, with serious implications for China's neighbors and concerned powers including the United States. China seemed to expand the scope of the confrontations by causing a serious crisis with the unannounced deployment of an oil rig for exploration in the Paracel Islands disputed with Vietnam in May 2014. The result was a protracted face-off of massed Chinese and Vietnamese coast guard and fishing boats and demonstrations in Vietnam that turned violent and destroyed Chinese properties and killed four Chinese.[2] China's avowed success in advancing its claims against the Philippines and Vietnam and in challenging Japan's control of disputed islands head the list of reasons why the new Chinese policy is likely to continue and perhaps intensify in the future. Only a few governments seem prepared to resist, and the United States and other concerned powers have yet to demonstrate viable ways to get China to stop.

China has established a pattern of employing force, short of military means, and other pressure in order to more actively assert claims over disputed maritime territories. The Philippines, and more recently Vietnam, continued to complain loudly, and Japan resisted firmly. But most concerned governments came to recognize that China's "win-win" formula emphasizing cooperation over common ground was premised on the foreign government eschewing actions acutely sensitive to China over Taiwan, Tibet, and Xinjiang, and that the scope of China's acute sensitivity had now been broadened to include the maritime disputes along China's rim.

China's neighbors and concerned powers like the United States have been required to calibrate more carefully their actions related to disputed maritime territories. Unfortunately, the parameters of China's acute concerns regarding maritime claims remain unclear. Meanwhile, the drivers of China's new toughness on maritime disputes include rising patriotic and nationalist sentiment in Chinese elite and public opinion and the growing capabilities of Chinese military, coast guard, fishery, and oil exploration forces. The latter are sure to grow in the coming years, foreshadowing greater Chinese willingness to use coercion in seeking advances in nearby seas.

For now, a pattern of varied regional acquiescence, protests, and resistance to China's new toughness on maritime claims seems likely. It raises the question about future Chinese assertiveness, challenging neighboring governments with disputes over Chinese claims and challenging American leadership in promoting stability and opposing unilateral and coercive means to change the regional status quo.

There are forecasts of inevitable conflict between the United States and China as they compete for influence in the Asia-Pacific, or of a U.S. retreat in the Asia-Pacific in the face of China's assertiveness.[3] Such forecasts are offset in this writer's opinion by circumstances in China and abroad that will continue to constrict China's leaders. The circumstances are seen to hold back Chinese leaders even if they, like much of Chinese elite and public opinion, personally favor a tough approach in order to secure interests in the Asia-Pacific.

CONSTRAINTS ON CHINESE ASSERTIVENESS

There are three sets of restraints on China's tough measures in foreign affairs related to the United States that are strong and are unlikely to diminish in the foreseeable future.

Domestic Preoccupations[4]

The first relates to Chinese leaders' domestic priorities. There is a general consensus among specialists in China and abroad about some of the key objectives of Chinese leaders. They want to sustain one-party rule, and to do so they require continued economic growth that advances the material benefits of the Chinese people and assures general public support and legitimacy for the communist government. Such economic growth and continued one-party rule require stability at home and abroad, especially in nearby Asia where conflict and confrontation would have a serious negative impact on Chinese economic growth. At the same time, the need for vigilance in protecting Chinese security and sovereignty remains among the top leadership concerns as evidenced by the long and costly buildup of military forces to deal with a Taiwan contingency involving the United States and more recent use of various means of state power to advance territorial claims in nearby disputed seas. There is less clarity among specialists as to where Chinese international ambitions for regional and global leadership fit in the current priorities of Beijing's leaders, but there is little doubt that domestic concerns get overall priority.

On this basis, analysts see a wide range of domestic concerns preoccupying the Xi Jinping leadership and earlier Chinese leaders. They involve the following:

- weak leadership legitimacy highly dependent on how the leaders' performance is seen at any given time;
- pervasive corruption viewed as sapping public support and undermining administrative efficiency;
- widening income gaps posing challenges to the communist regime ostensibly dedicated to advancing the disadvantaged;
- widespread social turmoil reportedly involving one hundred thousand to two hundred thousand mass incidents annually that are usually directed at

government officials or aspects of state policies; managing such incidents and related domestic control measures involve budget outlays greater than China's impressive national defense budget[5];

- a highly resource-intensive economy (e.g., China uses four times the amount of oil to advance its economic growth to a certain level than does the United States, even though the United States is notoriously inefficient and arguably wasteful in how it uses oil)[6]; enormous and rapidly growing environmental damage is being done in China as a result of such intensive resource use; and
- the need for major reform of an economic model in use in China for over three decades that is widely seen to have reached a point of diminishing returns.

The Chinese leadership set forth in November 2013 an ambitious and wide-ranging agenda of economic and related domestic reforms. These proposed actions will deal with the problems noted above, among other things. How the more than sixty clusters of measures set forth for reform will in fact be implemented and how they will be made to interact effectively with one another are widely seen to require a strong and sustained effort of top Chinese leaders, probably for many years.[7] Under these circumstances, those same leaders would seem unlikely to seek confrontation with the United States. Xi Jinping's accommodation of President Obama in meeting in California in 2013 and his leadership's continued public emphasis on the positive in U.S.-China relations in seeking a new kind of major power relationship underlines this trend. Xi has also presided over China's greater assertiveness on maritime territorial issues that involve the United States, but thus far the Chinese probes generally have been crafted to avoid direct confrontation with the superpower.

Whether or not the many domestic priorities preoccupying Chinese leaders noted above can be equated with President Obama's domestic preoccupations arguing for a continued pragmatic American approach to China remains to be seen. On balance, they incline Chinese leaders toward caution and pragmatism.

Strong Interdependence

The second set of constraints on tough Chinese measures against the United States involves strong and ever-growing interdependence in U.S.-Chinese relations. As reviewed in chapter 3, at the start of the twenty-first century, growing economic interdependence reinforced each government's tendency to emphasize the positive and pursue constructive relations with one another. A pattern of dualism in U.S.-China relations arose as part of the developing positive equilibrium. The pattern involved constructive and cooperative engagement on the one hand and contingency planning or hedging on the other. It reflected a mix of converging and competing interests and prevailing leadership suspicions and cooperation.

The dualism showed as each government used engagement to build positive and cooperative ties while at the same time seeking to use these ties to build interdependencies and webs of relationships that had the effect of constraining the other power from taking actions that opposed its interests. The Council on Foreign Relations was explicit about this approach in a book titled *Weaving the Net* arguing for engagement that would over time compel changes in Chinese policies in accord with norms supported by the United States. While the analogy is not precise, the policies of engagement pursued by the United States and China toward one another featured respective "Gulliver strategies" that were designed to tie down the aggressive, assertive, and other negative policy tendencies of the other power through webs of interdependence in bilateral and multilateral relationships. [8]

The power of interdependence and dualism to constrain assertive and disruptive actions has limits. Thus, in the late 1990s, some specialists in China and the United States judged that the more moderate Chinese approach to the United States at that time would be reciprocated by the United States, leading to growing convergence. [9] As it turned out, other Chinese and American specialists who judged that the circumstances surrounding Chinese foreign policy and Chinese policy toward the United States had remained far too uncertain to posit a truly lasting Chinese strategy of cooperation and convergence with the United States were proven correct. [10] Changing international circumstances mix with patriotic and often strongly nationalistic sentiment among Chinese elite and public opinion and expanding Chinese military capabilities and coercive power to support stronger Chinese measures to protect and advance Chinese interests in the face of perceived outside intrusions and pressures. Chinese leaders adjust to such changing circumstances, weighing in each instance the costs and benefits of maintaining or altering policies. [11]

In recent years, Chinese leaders are seen by this group of analysts as continuing to hedge their bets as they endeavor to persuade the United States and other important world powers of China's avowed determination to pursue the road of peace and development. Thus, the new thinking seen in greater Chinese international activism and positivism regarding multilateral organizations and world politics appears to be only one part of recent Chinese foreign policy. Such new Chinese diplomatic and international activism and positivism not only foster a positive and beneficent image for China; they are seen by these analysts as serving an important practical objective of fostering norms and practices in regional and international organizations and circumstances that create a buffer against suspected U.S. efforts to "contain" China and to impede China's rising power. Roughly consistent with the image of the "Gulliver strategy" noted earlier, they foster webs of interdependent relationships that tie down and hamper unilateral or other actions by the U.S. superpower that could intrude on important Chinese interests in Asian and world affairs.[12]

In sum, the American approach to China seeks engagement for its own sake, but it also seeks to intertwine China into what the Council on Foreign Relations called a "web" woven by the United States and its allies and associates to ensure that rising China conforms more to international norms backed by the United States as it rises in world prominence. For its part, China deliberately builds interdependence with the United States and with regional and international organizations involving the United States as a means to buffer against and constrain possibly harsh U.S. measures against China. As time passed, both sides became increasingly aware of how their respective interests were tied to the well-being and success of the other, thereby limiting the tendency of the past to apply pressure on one another. In effect, interdependence has worked to constrain both sides against taking forceful action against each other.

China's Insecure Position in the Asia-Pacific

The third set of constraints on tough Chinese measures against the United States involves China's insecure position in the Asia-Pacific region. This factor does not receive the attention it deserves. Major American government and nongovernment studies of China's military challenge to the United States do not consider how China's insecure position in Asia reduces the likelihood that Beijing would seek a military challenge and confrontation with the United States.[13] Even after over two decades of repeated efforts, China's rise in the region remains encumbered and has a long way to go to challenge U.S. regional leadership. Nearby Asia is the world area where China has always exerted the greatest influence and where China devotes the lion's share of its foreign policy attention. The region contains security and sovereignty issues (e.g., Taiwan) of top importance for China. It is the main arena of interaction with the United States. This is the world area where the People's Liberation Army (PLA) is most active and exerts its greatest international influence. The region's economic importance far surpasses the rest of the world (China is Africa's biggest trader, but it does more trade with South Korea). Stability along the rim of China is essential for China's continued economic growth—the linchpin of leadership legitimacy and continued communist rule. Against this background, without a secure foundation in nearby Asia, China will be inclined to avoid serious confrontation with the United States.[14]

Among Chinese strengths in the Asia-Pacific region are the following:

- China's position as the leading trading partner with most neighboring countries and the heavy investment many of those countries make in China;
- China's growing web of road, rail, river, electric power, pipeline, and other linkages promoting economic and other interchange with nearby countries;
- China's prominent leadership attention and active diplomacy in interaction with neighboring countries both bilaterally and multilaterally; and
- China's expanding military capabilities and related civilian security capabilities.

Nevertheless, these strengths are offset by various weaknesses and limitations. First, some Chinese practices alienate nearby governments, which broadly favor key aspects of U.S. regional leadership. Thus, leadership in the region involves often costly and risky efforts to support common goals involving regional security and development. In contrast, Chinese behavior shows a well-developed tendency to avoid risks, costs, or commitments to the common good unless there is adequate benefit for a narrow set of tangible Chinese interests. Although it has around $4 trillion in foreign exchange reserves, China continues to run a substantial trade surplus and to accumulate large foreign exchange reserves supported by currency policies widely seen to disadvantage trading competitors in the Asia-Pacific and elsewhere. Despite its economic progress and role as an international creditor comparable to international financial institutions, China annually receives over $6 billion a year in foreign assistance loans and lesser grants that presumably would otherwise be available for other deserving clients in the Asia-Pacific and the world. It carefully adheres to UN budget formulas that keep Chinese dues and other payments remarkably low. It tends to assure that its contributions to the broader good of the international order (e.g., extensive use of Chinese personnel in UN peacekeeping operations) are paid for by others. At bottom, the "win-win" principle that undergirds recent Chinese foreign policy means that Chinese officials make sure that Chinese policies and practices provide a "win" for generally narrowly defined national interests of China. They eschew the kinds of risky and costly commitments for the broader regional and global common good that Asian leaders have come to look to U.S. leadership to provide. A major reason for China's continued reluctance to undertake costs and commitments for the sake of the common good of the Asia-Pacific and broader international affairs is the long array of domestic challenges and preoccupations faced by Chinese leaders. The actual impact of these domestic issues on the calculations of Chinese leaders is hard to measure with any precision, though their overall impact appears substantial.

Second, recent episodes of Chinese assertiveness toward several neighbors and the United States have put nearby governments on guard and weakened Chinese regional influence. They have reminded China's neighbors that the sixty-year history of the People's Republic of China (PRC) has much more often than not featured China acting in disruptive and domineering ways in the region.[15] Notably, Mao Zedong and Deng Xiaoping repeatedly conflicted with and invaded neighboring countries either with Chinese forces or with insurgents organized, armed, and trained by China.

Third, the record of China's success in reassuring neighbors and advancing influence in the Asia-Pacific in the post–Cold War period—a period now extending twenty-five years—is mediocre. China faces major impediments, many homegrown. China's long-standing practice of building an image of consistent and righteous behavior in foreign affairs blocks realistic appraisal of the wary view of China held by officials in most neighboring countries and the United States. The latter countries fear another in the long series of historical shifts in Chinese policy away from the current emphasis on reassurance and toward past practices of intimidation and aggression.

Chinese elite and public opinion is well conditioned by China's extensive education-propaganda apparatus; they know little about this negative Chinese legacy of past widespread intimidation and aggression. Absorbed in Chinese publicity regarding China's allegedly exceptional position of consistent, moral, and benign foreign behavior, Chinese elites and public opinion have a poor appreciation of regional and American concerns. Elite and public opinion restricts more realistic Chinese policies when dealing with disputes and differences with neighbors and the United States.

Most notably, the Chinese government has the exceptional position among major powers of having never acknowledged making a mistake in foreign policy. Analysis shows that the Chinese sense of exceptionalism and righteousness is much stronger even than that prevailing in the United States, known for its exceptionalism in foreign affairs. However, free media, open politics, regularly scheduled elections, and changes in administrations lead repeatedly to U.S. recognition of foreign policy failures in pursuit of new directions. Roughly comparable to China's outlook is that seen in my beloved but flawed church, the Roman Catholic Church, when the pope issues directives on faith and dogma. Thus Beijing joins the Vatican with Chinese exceptional exceptionalism, which reinforces among Chinese people and elites the Chinese government–fostered worldview of China always following a correct stance.

As a result, when China encounters a dispute with neighbors, the fault never lies with China. If Beijing chooses not to blame the neighbor, its default position is to blame larger forces, usually involving the United States. Adding to this peculiar negative mix, Chinese elites and public opinion remain heavily influenced by prevailing Chinese media and other emphases on China's historic victimization at the hands of outside powers such as the

United States, Japan, and others. In sum, they are quick to find offense and impervious to the need for change and recognition of fault on their part. [16]

Measuring China's Relationships

Measuring significant limitations and shortcomings seen in China's recent relations in the Asia-Pacific—even after twenty-five years of efforts in the post–Cold War period—can start with China's relationship with Japan, arguably Asia's richest country and the key ally of the United States in the region. The record shows that China usually has been unsuccessful in winning greater support, and relations seriously worsened to their lowest point because of disputes involving Japanese missteps and widespread Chinese violence, extralegal trade sanctions, and intimidation well beyond accepted international norms over territorial and resource claims in the East China Sea. [17]

India's interest in accommodation with China has been offset by border frictions and competition for influence among the countries surrounding India and in Southeast Asia and Central Asia. The limited progress in Sino-Indian relations became overshadowed by a remarkable upswing in India's strategic cooperation with the United States during the past decade. [18] Meanwhile, Russian and Chinese interest in close alignment has waxed and waned and often has appeared to depend on their respective relationships with the West. [19]

Until recently, China had a very negative record in relations with Taiwan. The election of a new Taiwan government in 2008 bent on reassuring Beijing changed relations for the better. China's economic, diplomatic, and military influence over Taiwan grew. The government was reelected in 2012, but the political opposition in Taiwan remained opposed to recent trends and improved its standing with Taiwan voters as the percentage approval of the ruling president sometimes dropped to single digits. [20]

Despite close Sino–South Korean economic ties, South Korean opinion of China declined sharply from a high point in 2004, initially because of historical disputes. South Koreans also opposed Chinese support for North Korea, which seemed designed to sustain a viable North Korean state friendly to China—an objective at odds with South Korea's goal of reunifying North and South Korea, with South Korea being dominant. China's refusal in 2010 to condemn North Korea's killing of forty-six South Korean sailors in the sinking of a South Korean warship and its killing of South Korean soldiers and civilians in an artillery attack strongly reinforced anti-China sentiment. Chinese efforts to improve ties with a new South Korean president in 2013 were sidetracked by provocations from North Korea and Chinese advances in disputed territory claimed by South Korea. [21]

Chinese diplomacy at various times endeavored to play down Chinese territorial disputes in Southeast Asian countries, but differences have become more prominent in recent years, especially over disputed claims in the South China Sea, seriously complicating Chinese relations with the region. China's remarkable military modernization and its sometimes secretive and authoritarian political system raised suspicions and wariness on the part of a number of China's neighbors, including such middle powers as Australia.[22] These countries have endeavored to build their own military power and to work cooperatively with one another and the United States in the face of China's military advances.

The People's Republic of China's record of repeated aggression and assertiveness during the forty years' rule of Mao Zedong and Deng Xiaoping toward many Asian countries means that China has had few positive connections on which to build friendly ties with its neighbors. Chinese interchange with Asian neighbors has depended heavily on the direction and leadership of the Chinese government. Nongovernment channels of communication and influence have been limited. The so-called overseas Chinese communities in Southeast Asian countries have provided important investment and technical assistance to China's development and have represented political forces supportive of their home country's good relations with China. At the same time, however, the dominant ethnic, cultural, and religious groups in Southeast Asia often have a long history of wariness of China and sometimes have promoted violent actions and other discrimination against ethnic Chinese.[23]

Limitations and complications also showed up in the areas of greatest Chinese strength in Asia—economic relations and diplomacy.[24] Double counting associated with processing trade exaggerated Chinese trade figures. As half of Chinese trade was conducted by foreign invested enterprises in China, the resulting processing trade saw China often add only a small amount to the product, and the finished product often depended on sales to the United States or the European Union. A Singaporean ambassador told Chinese media in August 2013 that 60 percent of the goods that are exported from China and ASEAN are ultimately manufactures that go to the United States, Europe, and Japan. Only 22 percent of these goods stay in the China-ASEAN region.[25] Taken together, these facts seemed to underscore Chinese interdependence with the United States and allied countries and to represent a major caveat regarding China's stature in Asia as a powerful trading country.

The large amount of Asian and international investment that went to China did not go to other Asian countries, hurting their economic development. Until very recently, China invested little in Asia apart from Hong Kong, a reputed tax haven and source of "round-trip" monies leaving China and then returning to China as foreign investment. China in 2013 and 2014 repeatedly pledged tens of billions of dollars worth of Chinese investment for infrastructure development in countries along China's periphery. The pledges seemed credible given China's large foreign exchange reserves, and interest among countries in the region in using the funds was strong. It remained to be seen how China and its various neighbors would work out mutually agreeable arrangements that would accord with China's ubiquitous "win-win" formula that required a clear advantage for a narrowly defined Chinese win-set before China would move forward with such foreign assistance.

Chinese aid figures are not clearly presented by the Chinese government. What is known shows that China's aid (as opposed to financing arrangements that require repayment in cash or kind) to Asia is very small, especially in comparison to other donors, with the exception of Chinese secret but reportedly substantial aid to North Korea and, at least until recently, Myanmar. In keeping with China's "win-win" diplomacy, the sometimes dizzying array of meetings, agreements, and pronouncements in active Chinese diplomacy in Asia did not hide the fact that China remained reluctant to undertake significant costs, risks, or commitments in dealing with difficult regional issues.

North Korea reflects an unusual mix of Chinese strengths and weaknesses in Asia. On the one hand, China provides considerable food aid, oil, and other material support. China is North Korea's largest trading partner and foreign investor. China often shields Pyongyang from U.S.-led efforts at the United Nations to sanction or otherwise punish North Korea over its nuclear weapons development, ballistic missile development, proliferation activities, and military aggression against South Korea. At times, the United States and other participants in the six-party talks relied on China to use its standing as the foreign power with the most influence in North Korea to get Pyongyang to engage in negotiations over its weapons development and proliferation activities. On the other hand, North Korea repeatedly rejects Chinese advice and warnings. North Korean officials tell American and other officials of their disdain for China. Nonetheless, Chinese leaders are reluctant to cut off their aid. An increase in pressure on North Korea to conform to international norms could cause a backlash from the Pyongyang regime that would undermine Chinese interests in preserving stability on the Korean Peninsula and in northeastern Asia. The net effect of these contradictions is that while China's influence in North Korea is greater than that of other major powers, it is encumbered and limited. [26]

CHINA IN THE SHADOW OF U.S. LEADERSHIP IN THE ASIA-PACIFIC

A comparison of Chinese policies and practices in the Asia-Pacific with those of the United States underlines how far China has to go despite over two decades of efforts to secure its position in Asia if it intends to be successful in seriously confronting and challenging the United States. Without a secure periphery, and facing formidable American presence and influence, China almost certainly calculates that challenging the United States poses grave dangers for the PRC regime.[27]

U.S. weaknesses in the Asia-Pacific included the foreign policies of the George W. Bush administration, which were very unpopular with regional elites and public opinion. As the Barack Obama government has refocused U.S. attention positively on the Asia-Pacific region, regional concerns shifted to worry that U.S. budget difficulties and political gridlock in Washington would undermine the ability of the United States to sustain support for regional responsibilities.

As seen in the Obama government's rebalance policy reviewed in chapter 4 and in recent American practice, U.S. priorities, behavior, and power mesh well with the interests of the majority of Asia-Pacific governments that seek legitimacy through development and nation building in an uncertain security environment and an interdependent world economic order. The drivers of America undertaking leadership responsibilities in the Asia-Pacific region remain strong:

- The region is an area of ever-greater strategic and economic importance for the United States.
- The United States remains strongly committed to long-standing U.S. goals of supporting stability and balance of power, sustaining smooth economic access, and promoting U.S. values and accepted international norms in this increasingly important world area.

The basic determinants of U.S. strength and influence in the Asia-Pacific region involve the factors discussed below.[28]

Security

In most of Asia, governments are strong and viable and are able to make the decisions that determine the direction of foreign affairs. In general, officials see their governments' legitimacy and success resting on nation building and economic development, which require a stable and secure international environment. Unfortunately, Asia is not particularly stable, and most regional governments are privately wary of and tend not to trust each other. As a result, they look to the United States to provide the security they need. They recognize that the U.S. security role is very expensive and involves great risk, including large-scale casualties if necessary. They also recognize that neither China nor any other Asian power or coalition of powers is able or willing to undertake even a fraction of these risks, costs, and responsibilities.

Economic

The nation-building priority of most Asian governments depends importantly on export-oriented growth. As noted above, much of Chinese and Asian trade heavily depends on exports to developed countries, notably the United States. The United States has run a massive trade deficit with China, and a total annual trade deficit with Asia valued at over $400 billion. Asian government officials recognize that China, which runs an overall trade surplus, and other trading partners of Asia are unwilling and unable to bear even a fraction of the cost of such large trade deficits, which nonetheless are very important for Asian governments.

Government Engagement

The Bush administration was generally effective in interaction with Asia's powers. The Obama government has built on these strengths. The Obama government's wide-ranging rebalancing with regional governments and multilateral organizations has a scope going from India to the Pacific Island states to Korea and Japan. Its emphasis on consultation and inclusion of international stakeholders before coming to policy decisions on issues of importance to Asia and the Pacific has also been broadly welcomed and stands in contrast with the previously perceived unilateralism of the Bush government.

Meanwhile, the U.S. Pacific Command and other U.S. military commands and security and intelligence organizations have been at the edge of wide-ranging and growing U.S. efforts to build and strengthen webs of military and related intelligence and security relationships throughout the region.

Nongovernment Engagement and Immigration

The United States has long engaged the Asia-Pacific through business, religious, educational, media, and other interchange. Such active nongovernment interaction puts the United States in a unique position and reinforces overall U.S. influence. During a speech in Manila in December 2013, Secretary of State John Kerry highlighted the millions of dollars of assistance to Philippine storm victims coming from such U.S. business partners as Coca-Cola, Proctor & Gamble, Dow Chemical, FedEx, Cargill, and Citibank.[29] Meanwhile, almost fifty years of generally color-blind U.S. immigration policy since the ending of discriminatory U.S. restrictions on Asian immigration in 1965 has resulted in the influx of millions of Asia-Pacific migrants who call America home and who interact with their countries of origin in ways that undergird and reflect well on the American position in the region. Kerry noted that there are now over four million Filipino-Americans and over 350,000 American residents in the country.

Asia-Pacific Contingency Planning

Part of the reason for the success of U.S. efforts to build webs of security-related and other relationships with Asia-Pacific countries has to do with active contingency planning by many Asia-Pacific governments. As power relations change in the region, notably on account of China's rise, regional governments generally seek to work positively and pragmatically with rising China on the one hand, but on the other hand they seek the reassurance of close security, intelligence, and other ties with the United States in case rising China shifts from its current avowed benign approach to one of greater assertiveness or dominance.

Against the background of recent Chinese assertiveness, the Asia-Pacific governments' interest in closer ties with the United States meshed well with the Obama government's engagement with regional governments and multilateral organizations. The U.S. concern to maintain stability while fostering economic growth overlapped constructively with the priorities of the vast majority of regional governments as they pursued their respective nation-building agendas.

ASIAN-PACIFIC DYNAMICS AND U.S.-CHINA RELATIONS

The circumstances discussed above underline the judgment that China is constrained in the Asia-Pacific region and is not in a position to confront the United States. The forecast explained in this section also adds to evidence showing that the Obama government's rebalance toward the Asia-Pacific region fits well with Asia-Pacific dynamics while China's approach remains conflicted between reassurance and assertiveness in ways that reinforce regional interest in sustaining and advancing closer ties with the United States. It is judged that U.S. leaders will see their interests best served by supporting stability and avoiding offensive actions, thus reinforcing the conclusion that the main element leading to instability and possible U.S.-China conflict—rising China and its assertiveness—will be held in check.

As noted in the introduction, post–Cold War dynamics in Asia are seen as determined by five sets of factors[30]:

1. the changing power relationships among Asia's leading countries (e.g., the rise of China and India; change in Japan; rising or reviving middle powers—South Korea, Indonesia, and Australia);
2. the growing impact of economic globalization and related international information interchange;
3. the ebb and flow of tensions in the Korean Peninsula, southwestern Asia, and the broader U.S.-backed efforts against terrorism and proliferation of weapons of mass destruction;

4. the rise of Asian multilateralism; and
5. the changing extent of U.S. engagement with and withdrawal from involvement in Asian matters.

In addition, a survey of leadership debates over foreign policy among Asian-Pacific leaders[31] shows movement toward perspectives of realism in international relations theory in the United States, China, Japan, Russia, India, and several middle and smaller powers including Indonesia, Australia, South Korea, Vietnam, Malaysia, and Singapore.[32] Such perspectives are important in how these leaders view the changing power dynamics and security issues seen notably in factors 1, 3, and 5.

While vigilant regarding changing circumstances that could have an impact on their security, sovereignty, and other important interests, the government leaders also clearly recognize the importance of economic development, the linchpin of their political legitimacy. Thus they endeavor to use the liberal international economic order in ways that benefit them and their countries, and in so doing they subscribe in various ways and to varying degree to aspects of liberalism in international relations theory.

Asian-Pacific leaders also show support for aspects of the international relations theory of constructivism. Such support is manifest in their ongoing efforts to build regional and international organizations and to support international norms as effective means to manage interstate tensions and differences and to promote greater interstate cooperation. Domestically, most Asian-Pacific governments also foster a strong identity for their nations as independent actors in regional and global affairs representing the interests and qualities of the peoples of their respective countries. Supporting such an identity is an important element in their continued political legitimacy.[33]

The Obama government's rebalancing initiatives fit well with most of these regional dynamics. And U.S. strengths look even stronger when compared with China's recent approaches.

The United States has a proven record of bearing the costs and risks of sustaining the regional stability that is essential for the development and nation building sought by regional government leaders. There is little perceived danger of offensive U.S. military, economic, or other policy actions amid repeated stress by American leaders against unilateral change in the status quo.

By contrast, China has accompanied its rise in regional prominence with a conflicted message of closer economic cooperation on a mutually beneficial (win-win) basis and often strident Chinese threats and coercive actions backed by civilian and military government power against neighbors that disagree with China, especially on issues of sovereignty and security. The fact that China's stridency on these matters has grown with the expansion of coercive civilian and military power alarms many Asian neighbors who seek reassurance from closer relations with the United States in a variety of forms, thereby deepening and strengthening American integration with the region. Meanwhile, Chinese leaders continue to focus on a narrow win-set of Chinese interests. They avoid the kinds of costs and risks borne by the United States in support of perceived American interests in the broader regional order that are well recognized by regional governments, reinforcing those governments' support for closer American involvement in regional affairs. Asian leaders watch closely for signs of U.S. military withdrawal or flagging American interest in sustaining regional stability. The Obama government has affirmed its commitment to sustain the robust American security presence involving close military cooperation with the vast majority of Asian-Pacific governments built during the post–Cold War period.

China's role as a trader, site for investment, and increasingly important foreign investor continues to grow in regional affairs. Unlike the United States, China has a great deal of money that could be used to the benefit of its neighbors, and neighboring governments see their interests well served by interchange with Chinese counterparts in finding possible ways that such resources could be used in ways of mutual benefit according to China's "win-win" formula. China's location and advancing infrastructure connecting China to its neighbors are major positive attributes supporting closer Chinese relations with neighboring states. Of course, much of the trade is dependent on foreign investment and access to markets in the United States in particular. The United States sustains a very large trade deficit that undergirds the export-oriented economies of the region. Asian leaders are watchful for signs of American protectionism, but the Obama government's rebalance features strong emphasis on ever-greater American commitment to openness and free trade. By contrast, China's commitment to free trade seems more selective and narrow. Beijing is prone to go well beyond international norms in retaliating against others over trade and other issues. Its cybertheft of trade and economic information and property is enormous. Its currency manipulation and other neomercantilist practices disadvantage neighboring economies along with the United States.[34] China has also put extraordinary pressure on Japan for the sake of territorial claims, risking enormous negative consequences for regional economic growth. In contrast, the United States has endeavored to calm the tensions by playing a stabilizing role highly valued by most regional governments.

The growth of U.S. security, economic, and political relationships with a wide range of Asian-Pacific governments under the terms of the Obama government rebalance has the effect of strengthening these governments and countries, reinforcing their independence and identity. While many of these governments disagree with U.S. policies regarding the Middle East peace process, electronic spying, and other issues, American interests in preserving a favorable balance of power in the region are supported by the prevalence of such strengthened independent actors. By contrast, China's assertiveness shows its neighbors that Beijing expects them to accommodate a growing range of Chinese concerns, even to the point of sacrificing territory. Strengthening those in the region that resist China's pressure is seen in Beijing as a hostile act. It is important to reiterate here that most Asian-Pacific governments expect the Obama government to carry out its improvement of relations in the region in ways that do not exacerbate China-U.S. tensions and thereby disrupt the Asia-Pacific region. Adjustments in the Obama rebalance policy, giving less public emphasis to competition with China and military dimensions while stressing and carrying out an extraordinary series of top-level engagement efforts with China, serve to manage tensions in line with regional concerns.

The Obama government has also markedly advanced U.S. relations with the various regional organizations valued by Asian governments as part of their "constructivist" efforts to create and build institutions to ease interstate rivalries and promote cooperative relations. The Obama government seems sincere in pursuing interchange that is respectful of the regional bodies. China also shows close alignment with these groups, though more assertive Chinese ambitions regarding disputed territories have seen Chinese leaders grossly manipulate these bodies or resort to coercion and intimidation.

OTHER CONTEMPORARY ISSUES AND THEIR IMPLICATIONS

The combination of the Obama government's rebalance policy and China's rising assertiveness in Asia rightfully places emphasis on growing Sino-American competition for influence in the Asia-Pacific as the focus of uncertainty, potential instability, and possible fracturing of the fragile post–Cold War equilibrium in U.S.-Chinese relations. Meanwhile, the twists and turns of U.S.-Chinese relations in the post–Cold War period reviewed in chapter 3 underline the multifaceted major differences between the world's leading powers that have a seemingly ever-present ability to disrupt and possibly derail the relationship under varied circumstances.

The Obama administration has over six years of dealing with a rising China. Experience shows that U.S. expectations of significant positive breakthroughs in the relationship are justifiably low. The Chinese have proven to be difficult partners. The Chinese harbor objectives strongly at odds with important American interests. Specifically, Beijing explicitly favors a multipolar international order at odds with U.S. leadership in world affairs. It opposes the strengthening U.S. alliance system and the behavior of American security and other forces as the leading power along the rim of China. It builds and deploys an impressive array of military forces designed to counter and, if necessary, confront the American military along China's rim. It sharply criticizes American support for Taiwan, especially arms sales, and it attacks U.S. support for China's neighbors that contest expansive Chinese claims to territory in the disputed seas along China's periphery. The Chinese government is highly sensitive to signals of U.S. support for the Dalai Lama, ethnic Uyghur dissidents in China's Xinjiang region, and other domestic Chinese oppositionists. State-directed Chinese outlets routinely portray U.S. policy intentions in worst-case assessments, seeing Washington as seeking to bring down the one-party system in China as it fosters regional efforts to contain Chinese power. Prevalent negative depictions of U.S. intentions are married with media-propaganda campaigns establishing China's identity as resisting many aspects of American leadership while reinforcing Chinese self-righteousness.

Against this background, salient issues in Sino-American relations will not be resolved soon or easily. In addition to the recent disputes over maritime issues discussed above, these issues focus on important security and economic questions, Taiwan, and human rights, democracy, and other international norms favored by the United States.[35]

Security Issues

In the course of U.S. normalization with China since the late 1960s, security issues moved from being the main source of converging interests between the United States and China to the main source of divergence and mutual distrust between the two countries. Throughout the entire period, security issues have never been uniformly positive or negative for the relationship; their implications usually have been mixed. However, the broad pattern shows important convergence of Sino-American security interests against the Soviet Union in the period from the late 1960s through the early 1980s. U.S.-China security ties were cut drastically after the 1989 Tiananmen crackdown. Since then, the United States and China have restored businesslike security ties and developed common ground on a variety of international security questions. These positive elements, however, were offset by differences on a range of security issues.

The differences arose against a background of changing Asian and international power relations caused in part by China's rising power and prominence in international affairs, particularly by China's strong military modernization focused on Asian issues of key concern to the United States. Thus a security dilemma has emerged in the respective Chinese and U.S. military buildups focused on Taiwan since the 1990s. The scope of the Sino-American security dilemma has broadened in recent years to include the contested maritime areas along China's periphery, with China more assertively using military means to support other mechanisms of state power to coerce neighbors to accept China's claims in the disputed East and South

China Seas. The United States has deployed military forces, carried out extensive surveillance of Chinese deployments, and used numerous military exercises and other security measures to support its allies and associates facing Chinese coercion and to deter further Chinese assertiveness. The broad security dilemma involves forces directly committed to the Asia-Pacific region supported by expanding Chinese and substantial American nuclear weapons; growing cyber, space, and other unconventional attack capabilities; and espionage directed at one another.

Economic Issues

The rapid growth of the Chinese economy and close integration of Chinese development into the global economy have been the most salient accomplishments of the reforms pursued by Chinese leaders since the death of Mao. The rapid growth of China's economy and U.S.-China economic relations has in varying degrees conformed with and been driven by forces of international economic globalization. The overall impact of Chinese growth, closer U.S.-China economic relations, and international economic globalization has been profound. It has had both positive and negative effects on broad swaths of opinion, economic, and other interest groups, not to mention political leaders, in both societies. On the whole, the impact has been highly beneficial to China's interests.

Complaints and initiatives to change existing economic relations have come in recent years largely from the U.S. side of the Sino-American relationship. Recent U.S. initiatives and complaints reflect a wide range of American interests and constituencies concerned with perceived unfair or disadvantageous aspects of the massive U.S.-China economic relationship. They focus on the unprecedented U.S. trade deficit with China seen as caused by currency manipulation, massive cyber and other theft of commercial know-how and intellectual property, state-sponsored subsidies, coercion and intimidation to force the sharing of sensitive technology, and refusal to abide by pledges made in China's accession to the WTO to open restricted sectors of China's markets where American companies would be competitive. Suspicions of Chinese espionage color the American reaction to China's expanding investment in the United States, and some Americans argue against U.S. reliance on China to purchase American government securities. The salience of these issues in American domestic politics has varied over time. As noted in chapter 3, often heated criticism of China in the 2012 U.S. election campaign focused on economic complaints more than any other set of issues, and recent public opinion polls show that Americans have a greater concern with China's economic threat, as opposed to its security or political threat, to American interests.[36]

Taiwan Issues

From the outset of U.S. normalization with China, Chinese officials have repeatedly pointed to Taiwan issues as the most important obstacle to improving Sino-American relations. There was a major cross-strait crisis involving the Chinese and American military forces in 1995–1996, and strong tensions rose to the surface several times during the leadership of Taiwan by presidents Lee Teng-hui and Chen Shui-bian who steered the government in the direction of separation and independence from China. Under President Ma Ying-jeou, in power since 2008, the Taiwan government has reversed course and sought to accommodate and interact more frequently and closely with mainland China. Tensions in contemporary U.S.-China relations over Taiwan have eased remarkably. As noted briefly in chapters 1 and 3, general satisfaction of the governments in China and the United States over the improvements in cross-strait relations in recent years has helped to offset the impact of rising Sino-American differences over China's tough measures on territorial disputes in the East and South China Seas, North Korea's developing nuclear weapons, and America's more competitive regional posture under President Obama's rebalance policy.

Nevertheless, the interests, policies, and practices of the United States and China usually have been at odds over Taiwan and remain so today in important ways. Notably, the Chinese authorities continue an impressive buildup of military forces targeting Taiwan and American forces that they believe will come to Taiwan's assistance in the event of conflict over Taiwan. The Americans carefully monitor the Chinese buildup as they prepare forces to counter and destroy Chinese combatants that would impede U.S. response in a Taiwan conflict. The military strengthening on both sides underlines the position of Taiwan as one of only a few areas where the world's number-one and number-two powers could come to blows, with devastating implications for them and international affairs.

Such confrontation and conflict likely will continue to be avoided provided the Taiwan government continues its recent policies of accommodation and closer engagement with China. Circumstances could change, however. Domestic politics in Taiwan remain volatile. The Ma government has become very unpopular. Mass movements accompanied by large public demonstrations emerge repeatedly to show dissatisfaction with governance at home and abroad, including management of Taiwan's relations with China. The political opposition has revived from its election losses in 2008 and 2012. It remains opposed to many current cross-strait policies. It is viewed with great suspicion by China. Taken together, these trends reinforce the chances of the election in 2016 of an opposition party leader favoring greater separatism and independence from China. A crisis could ensue if China responded with greater coercion and intimidation that in turn could result in American intervention and possible U.S.-China confrontation.

Meanwhile, American concern with China's use of military-backed intimidation and coercion to advance its control in disputed territories in the East and South China Seas has been accompanied by greater strategic interest in Taiwan. In contrast with previous reluctance of U.S. leaders to include Taiwan within the scope of the Obama government rebalance policy, administration representatives have in the past year mentioned Taiwan explicitly within the scope of the rebalance. Some specialists outside the U.S. government as well as officials in Congress have discussed Taiwan's military importance as a key link in the array of American-backed security structures and arrangements designed to dissuade China from further expansionism in disputed maritime territories. Some call for U.S. sales of advanced F-16 fighters to Taiwan and closer U.S. military cooperation with Taiwan as a way to signal to Chinese leaders that their assertive actions in the East and South China Seas could result in American actions elsewhere posing major costs for Chinese interests.[37]

Human Rights and International Norms

Issues of human rights in U.S.-China relations reflect a wide range of values dealing with economic, social, political, cultural, and other interests and concerns of groups and individuals. Differences over human rights issues have long characterized Sino-American relations. The differences have their roots in the respective backgrounds of the American and Chinese societies, governments, and peoples. Those backgrounds foster values that are often at odds.

In general, since the opening of Sino-American relations in the early 1970s, the Chinese and American governments have endeavored to manage these differences in ways that do not block progress in other important areas of Sino-American relations. At times when one side or the other has focused high priority on human rights issues, as the United States did following the Tiananmen crackdown of 1989, U.S.-China relations have tended to stall or retrogress. As U.S. and Chinese leaders more often have devoted only secondary consideration to human rights differences, the obstacles posed by these issues for Sino-American relations have also been less significant.

The importance of human rights differences between the United States and China has also been influenced by changes in policies and practices, especially on the part of China. In a broad sense, the United States has sought to prompt the Chinese authorities to adopt policies and practices in line with the international values and norms prevalent in modern developed countries of the West. In general, Chinese leaders have seen their interests better served by conforming more to international norms. Economically, China's government has embraced many of the norms of the globalized international economy and has adapted comprehensively to economic market demands. Significant benchmarks in this process were capped by China's decision to join the WTO with an agreement demanding extensive changes in Chinese economic policies and practices. As noted above, evidence of shortcomings in the process include rising complaints by Americans and others regarding China's failure to live up to WTO commitments. Meanwhile, China's conformity to world norms in the security area has been slower but substantial, especially in areas involving such sensitive issues as the proliferation of weapons of mass destruction.

China's leadership has also endeavored to appear more in line with international norms regarding issues affecting political power and processes in China. Chinese officials have engaged in a broad range of discussions, dialogues, and agreements with various countries and international organizations designed to advance political rights in line with world norms supported by the United States. China has signed international covenants dealing with economic, social, and political rights. Chinese leaders routinely pledge cooperation with other countries in promoting human rights. They have fostered reforms emphasizing the rule of law, creating greater transparency and accountability, and promoting democracy and democratic decision making in handling various human rights concerns in China. The process of Chinese reform in these areas has encouraged some Chinese and foreign specialists to anticipate continued progress leading to the transformation of China's authoritarian one-party political system. However, other specialists in China and abroad see the Chinese leadership as following policies of adaptation and adjustment in the area of political reform and related human rights. The reforms in these areas are seen as not undermining Chinese leadership control of political power in China or the key concern of Chinese leaders of sustaining and strengthening one-party rule in China through authoritarian as well as more liberal means. The result is continuing disagreement and controversy in U.S.-China relations over these issues.

Looking ahead, it appears that Chinese capabilities will grow, and as they do, Beijing is likely to take actions that will further challenge the United States regarding the above-noted issues and the broad international order supported by the United States.[38] The challenges to the security and stability of the Asia-Pacific have been clear and seem primed to continue and perhaps advance. China's erosion of international economic norms is more hidden. China seems to support free trade by the United States and others in its ongoing efforts to exploit this open environment with state-directed means, widespread theft, and intimidation and coercion of companies and governments in a wholesale grab of technology, know-how, capital, and competitive advantage in a headlong drive for economic development at the expense of others.

Americans will face continuing impediments from China in dealing with nuclear proliferation by North Korea and Iran, and China was of little help in dealing with Syria's use of chemical weapons or with Russia's coercion of Ukraine and acquisition of Crimea. Chinese leaders remain determined to support the Leninist one-party system in China that treats human rights selectively and capriciously, with an eye always focused on sustaining the communist state.

Taken together, these difficulties, frictions, and frustrations represent the focus of the overall China challenge for the United States in the period ahead. They promise numerous headaches and problems for U.S. policy makers, and American officials may grow somewhat weary in efforts to deal with various Chinese probes and machinations. However, the above assessment shows that the China challenge is not a fundamental one, at least not yet. The United States can have some confidence that prevailing circumstances and constraints seem to preclude China from seeking confrontation with America or a power shift in Asia. Some aver that China has adopted a slow and steady pace as it seeks to spread its influence and undermine that of the United States, especially in the all-important Asia-Pacific region.[39] Maybe so, but the record of Chinese advances over the past twenty-five years shows such mediocre results and conflicted approaches that the prospect of Chinese leadership in the Asia-Pacific region seems remote. More likely, China will continue to rise in the shadow of a United States increasingly integrated among a wide range of independent-minded Asian-Pacific governments that view the United States as critically important to their stability, growth, and identity.

NOTES

1. Among treatments of this subject, see Timothy Adamson, "China's Response to the U.S. Rebalance," in *Balancing Acts: The U.S. Rebalance and Asia-Pacific Stability*, by Robert Sutter, Michael Brown, and Timothy Adamson, 39–43 (Washington, DC, George Washington University, Elliott School of International Affairs, 2013).

2. "China-Southeast Asia Relations," *Comparative Connections* 16, no. 2 (September 2014): 59–61.

3. Aaron L. Friedberg, *A Contest for Supremacy: China, America and the Struggle for Mastery in Asia* (New York: Norton, 2011); Hugh White, "The China Choice," book review by Andrew Nathan, *Foreign Affairs*, January–February 2013, http://www.foreignaffairs.com/articles/138661/hugh-white/the-china-choice-why-america-should-share-power.

4. See the treatment of these preoccupations in, among others, David M. Lampton, *Following the Leader: Ruling China from Deng Xiaoping to Xi Jinping* (Berkeley: University of California Press, 2014), and Andrew J. Nathan and Andrew Scobell, *China's Search for Security* (New York: Columbia University Press, 2012).

5. Ben Blanchard and John Ruwitch, "China Hikes Defense Budget, to Spend More in Internal Security," Reuters, March 5, 2013, http://www.reuters.com/article/2013/03/05/us-china-parliament-defence-idUSBRE92403620130305.

6. Feng Zhaokui, "China Still a Developing Nation," *China Daily*, May 6, 2010, 12.

7. Stephen Roach, "China's Policy Disharmony," *Project Syndicate*, December 31, 2013, http://www.project-syndicate.org.

8. This dualism and respective Gulliver strategies are discussed in Robert Sutter, "China and U.S. Security and Economic Interests: Opportunities and Challenges," in *U.S.-China-EU Relations: Managing the New World Order*, ed. Robert Ross and Oystein Tunsjo (London: Routledge, 2010); James Shinn, *Weaving the Net* (New York: Council on Foreign Relations, 1996).

9. Avery Goldstein, *Rising to the Challenge: China's Grand Strategy and International Security* (Stanford, CA: Stanford University Press, 2005).

10. Susan Shirk, *China: Fragile Superpower* (New York: Oxford University Press, 2007).

11. Robert Sutter, *Chinese Foreign Relations: Power and Policy since the Cold War*, 3rd ed. (Lanham, MD: Rowman & Littlefield, 2012), 3–13.

12. Phillip Saunders, "China's Global Activism: Strategy, Drivers, and Tools" (occasional paper, National Defense University Press Institute for National Strategic Studies, Washington, DC, June 4, 2006), 8–9.

13. Such assessments of Chinese military capabilities include those by the Department of Defense, the Congressional Research Service (CRS), CSIS, and the Carnegie Endowment, which portray growing challenges and sometimes dire implications for the United States. The Defense Department assessments are annual; see http://www.defense.gov/pubs/2013_china_report_final.pdf. The CRS report is updated regularly; see http://fpc.state.gov/documents/organization/207068.pdf. The CSIS report is available at http://csis.org/publication/chinese-military-modernization-and-force-development-1; the Carnegie report is available at http://carnegieendowment.org/files/net_assessment_full.pdf.

14. Mark E. Manyin, Stephen Daggett, Ben Dolven, Susan V. Lawrence, Michael F. Martin, Ronald O'Rourke, and Bruce Vaughn, "Pivot to the Pacific? The Obama Administration's 'Rebalancing' toward Asia" (Washington, DC: Congressional Research Service, March 28, 2012); Philip Saunders, *The Rebalance to Asia: U.S.-China Relations and Regional Security* (Washington, DC: National Defense University, Institute for National Security Studies, 2012). This section summarizes findings in Robert Sutter, *Foreign Relations of the PRC* (Lanham, MD: Rowman & Littlefield, 2013), 1–26, 311–27.

15. For a more detailed explanation of these findings, see Sutter, *Foreign Relations of the PRC*, 13–14.

16. Gilbert Rozman, *East Asian National Identities: Common Roots and Chinese Exceptionalism* (Stanford, CA: Stanford University Press, 2013).

17. Peter Ford, "Japan Abandons Bid to Make China a Key Pillar of Its Foreign Policy," *Christian Science Monitor*, November 17, 2010, http://www.csmonitor.com; James Przystup, "Japan-China Relations," *Comparative Connections* 14, no. 3 (January 2013): 109–17.

18. Lawrence Saez and Crystal Chang, "China and South Asia: Strategic Implications and Economic Imperatives," in *China, the Developing World, and the New Global Dynamic*, ed. Lowell Dittmer and George Yu, 83–108 (Boulder, CO: Lynne Rienner, 2010); John Garver and Fei-ling Wang, "China's Anti-encirclement Struggle," *Asian Security* 6, no. 3 (2010): 238–63.

19. Yu Bin, "China-Russia Relations: Guns and Games of August; Tales of Two Strategic Partners," *Comparative Connections* 10, no. 3 (October 2008): 131–38; Yu Bin, "China-Russia Relations: Putin's Glory and Xi's Dream," *Comparative Connections* 14, no. 1 (May 2014): 121–33.

20. Richard Bush, *Unchartered Strait* (Washington, DC: Brookings Institution, 2013).

21. Scott Snyder, "China-Korea Relations," *Comparative Connections* 12, no. 4 (January 2011), http://www.csis.org/pacfor; Scott Snyder, "China-Korea Relations," *Comparative Connections* 14, no. 1 (May 2014): 87–94.

22. Linda Jacobson, "Australia-China Ties: In Search of Political Trust," *Policy Brief* (Sydney: Lowy Institute, June 2012).

23. Sutter, *Foreign Relations of the PRC*, 319.

24. Yu Yongding, "A Different Road Forward," *China Daily*, December 23, 2010, 9.

25. Pu Zhendong, "Singapore Supports Strengthened Free-Trade Agreement with Beijing," *China Daily*, August 30, 2013, http://usa.chinadaily.com.cn/epaper/2013-08/30/content_16932418.htm.

26. Scott Snyder, "China's Post-Kim Jong Il Debate," *Comparative Connections* 12, no. 1 (May 2012): 107–14; Scott Snyder, "China-Korea Relations," *Comparative Connections* 14, no. 1 (May 2014): 87–94.

27. Robert Sutter, "Assessing China's Rise and U.S. Influence in Asia: Growing Maturity and Balance," *Journal of Contemporary China* 19, no. 65 (June 2010): 591–604; Sutter, *Foreign Relations of the PRC*, 321–26.

28. Author's findings based on interviews with over two hundred officials from ten Asia-Pacific countries discussed most recently in Sutter, *Foreign Relations of the PRC*, 321–26.

29. "Kerry Speaks in the Philippines," *Asian American Press*, December 17, 2013, http://aapress.com/ethnicity/filipino/kerry-speaks-in-the-philippines.

30. This assessment builds on Robert Sutter, *The United States in Asia* (Lanham, MD: Rowman & Littlefield, 2009), 154–66; Suisheng Zhao, "Shaping the Regional Context of China's Rise: How the Obama Administration Brought Back Hedge in Its Engagement with China," *Journal of Contemporary China* 21, no. 75 (May 2012): 369–90; and Robert Sutter, "Rebalancing, China and Asian Dynamics: Obama's Good Fit," *PacNet*, no. 1 (January 5, 2014), http://csis.org/files/publication/Pac1401.pdf.

31. Henry Nau and Deepa Ollapally, eds., *World Views of Aspiring Powers* (New York: Oxford University Press, 2012).

32. Author interviews in Sutter, *Foreign Relations of the PRC*.

33. Gilbert Rozman, *East Asian National Identities: Common Roots and Chinese Exceptionalism* (Stanford, CA: Stanford University Press, 2012).

34. Wayne Morrison, *China-U.S. Trade Issues*, Report RL33536 (Washington, DC: Library of Congress, Congressional Research Service, December 16, 2013).

35. On Sino-American differences over these issues, see Susan Lawrence, *U.S.-China Relations: An Overview of Policy Issues*, Report R41108 (Washington, DC: Library of Congress, Congressional Research Service, August 1, 2013); Robert Sutter, *U.S.-Chinese Relations: Perilous Past, Pragmatic Present*, 2nd ed. (Lanham, MD: Rowman & Littlefield, 2013), 183–272.

36. Andrew Dugan, "Americans View China Mostly Unfavorably," Gallup Politics, February 20, 2014, http://www.gallup.com/poll/167498/americans-view-china-mostly-unfavorably.aspx.

37. Vance Serchuk, "Obama's Silence on Taiwan Masks Its Significance in U.S. Relations with China," *Washington Post*, May 23, 2013, http://www.washingtonpost.com/opinions/obamas-silence-on-taiwan-masks-its-significance-in-us-relations-with-china/2013/05/23/a1b40470-c243-11e2-914f-a7aba60512a7_story.html; Daniel Russel, "U.S. Policy towards East Asia and the Pacific: Remarks at Baltimore Council on Foreign Affairs," Department of State Diplomacy in Action, May 29, 2014, http://www.state.gov/p/eap/rls/rm/2014/05/226887.htm; U.S. China Economic and Security Review Commission Hearing, "China and the Evolving Security Dynamics in East Asia," March 13, 2014, http://origin.www.uscc.gov/sites/default/files/transcripts/Hearing%20Transcript_March%2013%2C2014_0.pdf.

38. For a review of the issues and disputes, see Susan Lawrence, *U.S.-China Relations: An Overview of Policy Issues*, Report R41108 (Washington, DC: Library of Congress, Congressional Research Service, August 1, 2013).

39. Friedberg, *Contest for Asia*; White, *The China Choice*.

Chapter Six

U.S. Relations with Korea

The mix of U.S. interests on the Korean Peninsula feature major security concerns that can be understood with the perspective of realist international relations theory. Asymmetrical U.S. alliance relations with South Korea to deter North Korean aggression have provided the basis for American relations with the Korean Peninsula since the Korean War over sixty years ago. The growth of South Korea's economic progress, political pluralism, and democracy has reinforced American interests and close ties. This growth reflects determinants that can be explained by liberal international relations perspectives. Meanwhile, South Korean nationalism and identity formation along with North Korea's uniquely strenuous efforts at identity featuring strident self-reliance are key determinants in U.S. relations with both governments. They represent aspects of world politics explained by the constructivist school of thought in international relations theory.

Strong U.S. interest in Korea began with the Korean War (1950–1953).[1] The United States suffered over thirty-three thousand killed and over one hundred thousand wounded in the war. The U.S. government agreed to defend South Korea from external aggression in the 1954 Mutual Defense Treaty, and U.S. leaders repeatedly affirmed that commitment in subsequent years. The commitment involves the possible American use of nuclear weapons to protect South Korea under the so-called U.S. nuclear umbrella in which the nuclear armed United States extends a security guarantee to nonnuclear alliance partners. In 2014, the United States maintained about 28,000 troops in South Korea to supplement the 650,000-strong South Korean armed forces. This force was intended to deter North Korea's numerically large (1.2 million troops) army. South Korea reciprocated American backing, notably by supporting, with combat troops when required, U.S. military actions abroad. Tens of thousands of South Korean forces were an important part of

U.S.-led efforts during the Vietnam War. In recent years, South Korea deployed over three thousand troops in support of the U.S.-led war in Iraq and also deployed some military forces to help the U.S.-led military effort in Afghanistan.

U.S. economic aid to South Korea since 1945 has totaled over $6 billion. Most economic aid ended in the mid-1970s as South Korea reached higher levels of economic development. U.S. military aid in this period totaled $9 billion.

South Korea is a major economic partner of the United States. In 2013, two-way trade between the countries was about $100 billion, making South Korea the United States' sixth-largest trading partner. South Korea is far more dependent economically on the United States than the United States is on South Korea. In 2013, the United States was South Korea's third-largest trading partner, second-largest export market, and third-largest source of imports. It is among South Korea's largest suppliers of foreign direct investment (FDI). The United States used to be South Korea's largest trade partner, but that position went to China in 2003, and in 2005 the value of South Korea–Japan trade also surpassed the value of South Korea–U.S. trade, putting the United States in third place among South Korea's trading partners.[2]

Political, cultural, and personal ties between South Korea and the United States have deep roots and have remained strong. With the change of U.S. immigration policies and laws in the mid-1960s, large numbers of South Koreans settled permanently in the United States. Many became citizens and raised their children to be American citizens. Numbering 1.7 million in 2014,[3] Koreans are one of the larger groups in the ethnically pluralistic contemporary U.S. society. Religious, educational, and business ties also are deeply rooted with many decades of constructive interaction.

Many important nongovernment American organizations were ahead of the U.S. government in encouraging and welcoming economic, social, and political change in South Korea. They supported South Korea's strong economic growth in the 1970s and 1980s, and they were in the lead in backing South Korea's turbulent transition from political authoritarianism to democracy in the 1980s. The U.S. Catholic Conference of Bishops was among many American church groups that played an important role in support of South Korean activists and demonstrators seeking democratic reform in the face of sometimes harsh suppression by the authoritarian South Korean administration in the 1980s. They followed the lead of Pope John Paul II, who along with U.S. and other world leaders intervened with the authoritarian South Korean government to stop the planned execution of prominent political dissident and later president Kim Dae Jung, a devout Catholic.[4] During that difficult period of frequent demonstrations and suppression in the South Korean capital, the Catholic cathedral in Seoul provided a sanctuary for the demonstrators, who were supported by Catholics, other Christians, and other concerned American citizens.

U.S. issues and concerns on the Korean Peninsula in the post–Cold War period have focused on security issues with special emphasis on the threat from North Korea.[5] North Korea has remained a serious threat to South Korea and regional stability. For over two decades, North Korean forces deployed along the South Korean border have been seen as having the ability to launch massive artillery and rocket barrages against the South Korean capital, Seoul, a city of over ten million people with a metropolitan population of over twenty million people, including many Americans among its over six hundred thousand foreign residents. The potential resulting casualties were viewed as comparable to a nuclear weapon attack.[6]

North Korea's development of nuclear weapons, ballistic missiles, and other weapons of mass destruction (WMD) has added to the regional threat while posing a critical danger of proliferation to international terrorists targeting the United States and its allies. Meanwhile, North Korea's domestic conditions of periodic famine, negative growth, governance failure, and life-or-death power struggles amid a fragile dynastic leadership succession foreshadow possible internal violence and collapse. The United States and ally South Korea would face great uncertainty in dealing with a North Korean collapse and the reaction of Pyongyang's sole ally, China, to the unstable situation that would result. The U.S.–South Korean military advance into North Korea in 1950 prompted a massive Chinese counterattack and over two and a half years of bloody combat in the Korean War.

North Korea advanced its nuclear weapons program amid adverse conditions after the Cold War. North Korea's main international backer, the Soviet Union, cut back economic and political support before it collapsed in 1991. Remaining ally China continued food, oil, and other assistance to North Korea on the one hand as it increased attention to developing mutually beneficial economic and other relations with South Korea on the other.

The United States has given top priority to restricting and ending North Korea's nuclear weapons program and development of ballistic missiles. The priority was reinforced by the terrorist attack on America on September 11, 2001, and the now vividly perceived danger that terrorists could obtain nuclear weapons from North Korea and use them against the United States. American leaders debated intensely and swung widely in approaching North Korea as they reacted to sometimes abrupt changes in North Korean behavior from confrontation to accommodation and back. There were episodes of strong U.S. pressure backed by military force along with episodes of negotiation and even high-level engagement.

American debates on how best to deal with the North Korean threat were also complicated by periodic U.S. frictions with South Korean governments reacting in ways different from the United States to North Korea's threats.[7]

U.S. relations with South Korea deteriorated sharply at the start of the twenty-first century, with various differences in dealing with North Korea, as well as issues regarding U.S. troop deployments in South Korea, defense burden sharing questions, and trade issues. A prevailing pattern in the early twenty-first century saw U.S. relations with both North Korea and South Korea facing periodic crises that seemed difficult to resolve. U.S.–South Korean relations improved markedly during the government of President Lee Myung Bak (2008–2013). His conservative administration sought to deepen close alliance relations with the United States while adopting a tougher stance toward North Korea than the left-of-center governments of presidents Kim Dae Jung (1998–2003) and Roh Moo Hyun (2003–2008). The latter two leaders pursued policies of asymmetrical South Korean accommodation with North Korea known as the "sunshine policy," which the George W. Bush administration tended to view as naive and counterproductive.[8]

U.S.–NORTH KOREAN RELATIONS

Nuclear Crisis after the Cold War

A crisis on the Korean Peninsula emerged in the early 1990s over North Korea's violation of past nonproliferation pledges and suspected development of nuclear weapons. The crisis led to U.S.–North Korean negotiations and the so-called Agreed Framework of 1994. The Agreed Framework was controversial in the United States, and suspected North Korean cheating along with provocative ballistic missile testing prompted renewed negotiations with North Korea led by former U.S. defense secretary William Perry in 1999.

The 1994 Agreed Framework. Concerned over reports in the late 1980s and early 1990s of North Korea's possible development of nuclear weapons, the George H. W. Bush administration took several actions aimed at securing from North Korea adherence to Pyongyang's obligations as a signatory of the Nuclear Nonproliferation Treaty (NPT); North Korea had signed the treaty in 1985. Bush administration actions included the withdrawal of U.S. nuclear weapons from South Korea in late 1991. North Korea entered into two agreements, which specified nuclear obligations. In a denuclearization agreement signed in December 1991, North Korea and South Korea pledged not to possess nuclear weapons, not to possess plutonium reprocessing or uranium enrichment facilities, and to negotiate a mutual nuclear inspection system. In January 1992, North Korea signed a safeguards agreement with the International Atomic Energy Agency (IAEA), providing for regular IAEA inspections of nuclear facilities. In 1992, North Korea rebuffed South Korea regarding implementation of the denuclearization agreement, but it did allow the IAEA to conduct six inspections from June 1992 to February 1993.[9]

In late 1992, the IAEA found evidence that North Korea had reprocessed more plutonium (potentially useful in producing a nuclear weapon) than the eighty grams it had disclosed to the agency. In February 1993, the IAEA invoked a provision in the safeguards agreement and called for a "special inspection" of two concealed but apparent nuclear waste sites at Yongbyon, North Korea. The IAEA believed that a special inspection would uncover information on the amount of plutonium North Korea had produced since 1989. North Korea rejected the IAEA request and announced on March 12, 1993, an intention to withdraw from the NPT. [10]

The NPT withdrawal threat led to diplomatic talks between North Korea and the Clinton administration. North Korea "suspended" its withdrawal from the NPT when the Clinton administration agreed to a high-level meeting in June 1993. However, North Korea continued to refuse both special inspections and IAEA regular inspections of facilities designated under the safeguards agreement. In May 1994, North Korea refused to allow the IAEA to inspect the eight thousand fuel rods that it had removed from its five-megawatt reactor. In June 1994, North Korea's President Kim Il Sung reactivated a long-standing invitation to former U.S. president Jimmy Carter to visit Pyongyang. Kim offered Carter a freeze of North Korea's nuclear facilities and operations. Kim took this initiative after China reportedly informed him that it would not veto a first round of economic sanctions, which the Clinton administration had proposed to members of the UN Security Council.

The Clinton administration reacted to Kim's proposal by dropping its sanctions proposal and entering into a new round of high-level negotiations with North Korea, which led to the Agreed Framework of October 21, 1994. Two amending agreements were concluded in 1995: a U.S.–North Korean statement in Kuala Lumpur, Malaysia, in June and a supply contract for the provision of nuclear reactors to North Korea, concluded in December.

The heart of the Agreed Framework and the amending accords was a deal under which the United States would provide North Korea with a package of nuclear, energy, economic, and diplomatic benefits; in return, North Korea would halt the operations and infrastructure development of its nuclear program.

U.S. officials emphasized that the key policy objective of the Clinton administration was to secure a freeze of North Korea's nuclear program in order to prevent North Korea from producing large quantities of nuclear weapons–grade plutonium through the operations of its planned fifty- and two-hundred-megawatt reactors and the existing plutonium reprocessing plant at Yongbyon. However, the Agreed Framework did not resolve the question of North Korea's existing achievements regarding the production and acquisition of plutonium and the production of nuclear weapons. The freeze did not prevent North Korea from producing a few nuclear weapons if, according to U.S. and foreign intelligence reports, North Korea had enough plutonium and sufficient technology to manufacture them. This shortcoming appeared to be a major weakness of the Agreed Framework that was cited by U.S. and other critics. Critics also balked at the benefits provided to North Korea, including U.S.-supplied shipments of five hundred thousand metric tons of oil annually to North Korea and provision of two light water nuclear power reactors that were to be paid for mainly by South Korea and Japan. The accord also called for establishing full diplomatic relations and ending the U.S. economic embargo of North Korea, steps that critics in Congress and elsewhere were reluctant to take without major change in North Korea's internationally aggressive and internally repressive policies and practices.

The Perry Initiative

In September 1998, North Korea launched a long-range ballistic missile over Japan, prompting great concern there. Concurrently there were disclosures of a possible hidden North Korean nuclear weapons site at Kumchangri, North Korea. These developments prompted the Clinton administration to reassess its policy toward North Korea. The result was the Perry initiative. William Perry, former secretary of defense and special adviser to the president and secretary of state on North Korea, outlined a revised U.S. strategy in an October 1999 report. The Perry report asserted that the Agreed Framework should continue in order to prevent North Korea from producing a "significant number of nuclear weapons." It recommended two sets of new U.S.–North Korea negotiations with the objectives of securing (1) "verifiable assurances" that North Korea does not have a secret nuclear weapons program, and (2) "verifiable cessation" of North Korea's missile program. Perry recommended a step-by-step negotiating process. He proposed that, in return for commitments by North Korea on the nuclear and missile issues, the United States should normalize diplomatic relations with North Korea, relax economic sanctions against it, and "take other positive steps" to "provide opportunities" for North Korea. Perry stated that such U.S. initiatives should be coordinated with similar actions by Japan and South Korea.[11]

The Clinton administration took an initial step in line with Perry's recommendations when it negotiated an agreement with North Korea in Berlin in September 1999 in which North Korea agreed to defer further missile launch tests in return for actions by the Clinton administration to lift major U.S. economic sanctions. The next planned step, a high-level North Korean visit to Washington, was stalemated over North Korea's demand for preconditions.

High-Level Dialogue 2000

North Korea's abrupt shift toward reconciliation with South Korea, leading to a Pyongyang summit between North and South Korean leaders in 2000, had an important if temporary impact on the U.S. approach to North Korea. For a time, senior leaders of the Clinton administration sought improved relations through widely publicized high-level dialogues. What had heretofore been widely considered as the most dangerous regional "hot spot" now became a focal point of speculation as to how far the thaw on the peninsula would go and what would be the implications for broader regional security concerns. Most notably, the changes in North-South Korean relations, highlighted during the summit meeting of the two top Korean leaders in Pyongyang on June 2000, led to a flurry of diplomatic activity as all major powers with concerns on the peninsula maneuvered for an advantageous position in the new, more fluid policy environment. The North-South changes also caused the United States and its allies in Seoul and Tokyo to consider whether and how the thaw on the peninsula would affect the size and scope of the U.S. military presence in South Korea and Japan, which focused heavily on the duties required in a possible Korean contingency. [12]

In June 2000, the Clinton administration announced officially the lifting of some economic sanctions against North Korea. North Korea responded by reaffirming its agreement to defer missile launch tests. North Korea sent a high-level official to Washington in October 2000, and this was followed by Secretary of State Madeleine Albright's visit to North Korea. These talks focused on the missile issue, particularly on a North Korean proposal made by North Korean leader Kim Jong Il to Russian president Vladimir Putin. According to Putin, Kim Jong Il offered to make concessions on the missile issue (the scope of the proposed concessions was unclear) if the United States would organize a program to launch North Korean satellites into orbit. [13]

In ongoing bilateral talks, North Korea was also seeking removal from the U.S. list of state sponsors of terrorism, which prevented U.S. backing of Pyongyang's membership in international aid organizations. For its part, the United States was pressing Pyongyang to make permanent its temporary moratorium on missile programs, to demonstrate a commitment to nonproliferation, and to provide evidence that it was no longer supporting terrorist groups. [14]

In the United States there was considerable debate over the wisdom of the U.S. engagement of North Korea under terms of the 1994 Agreed Framework, the so-called Perry process, and other diplomatic interactions and negotiations. Although Congress ultimately approved appropriations for assistance to North Korea that made it by far the largest recipient of U.S. aid in East Asia, this occurred amid considerable grumbling and controversy. Critics in Congress and elsewhere were quick to note that the North Korean military threat had not significantly changed; that Pyongyang continued to proliferate ballistic missiles and other weapons of mass destruction to sensitive developing countries, and to develop its own missile and other WMD programs; and that North Korea's tight authoritarianism came at the expense of basic human rights, including the starvation of hundreds of thousands of its citizens. The Clinton administration's consideration of a possible U.S. presidential trip following Secretary of State Madeleine Albright's October 2000 visit to Pyongyang elicited an outpouring of criticism both within and outside of the U.S. government that the United States was going too far in "rewarding" North Korea with a high-level U.S. official visit while Pyongyang still threatened the South and its allies and oppressed its people.[15] In the event, North Korea dithered, and Clinton ran out of time for a meaningful visit.

TWENTY-FIRST-CENTURY DEVELOPMENTS

The new U.S. administration of George W. Bush was divided and generally more wary than the Clinton government regarding the North Korean regime. A harder U.S. line stalled progress in American relations with North Korea. Relations sharply declined in late 2002 when North Korea responded harshly to U.S. accusations that North Korea was secretly developing a highly enriched uranium nuclear weapons program and a U.S. cutoff of oil to North Korea provided under the terms of the Agreed Framework. North Korea broke its promises in the Agreed Framework, withdrew from the Nuclear Nonproliferation Treaty, and proceeded with openly producing nuclear weapons.[16]

In a subsequent mix of U.S. pressure and negotiations that seemed to reflect continued strong differences within the Bush administration on how to deal with North Korea, officials worked with China, and later with Japan, South Korea, and Russia, in multilateral talks, the six-party talks, seeking to curb and end North Korea's nuclear weapons program. Those talks went through ups and downs, mainly in reaction to North Korean moves, which in turn seemed to be in reaction to U.S. steps that sometimes stressed a hard line to North Korea and sometimes a more flexible approach. North Korea stayed away from the six-party talks for much of 2004 and 2005. An agreement on principles governing a settlement of the North Korean nuclear issues was reached in the six-party talks in Beijing in September 2005. There was little progress after that.

A high point in tensions emerged when North Korea conducted seven ballistic missile firings in July 2006, and on October 9, 2006, North Korea conducted its first nuclear weapons test. This was followed by North Korea agreeing on November 1, 2006, to return to the six-party talks and an agreement in those talks on February 13, 2007, that outlined steps to meet U.S. and North Korean concerns regarding the North Korea nuclear program and related issues. The February 2007 agreement was widely seen as a first step in an uncertain process designed from the U.S. perspective to manage the consequences of North Korea's nuclear weapons development and over time to curb and ultimately end North Korea's nuclear weapons. North Korea, the United States, and the other participants in the six-party talks followed through with actions in 2007 that saw the disabling of North Korea's overt nuclear installations and provision of aid to North Korea by the United States and other powers. [17]

In 2008, newly installed South Korean president Lee Myung Bak initiated a more conservative policy toward North Korea, ending the asymmetrical accommodation of the North Korean government carried out by his two predecessors. The Barack Obama administration took power in Washington in January 2009 and signaled a shift toward a more detached and steady policy of "strategic patience," in effect waiting for North Korea to take substantive action to curb its nuclear program. In 2008, North Korean leader Kim Jong Il suffered a stroke. He undertook initiatives at home and abroad to ensure the succession to top North Korean leadership for his young and inexperienced son Kim Jong Un. Against this background, North Korea in 2009 conducted its second nuclear weapons test. In 2010 it took a series of provocative actions—notably the sinking of a South Korean warship, killing forty-six, and the shelling of a South Korean–occupied border island, killing four—that raised tensions and ended prospects for progress in North Korean relations with South Korea and the United States. The provocations, including another nuclear weapons test in 2013, continued as Kim Jong Un succeeded his father, who died in December 2011.

NORTH KOREAN PRIORITIES

Periods of high tension and periods of remarkable thaw on the Korean Peninsula have been hard to predict in the post–Cold War years. They have come about as a result of the policies and actions of South Korea as well as the United States, China, Japan, and Russia, the four powers most involved with Korean issues. At bottom, however, they have depended on the policies and actions of the North Korean leaders. [18]

Though the weakest of the six governments directly involved with Korean affairs, the North Korean administrations of Kim Il Sung (d. 1994), Kim Jong Il (1994–2011), and Kim Jong Un (2011–) have more often than not been in the lead in determining whether developments on the peninsula would move toward greater friction and confrontation or greater moderation and accommodation. North Korea in the early 1990s created a major nuclear weapons crisis that was eventually eased with the Agreed Framework accord of 1994. In 2000, it shifted sharply in favor of accommodation with the South Korean government of President Kim Dae Jung. It hosted a summit with the South Korean leader in Pyongyang. This set off rounds of high-level North Korean dialogue and détente with South Korea, the United States, and other concerned powers. In the face of the more hard-line U.S. posture of the incoming George W. Bush administration, North Korea created a major international crisis by breaking previous agreements and overtly pursuing nuclear weapons development. The six-party negotiating process went on for a few years but failed with North Korea's nuclear weapons test of 2006. A revitalized six-party talks featuring intensive U.S. negotiations with North Korea failed to bridge the gap. Often acute tensions have prevailed since 2009, a period marked by two North Korean nuclear weapons tests (2009 and 2013) and other notable provocations.

In general, the governments concerned with Korean Peninsula affairs apart from North Korea have found their policy choices bounded by strong interests that would be affected by major changes in their policies. Because of its status as a strict and authoritarian dictatorship with less commitment to existing policies and often with much to gain by shifting course, the North Korean government has been freer and less constrained than the other powers in changing course on the Korean Peninsula.[19]

North Korea has one of the most secretive governments in world affairs. As a result, North Korea's motives and goals have continued to be matters of discussion and debate. Given the structure of power in North Korea, a great deal has appeared to depend on the calculus of one person, the senior leader—Kim Il Sung, Kim Jong Il, and Kim Jung Un—whose thinking has not been well known or understood.

Available circumstantial evidence and assessments by specialists[20] have shown North Korean motives to be focused on regime survival. This focus appeared to require enormous military preparations for a country of North Korea's size and the development of weapons of mass destruction sufficient to deter the United States and other powers from attacking or forcing regime change. North Korea also seemed determined to use its growing WMD capabilities in order to bargain for international prominence, leverage, and material profit. Meanwhile, it used the specter of regime decay and collapse in North Korea to prompt neighboring countries, notably South Korea and China, to provide advantageous trade and foreign assistance. The alternative was seen as mass refugee flows to and disruption of these neighboring countries. Indeed, North Korea endured economic collapse beginning in the 1990s that saw famine kill more than a million people by some estimates. The international response was large amounts of food aid and related assistance. These features suggested that North Korea was a failing state and was highly dependent on international assistance. However, the North Korean government proved to be resilient, and outside aid givers seemed to have little success in using aid as a means to change North Korea's nuclear weapons program and other North Korean policies and actions deemed undesirable by donor governments.

Throughout the post–Cold War period, the North Korean leaders sought direct dialogue with the United States. Such dialogue presumably was a means to constrain the United States from using pressure to foster regime change in North Korea, thereby strengthening the security of the North Korean regime. The United States was also critically important in the approval of any international aid program to North Korea on the part of major international financial institutions, and the United States would presumably exert considerable influence on any Japanese decision to follow through with stalled efforts to normalize relations with North Korea by paying large amounts of foreign assistance. U.S. engagement with and recognition of the North Korean regime also seemed likely to add greatly to the legitimacy of the North Korean administration both at home and abroad. [21] Over the longer term, some specialists discerned North Korean goals to use its WMD capabilities and international prominence in interaction with the United States in order to sustain an independent position vis-à-vis the much more powerful and prosperous South Korea, and possibly to advance North Korean influence at the expense of the South. [22]

Kim Jong Il's Control and Calculus

Kim Jong Il used purges and other means to solidify his personal rule following the death of Kim Il Sung in 1994. His regime endured the multiyear famine in the 1990s with the support of foreign food aid. In 2000, he used summits with Chinese, South Korean, and Russian leaders, and high-level meetings with the United States, to reflect his ability to use personal diplomacy to secure important benefits for North Korea. He did so while preserving key interests involving internal regime control, military preparedness, WMD capabilities, and long-term goals regarding Korean unification. [23]

Kim Jong Il was long seen to be committed to regime preservation, economic recovery, and ultimately a unified Korea in which the North was preeminent. Many specialists on Korean affairs were surprised by his changed approach to South Korea in 2000. Kim presumably judged that through greater détente with South Korea, the North Korean government could seek economic improvements. South Korea reportedly smoothed the way for the summit with secret payments of several hundred million dollars. Kim also may have sought greater North-South agreement that Korea's future should involve two separate states for the foreseeable future. Kim Jong Il's success with and satisfaction over the initial openings to South Korea and the international community might have provided momentum for further advances—the North Korean leader may have been undertaking a major change in policy direction that would have led to an extensive and constructive outreach to South Korea and foreign powers. However, Kim remained preoccupied with maintaining the existing power structure at minimum risk, and his approach was subject to abrupt change. Indeed, in the face of the tougher U.S. posture of the George W. Bush administration, Kim shifted to a much tougher stance toward South Korea while openly pushing ahead with nuclear weapons development. [24]

To meet economic requirements needed to sustain the regime, Kim Jong Il relaxed some domestic economic controls and promoted economic interactions with South Korea and other donors. Food, fertilizer, electric power, foreign investment, and hard currency headed the list of regime needs. Positive movement in North Korea's relations with the United States, Japan, international financial institutions, and other possible donors reinforced positive North-South momentum. Such improvement with the outside world was also used by the North as leverage to extract more material benefit from the South Korean government that did not wish to lose its position as a primary conduit to the North. [25]

Kim's determination to maintain tight control of major developments in North Korea—control that inevitably would be challenged if Pyongyang opened to outside economic and other exchanges—posed a major brake on forward movement in relations with the United States and its allies. Moreover, South Korea, Japan, the United States, and other powers failed to meet Kim Jong Il's expectations for compensation. Meanwhile, bureaucratic and other differences emerged from time to time in North Korea over the implications of détente with South Korea and the Western-aligned countries that in turn impeded advances in North-South relations. Though there is little reliable information about such differences, some North Korean elites, including those in the North Korean military, an institution that has exerted greater internal influence in recent years, placed extraordinary emphasis on North Korean military and security preparedness and independence from foreign powers.

Weaknesses in Kim Jong Il's Approach

Despite its leading role in setting the agenda in international consideration of Korean Peninsula issues, the Kim Jong Il regime made mistakes as it maneuvered for tactical advantage and demonstrated greater tolerance of tension and confrontation than South Korea and the other powers concerned with the Korean Peninsula. Kim Jong Il waited too long following the visit by U.S. Secretary of State Madeleine Albright to Pyongyang in 2000 to come to an agreement on a proposed visit to North Korea by President Bill Clinton.

Other perceived mistakes under Kim's guidance included North Korean negotiators' admission to U.S. counterparts in October 2002 that North Korea did indeed have a clandestine highly enriched uranium program for developing nuclear weapons. The admission was used by Bush administration officials to place North Korea on the defensive and to strengthen international pressure against North Korea's WMD efforts.[26] Kim Jong Il's admission to Japanese prime minister Junichiro Koizumi in September 2002 that North Korea had indeed abducted Japanese citizens did not improve North Korean–Japanese relations but actually hardened Japanese attitudes against the North Korean regime.[27] North Korean efforts to develop a special economic zone along China's border without adequate consultation with China prompted Beijing in 2002 to arrest the Chinese citizen slated to lead the North Korean zone.[28]

On the one hand, North Korea's frequently confrontational and erratic maneuvers have served to isolate North Korea from the other concerned powers that—with the possible exception of the United States—have been heavily focused on nation-building agendas requiring regional peace and stability. On the other hand, the North Korean regime has more or less effectively used three main cards—its WMD programs, the massive military deployments along the Korean Demilitarized Zone (DMZ), and the specter of North Korean collapse—to garner international leverage, recognition, and material advantage in the post–Cold War years.

Leadership Succession and Repeated Provocations

The firm approach of the Lee Myung Bak and Obama governments to North Korea coincided with Kim Jong Il's debilitation after a stroke and the hurried efforts to secure the succession of his inexperienced son Kim Jong Un. Foreign specialists widely saw a connection between the rushed succession arrangements and a string of provocations from North Korea that were interpreted as signs of military strength and independence designed to solidify the younger Kim's leadership position.

On April 5, 2009, North Korea conducted a ballistic missile test couched as a satellite launch that was contrary to existing United Nations sanctions and prompted criticism from the UN Security Council. North Korea then announced that it was withdrawing from the six-party talks on North Korea's nuclear programs as a result of the Security Council criticism. The Security Council statement, issued by the president of the Security Council, said that the missile test violated Security Resolution 1718 of October 2006, which banned tests of long-range North Korean missiles. The statement called on members of the United Nations to enforce sanctions against North Korea adopted in Resolution 1718.[29] North Korea claimed that the missile test was a legitimate launching of a satellite into space. North Korea warned prior to the April 5 test that it would withdraw from the six-party talks if the Security Council took any action against it over the missile test.

North Korea had staged boycotts of the six-party talks on two previous occasions, in 2004–2005 and 2005–2006, each for nearly one year. North Korea's announcement of April 13, 2009, and subsequent statements, however, contained a more absolute rejection of the six-party talks than was the case in the prior boycotts. The April 13 announcement also said that North Korea "will take steps to restore disabled nuclear facilities" and "revive nuclear facilities and reprocess used nuclear fuel rods." North Korea thus threatened to restore operation of its plutonium nuclear installations at Yongbyon that had been shut down since mid-2007 under agreements between North Korea and the Bush administration for the disablement of the Yongbyon facilities.[30] By early 2009, the disablement process was about 80 percent completed. Following the announcement, North Korea expelled from Yongbyon technicians and monitors from the United States and the International Atomic Energy Agency who had been there since 2007.

On May 25, 2009, North Korea announced that it had conducted a second test of a nuclear bomb. U.S. and foreign officials said afterward that initial detected soundings indicated that a nuclear test had taken place. Most U.S. and foreign nuclear experts estimated the explosive power of the bomb at between four and five kilotons. By comparison, the first North Korean test of October 2006 had an explosive yield of less than one kiloton.[31] North Korean statements indicated that this second test had achieved technical advances over the first test. A North Korean diplomat in Moscow predicted that there would be further tests.

The Obama administration responded to North Korea's nuclear test by seeking another UN Security Council resolution penalizing Pyongyang. On June 12, 2009, the UN Security Council approved Resolution 1874. It called on UN member states to apply several sets of sanctions against North Korea.

In his presidential campaign and inaugural address, President Obama had indicated willingness to engage with "rogue" governments. As North Korea beginning in 2009 carried out a series of provocative acts, the Obama administration has maintained a policy toward North Korea known as "strategic patience," which essentially waits for North Korea to come back to the negotiating table while maintaining pressure on the regime. The main elements of the policy involve insisting that Pyongyang commit to steps toward denuclearization and mend relations with Seoul as a prelude to returning to the six-party talks; attempting to convince China to take a tougher line on North Korea; and applying pressure on Pyongyang through arms interdictions and sanctions. Obama administration officials have stated that, under the right conditions, they would seek a comprehensive package deal for North Korea's complete denuclearization in return for normalization of relations and significant aid. This policy has been closely coordinated with South Korea and accompanied by large-scale military exercises designed to demonstrate the strength of the U.S.-ROK alliance.

The collapse of the denuclearization talks intensified American concerns about proliferation. Critics claimed that the "strategic patience" approach allowed Pyongyang to control the situation and steadily improve its missile and nuclear programs. North Korea's poor economic performance added to fears that Pyongyang would sell nuclear technology to another country, a terrorist group, or other nonstate actor. Evidence of some North Korean cooperation with Syria, Libya, and potentially Myanmar alarmed national security experts. The Israeli bombing of a nuclear facility in Syria in 2007 raised concerns about North Korean collaboration on a nuclear reactor with the Syrians. Despite speculation in the media about Iran-DPRK proliferation, the official position of the U.S. Intelligence Community was that North Korea and Iran were not cooperating on nuclear weapons development.

In moves seen related to North Korea's leadership succession, provocations from Pyongyang continued. In March 2010, a North Korean torpedo sank a South Korean warship, killing forty-six; and in November 2010, a North Korean artillery barrage hit a South Korean–controlled island, killing civilians and service people. Meanwhile, throughout the succession period, China endeavored to consolidate its ties with the new North Korean leadership. All senior Chinese leaders, including incoming party and government leader Xi Jinping, made speeches or took other steps in support of Chinese–North Korean solidarity. China ensured that UN sanctions against North Korea over the attacks on South Korea and other provocations were weakened or blocked. In meeting with his Chinese counterpart in 2010, President Obama accused the Chinese of "willful blindness" in the face of North Korean provocations. Nevertheless, Chinese support continued, including significant expansion of trade and investment with North Korea.[32]

Following Kim Jong Il's death in December 2011, Kim Jong Un undertook a new round of provocations in 2012. The provocations came on the heels of a surprise agreement with the United States in February 2012 to halt nuclear weapons activities in return for U.S. food aid. That agreement quickly unraveled. The provocations involved North Korea ballistic missile tests couched as satellite launches in April and December 2012, followed by North Korea's third nuclear weapons test in February 2013. The results were harsher sanctions from the UN Security Council, with China going along with the anti–North Korean moves. Subsequent developments saw periodic outbursts of intense North Korean hostility against South Korea and the United States. China's influence with Pyongyang suffered a serious setback when Jang Song Tek, the North Korean leader seen as second only to Kim Jong Il and close to China, was abruptly purged and executed in December 2013.[33]

U.S.–SOUTH KOREAN RELATIONS

South Korean Priorities

South Korean government priorities have been pulled in sometimes different directions in the post–Cold War period. The greater role South Korea has endeavored to play in regional and international affairs, notably managing and resolving tensions on the Korean Peninsula, was accompanied by changes and uncertainties regarding South Korea's relations with its three main partners:

* vacillation in South Korea's continuing commitment to the alliance with the United States;
* a mix of simmering frictions, closer economic interdependence, and greater cultural ties with Japan; and
* on-again, off-again enthusiasm over the rising importance of China for South Korea's economic growth, national security, and broader influence in Korean and Asian affairs. [34]

Domestic preoccupations focused on sustaining economic growth amid a very competitive international environment of economic globalization and the usually intense political competition among more conservative and more progressive political parties that was fed by various interest groups and the aggressive South Korean media. These domestic factors frequently overrode international concerns for Korean voters and political leaders. [35]

Regarding Korean Peninsula concerns, President Kim Dae Jung's (1998–2003) sunshine policy of asymmetrical accommodation of North Korea lasted through the Roh Moo Hyun (2003–2008) administration and has remained influential among substantial segments of South Korean opinion up to the present. [36] Of course, South Korea, like the United States, Japan, and China, has more often than not been in a reactive position in the face of North Korean maneuvers, and South Korea at times has been compelled to adjust to shifts in the policies of other powers.

South Korean decision making on Korean Peninsula issues remains divided. There has been a wide gap on a range of important subjects between the administrations of Kim Dae Jung and Roh Moo Hyun on one side and their conservative opponents in the Lee Myung Bak government on the other. The senior officials of the new presidency of President Park Geun Hye (2013–) come from the conservative political wing in South Korean politics. Nevertheless, President Park has endeavored to bridge the gap in South Korean opinion regarding North Korea, though her efforts to promote greater engagement with the North have been thwarted by North Korean belligerence and provocations.

The gap in South Korea politics sometimes gives pride of place to issues regarding the alliance relationship with the United States. During the Kim and Roh presidencies, Seoul showed a tendency to move away from a close alignment with the United States. During much of the George W. Bush administration, the two governments were clearly at odds in their respective approaches to North Korea. Younger South Korean voters were in the lead in South Korean opinion that saw North Korea less as a threat and more as a needy brother requiring assistance. This view posed a stark contrast with Bush administration hard-line statements against the threats posed by Pyongyang. Broader South Korean opinion also recognized that South Korea was in no position to handle the consequences of a collapse and absorption of indigent North Korea; South Korea thus sought to avoid regime change and reunification until well into the future. Meanwhile, in the period 2002–2004, U.S.–South Korea alliance frictions added to bad feeling and contrasted markedly with improved South Korean relations with China. This prompted some in South Korea to view relying on China as an alternative to the alliance with the United States, and some South Korean leaders advocated a role for South Korea as a mediator or balancer between the two powers.[37]

Working against a serious split in South Korea's alliance with the United States were economic realities that required a strong alliance against North Korea if South Korea were to appear stable enough to attract needed foreign investment. The left-of-center Roh government endeavored to improve the alliance by agreeing to send three thousand combat troops to assist the U.S.-led stabilization in Iraq and by seeking a free trade agreement with the United States that was signed in 2007. The change toward direct negotiation in Bush administration policy on North Korea following North Korea's first nuclear weapons test in 2006 converged with the approach favored by the Roh government. The so-called silent majority of middle-aged and older South Korean voters viewed South Korea going alone or relying on China as too dangerous in view of South Korea's relative small size and perceived need for U.S. backing to deal with North Korea and other sometimes difficult neighbors.[38]

Meanwhile, South Korean relations with China cooled after reaching a high point in 2004. China loomed more as an international competitor to South Korean manufacturers. There were recurring differences with China over interpretations of historical territorial claims that received wide publicity in South Korea and were of great importance to South Korean leaders. Some in South Korea also saw China's growing economic interchange with North Korea as opposed to South Korea's long-term goal of reunification. The Chinese actions were interpreted as efforts to shore up a North Korean administration that would lean to China and avoid reunification with South Korea.[39]

President Lee Myung Bak (2008–2013) changed policies in directions favored by the United States. The Lee and Obama governments coordinated closely over their respectively firm policies toward North Korea. The two presidents reportedly developed a close personal bond as they sought ways to broaden the alliance relationship from its focus on North Korea to a broad-ranging strategic partnership. President Park Geun Hye (2013–) comes from the same conservative party as President Lee, though she has emphasized a more flexible policy toward North Korea and more interest in developing ties with China, providing less opportunity for emphasis on ties with the United States.

South Korean relations with Japan continued to deepen economic interdependence and cultural and personal exchanges despite often intense differences over historical and territorial issues. Frictions subsided under the leadership of President Kim Dae Jung, rose in response to Japanese prime minister Junichiro Koizumi (2001–2006) and his insistence on visiting annually the controversial Yasukuni Shrine, and subsided with the more moderate and accommodating stance on historical issues adopted by later Japanese leaders. [40]

Tensions took a turn for the worse in 2012 over the disputed islands of Dokdo/Takeshima, which are controlled by South Korea but also claimed by Japan. Lee Myung Bak made an unprecedented presidential visit to the territory in response to reiterated official Japanese claims to the territory. The return of conservative Japanese leader Shinzo Abe as Japan's prime minister in 2012 was accompanied by inflammatory remarks by some in his cabinet about Japan's conduct in World War II, including the coercion of Korean women to serve as sex workers for Japanese soldiers. Abe visited the Yasukuni Shrine in December 2013, causing a major rift with President Park Geun Hye. [41]

The South Korean–Japan rift seriously complicated ongoing U.S. efforts to strengthen U.S.–Japan–South Korean alliance cooperation in the face of threats and provocations from North Korea and in the face of Chinese actions using coast guard forces, government edicts, and other coercive means to assert territorial claims in the Senkaku/Diaoyu Islands controlled by Japan but claimed by China. In November 2013 China announced the establishment of an air defense identification zone over the East China Sea including the disputed islands, and also including sea areas and an islet claimed by South Korea. South Korea joined the United States and allies Japan and Australia in protesting the Chinese action. [42]

China's solidifying relations with North Korea saw Beijing protect North Korea in the face of accusations and sanctions sought by South Korea after North Korean forces killed South Korean military and civilian personnel in incidents in 2010. The result was a serious split between Beijing and Seoul. On taking office in 2013, President Park Geun Hye reached out to her Chinese counterpart, incoming president Xi Jinping, and relations improved, though North Korea's repeated threats and the Chinese air defense identification zone including South Korean territory complicated and slowed the process. [43]

In the end, South Korea's priorities appeared to focus on sustaining economic development amid continued intense political competition in South Korean domestic politics. The Lee Myung Bak government sought to avoid conflict but was unwilling to carry out concessions and gestures to North Korea that were not reciprocated. President Lee sharply diverged from the sunshine policy of his two predecessors. South Korea continued to rely on the alliance relationship with the United States and to develop closer ties with both Japan and China, with clear awareness of the differences South Korea had with both Asian neighbors. In 2014, the differences with Japan posed a major handicap to improved relations at least in the near future.

U.S. POLICY PRIORITIES

The United States has maintained a strong, multifaceted alliance relationship with South Korea that has for decades served vital interests of both sides. Beginning in the late 1990s, major changes in South Korean politics, public opinion, and elite viewpoints saw a major shift in South Korea's approach to North Korea and South Korea's attitude toward and interest in its alliance relationship with the United States. Under the George W. Bush administration, frictions in South Korean–U.S. differences over policy toward North Korea, military alliance issues, trade policies, and other questions periodically reached crisis proportions. The differences subsided under President Lee Myung Bak and President Barack Obama, ushering in a period where relations were said to be exceptionally close. The meetings of President Obama with President Park Geun Hye also reflected close alliance relations. Nonetheless, some serious differences remained. [44]

Dealing with North Korea

The twists and turns in South Korean and U.S. interchanges with North Korea since the end of the Cold War are recounted earlier in this chapter and show major divergence between Seoul and Washington during the first six years of the George W. Bush administration. Those differences began to narrow with initiatives on both sides to ease tensions and preserve the alliance relationship. Lee Myung Bak's seeking greater reciprocity from North Korea meshed well with Barack Obama's strategic patience. Whether Park Geun Hye's seeking greater confidence-building measures in order to create a "new era" on the peninsula will diverge from Obama's policies seems moot for the time being. North Korean provocations have made for slow going in Park's proposed new policy direction.

Military Issues and Alliance Relations

From the late 1990s until 2008, South Korean government leaders and broad segments of opinion differed strongly with U.S. government leaders over the threat posed by North Korea. This exacerbated differences on how to deal with the North Korean nuclear weapons program in the six-party talks and on whether to adopt a policy of engagement or containment in dealing with North Korea on other matters in international affairs and bilateral relations. In the past, there was close common understanding between U.S. and South Korean leaders on the prime mission of the U.S.–South Korean alliance— deterring the North Korean military threat. The George W. Bush administration strongly emphasized the threat posed by North Korea's nuclear weapons development, ballistic missile development and proliferation, and large conventional forces forward deployed near the Demilitarized Zone separating North and South Korea. By contrast, South Korean leaders and public opinion tended to play down concern over the military threat from North Korea. The end of the Cold War and of support for North Korea by the Soviet Union, marked decline in North Korea's economy, and progress in North-South relations headed the list of factors that prompted South Korean leaders and public opinion to adopt a more moderate attitude toward the North Korean threat than the U.S. government did.

Declining South Korean fears of a North Korean invasion and threat, and progress in inter-Korean dialogue, added to the debate in South Korea over perceived negative implications for South Korea posed by the large U.S. military presence and other aspects of the alliance relationship. Long-standing opposition by some groups in South Korea to sensitive aspects of the U.S. military presence and of U.S. alliance relations was reinforced by a younger generation of South Koreans who came of age under the authoritarian South Korean regimes, which the young South Koreans tended to view unfavorably. These younger South Koreans came into positions of power in the administrations of Kim Dae Jung and Roh Moo Hyun, and they held negative views of U.S. government support for previous South Korean authoritarian governments.[45]

Changing South Korean government and public attitudes toward the alliance with the United States meant that various incidents and issues resulted in strong South Korean public criticism. In the late 1990s, one issue was perceived U.S. resistance to South Korean government demands that the bilateral Status of Forces Agreement (SOFA) be amended to give South Korea greater jurisdiction over U.S. servicemen accused of crimes. The SOFA was ultimately amended to the at least temporary satisfaction of both governments in early 2001. Other contentious issues at that time were an errant U.S. bombing exercise that damaged a South Korean village and the disclosure that the U.S. Military Command had dumped dangerous chemicals in the Han River, which flows through Seoul. The United States and South Korea also engaged in tough negotiations over South Korea's desire to develop missiles with nearly double the range of the 180-kilometer limit established by a U.S.–South Korean agreement in 1979. The two governments, too, had to respond to reports that surfaced in 1999 that, during the 1950–1953 Korean War, U.S. troops committed several atrocities on South Korean citizens or allowed South Korean troops under U.S. command to commit atrocities.[46]

In 2002, massive South Korean protests erupted when a U.S. military vehicle killed two South Korean schoolgirls and the U.S. military personnel driving the vehicle were acquitted in a U.S. court-martial. Presidential candidate Roh Moo Hyun was elected in December 2002 after strongly criticizing the United States during his campaign. By 2004, polls found that more South Koreans viewed the United States as the biggest threat to South Korea as compared to those who viewed North Korea as the principal threat.[47]

Against the backdrop of these tensions in South Korean–U.S. alliance relations, the Bush administration in 2003 began a series of steps to alter the U.S. military presence in South Korea with the aim of bringing U.S. deployments there more into line with American plans in the Korean Peninsula and with U.S. troop realignments in Asian and world affairs. The steps added to U.S.–South Korean friction and differences over their alliance relationship. The U.S. actions called for the withdrawal of the U.S. Second Division of about fifteen thousand troops from a position just below the DMZ to bases about seventy-five miles south, and the relocation of the U.S. base at Yongsan, housing about eight thousand U.S. military personnel in the center of Seoul, away from the city. (A 1991 agreement to relocate Yongsan was never implemented.) In mid-2004, the Pentagon disclosed a plan to withdraw 12,500 U.S. troops from South Korea by the end of 2005, and the United States rapidly withdrew one of two combat brigades of the Second Division to Iraq. Under South Korean pressure, the United States agreed to slow the withdrawal, but by 2008 U.S. forces in South Korea were to decline from thirty-seven thousand to twenty-four thousand. Proposed U.S. compensation efforts included upgrades worth $11 billion for U.S. forces in South Korea.[48]

The South Korean government voiced strong reservations over some of the U.S. decisions, though it eventually concluded agreements to facilitate the relocations and agreed in 2004 to assume the estimated $3 to $4 billion cost of relocating the Yongsan garrison. By 2014, U.S. forces in Korea numbered twenty-eight thousand. The relocation of U.S. forces to the south of the DMZ was progressing slowly and was expected not to be completed until 2020. The cost to South Korea of the relocation was more than the original estimate of $4 billion. Meanwhile, South Korea also continued some support for the cost of U.S. troops in South Korea. The cost in 2005 was about $3 billion annually, and South Korea's direct financial contribution for 2005 and 2006 was $681 million. In 2012 it was reported that South Korea provided about 40 to 45 percent of the U.S. nonpersonnel stationing costs for the U.S. troop presence in Korea.[49]

The changes in U.S. force deployments were accompanied by changes in the U.S. military command structure in Korea. During a summit meeting in September 2006, President Bush expressed support for President Roh Moo Hyun's declared policy of regaining operational command from the United States over South Korea's armed forces during wartime. They agreed that the timing of the transfer should not become a political issue. This supported the South Korean president against domestic critics who feared a weakening of the U.S.–South Korean alliance. Bush affirmed that South Korea should not worry about American support during an emergency. He declared, "My message to the Korean people is that the United States is committed to the security of the Korean Peninsula."[50]

For South Korea, the transfer represented recognition of the country's independent defense capabilities and affirmed its equal role within the U.S.–South Korean alliance. President Roh proposed a 2012 transfer date. The U.S. military indicated in September 2006 that it was prepared to complete the transfer by 2009. The U.S. and South Korean defense ministers said following their meeting at the Pentagon in late September 2006 that the transfer would take place after October 15, 2009, but before March 15, 2012. Later developments saw the two sides agree to delay the transfer until 2015. The decisions came amid concerns voiced by specialists on both sides that South Korea needed more capabilities to operate wartime command. Such concerns caused the transfer to be delayed again, with the joint statement marking President Obama's April 2014 visit to South Korea affirming that the "enduring North Korean nuclear and missile threat" warranted reconsideration of the 2015 transfer date.[51]

Political Issues

From one perspective, U.S. support for democratization in South Korea was a great success for U.S. policy. As South Korea moved from the authoritarian regimes of the past to more democratically based governments, U.S. officials were prominent in encouraging greater pluralism and democratic process. However, the process of democratization resulted in greater political instability and uncertainty in South Korea, exacerbating differences in the alliance relationship and raising questions for U.S. policy makers about the South Korean government's ability to carry out burden sharing and economic reform programs sought by the United States. The George W. Bush administration put priority on developing close relations with U.S. allies in East Asia and elsewhere, and relations with South Korean leaders received careful attention. However, as noted above, major differences emerged on how to deal with North Korea and regarding sensitive issues in alliance relations amid an upswing in negative public opinion polls in South Korea regarding the United States.[52]

Beginning in 2005, the United States was somewhat less in the negative spotlight of South Korean nationalistic public opinion as attention in South Korea focused on territorial and historical disputes with Japan. The rising South Korean infatuation with China also reached a plateau and appeared to take a dive when it became clearer that China disputed nationalistic Korean views on a historical kingdom ruling the peninsula and parts of what is now northeastern China.

Meanwhile, Christopher Hill, the U.S. ambassador to Seoul whose brief record in U.S.–South Korean relations was the most positive in recent years, was appointed leading U.S. negotiator in the six-party talks and concurrently assistant secretary of state for East Asian affairs. He and his South Korean counterparts endeavored to play down obvious differences between the two governments over policy toward North Korea in the interests of reaching agreements acceptable to all in the multilateral negotiations. Hill was replaced as U.S. ambassador to South Korea by the previous U.S. ambassador to Russia, a move that demonstrated the importance the U.S. government gave to this post and appealed to South Korean national pride. A later U.S. appointment was Ambassador Sung Y. Kim (2011–2014), whose deep involvement with Korean affairs and negotiations with North Korea added to the strengths of this first Korean-American U.S. ambassador to Seoul.

Political relations also improved as U.S. and South Korean defense officials made progress amid continuing differences on burden sharing issues while the United States continued the realignment and streamlining of its forces on the peninsula. President Bush generally emphasized the positive in his regularly scheduled meetings with his South Korean counterpart. The Lee Myung Bak and Obama administrations reached strong accord on a variety of foreign policy issues ranging from North Korea to international terrorism and economic development. The conservative Park Geun Hye seemed more likely to continue along cooperative paths with the United States, even though she also sought closer ties with China. The main exception was the strong friction between South Korea and Japan over historical and territorial matters. The disputes posed a serious obstacle to persisting Obama government efforts to foster closer trilateral cooperation among Seoul, Tokyo, and Washington.[53]

Economic Issues

The Asian economic crisis of 1997–1998 had a major negative effect on the South Korean economy. South Korea took remedial actions, and growth recovered in 1999. As U.S. trade and trade deficits with South Korea grew, U.S. administration officials focused less on the overall trade deficit and more on South Korea's continued restrictions on market access for U.S. goods and services. Salient issues also included U.S. concerns over steel imports from South Korea and South Korean restrictions on U.S. beef exports to the country.[54] On the whole, the intensity of U.S.–South Korea trade disputes diminished.[55]

Against this background, U.S. and South Korean officials announced in February 2006 their intention to negotiate a Korea-U.S. free trade agreement (KORUSFTA). The negotiations began later in the year and were completed in mid-2007. The accord faced serious hurdles to implementation, which finally took place in 2012. The accord was the second largest FTA in which the United States is a participant and the largest in which South Korea is a participant. Meanwhile, the Obama government saw its interests well served with a high-standard Asia-Pacific FTA called the Trans-Pacific Partnership. In 2014, South Korean officials showed some interest in joining the grouping then composed of twelve Asian-Pacific countries.[56]

The issue of reprocessing U.S.-controlled nuclear fuel in South Korea complicated negotiations on an extension of an existing agreement on civilian nuclear cooperation between the United States and South Korea. South Korea had become a major user and builder of nuclear power and reportedly wished to reprocess spent fuel with less cumbersome procedures than under the existing agreement. The United States had a strong interest in curbing international reprocessing of spent nuclear fuel. The existing agreement was extended for two years in 2013 as the two sides tried to iron out their differences.[57]

PRIORITIES OF CHINA, JAPAN, AND RUSSIA

The United States and China are the outside powers that have exerted the most important influence on the Korean Peninsula in recent years. China's priorities have been to sustain stability and avoid conflict on the peninsula. The danger of U.S.–North Korea conflict seemed high in 2003, prompting China to take a more active role as a mediator in the three-party and later six-party negotiations. China sees North Korea's nuclear weapons program as against its interests in regional stability, but it also opposes pressure on North Korea for fear that Pyongyang will lash out with dangerous consequences. China also fears that a North Korean collapse would have major negative consequences for nearby areas of China and could lead to the absorption of North Korea by South Korea backed by the United States.[58]

Among the foreign powers concerned with Korean affairs, China has the most effective relationships with North and South Korea. The obvious signs of friction between China and North Korea diminish but do not offset the fact that China maintains the position as the outside power with the best relationship with Pyongyang. The costs to China include substantial aid and investment in North Korea.[59] Meanwhile, China's economic, political, and sociocultural ties with South Korea have grown by leaps and bounds over the past decades. For a time, the improvement in China's relationship with South Korea was one of the most significant advances in Chinese foreign relations in the post–Cold War period, though, as noted earlier, South Korean wariness of China has grown in recent years.[60]

By virtue of its location and wealth, Japan should be playing an influential role on the Korean Peninsula. In fact, Japan has generally been shunned by North Korea, while its relations with South Korea have been negatively affected by historical and territorial issues. In common with other concerned powers, Japan seeks stability and the avoidance of war. It views North Korea's WMD programs as a serious and growing national security threat. Its ability to negotiate with North Korea is seriously hampered by the unresolved issues of Japanese abducted by North Korea. In general, the Japanese government aligned with the tough posture of the Bush administration; it was somewhat upset by the Bush administration shift in 2006 toward greater engagement and accommodation of North Korea without any concession by the North Korean side. But such engagement ended with North Korean provocations and the Obama government's firmer policy of "strategic patience." Over the longer term, Japanese officials are worried by China's rising influence in Korean affairs and have tried from time to time, with little apparent success, to position Japan more advantageously in relation to North and South Korea. Efforts by the Obama government to strengthen trilateral cooperation and coordination among the three allies in the face of dangers posed by North Korea and by recent Chinese assertiveness over disputed maritime territorial issues have flagged in the face of continued strong disputes between Japan and South Korea over historical and territorial issues.[61]

Because of economic problems and domestic and other international preoccupations, Russia has not been in a good position of influence in Korean affairs. It sought international prominence in the six-party talks. It sees some possible economic advantages for Russia in transportation and other schemes involving Korea. It favored the past South Korean approach of asymmetrical engagement with North Korea and negotiations as the best way to deal with the dangers posed by North Korean WMD programs.[62]

NOTES

1. White House, Office of the Press Secretary, *Joint Fact Sheet: The United States–Republic of Korea Alliance: A Global Partnership*, April 25, 2014, http://www. whitehouse.gov/the-press-office/2014/04/25/joint-fact-sheet-united-states-republic-korea-alliance-global-partnershi; Scott Snyder, "The U.S.-ROK Alliance and the U.S. Rebalance to Asia," in *Strategic Asia 2014–2015: U.S. Alliances and Partnerships at the Center of Global Power*, ed. Ashley Tellis, Abraham Denmark, and Greg Chaffin, 61–86 (Seattle, WA: National Bureau of Asian Research, 2014); Katherine Moon, *Protesting America: Democracy and the U.S.-Korea Alliance* (Berkeley: University of California Press, 2013); Scott Snyder, *The U.S.-South Korean Alliance: Meeting New Security Challenges* (Boulder, CO: Lynne Rienner, 2012); Sunhyuk Kim and Wonhyuk Lim, "How to Deal with South Korea," *Washington Quarterly* 30, no. 2 (Spring 2007): 71–82.

2. William Cooper and Mark Manyin, *The Proposed South Korea–US Free Trade Agreement (KORUSFTA)*, Report RL33435 (Washington, DC: Library of Congress, Congressional Research Service, May 24, 2006), 2–5; U.S. Trade Representative Office, *Korea Factsheet*, May 16, 2014, http://www.ustr.gov/countries-regions/japan-korea-apec/korea.

3. White House, Office of the Press Secretary, *Joint Fact Sheet: The United States–Republic of Korea Alliance—A Global Perspective*.

4. "John Paul II's Appeal Saved Future Korean President from Death Sentence," Catholic News Agency, May 21, 2009, http://www.catholicnewsagency.com/news/john_paul_iis_appeal_saved_future_korean_president_from_death_sentence.

5. Kyung-Ae Park and Scott Snyder, eds., *North Korea in Transition* (Lanham, MD: Rowman & Littlefield, 2013); Victor Cha, *The Impossible State: North Korea Past and Future* (New York: HarperCollins, 2012); Jonathan Pollack, *No Exit: North Korea, Nuclear Weapons and International Security* (London: Routledge and International Institute for Strategic Studies, 2011); Bruce Cumings, *North Korea: Another Country* (New York: New Press, 2004); Robert Carlin and Joel Wit, *North Korean Reform*, Adelphi Paper 382 (London: Routledge and International Institute for Strategic Studies, 2006).

6. Eric Talmadge, "A Look at North Korea's Artillery Shows Why No One Wants War," Associated Press, April 7, 2013, http://www.businessinsider.com/why-no-one-in-korea-wants-war-2013-4.

7. Larry Niksch, *North Korea's Nuclear Weapons Program*, Report RL33590 (Washington, DC: Library of Congress, Congressional Research Service, August 1, 2006); Emma Chanlett-Avery and Ian E. Rinehart, *North Korea: U.S. Relations, Nuclear Diplomacy, and Internal Situation*, Report R41259 (Washington, DC: Library of Congress, Congressional Research Service, January 15, 2014).

8. Victor Cha, "Korea: A Peninsula in Crisis and Flux," in *Strategic Asia 2004–2005*, ed. Ashley Tellis and Michael Wills, 139–62 (Seattle, WA: National Bureau of Asian Research, 2004); Jonathan Pollack, "The Korean Peninsula in U.S. Strategy: Policy Issues for the Next President," in *Strategic Asia 2008–2009*, ed. Ashley Tellis, Mercy Kuo, and Andrew Marble, 135–66 (Seattle, WA: National Bureau of Asian Research, 2008).

9. Pollack, *No Exit*; Donald Oberdorfer, *The Two Koreas* (Reading, MA: Addison-Wesley, 1997); Nicholas Eberstadt, *The End of North Korea* (Washington, DC: AEI Press, 1999).

10. The account here is based on Niksch, *North Korea's Nuclear Weapons Program*. See also Joel Wit, Daniel Poneman, and Robert Gallucci, *Going Critical: The First North Korean Crisis* (Washington, DC: Brookings Institution, 2004), and Charles Pritchard, *Failed Diplomacy: The Tragic Story of How North Korea Got the Bomb* (Washington, DC: Brookings Institution, 2007).

11. William Perry, *Review of United States Policy toward North Korea: Findings and Recommendations* (Washington, DC: U.S. Department of State, Office of the North Korea Policy Coordinator, October 12, 1999).

12. *North Korea's Engagement: Perspectives, Outlook, and Implications*, Conference Report CR2001-01 (Washington, DC: U.S. National Intelligence Council, May 2001).

13. Donald Gross, "Progress on All Fronts," *Comparative Connections* 2, no. 4 (October–December 2000), http://www.csis.org/pacfor.

14. Victor Cha, "Engaging North Korea Credibly," *Survival* 42, no. 2 (Summer 2000): 136–55.

15. Daniel Bob, *The 107th Congress: Asia Pacific Policy Outlook*, NBR Briefing No. 10 (Seattle, WA: National Bureau of Asian Research, February 2001), 8–9.

16. Pritchard, *Failed Diplomacy*, 25–44.

17. Larry Niksch, *North Korea's Nuclear Weapons Developments and Diplomacy*, Report RL33590 (Washington, DC: Library of Congress, Congressional Research Service, September 10, 2007).

18. Samuel Kim, *The Two Koreas and the Great Powers* (New York: Cambridge University Press, 2006).

19. *North Korea's Engagement: Perspectives, Outlook, and Implications*, 3–6.

20. Oberdorfer, *The Two Koreas*; Pollack, *No Exit*; Victor Cha and David Kang, *Nuclear North Korea* (New York: Columbia University Press, 2003); Carlin and Wit, *North Korean Reform*; Cha, *The Impossible State*.

21. Mitchell Reiss, "Avoiding *Déjà vu* All over Again: Some Lessons from U.S.-DPRK Engagement," in National Intelligence Council, *North Korean Engagement: Perspectives, Outlook, and Implications*, Conference Report CR 2001-01 (Washington, DC: Government Printing Office, 2001), 11–25; Pollack, *No Exit*, 191.

22. Daryl Plunk, "The New U.S. Administration and North Korea Policy: A Time for Review and Adjustment," in National Intelligence Council, *North Korean Engagement: Perspectives, Outlook, and Implications*, Conference Report CR 2001-01 (Washington, DC: Government Printing Office, 2001), 27–38; Pollack, *No Exit*, 188–95.

23. Pollack, *No Exit*, 99–182.

24. On varying perspectives on Kim's motives and goals, see, among others, Cha and Kang, *Nuclear North Korea*.

25. International Crisis Group, *Korea Backgrounder: How South Korea Views Its Brother from Another Planet* (Brussels: International Crisis Group, December 14, 2004).

26. Pritchard, *Failed Diplomacy*, 40–44.

27. Ibid., 39.

28. Ming Liu, "China and the North Korean Crisis," *Pacific Affairs* 76, no. 3 (Fall 2003): 370–72.

29. "UN Council Demands Enforcement of N. Korea Sanctions," Reuters, April 13, 2009, http://in.reuters.com/article/2009/04/13/idINIndia-39025620090413.

30. Evan Ramstad and David Crawford, "North Korea Leaves Six-Party Talks," *Wall Street Journal Asia*, April 15, 2009, 1; "North Korea Quits Nuclear Talks, to Restart Plant," Reuters, April 14, 2009, http://www.reuters.com/article/2009/04/14/us-korea-north-idUSTRE53 C42820090414.

31. Sigfried Hecker, "From Pyongyang to Tehran, with Nukes," ForeignPolicy.com, May 26, 2009, http://experts.foreignpolicy.com/posts/2009/05/26/from_pyongyang_to_tehran.

32. Jeffrey Bader, *Obama and China's Rise* (Washington, DC: Brookings Institution, 2011), 26–39, 83–93.

33. Scott Snyder, "The Korean Peninsula and Northeast Asian Stability," in *International Relations of Asia*, ed. David Shambaugh and Michael Yahuda, 302–4, 306–8 (Lanham, MD: Rowman & Littlefield, 2014); Scott Snyder, "China-Korea Relations," *Comparative Connections* 15, no. 3 (January 2014), 87.

34. Mark Manyin, Mary Beth Nikitin, Emma Chanlett-Avery, Ian Rinehart, and William Cooper, *U.S.-South Korea Relations*, Report R41481 (Washington, DC: Library of Congress, Congressional Research Service, February 12, 2014).

35. Samuel Kim, "The Two Koreas: Making Grand Strategy amid Changing Domestic Politics," in *Strategic Asia 2007–2008*, ed. Ashley Tellis and Michael Wills, 113–38 (Seattle, WA: National Bureau of Asian Research, 2007); David Kang, "South Korea's Embrace of Interdependence in Pursuit of Security," in Ashley Tellis and Michael Wills, *Strategic Asia 2006–2007*, 139–72 (Seattle, WA: National Bureau of Asian Research, 2006).

36. Jiyoon Kim and Karl Friedhoff, *South Korean Public Opinion on North Korea & the Nations of the Six-Party Talks* (Seoul: Asan Institute, October 2011).

37. Kang, "South Korea's Embrace of Interdependence in Pursuit of Security."

38. Jae Ho Chung, *Between Ally and Partner: Korea-China Relations and the United States* (New York: Columbia University Press, 2006).

39. Scott Snyder, "China-Korea Relations," *Comparative Connections* 9, no. 3 (October 2007): 107–12.

40. David Kang and Ji-Young Lee, "Japan-Korea Relations," *Comparative Connections* 9, no. 3 (October 2007): 125–31.

41. David Kang and Jiun Bang, "Japan-Korea Relations," *Comparative Connections* 15, no. 3 (January 2014): 111, 116–17.

42. Ibid., 114.

43. Jin Kai, "South Korea–Japan Relations: America's Achilles' Heel?," *The Diplomat*, December 4, 2014, http://thediplomat.com/tag/china-south-korea-relations.

44. Moon, *Protesting America*; Victor Cha, "South Korea: Anchored or Adrift?," in *Strategic Asia 2003–2004*, ed. Richard Ellings and Aaron Friedberg, 109–30 (Seattle, WA: National Bureau of Asian Research, 2003); Mark Manyin et al., *U.S.–South Korean Relations*.

45. Larry Niksch, *Korea: U.S.–South Korean Relations—Issues for Congress*, CRS Issue Brief IB98045 (Washington, DC: Library of Congress, Congressional Research Service, July 16, 2005), 6.

46. Richard Baker and Charles Morrison, *Asia Pacific Security Outlook 2000* (New York: Japan Center for International Exchange, 2000), 103–11.

47. Niksch, *Korea: U.S.–South Korean Relations*, 12; for an overall assessment, see Moon, *Protesting America*.

48. Niksch, *Korea: U.S.–South Korean Relations*, 12–13.

49. Manyin et al., *U.S.–South Korea Relations*, 19.

50. "The United States and Asia in 2006," *Asian Survey* 47, no. 1 (January–February 2007): 17.

51. *Joint Fact Sheet: The United States-Republic of Korea Alliance—A Global Perspective*.

52. Cha, "South Korea: Anchored or Adrift?"

53. Xenia Dormandy with Rory Kinane, *Asia-Pacific Security: A Changing Role for the United States* (London: Chatham House, Royal Institute of International Affairs, April 2014), 12–13; Manyin et al., *U.S.–South Korea Relations*, 31–32.

54. Donald Gross, "Good Sense in Washington, a Big Question Mark in Pyongyang," *Comparative Connections*, April–June 2001, http://www.csis.org/pacfor.

55. William Cooper, coordinator, *The U.S.–South Korean Free Trade Agreement*, Report RL34330 (Washington, DC: Library of Congress, Congressional Research Service, March 7, 2013), 7–9.

56. "S. Korea's Top FTA Negotiator Says More Talks Required before Joining TPP," *Yonhap News*, February 12, 2014.

57. Manyin et al., *U.S.–South Korea Relations*, 3.

58. Kim, *The Two Koreas and the Great Powers*, 42–101; Pollack, *No Exit*, 168–75.

59. Ming Liu, "China and the North Korean Crisis," *Pacific Affairs* 76, no. 3 (Fall 2003): 347–73; Scott Snyder, "China's Post–Kim Jong Il Debate," Council on Foreign Relations, May 14, 2012, http://www.cfr.org/north-korea/china-korea-relations-chinas-post-kim-jong-il-debate/p28282.

60. Scott Snyder, "China-Korea Relations," *Comparative Connections*, July 2007, 121–30, http://www.csis.org/pacfor.

61. David Kang and Jiun Bang, "Japan-Korea Relations," *Comparative Connections* 16, no. 1 (May 2014): 135.

62. Kim, *The Two Koreas and the Great Powers*, 102–56.

Chapter Seven

U.S. Relations with Japan

Japan is America's most important ally in the Asia-Pacific region, the world's third-largest economy closely interacting with the United States, and a regional leader determining policy directions affecting its neighbors and American interests. Japan's importance has declined from the late Cold War period when U.S. ambassador to Japan Mike Mansfield (1977–1988) routinely referred to U.S.-Japan ties as unquestionably America's most important bilateral relationship. The assertion was debatable at the time, and the subsequent rise of Chinese power and decline of Japan's economic performance head the list of reasons for a remarkable power shift between these two Asian powers since that time and the resulting shift in American attention and priorities. Nevertheless, American leaders continue to devote high priority to deepening the alliance and other relations, seeing Japan as the "cornerstone" of American ability to influence developments and advance its security, economic, and political interests in Northeast Asia and the broader Asia-Pacific.[1]

Thus, American alignment with Japan is determined by realism in regional and world power politics. Japan also comes closer than most major countries to cooperating with the United States in establishing a rules-based liberal economic order of open trading and investment exchanges. Meanwhile, constructivist influences in U.S.-Japan relations see the Japanese government adhere to major Western values and encourage an identity in Japan in line with the community of developed countries centered in Europe and North America.

U.S. relations with Japan have significant areas of friction and frustration for both countries, but these difficulties are overshadowed by converging interests and values. Relations with Japan have remained of central importance in American policy toward the region in the post–Cold War period, and they represent a major element in the Barack Obama administration's rebalance policy toward the Asia-Pacific.

Over the years, American policy makers, specialists, and opinion leaders have disagreed on Japan's priority in U.S. foreign policy. In broad terms, U.S. policy toward the Asia-Pacific since the 1960s saw President Richard Nixon and some later presidents give top priority to developing cooperative U.S. relations with China, and in the process they neglected or downgraded U.S. relations with Japan. In the post–Cold War period, as Japan was economically stagnating and its political leadership sometimes appeared weak, some in and out of government believed that the United States was better off seeking to enhance its interests and influence in the Asia-Pacific by working more closely with rising regional powers, notably China. Others strongly disagreed, however, and stressed that without Japan as an ally and without access to military bases in Japan, U.S. influence in the Asia-Pacific would be severely constrained. According to this view, China's rapidly growing economic and military power represented major challenges as well as opportunities for the United States. To manage the challenges effectively in line with American interests appeared to require close U.S. cooperation with Japan. Common interests and values were said to bind the United States closely to Japan in an alliance relationship demonstrating mutual trust deemed essential in sustaining American security, economic, and political interests in the Asia-Pacific region.[2]

The George W. Bush administration in its early years clearly favored the latter view. Reflecting the judgments of a cohort of strongly pro-Japan leaders headed by Deputy Secretary of State Richard Armitage, the Bush administration's relations with Japan were given top priority in the Asia-Pacific and probably received more favorable U.S. administration attention than any other U.S. bilateral relationship during the early years of Bush's presidency. The improvement in U.S.-Japan relations was a notable bright spot in the administration's foreign policy record, which became mired in controversy and recriminations, particularly as a result of its decision to invade Iraq.[3]

In its later years, however, Bush administration leaders came increasingly to rely on consultations and coordination with Chinese counterparts to manage salient Asia-Pacific hot spots, notably North Korea's nuclear weapons program and the Taiwan situation. On the one hand, U.S. leaders and Japanese leaders continued to reinforce political and economic cooperation and closer security ties, some of which served as a hedge against rising Chinese power and influence. On the other hand, American officials also came increasingly to rely on China to help keep the North Korean and Taiwan situations stable as Bush administration leaders focused on other issues, especially the deep crisis posed by the U.S.-led conflict in Iraq and related turmoil in the Middle East and Afghanistan.[4]

As discussed in chapter 5, the Barack Obama government sought to advance the Bush government's positive engagement and attention to China. China's role loomed large in administration calculations dealing with such salient issues as the global economic crisis, climate change, efforts to thwart the spread of nuclear weapons involving North Korea and Iran, and struggles against terrorism.

By contrast, Japan became a more negative element in American policy calculations. Political uncertainty accompanied major leadership change in Japan. The election victory of the Democratic Party of Japan (DPJ) in 2009 challenged U.S. alliance relations in serious ways. DPJ leader Yukio Hatoyama campaigned with pledges to reexamine the planned realignment of U.S. forces in Japan agreed to by previous Japanese governments and to pursue a more balanced foreign policy between the United States and Japan's neighbors.

On entering office, Prime Minister Hatoyama moved quickly to reassess a 2006 Japan-U.S. agreement to realign U.S. troops in Japan, with a particular focus on the large and controversial U.S. bases in Okinawa, and to revise the U.S.-Japan Status of Forces Agreement (SOFA). Both topics were keenly sensitive issues in alliance relations. The 2006 agreement represented a delicate compromise reached after protracted negotiations that had a number of provisions calling for actions in future years that appeared difficult to implement. Hatoyama was pressured by his party's coalition partners, the Social Democratic Party and the People's New Party which held swing votes in Japan's upper house, to switch that part of the 2006 agreement involving the U.S. Marine Corps Air Station (MCAS) Futenma Replacement Facility (FRF) in Okinawa. Thus, Hatoyama urged that the FRF site be switched from Henoko Bay, Okinawa—the location stipulated in the U.S.-Japan arrangements in the 2006 agreement—to some location off the island of Okinawa. He pressed his case publicly in initial official meetings with President Obama. The U.S. government remained firm in support of the provisions stipulated in the 2006 agreement. The FRF issue became the most important problem in U.S.-Japan relations and ultimately led to Prime Minister Hatoyama's resignation in 2010.[5]

Hatoyama and other DPJ leaders' calls for a more balanced Japanese foreign policy seemingly less closely aligned with the United States and more attentive to China and other neighbors resulted in various calls by the new Japanese government for an East Asian Community that initially seemed to leave the United States outside the grouping. The DPJ found China to be wary of these Japanese initiatives, as Beijing saw them as a means for Japan to assert leadership in regional affairs in competition with China.[6] The party's efforts to promote closer Sino-Japanese relations subsequently foundered over the increasingly contentious territorial disputes over the Senkaku (Diaoyu) Islands, which became acute when Japan arrested a Chinese fishing boat captain for ramming Japanese coast guard ships in 2010. Two years later, DPJ prime minister Yosihiko Noda endeavored to limit the damage to Japan-China relations caused by Japanese right-wing elements under the leadership of Tokyo governor Shintara Ishihara seeking to purchase some of the disputed islands and use them in ways sure to antagonize China. Noda decided in September 2012 to have the Japanese government purchase the islands instead.

As noted earlier, the Chinese reaction was truly extraordinary. It pushed Sino-Japanese relations to their lowest point since the start of the Cold War. An intense and massive propaganda barrage against Japan featured authoritative government, party, and military pronouncements and remarks by a broad array of top leaders urging Chinese people to register their "righteous indignation" over the Noda decision. In response, a spectacle not seen in China since the depths of the Cultural Revolution showed mass demonstrations in 120 Chinese cities over the course of one week, with associated violence including the burning and looting of Japanese properties.[7]

Unfortunately for Prime Minister Noda, his seemingly pragmatic decisions came amid heightened public Chinese determination to defend territorial claims along China's maritime rim and followed China's successful use of coercion and intimidation to force Philippine fishing boats and security forces out of the disputed Scarborough Shoal in the South China Sea in mid-2012. This new pattern of Chinese assertiveness now had a much more important target than the Philippines. There ensued repeated Chinese use of coast guard forces, legal and administrative measures, trade pressures, diplomatic threats, and other means to force Japan to reverse its actions and negotiate with China over the disputed islands. The acute crisis with China added to DPJ woes and contributed to the landslide election victory of the Liberal Democratic Party (LDP) under Shinzo Abe in late 2012. Abe was firm in the face of Chinese pressure, setting the stage for protracted tensions unseen in Sino-Japanese relations since the end of the Japanese Empire.[8]

The Obama government welcomed Abe's ascendance. The LDP administration promised better adherence to past agreements, including those involving U.S. forces in Okinawa, and a strong Japanese emphasis on the importance of the alliance. American interest in calming the disputes in the East and South China Seas while avoiding taking a position on sovereignty was soon followed by a tougher U.S. stance. The United States reacted negatively to incremental Chinese advances to control more territory and otherwise advance Beijing's interests through various use of coercion, intimidation, and pressure short of direct use of military force. The U.S. government, including Secretary of State John Kerry and Secretary of Defense Chuck Hagel, repeatedly condemned the Chinese actions as provocative; it eventually warned of serious consequences for U.S.-Chinese relations.[9]

The tougher U.S. stance overlapped closely with Abe's defensive but firm stance toward China. Chinese criticism endeavored to demonize Abe as he sought to balance against Chinese pressures by strengthening defense at home and seeking support in visits to all members of ASEAN as well as India, Australia, and others. In contrast, President Obama visiting Japan in April 2014 embraced close collaboration with Japan in building Japanese-American influence in Asia while he underlined America's defense commitment to all areas under Japanese administrative control including the Senkaku (Diaoyu) Islands.[10]

Of course Abe's leadership was not without problems for the United States. His visit to the Yasukuni Shrine in December 2013 antagonized China and further upset relations with South Korea that were already frayed as a result of comments from Abe and senior associates dealing with issues left over from history, notably the Japanese wartime use of "comfort women" sex slaves involving many Koreans. The actions ran against U.S. efforts to build synergies in the U.S. alliances with Japan and South Korea in the face of dangers posed by North Korea's nuclear weapons developments and other provocations and challenges posed notably by Chinese assertiveness. In the U.S. view, they added unhelpful complications to U.S. efforts to work cooperatively with Japan in dealing with assertive Chinese actions.[11]

JAPANESE GOVERNMENT PRIORITIES

Japanese government priorities and behavior in foreign affairs after the Cold War have reflected changes at home and abroad that pulled Japanese policies in often contradictory directions and led to a general reduction in Japan's influence in Asian and world affairs. Japan's economic growth, the foundation of Japanese international influence in previous years, stalled as Asia's other large economies, notably China and India, rose in prominence. Reviving the Japanese economy required closer integration with China, South Korea, and other Asian economies, but Japanese relations with China and Korea were seriously complicated by burgeoning Japanese nationalism, which featured patriotic demonstrations by Japanese leaders that were grossly offensive to the peoples and leaders of those countries. Japanese officials and public opinion saw growing security threats to Japan posed by North Korea and China. This pushed Japan into a closer military relationship with the United States, even though Japanese leaders continued to be concerned that future shifts in U.S. policies could see the United States give less priority to Japan as it sought U.S. interests in Asian and world affairs.[12]

That the Japanese leaders were not determined on a clear set of post–Cold War priorities was reflected in scholarly assessments by Western specialists.[13] Japan was seen at first as a reactive state, responding to the course of world events rather than shaping them.[14] Some specialists emphasized that Japan was becoming what was labeled a "reluctant realist," pursuing the more assertive and nationalist foreign policies advocated by Japanese conservatives.[15] At the same time, however, other specialists saw continued Japanese tendencies to eschew military power in favor of diplomacy and international cooperation. Japan continued to secure access to outside markets through nonmilitary means such as diplomacy, trade, and foreign aid and tried to maintain diplomatic and trade relations with all nations as much as possible.[16]

For many years, Japanese and foreign specialists debated whether significant change was actually occurring in Japan. The debate focused on how significant the change was, how fast it would develop, how far it would go, what its principal drivers were, and what it might mean for the United States. The political system has been undergoing major transformation, marked by the obsolescence of the one-party system, diminished bureaucratic power, increased influence of politicians, strained corporate-political ties, the unprecedented volatility of the voting public, and the unpredictability of politician behavior. In this environment, the United States has fewer direct levers of influence, a reality seen in American government frustrations in endeavoring to deal with the newly installed DPJ leadership of Prime Minister Hatoyama in 2009.[17]

ECONOMIC TRENDS

Japan's economic development appears to be the key to determining Japanese government priorities. While losing out to rising China as the world's second economic power, Japan remains important to regional and global economic trends, but less so than in the past. Stalled growth from the early 1990s reduced Japan's international stature and undermined the confidence of Japanese business and government leaders. Globalization also forced Japanese economic elites to conduct more unconventional and pluralistic decision making in pursuit of policies that will work effectively in the new environment. They have been compelled to conform more to Western norms of behavior that depart from the past methods of "Japan Incorporated," but the record of reform remains mixed. Corporations and politicians are increasingly learning the lessons needed to restructure and are looking to outside experts for assistance. Still, the established rules and practices in Japan slow the economy's restructuring and serve to keep Japan from full engagement in the global trend to let the market dictate winners and losers.[18]

Economic experts continue to forecast a slow economic recovery in Japan. They doubt that the incremental and partial reforms seen thus far will be sufficient to significantly improve Japan's position as a leader in the global market. Factors that impede effective Japanese growth included heavy government and private indebtedness, a persisting dual economy consisting of a competitive export-oriented business sector and less competitive domestic enterprises, an aging society, and the perceived absence of an entrepreneurial spirit. Some economic experts see a more gloomy future of protracted stagnation caused by deflation, an aging society, and tense relations with China.[19]

The major problems of the Japanese economy were clear at the start of the twenty-first century. During the previous decade, Japan—after more than three decades of sustained high levels of economic growth—was mired in an economic slump that the government was ineffective in correcting. Poor economic performance put pressure on Japan's political system and depressed growth prospects in Asia. The Japanese government remained hard-pressed to implement a sweeping reform strategy because aggressive efforts to restructure Japan's economy would initially cause economic instability in the form of bankruptcies, unemployment, and probably recession.

Weak demand was producing a deflationary environment and eroding household and corporate balance sheets that were already burdened by large debt. Deflation reinforced the Japanese cultural emphasis on saving, making government efforts to boost consumer spending increasingly difficult. The slowdown in the world economy in general, and the U.S. economy in particular, limited the boost that Japan was likely to receive from foreign purchases of its goods and services. Continued government efforts at fiscal stimulation may have been an effective tool for avoiding a steep downturn, but they were not able to restore growth. Increasing budget deficits added to the gross public debt, which was over twice the value of Japan's gross domestic product (GDP) in 2013.[20]

Structural and political barriers to economic recovery complicated Japan's efforts to achieve even modest levels of economic growth. Efforts to place the banking system on a solid financial foundation were associated with bank closures and unemployment. Likewise, corporate restructuring was difficult because of the traditional reluctance of managers to cut jobs. Gradual restructuring ensued, slowing new hiring and leading to unemployment, which reinforced deflationary pressures.[21]

Japan is an important economic partner of the United States, but its importance has slid as it has been edged out by other partners. Japan was the United States' fourth-largest merchandise export market (behind Canada, Mexico, and China) and the fourth-largest source for U.S. merchandise imports (behind China, Canada, and Mexico) at the end of 2013. These numbers probably underestimate the importance of Japan in U.S. trade since Japan exports intermediate goods to China that are then used to manufacture finished goods that China exports to the United States.[22]

The United States was Japan's largest export market and second-largest source of imports as of the end of 2013. The global economic downturn had a significant impact on U.S.-Japan trade: both exports and imports declined in 2009 from 2008. U.S.-Japan bilateral trade increased since 2009 and until 2012, but declined in 2013.

Despite some outstanding issues, tensions in the U.S.-Japan bilateral economic relationship have been much lower than was the case in the 1970s, 1980s, and early 1990s. A number of factors may have contributed to this trend:

- Japan's slow, if not stagnant, economic growth began with the burst of the asset bubble in the latter half of the 1990s and continued as a result of the 2008–2009 economic downturn and the 2011 disasters associated with the earthquake, tsunami, and nuclear reactor meltdown in Fukushima in northeastern Japan. Such developments changed the general U.S. perception of Japan from one as an economic competitor to one as a "humbled" economic power.
- The rise of China as an economic power and trade partner has caused U.S. policy makers to shift attention from Japan to China as a source of concern.
- The increased use by both Japan and the United States of the WTO as a forum for resolving trade disputes has depoliticized disputes and helped to reduce friction.
- Shifts in U.S. and Japanese trade strategies that have expanded the formation of bilateral and regional trade areas with other countries have lessened the focus on their bilateral ties.
- The rise of China as a military power and the continued threat of North Korea have forced U.S. and Japanese leaders to give more weight to security issues within the bilateral alliance.

During the global financial crisis which began in 2008 and intensified in 2009, Japan was hit hard by the decline in global demand for its exports, particularly in the United States and Europe. Japan had become dependent on net export growth as the engine for overall GDP growth, as domestic consumer demand and investment lagged.

The March 11, 2011, earthquake, tsunami, and nuclear reactor meltdowns in northeast Japan became known as the "Triple Disaster." On March 11, 2011, a magnitude 9.0 earthquake jolted a wide swath of Honshu, Japan's largest island. The quake, with an epicenter located about 230 miles northeast of Tokyo, generated a tsunami that pounded Honshu's northeastern coast, causing widespread destruction in Miyagi, Iwate, Ibaraki, and Fukushima Prefectures. Some twenty thousand lives were lost, and entire towns were washed away; over five hundred thousand homes and other buildings and around 3,600 roads were damaged or destroyed. Up to half a million Japanese were displaced. Damage to several reactors at the Fukushima Dai-ichi nuclear power plant complex led the government to declare a state of emergency and evacuate nearly eighty thousand residents within a twenty-kilometer radius due to dangerous radiation levels.[23]

In many respects, Japan's response to the multifaceted disaster was remarkable. Over one hundred thousand troops from the Self-Defense Force (SDF), Japan's military, were deployed quickly to the region. After rescuing nearly twenty thousand individuals in the first week, the troops turned to a humanitarian relief mission in the displaced communities. Construction of temporary housing began a week after the quake. Foreign commentators marveled at Japanese citizens' calm resilience, the lack of looting, and the orderly response to the strongest earthquake in the nation's modern history.[24]

Japan's preparedness—strict building codes, a tsunami warning system that alerted many to seek higher ground, and years of public drills—likely saved tens of thousands of lives. Appreciation for the U.S.-Japan alliance surged after the two militaries worked effectively together to respond to the earthquake and tsunami. Years of joint training and many interoperable assets facilitated the integrated alliance effort. Operation Tomodachi, using the Japanese word for "friend," was the first time that Self-Defense Force helicopters used U.S. aircraft carriers to respond to a crisis. The USS *Ronald Reagan* aircraft carrier provided a platform for air operations as well as a refueling base for Japanese SDF and coast guard helicopters. Other U.S. vessels transported SDF troops and equipment to the disaster-stricken areas. Communication between the allied forces functioned effectively, according to military observers. For the first time, U.S. military units operated under Japanese command in actual operations. Specifically dedicated liaison officers helped to smooth communication. Although the U.S. military played a critical role, the Americans were careful to emphasize that the Japanese authorities were in the lead.[25]

Despite this response to the initial event, the uncertainty surrounding the nuclear reactor meltdown and the failure to present longer-term reconstruction plans led many to question the government's handling of the disaster. As reports mounted about heightened levels of radiation in the air, tap water, and produce, criticism emerged regarding the lack of clear guidance from political leadership. Concerns about the government's excessive dependence on information from Tokyo Electric Power Company (TEPCO), the firm that owns and operates the power plant, amplified public skepticism and elevated criticism about conflicts of interest between regulators and utilities.

The Japanese government has responded with a series of four supplemental fiscal packages to finance reconstruction. The implementation of the reconstruction efforts has been slower than expected, dampening the stimulus effect on economic growth. In addition, the country has had to cope with electricity shortages and search for alternative sources of power, including increased fossil fuel imports. [26]

The two crises and the economic problems in Europe, among other factors, have adversely affected Japan's economic growth. Japan incurred negative growth rates of -1.1 percent in 2008 and -5.5 percent in 2009 but recovered in 2010 to expand by 4.7 percent. The recovery proved short-lived as Japan experienced -0.4 percent growth in 2011, only 1.4 percent in 2012, and 1.6 percent in 2013. [27]

Prime Minister Abe has made it a priority of his administration to boost economic growth and to eliminate deflation, which has plagued Japan for many years. Abe is promoting a three-pronged, or "three arrow," economic program. The first arrow consisted of a $122 billion fiscal stimulus package aimed at spending on infrastructure, particularly in areas affected by the March 2011 disaster. While the package boosted growth somewhat, its effects appear to have largely run their course, and it added to Japan's already large public debt, which continued to rise to over 200 percent of the country's GDP—the highest of any advanced economy. [28]

The second arrow consists of monetary stimulus to arrest deflation. Under pressure from the prime minister, the independent central bank (Bank of Japan, or BOJ) announced in the spring of 2013 a continued loose monetary policy with interest rates of 0 percent, quantitative easing measures, and a target inflation rate of 2 percent. In response, the Japanese yen rapidly dropped in value against the U.S. dollar and other major currencies. Although the bank's target may take time to reach, it appeared that inflationary pressures have reemerged in the economy, at least in part due to the rise in import prices resulting from the yen's depreciation.

The third arrow consists of economic reforms, notably restructuring the agricultural, medical services, and electricity sectors (among others) and the promotion of new services and industries. Prime Minister Abe viewed Japan's participation in the U.S.-led Trans-Pacific Partnership (TPP) trade framework as a catalyst for those growth-promoting reforms, but many of the established economic interests remain deeply entrenched, particularly within Abe's party, the LDP. On balance, Abe has pursued structural reforms cautiously and has backtracked on many of them, such as liberalizing the sale of pharmaceuticals.

A likely by-product of these measures will be the weakening of the yen. In the five years leading to Abe's reforms in 2012, the yen exhibited unprecedented strength in terms of the dollar. In January 2007 the yen's average value was ¥120.46 = $1 during the month, but after rapid appreciation, it reached as high as ¥76.65 = $1 in October 2011. Since that time, it has depreciated to ¥121 = $1 during 2014. [29]

Structural and political barriers to economic recovery complicate Japan's efforts to achieve even modest levels of economic growth. The Japanese economy is still regulated and insulated when compared to the United States and some other Western-oriented economies. Past practice showed an incremental trend to reduce the role of the state, allowing market forces to operate in the interests of greater efficiency.

Looking forward, monetary and fiscal policies need to be managed in ways that promote sustainable growth. Japanese fiscal authorities face large deficits, but tightening the monetary or fiscal policies prematurely or too severely could halt the recent progress. Higher energy and natural resources prices negatively affect the energy- and resource-intensive sectors of the economy. A major long-term brake on Japanese growth is the aging Japanese population and overall decline in the Japanese workforce. The Japanese government anticipates that the workforce will decline 0.7 percent per year and that the total population could decline from 128 million to 100 million by 2050. These trends will almost certainly hold back the expansion of the Japanese economy, though their negative effects can be offset to some degree by increases in worker productivity, and Japan may see more employment for women and immigrants. [30]

The implications of these trends for U.S. and international interests seem generally clear. Incremental reform and a possibly mixed record on sustaining economic growth will probably restrict or at least complicate vigorous Japanese participation in international political and security affairs. The earlier postwar era of rather extreme Japanese passivity in global affairs is certainly over, but the nature of Japan's future participation remains uncertain. A scenario of partial reform could also leave the Japanese government favoring an international agenda that runs counter to the U.S.-backed global trend toward reinforcement of market principles.

A similar story could be told regarding international trade, depending most immediately on how supportive the Abe government is regarding the TPP. The bilateral trade deficit persists as an issue with the United States. As more U.S. and other foreign companies invest in and participate in Japan's economy as a result of recent reforms, the United States has become more invested in the process and has a greater stake in the overall stability of the U.S.-Japan economic relationship. [31]

Incremental reform and slow growth hold potential negative consequences for strategic policy as well. Japanese leaders worried about the large fiscal deficit despite weak economic performance may seek to cut spending. In this environment, expensive new military equipment development or procurement is problematic. This situation could cause difficulties if, for example, the U.S. government wants Japan to participate more actively in expensive projects related to upgraded roles and missions in the bilateral relationship. On the whole, however, economic trends probably will have only marginal implications for Japanese-U.S. security relations. The bilateral strategic relationship is not prone to sudden reversals, in part because there exist

numerous brakes on abrupt changes in security policy, including strong domestic support for the U.S. alliance, cautious and status quo–oriented leaders,
the requirement for consensus building, and continued strong pacifist sentiment.[32]

CHANGES IN JAPAN'S SECURITY POSTURE

Continuing serious economic concerns combine with a number of recent
security and other challenges to raise grave questions in Japan about the
viability of its long-standing post–World War II national development-security strategy. The goal of Japan's postwar national strategy as laid out by
Prime Minister Shigeru Yoshida was to gradually reestablish Japan's national power and preeminence. The strategy emphasized economic recovery and
expansion to rebuild Japanese national wealth and, with that wealth, power
and influence. The primacy of economics fit well with widespread Japanese
postwar aversion to militarism and the use of force. But with the bipolar Cold
War heating up, Japan could pursue economic growth only if its security
were guaranteed. It thus relied on the United States for external security in
exchange for hosting a large, permanent U.S. military presence.[33]

Japan's strategy was successful. Legally, politically, and socially constrained from rebuilding a credible military capability, Japan grew and became an economic superpower and leader by the 1980s. Not only did this
strategy benefit Japan, but the bilateral security arrangement also supported
the U.S. Cold War security strategy in the Pacific and was quietly endorsed
by the rest of Asia as a check against future Japanese militarism.

Since the 1990s, this national development-security strategy has come
under challenge and undergone change because of several key factors, described below.[34]

Post–Cold War Threats and Uncertainties

The end of the Cold War and collapse of the Soviet Union altered Japan's
threat environment. It dismantled the Cold War strategic framework for the
East Asian security equation, removed Japan's number-one security threat
against which Japan's force structure had been configured, and took away the
initial rationale for Japan's post–World War II geostrategic bargain with the
United States.

Japanese leaders view the strategic situation in East Asia as being more
unsettled than during the Cold War, with a number of near-term flash points
and longer-term uncertainties shaping Japan's security calculus now and
probably in the coming years:

- North Korea is the most pressing security issue. Pyongyang's nuclear weapons tests and ballistic missile tests over Japan head the long list of reasons for Japanese angst. Japan had previously viewed North Korea as posing an indirect threat in terms of regional instability and refugee flows, as well as a potential problem for the alliance should rifts emerge with the United States over expected Japanese involvement in a Korean contingency. Polling data and media reporting now indicate that recent repeated North Korean provocations leave Japan with a greater sense of immediate danger and highlight limitations of the U.S. alliance in deterring threats to Japan. Japanese attitudes toward North Korea have hardened as a result of the protracted crisis over North Korea's nuclear weapons program beginning in 2003 as well as the issue of accounting for Japanese citizens abducted by North Korean agents and detained in North Korea. [35]
- Japanese cooperation in U.S.-backed efforts to promote efficiencies and synergy in trilateral Japan–South Korea–U.S. allied cooperation against North Korea remains hampered by distrust from the past negative history between Korea and Japan. The prospect of a unified Korea bears on Japan's efforts to prepare for future uncertainty. History makes Korea an important security concern for Japan. As Japan and South Korea remain suspicious of one another, the external orientation of a future unified Korea—how it relates to Beijing, the type of military capability it possesses, and the posture it assumes toward Japan—is seen in Japan as a major factor in the future security equation in Northeast Asia. [36]
- Taiwan is also a serious concern. Japanese leaders are aware that an outbreak of hostilities in the Taiwan Strait involving U.S. forces could easily draw Japan into it under the U.S.-Japan defense guidelines. The extent and role of Japanese involvement in a China-Taiwan-U.S. military conflict would require difficult decisions of Japan, weighing the need to support its ally against the costs such actions would entail for its future relationship with China. Japan faces the probability that it would emerge from a Taiwan crisis with either its U.S. or China relationship—or perhaps both—seriously damaged. In recent years, Tokyo has tilted against China as it has consulted closely with the United States in seeking to deter Chinese military action against Taiwan. As President Ma Ying-jeou since 2008 has accommodated China and brought about ever-closer ties with Beijing, Japanese strategists worry about Japan's strategic position should Taiwan be removed as an obstacle to China's expansion into the western Pacific.
- The confrontation with China over the disputed Senkaku (Diaoyu) Islands in the East China Sea underlines China as the largest and growing factor in Japan's security calculations. Encountering China's tougher approach to maritime territorial issues described in chapter 5, Japan continues to face a protracted struggle where China has employed sometimes extraordinary coercive measures short of direct use of military force to pressure Japan to

recognize China's claim, enter negotiations on terms agreeable to China, and follow conditions set by Beijing. Thus far, Japan seems prepared to resist, building its own strengths and working with the United States and others in the Asia-Pacific to offset the pressures from China. In the recent past, public opinion polls, as well as Japanese officials and academic experts, were prone to place China more as an uncertainty that Japan must actively position itself to deal with on many fronts rather than as a threat to be actively countered. Opinion has hardened as a result of China's perceived aggression and expansion at the expense of Japan.[37]

- Chinese expansion tops Japanese concerns over the stability of sea lines of communication and regional order in Southeast Asia and the South China Sea. Instability in Southeast Asia could jeopardize sea lines of communication, threaten Japanese nationals, and disrupt regional security dynamics. Japan's security interests are largely compatible with those of Southeast Asia—preventing regional hegemony, supporting a regional U.S. presence as a stabilizing force, and endeavoring to influence China's regional role as it grows in power. A stable and cooperative Southeast Asia can advance those interests better than a weak and divided region can. Recognizing the potential for broader instability, Tokyo has closely monitored and lent support where appropriate regarding the Philippines and Vietnam in their respective standoffs with China over disputed territory in the South China Sea.[38]
- Russia has been low on the list of Japan's security worries. The Northern Territories dispute remains a traditional security issue. Japan has competed with China over access to Russian oil. Speculation that Prime Minster Abe and Russian president Vladimir Putin would seek to improve relations as they respectively sought leverage against an ever more powerful China was undermined by the Russian annexation of Crimea at the expense of Ukraine and G-7 sanctions imposed on Russia and its leaders.[39]
- Long-term energy and economic concerns drive much of Japan's diplomatic and economic activity in the Middle East. The downgrading of nuclear power after the disaster at Fukushima means that Japan is ever more dependent on fossil energy imports from the Middle East and other suppliers. Japan looks to the United States to preserve stability and security lines of communication to the region following the U.S. military withdrawal from Iraq and Afghanistan.

Perceptions of U.S. Security Policy

U.S. security policy is a key question for Japan in the recent uncertain environment. Until the 1990s, Japanese policy makers appeared confident that the United States needed Japan—that the alliance was just as critical for Washington's security strategy as it was for Tokyo's. This confidence has been questioned, with Japan at times unsure of its value to the United States. This uncertainty stems from several factors:

- During the Bill Clinton administration, Japanese academic writings and media commentary indicated that Japan was unsure how Washington defined its strategic role in the post–Cold War era. Some saw inconsistency, unpredictability, and less strategic clarity in U.S. security calculations, which were seen as problematic to Japan. The updated U.S.-Japan Defense Guidelines and the strong pro-Japan leanings of the George W. Bush administration reassured Japanese leaders and helped to strongly solidify the U.S.-Japan alliance relationship. But Bush's later emphasis on close engagement with China and resort to confidential bilateral negotiations with North Korea after its 2006 nuclear weapons test disturbed Japanese strategists.
- The Obama government initially followed Bush's strong priority to China, while the DPJ prime ministers followed policies that tested American commitment and forbearance regarding Japan.[40] Japanese leaders have warmly welcomed the Barack Obama government's emphasis on improving relations with allies in its rebalance policy to Asia. Nonetheless, they are fully aware of American dissatisfaction with the Abe government regarding its handling of historical disputes with South Korea and Prime Minister Abe's 2013 visit to the controversial Yasukuni Shrine. They worry for one thing that the United States because of domestic and other international complications may prove to be weak and irresolute in standing up to Chinese expansion at Japan's expense; and they also worry that America may see its interests better served in accommodating a rising China rather than supporting a declining Japan.[41]
- Japanese leaders assess that Japan's economic stagnation and slow growth have made the country less important to the United States. Because Japan has calculated its own national power largely in terms of economic strength since World War II, it follows that Tokyo would view the loss of power and influence resulting from economic difficulties as decreasing its importance abroad, particularly without the Cold War backdrop.[42]

DOMESTIC POLITICAL ENVIRONMENT

The Japanese political system within which government policies and priorities have been framed and decided for much of the past fifty years has undergone major changes. The transformation of the political system is marked by the following:

- *Weakening of the party system.* Not only has the Liberal Democratic Party's monopoly on power been broken, but the structure of Japanese party politics has eroded as well. Coalition politics has become a feature of the political landscape, in an environment in which party affiliations are fragile and alliances transitory.
- *Voter unpredictability.* The volatility of the Japanese electorate has increased. Voter identification with political parties is weak, and traditional machine politics is dying. Social, economic, and technological changes have altered local political dynamics, leaving local elites unable to deliver the vote as in the past.
- *Decline of the bureaucrats.* The opening of the political system has increased the power of politicians at the expense of the bureaucrats—career subject experts who traditionally shaped public policy and were a strong force for continuity. Moreover, politician behavior increasingly reflects the volatile voting public.
- *Generational change.* A new generation of political leaders, reflecting generational change in Japanese society, is bringing new attitudes and policy concerns. Issues once considered taboo, such as constitutional revision, are now seriously debated and open to change.

The breakdown of the traditional political system has left a decision-making vacuum that is currently being filled by a variety of forces—public opinion, new interest groups, unusual tactical political alliances, and local political interests. In short, the political system is in flux, creating a decision-making environment that is more pluralistic and politically permissive and less predictable. The range of options has expanded, and policy outcomes cannot be taken for granted. Unexpected outcomes are increasingly possible.[43]

Generational change is producing new dynamics in how the Japanese think about their country. The population is proud of Japan's democracy and wants to demonstrate that pride. Japanese from various backgrounds are frustrated that Japan still seems to carry a pariah stigma; they believe it has earned the right to be a "normal" nation.

Nationalism in Japan is more of an expression of pride in Japan's postwar accomplishments and a desire to be viewed as a modern, responsible state than a desire for Japanese assertiveness or dominance, particularly in the security context. One component of this quest for normalcy is a greater popular acceptance of the Japan Self-Defense Force and more of a popular willingness to consider foreign missions for the SDF. The annual visits to the controversial Yasukuni war memorial by Prime Minister Junichiro Koizumi (2001–2006) and the December 2013 visit by Prime Minister Abe also were in line with this trend. Meanwhile, China's coercion and intimidation against Japan over the Senkaku (Diaoyu) Islands reinforces nationalist feelings in

Japan. Although a darker strain of nationalism does exist, it appears unlikely to grow significantly or gain popular acceptance unless there are dramatic changes in the regional situation and a major reordering of the political system.[44]

From 2007 to 2012, Japanese politics were plagued by instability. The premiership changed hands six times in those six years, and no party controlled both the lower and upper houses of the Parliament for more than a few months. This period of turmoil appeared to have been brought to an end with the LDP coalition's dominant election victories in December 2012 and July 2013. The former event, elections for Japan's lower house, returned the LDP and its coalition partner, the New Komeito Party, into power after three years in the minority. The latter consolidated the LDP coalition's hold by giving it a majority in the upper house. At the time of the election, Abe's public approval ratings were generally in the 60 to 70 percent range, which polls attributed to voters' support for his economic policies. The fact that parliamentary elections do not have to be held until the summer of 2016 presumably gives Abe and the LDP a relatively prolonged period in which to promote their agenda. Abe prompted elections for the lower house and an LDP win in December 2014. The results reinforced Abe's mandate by giving the prime minister a longer period in office. The LDP has ruled Japan for all but about four years since 1955.

Abe has made improving Japan's economy his top priority. In a previous stint as prime minister, from 2006 to 2007, widespread feelings that his government was paying insufficient attention to economic and social welfare issues contributed to low public approval ratings and the LDP's defeat in 2007 upper house elections. For much of 2013, Abe's cabinet enjoyed poll numbers above 60 percent. They declined slightly in the fall, in part due to unease among many Japanese about the LDP's passage of a new state secrets law and the manner in which the party pushed it through the Diet. By early 2014, the government's approval ratings began to decline.[45]

Abe's popularity is challenged due to some economic issues, notably the impacts of Japan's consumption tax increase from 5 to 8 percent, potentially curtailing economic growth. Also, Abe promises structural reforms, which remain controversial and unpopular with many. Abe has been acting on his pledges to boost Japan's security capabilities, such as through the creation of a national security council in the prime minister's office and the seeking of freedom to engage in collective self-defense with the United States in particular. These moves are generally popular in the LDP, which has steadily become more hawkish on national security matters, as well as more revisionist on historical matters over the past twenty years. They remain controversial in other segments of Japanese society.

Abe has said he will not prioritize his far-reaching proposals to amend the constitution's security-related clauses such as Article 9. The reasons for this decision seem clear. The July 2013 elections did not give the LDP the two-thirds majority that Abe would need to amend Japan's constitution. The LDP's coalition partner, New Komeito, opposes efforts to weaken or do away with Japan's collective self-defense ban, suggesting they would be more reluctant to undertake constitutional revision. While public support for amending the constitution's security provisions has increased in recent years, it remains a highly controversial topic that divides the Japanese electorate. [46]

ASSESSMENT

A balanced assessment of the likelihood of change in Japanese government priorities in policy areas important to the United States shows a variety of constraints that dampen the prospects for substantial reprioritization of Japanese policies, especially regarding relations with the United States. [47]

- Media and other reporting indicate a strong consensus that the U.S. alliance remains central to Japan's security, and public opinion polls show that popular support for the alliance remains high. Any deliberate actions that would directly undermine the alliance would be very controversial and unlikely to succeed.
- Consensus building in a democracy in which power is increasingly diffuse will be much more difficult to achieve than in a one-party-dominated, bureaucrat-controlled government, especially when virtually all subjects are debatable.
- Japanese leaders remain cautious and status quo oriented. In many ways, they are riding a wave of change, not driving it.
- Expected low economic growth will reinforce a status quo orientation and limit the resources available to substantially increase funding for Japan's current force modernization plans or other government spending initiatives.
- Although the political system is fluid, the political spectrum on key issues is generally bounded. On security issues, for example, the extreme left, as represented by the socialists, has been marginalized since the Soviet Union's collapse, leaving the political "center" somewhat more conservative. An abrupt upswing in leftist sentiment opposing the alliance is consequently less likely than other types of security shifts.
- Polling data indicates that antimilitarism and pacifist sentiment remain strong, especially among the elderly. This sentiment will dictate a cautious, incremental approach to any changes in how Japan uses its military, as demonstrated by the difficulties of achieving even relatively modest changes in Japan's legislation on these matters.

- Tokyo's appeal to the United States and Japan's neighbors for support in the face of a coercive China means that Japanese leaders also will be wary of drawing a negative reaction from Asian neighbors by moving unilaterally to increase defense capabilities or by taking steps that appear to pull away from the U.S. alliance.

The strength of these limitations on changes to Japanese priorities remains difficult to assess given the magnitude and pace of transformation occurring in Japanese society, politics, economics, and the regional security situation. Absent dramatic changes in the external environment that would greatly heighten Japan's sense of vulnerability, these factors will continue to limit the country's freedom of action on key issues. Should the external environment markedly worsen, however, most of these constraints probably would weaken, and some probably would be overwhelmed.

In such circumstances, developments that could prompt change in Japan substantially at odds with U.S. interests include Japanese anxiety about the depth of U.S. commitment to the alliance and about the asymmetry in the alliance, with Japan in a subordinate role. Japanese change at odds with U.S. interests might involve initiatives coming out of the wide-ranging debate over security policy, which features calls for revision of the constitution to allow for active national security policy and practice, calls for strong military action to deter North Korea and/or China, and even calls for Japan to consider development of nuclear weapons in order to keep sufficient deterrent in its own hands against such dangers as North Korea and China.

PRIORITIES AND ISSUES IN RECENT U.S. POLICY TOWARD JAPAN

The Obama administration rebalance policy puts a premium on improving relations with allies. In the case of Japan, the most important American ally in Asia, the policy has meant close attention to regional issues and related military and economic priorities. [48]

REGIONAL ISSUES

Prime Minister Abe has embraced the alliance with the United States and the Obama government rebalance policy initiatives. He increased Japan's defense budget for the first time in ten years, carried out defense reforms that enhanced Japanese military capabilities, and secured approval for the construction of a new U.S. Marine Corps base on Okinawa that was such a source of controversy during the DPJ government of Prime Minister Yukio Hatoyama (2009–2010). The LDP leader also entered Japan into the U.S.-led

Trans-Pacific Partnership free trade agreement negotiations, moved to restart Japan's economy, and sought economic reforms favored by many in the United States. Abe welcomed statements by President Obama and other senior leaders affirming strong support to Japan against Chinese pressure and intimidation and opposition to forceful change in the status quo in the Senkaku (Diaoyu) Islands.

Abe's December 2013 visit to the Yasukuni Shrine surprised American officials who had discouraged such action. As noted above, U.S. leaders had worked hard to bridge differences between South Korea and Japan over historical and territorial disputes. In particular, the United States sought to bring the three allies together in a united effort to deal with regional problems, notably North Korea and its development of nuclear weapons and other provocations. The trilateral arrangement was also deemed useful in strengthening the American officials as they tried to deter China from continuing its coercive expansion of control over disputed maritime territory at the expense of its neighbors.[49]

As noted earlier, China and South Korea are particularly sensitive to Japanese officials supporting this shrine which houses the spirits of several Class A war criminals from World War II along with those of Japanese who died in this and other wars. More broadly, China and South Korea see evidence that the Japanese government has neither sufficiently atoned for nor adequately compensated them for Japan's occupation and belligerence in the early twentieth century. Abe's cabinet includes a number of politicians well known for advocating nationalist, and in some cases ultranationalist, views that many argue appear to glorify Imperial Japan's actions. American officials reflect wariness that Abe or his associates may take steps or make statements about history that inflame regional relations, disrupt regional trade integration, threaten security cooperation among U.S. allies, and further disturb already tense relations with China.

In his first term as prime minister (2006–2007), Abe took a generally pragmatic approach to history issues and regional relations and had some success in mending poor relations with Seoul and Beijing. During his second term (2012–), Abe made, and then recanted, controversial statements that upset China and South Korea. In April 2013, his comments to the Diet suggested that his government would not reaffirm the apology for Japan's wartime actions issued by former prime minister Tomiichi Murayama in 1995, Japan's most significant official apology for wartime acts. Yet, from the earliest days of the Abe administration, his chief spokesman has said that the Abe government will abide by the Murayama statement.

Territorial Dispute with China

Abe inherited a tense confrontation with China over the disputed Senkaku (Diaoyu) Islands and has remained firm in resisting Chinese coercion and attempted intimidation. Coincident with the mass anti-Japanese demonstrations throughout China in reaction to the Japanese purchase of islands in September 2012, Beijing began regularly deploying maritime law enforcement ships near the islands and stepped up what it called "routine" patrols to assert jurisdiction in "China's territorial waters." Chinese military surveillance planes reportedly entered airspace that Japan considers its own, in what Japan's Defense Ministry called the first such incursion in fifty years. Encounters have become more frequent; both countries have scrambled fighter jets, and, according to the Japanese government, a Chinese navy ship locked its fire-control radar on a Japanese destroyer and a helicopter on two separate occasions.

The United States takes no position on the territorial disputes. However, it also has been U.S. policy since 1972 that the 1960 U.S.-Japan Security Treaty covers the islets, because Article 5 of the treaty stipulates that the United States is bound to protect "the territories under the Administration of Japan," and Japan administers the islets. China's increase in patrols appears to be an attempt to demonstrate that Beijing has a degree of administrative control over the islets and to underline that Japan must acknowledge that the territory is in dispute and begin negotiations with China on the dispute. Japan refuses to acknowledge that the islands are in dispute. The Abe government saw the Senkaku/Diaoyu conflict as part of a broader Chinese security challenge. The maritime confrontation with Beijing is a concrete manifestation of the threat Japan has faced for years from China's rising regional power. It also brings into relief Japan's dependence on the U.S. security guarantee and its anxiety that Washington will not defend Japanese territory if it risks going to war with China.

As discussed in chapter 5, the United States at first worked to calm the tensions once the active confrontations began in 2012 between China and Japan in the East China Sea and between China and the Philippines and Vietnam in the South China Sea. As time went on, China employed various tactics designed to intimidate Japan, the Philippines, and Vietnam that the United States viewed as provocative and destabilizing. While Washington remained neutral on which side had sovereignty over the territory, it took much sharper aim against Chinese coercive tactics against Japan as well as the South China Sea disputants. In effect, America took sides, publicly supporting its Japanese ally, as well as U.S. ally the Philippines and Vietnam in the South China Sea, against Chinese coercion and intimidation seen by Washington as out of line with international norms.

China's November 2013 announcement that it would establish an air defense identification zone (ADIZ) saw Washington weigh in publicly against Chinese actions. China had not consulted with affected countries, and so they were unprepared; the announcement used vague and ominous language that seemed to promise military enforcement within the zone; the requirements for flight notification in the ADIZ went beyond international norms and impinged on the freedom of navigation; and the overlap with other countries' ADIZs could lead to accidents or unintended clashes, thus raising the risk of conflict in the East China Sea. Outside of China, the ADIZ was widely interpreted as a challenge to Japanese administration of the Senkaku (Diaoyu) Islands. [50]

In response to the Chinese move, the United States and Japan tried to coordinate closely and at a high level in their individual and collective responses to the new situation. Secretary of Defense Chuck Hagel declared that the ADIZ was a destabilizing attempt to alter the status quo and would not change how the U.S. military conducts operations. At a press conference during his previously scheduled visit to Tokyo in early December 2013, Vice President Joseph Biden said, "We, the United States, are deeply concerned by the attempt to unilaterally change the status quo in the East China Sea. . . . I told the Prime Minister that we will remain steadfast in our alliance commitments."

American officials expressed appreciation for Japan's measured response in what could have been a combustible situation. Reportedly, the United States and Japan agreed to increase their reconnaissance and surveillance activities in the East China Sea, presumably to monitor Chinese practices in the new ADIZ. A minor U.S.-Japan disagreement showed when the State Department said on November 29, 2013, that the United States generally expects U.S. commercial air carriers to follow notices to airmen (NOTAMs), including Chinese requests for identification in the controversial ADIZ. This official guidance appeared to contradict the stated policy that the U.S. government does not accept China's requirements for operating in the ADIZ. On the instruction of the Japanese government, Japanese commercial airlines did not respond to Chinese identification requests when traveling through the newly declared ADIZ on routes that do not cross into Chinese airspace.

More recently, U.S. officials have taken a hard public line against Chinese assertiveness over disputes in the East and South China Seas. President Obama affirmed strong support for the alliance and affirmed the applicability of the U.S.-Japan alliance to the Senkaku (Diaoyu) Islands during his April 2014 visit to Japan. Tensions eased somewhat in the lead-up to a brief meeting between Abe and Chinese president Xi Jinping at the APEC meeting in Beijing in November 2014, though the outlook for Japan-China relations remained uncertain. [51]

Japan's Ties with Korea

North Korea

Japan's policy toward North Korea has hardened in recent years. Japan insisted on North Korea abandoning its nuclear weapons and development programs. At times, Japan promised substantial aid in return. The Japanese government took steps to squeeze North Korea with restrictions on economic and trade relations with Japan. It also participated in the U.S.-led Proliferation Security Initiative (PSI), which guards against proliferation of weapons of mass destruction (WMD) from North Korea and other international proliferators. Japan took the lead in seeking UN measures against North Korean ballistic missile tests in July 2006 and its nuclear weapons test in October 2006.

The issue of Japanese citizens kidnapped in the 1970s and 1980s by North Korean agents drove the governments of Prime Minister Koizumi (2001–2006) and the first administration of Prime Minister Abe (2006–2007) to a harder stance toward North Korea. The U.S. administration and the U.S. Congress supported Japan's insistence on a full accounting of the fate of those abducted. Subsequently, Japanese officials were dismayed by reports of rapid progress in confidential U.S.–North Korean negotiations marking an abrupt change in the Bush administration's theretofore hard-line approach to Pyongyang. The U.S. shift followed and was seen in Japan to reward North Korea following its first nuclear test. The U.S. position appeared at odds with Tokyo's continued hard line with Pyongyang over the Japanese abducted by North Korea and nuclear weapons issues.[52]

At times, Japan also adopted a more flexible position in talks with North Korea. Outside the framework of U.S.-led six-party talks, Koizumi pursued an independent channel of diplomacy with North Korea and held summits with North Korean leader Kim Jong Il in September 2002 and May 2004. Nonetheless, Koizumi and his successor Abe made normalization of Japan's relations with North Korea contingent on a settlement of the nuclear weapons and abduction issues.

During the Obama government beginning in 2009, Washington and Tokyo have been strongly united in their approach to North Korea. Their policies toward North Korea have also been more or less in sync with the conservative governments ruling in South Korea during this time. Pyongyang's string of provocations involving a nuclear weapons test and surprise attacks sinking a South Korean warship and bombarding a South Korean island in 2009–2010 forged a new consensus among Japan, South Korea, and the United States. North Korea's 2012 missile launches and the third nuclear weapons test in February 2013 helped to drive enhanced trilateral security cooperation among Washington, Tokyo, and Seoul.

As of late 2014, multilateral negotiations over North Korea's nuclear programs remain at a standstill. Tokyo has adopted a relatively hard-line policy against North Korea and has played a leadership role at the United Nations in pushing for stronger punishment of the Pyongyang regime for its military provocations and human rights abuses. Japan has imposed a virtual embargo on all trade with North Korea. North Korea's missile tests have demonstrated that a strike on Japan is well within range, spurring Japan to invest in ballistic missile defense (BMD) capabilities and to enhance BMD cooperation with the United States.

In addition to Japan's concern about North Korean missile and nuclear programs, the issue of the Japanese abductees remains a top priority for Tokyo. Japan pledged that it would not provide economic aid to North Korea without resolution of the abductees issue. In a surprising development, the Japanese government said in May 2014 that North Korea had agreed in recent secret bilateral talks to reopen investigations on the abductees. In return, Japan eased some sanctions against North Korea. Prime Minister Abe said the move was a "first step" toward resolving this issue. Other opinion was more reserved, influenced by the continuing erratic behavior of the Pyongyang regime.[53]

South Korea

Despite collaboration with Seoul and Washington over North Korea, Japan's relations with South Korea worsened in late 2013 and early 2014 over history issues in particular. Poor relations between Seoul and Tokyo continue to jeopardize U.S. interests by complicating trilateral cooperation on North Korea policy and other regional challenges. Tense relations also complicate the creation of an integrated U.S.–Japan–South Korea ballistic missile defense system. In 2012 Seoul abruptly canceled the signing of a military intelligence–sharing agreement with Tokyo, a pact long encouraged by the United States, due to public outcry in South Korea over the prospect of military cooperation with Japan.

South Korean leaders have objected to a series of statements and actions by Abe and his cabinet officials that have been interpreted as denying or even glorifying Imperial Japan's aggression in the early twentieth century. In particular, South Korean leaders stated that they would have difficulty holding a summit, or improving relations, unless Japan adopts a "correct understanding" of history. Abe's visit to Yasukuni in December 2013 underlined South Korean concerns.

Meanwhile, issues of Japanese history textbooks' interpretation of Japan's aggression and the territorial dispute between Japan and South Korea continue to periodically rile relations. A group of small islands in the Sea of Japan, known as Dokdo in Korean and Takeshima in Japanese (the U.S.

government calls them the Liancourt Rocks), are administered by South Korea but claimed by Japan.[54]

Japan's Relations with ASEAN, Australia, India, and Russia

In moves seen as designed to win support and gain leverage in the face of China's strong efforts to demonize and isolate him, Prime Minister Abe has visited all ten ASEAN states and has held high-level meetings with Australian, Indian, and Russian leaders. His rhetoric displays both power politics and an emphasis on democratic values, international laws, and norms. At the outset of his second term as prime minister, Abe released an article outlining his foreign and security policy strategy titled "Asia's Democratic Security Diamond," which described how the democracies Japan, Australia, India, and the United States could cooperate to deter Chinese aggression on its maritime periphery. In 2013, Japan held numerous high-level meetings with Asian countries to bolster relations and, in many cases, to enhance security ties. Abe had summit meetings in India, Russia, Great Britain, all ten countries in Southeast Asia, and several countries in the Middle East and Africa. This energetic diplomacy showed a desire to balance China's growing influence with a loose coalition of Asia-Pacific powers, but this strategy of realpolitik was couched in the rhetoric of international laws and democratic values. That President Obama embraced Japanese activism despite Chinese criticism came in a strong endorsement of U.S.-Japanese collaboration in advancing their collective interest and influence in Southeast Asia and the broader Asia-Pacific region in the official documents marking the president's 2014 visit to Japan.[55]

MILITARY AND ALLIANCE ISSUES[56]

Collective Self-Defense

Since the early 2000s, the United States and Japan have taken significant strides in improving the operational capability of the alliance as a combined force. As the two forces became more integrated in ways beneficial to both powers, Prime Minister Abe, a strong supporter of the alliance, has an ambitious agenda to increase the capability and flexibility of Japan's military. However, constitutional, legal, fiscal, and political barriers exist to significantly expanded defense cooperation. The most prominent debate involves relaxing or removing the self-imposed ban on Japanese forces participating in collective self-defense. Such measures face opposition from the public and from political parties. In addition, suspicion from Beijing and Seoul also complicates Japan's efforts to expand its security role.

Why collective self-defense is in American interests was explained by former Pacific commander and director of national intelligence Dennis Blair in a speech in Washington in April 2014.[57] In dealing with North Korean missile intimidation, Blair advised, Japanese and U.S. ballistic missile defense cruisers and destroyers should be part of a combined task group that includes U.S. satellite sensors and communications systems, both U.S. and Japanese shore-based radars, and Japanese and U.S. Patriot missile batteries in the region. South Korean systems should also be included in this defensive network.

The network should be deployed and operated so that it provides protection to the Republic of Korea, Japan, and the United States. Without an ability to exercise its right to collective self-defense, Japanese radars and missile systems may be employed only to protect Japan, thus precluding Tokyo from contributing to a regional air defense network.

In the event of major North Korean aggression against the Republic of Korea, Japanese contributions to defeating the attack would be vital, according to Blair. It is very much in the national interests of Japan, South Korea, and the United States to defeat North Korea quickly and decisively. As in the first Korean War, Japan would be the transportation and logistics rear base for American reinforcements to Combined Forces Command in Korea. Now, however, as many U.S. bases in Japan are ranged by North Korean missiles, the United States would expect Japan to defend those bases as part of a regional air and missile defense network. In addition, there would be an air and sea bridge from Japan to South Korea, and Japan would be expected to defend that bridge against air attacks, submarine attacks, and mining. To meet these expectations and conduct missions that would bring the conflict to an end more quickly, the Japanese SDF must be able to engage in collective self-defense.

Blair also showed the benefits of the integration of Japanese forces, engaging in collective self-defense, working with American and other forces in contingencies involving the East China Sea, Taiwan, and international peacekeeping. He concluded that in the past the capabilities of potential regional aggressors were relatively weak, so that the United States and Japan could achieve their common objectives without their forces operating together in an integrated fashion. Current trends and future projections are not positive, and unless collective self-defense can be realized, he advised that it will take much higher levels of force on both the American and Japanese sides to keep the level of operational risk from increasing.

U.S. Marine Corps Air Station Futenma Replacement Facility, Okinawa

The United States and Japan in December 2013 overcame an important obstacle in the controversial plan to relocate MCAS Futenma. The governor of Okinawa Prefecture approved construction of an offshore landfill necessary to build the replacement facility. This new base, located in a sparsely populated area, would replace the functions of MCAS Futenma, located in the center of a crowded town in southern Okinawa.

Despite still strong local opposition, the governor's approval of the landfill permit in theory allowed Washington and Tokyo to consummate their agreement to return the land occupied by MCAS Futenma to local authorities while retaining a similar level of military capability on Okinawa. A U.S.-Japan joint planning document in April 2013 indicated that the new base would be completed no earlier than 2022.

The relocation of the Futenma base is part of a larger bilateral agreement developed by the U.S.-Japan Special Action Committee on Okinawa (SACO) in 1996. In the SACO Final Report, the United States agreed to return approximately 20 percent of land used for U.S. facilities on Okinawa, including all or parts of a dozen sites. Handover of MCAS Futenma was contingent on providing FRF. The plan for implementing the SACO agreement evolved over the late 1990s and early 2000s until Washington and Tokyo settled on a "road map" in 2006: once Japan constructed the FRF, the United States would relocate roughly eight thousand marines from Okinawa to Guam, about half of the U.S. Marine Corps (USMC) presence then on Okinawa. In 2012, the allies revised the implementation plan to "delink" the Futenma relocation and the realignment of marines to Guam; in other words, the construction of a replacement facility was no longer a precondition for deploying marines off Okinawa.[58]

Burden Sharing Ties

The Japanese government without notable complications provides nearly $2 billion per year to offset the cost of stationing U.S. forces in Japan. The United States spends an additional $2 billion per year on nonpersonnel costs for troops stationed in Japan.[59]

ECONOMIC ISSUES

As discussed above, the long-standing U.S. complaints about the persisting trade deficit with Japan and related market access issues have subsided and have been overshadowed by much more serious American issues with China.

Japan and the TPP

Intense negotiations during President Obama's April 2014 visit to Japan failed to bridge gaps between the two governments over Japan's accession to the TPP. The U.S. government places high priority on the proposed multilateral agreement and Japan's participation. The TPP is now an agreement under negotiation among the original four countries (Singapore, New Zealand, Chile, and Brunei) plus the United States, Australia, Canada, Mexico, Peru, Malaysia, Vietnam, and Japan. The negotiators envision a comprehensive arrangement to liberalize trade and to cover a broad range of trade and trade-related activities. The TPP is also seen as a "twenty-first-century" framework for addressing cross-cutting issues including regulatory coherence; competitiveness and business facilitation, also known as transnational supply and production chains; issues pertaining to small and medium-sized companies; economic development; and the operations of state-owned enterprises. The United States and other TPP countries expect that other economies in the region will seek to join in those negotiations or will accede to the agreement after it has been concluded.

Prior to Japan's joining the TPP negotiations, the Obama administration identified three issues that Japan needed to address: Japanese restrictions on imports of U.S. beef, market access for U.S.-made cars, and insurance and express delivery issues. The beef issues were addressed in 2013, so the other two are to be resolved.[60]

Energy

The United States and Japan cooperate smoothly on environmental and energy issues. Japan used to rely on nuclear power for 30 percent of its power generation capacity. The March 2011 disaster saw all of Japan's fifty-four nuclear reactors shut down, resulting in an enormous increase in the use of fossil fuels, notably liquefied natural gas (LNG). Because of the expanded shale gas production in the United States, the price of American LNG is lower than that of other providers. Japan is anxious to sign agreements for future deliveries of such gas from yet-to-be-completed LNG export terminals in the United States.[61]

NOTES

1. Peter Ennis, "Why Japan Still Matters," *Brookings East Asia Commentary*, no. 49 (May 2001); Nicholas Szechenyi, "The U.S.-Japan Alliance: Prospects to Strengthen the Asia-Pacific Order," in *Strategic Asia 2014–2015: U.S. Alliances and Partnerships at the Center of Global Power*, ed. Ashley Tellis, Abraham Denmark, and Greg Chaffin, 35–60 (Seattle, WA: National Bureau of Asian Research, 2014).

2. Richard Armitage and Joseph Nye, *U.S.-Japan Alliance: Getting Asia Right through 2020* (Washington, DC: Center for Strategic and International Studies, 2007).

3. Robert Sutter, "The United States and Asia in 2006: Crisis Management, Holding Patterns, and Secondary Initiatives," *Asian Survey* 47, no. 1 (January–February 2007): 12.

4. Michael Green, "U.S.-Japanese Relations after Koizumi: Convergence or Cooling?" *Washington Quarterly* 29, no. 4 (Autumn 2006): 101–10.

5. Jeffrey Bader, *Obama and China's Rise* (Washington, DC: Brookings Institution, 2012), 42–43; David Allen, "Japan to Revisit Base Plan, SOFA," *Stars and Stripes*, September 11, 2009, http://www.stripes.com/news/japan-to-revisit-base-plan-sofa-1.94627.

6. John Hemmings, "Understanding Hatoyama's East Asia Community Idea," *East Asia Forum*, January 22, 2010, http://www.eastasiaforum.org/2010/01/22/understanding-hatoyamas-east-asian-community-idea.

7. James Przystup, "Japan-China Relations," *Comparative Connections* 14, no. 3 (January 2013): 109–11.

8. Kosuke Takahashi, "Shinzo Abe's Nationalist Strategy," *The Diplomat*, February 13, 2014, http://thediplomat.com/2014/02/shinzo-abes-nationalist-strategy.

9. Mark Valencia, "Asian Threats, Provocations Giving Rise to Wiffs of War," *Japan Times*, June 9, 2014, http://www.japantimes.co.jp/opinion/2014/06/09/commentary/world-commentary/asian-threats-provocations-giving-rise-whiffs-war/#.U6VP6JRdXxA.

10. White House Office of the Press Secretary, *Fact Sheet: U.S.-Japan Global and Regional Cooperation*, April 25, 2014.

11. Takashi Oshima, "Interviews: American Observers of Japan-U.S. Relations Divided over Abe's Yasukuni Visit," *Asahi Shimbun*, April 7, 2014, http://ajw.asahi.com/article/views/opinion/AJ201404070001.

12. Sheila Smith, "U.S. Alliances in Northeast Asia" (testimony before the Senate Foreign Relations Committee, March 4, 2014), http://www.cfr.org/asia-and-pacific/us-alliances-northeast-asia/p32533; Kent Calder, *Pacific Alliance: Reviving U.S.-Japan Relations* (New Haven, CT: Yale University Press, 2009); Kenneth Pyle, *Japan Rising: The Resurgence of Japanese Power and Purpose* (New York: Public Affairs, 2007); Richard Samuels, *Securing Japan: Tokyo's Grand Strategy and the Future of East Asia* (Ithaca, NY: Cornell University Press, 2007); Thomas Berger, ed., *Japan in International Politics: The Foreign Policies of an Adaptive State* (Boulder, CO: Lynne Rienner, 2006); Ellis Krauss and T. J. Pempel, eds., *The U.S.-Japan Relationship in the New Asia-Pacific* (Stanford, CA: Stanford University Press, 2004); Steven K. Vogel, *U.S.-Japan Relations in a Changing World* (Washington, DC: Brookings Institution, 2002); Michael J. Green, *Japan's Reluctant Realism* (New York: Palgrave, 2001).

13. Samuel Kim, *The Two Koreas and the Great Powers* (New York: Cambridge University Press, 2006), 161.

14. Kent Calder, *Crisis and Compensation* (Princeton, NJ: Princeton University Press, 1988).

15. Green, *Japan's Reluctant Realism*.

16. Thomas Berger, "Japan's International Relations: The Political and Security Dimensions," in *The International Relations of Northeast Asia*, ed. Samuel S. Kim, 135–69 (Lanham, MD: Rowman & Littlefield, 2004).

17. Martin Flacker and Mark Landler, "Ties to U.S. Played Role in Downfall of Japanese Leader," *New York Times*, June 2, 2010, http://www.nytimes.com/2010/06/03/world/asia/03japan.html.

18. Takatoshi Ito, Hugh Patrick, and David Weinstein, eds., *Reviving Japan's Economy: Problems and Prescriptions* (Cambridge, MA: MIT Press, 2005); "Japan and Abenomics: Taxing Times," *Economist*, October 5, 2013, http://www.economist.com/news/asia/21587242-prime-minister-raises-controversial-tax-needs-be-bolder-yet-taxing-times.

19. Atsushi Kodera, "Economy Faces Headwinds in 2014," *Japan Times*, January 3, 2014, http://www.japantimes.co.jp/news/2014/01/03/business/economy-business/economy-faces-headwinds-in-2014/#.U6VdcZRdXxA.

20. Adam Posen, "Pragmatic Policy Progress: Recent Changes in and the Outlook for Japanese Economic Policy," in National Intelligence Council, *Change in Japan: Implications for U.S. Interests*, Conference Report CR 2000-01 (Washington, DC: GPO, 2000), 9–22; Uri Dadush, "The Truth about Japan's Economic Decline," Carnegie Endowment for International

Peace, April 25, 2014, http://carnegieendowment.org/2014/04/25/truth-about-japan-s-economic-decline/h93f; "Abenomics: Not So Super," *Economist*, June 15, 2014, http://www.economist.com/news/leaders/21579464-third-arrow-reform-has-fallen-well-short-its-target-time-shinzo-abe-rethink-not.

21. Edward Lincoln, "Implications of Economic Reform in Japan for U.S. Economic Interests," in National Intelligence Council, *Change in Japan*, 49–58.

22. The following discussion is based on William Cooper, *U.S.-Japan Economic Relations: Significance, Prospects and Policy Options*, Report RL32649 (Washington, DC: Library of Congress, Congressional Research Service, February 18, 2014), 1–5, 8–9.

23. Emma Chanlett-Avery, William Cooper, Mark Manyin, and Ian Rinehart, *Japan-U.S. Relations: Issues for Congress*, Report RL33436 (Washington, DC: Library of Congress, Congressional Research Service, February 20, 2014), 15.

24. Ian Bremmer, "Japan's Year of Resilience," Reuters, February 15, 2012, http://blogs.reuters.com/ian-bremmer/2012/02/15/japan%E2%80%99s-year-of-resilience.

25. *Chronology of Operation Tomodachi*, National Bureau of Asian Research, April 2011, http://www.nbr.org/research/activity.aspx?id=121.

26. Ken Koyama, "Japan's Post-Fukushima Energy Policy Challenges," *Asian Economic Policy Review* 8, no. 2 (December 2013): 274–93.

27. Quarterly National Accounts, *OECD StatExtracts*, http://stats.oecd.org/Index.aspx?QueryName=350.

28. This and the following two paragraphs are taken from Cooper, *U.S.-Japan Economic Relations*, 3.

29. *X-RATES*, http://www.x-rates.com/table/?from=USD&amount=1.00 (accessed December 6, 2014).

30. Joshua Hausman and Johannes Wieland, *Abenomics Preliminary Analysis and Outlook* (Brookings Papers on Economic Activity, Spring 2014 Conference), http://www.brookings.edu/about/projects/bpea/papers/2014/abenomics-preliminary-analysis-and-outlook; "Japan's Changing Demography: Cloud or Silver Linings?," *Economist*, July 26, 2007, http://www.economist.com/node/9539825.

31. Cooper, *U.S.-Japan Economic Relations*, 11–14.

32. Richard Armitage and Joseph Nye, *U.S.-Japan Alliance: Getting Asia Right through 2020* (Washington, DC: Center for Strategic and International Studies, 2007).

33. Michael Yahuda, *The International Politics of the Asia-Pacific*, 3rd ed. (London: Routledge, 2011): 167.

34. These factors and developments are reviewed at length in, among others, Green, *Japan's Reluctant Realism*; Samuels, *Securing Japan*; Richard Bush, *The Perils of Proximity: China-Japan Security Relations* (Washington, DC: Brookings Institution, 2010); and Michael Swaine et al., *China's Military and the U.S.-Japan Alliance in 2030: A Strategic Net Assessment* (Washington, DC: Carnegie Endowment for International Peace, 2013).

35. Dick Nanto, *North Korea: Chronology of Provocations, 1950–2003*, Report RL30004 (Washington, DC: Library of Congress, Congressional Research Service, March 18, 2003).

36. Kim, *Two Koreas*, 157–224.

37. Minxin Pei and Michael Swaine, *Simmering Fire in Asia: Averting Sino-Japanese Strategic Conflict* (Washington, DC: Carnegie Endowment for International Peace, 2005); *Wall Street Journal*, "China-Japan Dispute," http://stream.wsj.com/story/china-japan-dispute/SS-2-58300/SS-2-60993/?mod=wsj_streaming_china-japan-dispute (accessed June 22, 2014).

38. Armitage and Nye, *U.S.-Japan Alliance*, 24; "Japan's Abe Turns to Southeast Asia to Counter China," Reuters, January 16, 2013, http://www.reuters.com/article/2013/01/16/us-japan-abe-asean-idUSBRE90F0LW20130116.

39. "G-7 Leaders Warn Russia of Fresh Sanctions over Ukraine," BBC News-Europe, June 5, 2014, http://www.bbc.com/news/world-europe-27707518.

40. Richard Samuels, "Japan's Goldilocks Strategy," *Washington Quarterly* 29, no. 4 (Autumn 2006); Michael Green and James Przystup, "The Abductee Issue Is a Test of America's Strategic Credibility," *PacNet*, no. 47 (Honolulu: CSIS Pacific Forum, November 15, 2007); Chanlett-Avery, Cooper, Manyin, and Rinehart, *Japan-U.S. Relations*.

41. Yo-jung Chen, "U.S.-Japan Relations and Obama's Visit to Japan," *The Diplomat*, April 23, 2014, http://thediplomat.com/2014/04/us-japan-relations-and-obamas-visit-to-japan.

42. Robert Sutter, *United States and East Asia* (Lanham, MD: Rowman & Littlefield, 2003), 133.

43. William Grimes, "The Changing Japanese Political System," *Journal of Japanese Studies* 33, no. 2 (Summer 2007): 565–69; "Japanese Politics: Moment of Reckoning," *Economist*, June 7, 2014, http://www.economist.com/news/asia/21603495-prime-ministers-attempts-reform-both-economy-and-pacifist-constitution-are-entering.

44. Benjamin Self, *The Dragon's Shadow: The Rise of China and Japan's New Nationalism* (Washington, DC: Stimson Center, 2006); Kosuke Takahashi, "Shinzo Abe's Nationalist Strategy," *The Diplomat*, February 13, 2014, http://thediplomat.com/2014/02/shinzo-abes-nationalist-strategy.

45. Jiro Yamaguchi, "Nationalistic Sentiment Keeps Abe's Popularity Ratings High," *Japan Times*, May 27, 2014, http://www.japantimes.co.jp/opinion/2014/05/27/commentary/japan-commentary/nationalistic-sentiment-keeps-abes-popularity-ratings-high/#.U6fVz5RdXxA.

46. Jeffrey Yellen, "Shinzo Abe's Constitutional Ambitions," *The Diplomat*, June 12, 2014, http://thediplomat.com/2014/06/shinzo-abes-constitutional-ambitions.

47. Szechenyi, "The U.S.-Japan Alliance."

48. White House Office of the Press Secretary, *Fact Sheet: U.S.-Japan Global and Regional Cooperation*, April 25, 2014; White House Office of the Press Secretary, *Fact Sheet: U.S.-Japan Bilateral Cooperation*, April 25, 2014; Szechenyi, "The U.S.-Japan Alliance"; Chanlette-Avery, Cooper, Manyin, and Rinehart, *Japan-U.S. Relations*.

49. Andrew Davis, "Kennedy Urges Japan, South Korea to Resolve Diplomatic Row," *Bloomberg*, March 6, 2014, http://www.bloomberg.com/news/2014-03-06/kennedy-urges-japan-south-korea-to-resolve-diplomatic-tensions.html.

50. Chanlette-Avery, Cooper, Manyin, and Rinehart, *Japan-U.S. Relations*, 2.

51. Michael Green and Nicholas Szechenyi, "US-Japan Relations," *Comparative Connections* 16, no. 1 (May 2014): 21–22; Michael Green and Nicholas Szechenyi, "US-Japan Relations," *Comparative Connections* 16, no. 3 (January 2015), http://www.csis.org/pacfor.

52. Robert Sutter, *The United States in Asia* (Lanham, MD: Rowman & Littlefield, 2009), 93.

53. Justin McCurry, "North Korea to Reopen Inquiry into Abductions during the Cold War," *The Guardian*, May 29, 2014, http://www.theguardian.com/world/2014/may/29/north-korea-reopen-inquiry-abductions-japanese-cold-war.

54. David Kang and Jiun Bang, "Japan-Korea Relations," *Comparative Connections* 16, no. 1 (May 2014): 129–31.

55. White House, *Fact Sheet: U.S.-Japan Global and Regional Cooperation*; Rory Medcalf, "Shizo Abe's Strategic Diamond," *The Diplomat*, January 15, 2013, http://thediplomat.com/2013/01/shinzo-abes-strategic-diamond.

56. Szechenyi, "The U.S.-Japan Alliance"; Chanlette-Avery, Cooper, Manyin, and Rinehart, *Japan-U.S. Relations*.

57. Dennis Blair, "Operational Impacts of Japan's New Security Strategy and Capabilities on the U.S.-Japan Alliance," speech, Sasakawa Peace Foundation, Washington, DC, April 30, 2014, http://www.spfusa.org/pdfs/2014/D.Blair_Speech-2014-4-30.pdf.

58. Chanlette-Avery, Cooper, Manyin, and Rinehart, *Japan-U.S. Relations*, 1–2, 19–22.

59. Ibid., 23–24.

60. White House, *Fact Sheet: U.S.-Japan Bilateral Cooperation*; Jonathan Soble and Shawn Donnan, "Obama and Abe Fail to Reach Trade Deal," *Financial Times*, April 25, 2014, http://www.ft.com/cms/s/0/6dde3056-cba9-11e3-8ccf-00144feabdc0.html#axzz35S61HTCE.

61. White House, *Fact Sheet: U.S.-Japan Bilateral Cooperation*.

Chapter Eight

U.S. Relations with Southeast Asia and the Pacific

After the high point of American strategic involvement in Southeast Asia during the failed war in Vietnam in the 1960s and 1970s, U.S. policy concerns in Southeast Asia and the nearby Pacific region were less important than the range of issues seen in U.S. relations with China, Japan, and Korea. In part this was because U.S. policy makers and opinion leaders generally saw less at stake for American interests in Southeast Asia and the Pacific than in Northeast Asia. U.S. military presence, trade and economic relations, and great power politics inevitably gave pride of place to Northeast Asia in American calculations. Facing demands from Philippine leaders, the United States closed its last military bases in Southeast Asia and withdrew in 1992. Opportunities for U.S. interests in Southeast Asia appeared limited. As the region recovered from the severe Asian economic crisis of 1997–1998, it remained subject to persistent political instability and economic uncertainty that curbed U.S. and other foreign investment. The instability and uncertainty also sapped the political power and importance of the Association of Southeast Asian Nations (ASEAN) and its leading members, adding to reasons for prevailing American skepticism about ASEAN's role at the center of growing Asian multilateral activism dealing with regional economic, political, and security issues.[1]

U.S. attention to the region rose in the first decade of the twenty-first century. The Bush administration–led global war on terrorism broadened and intensified U.S. involvement and concerns throughout Asia. Southeast Asia for a time became a "second front" in the U.S. struggle against terrorism. The United States worked closely with allies Australia, the Philippines, and Thailand, as well as with Singapore, Malaysia, and Indonesia, among others, in various efforts to curb terrorist activities in the region. These operations reinforced ongoing efforts by U.S. military, intelligence, and other security organizations to build closer relations with the vast majority of regional governments (Myanmar was the main exception).[2]

Following the Asian economic crisis, a variety of regional multilateral groupings centered on ASEAN and its Asian partners were formed and advanced significantly. China's stature and influence in these groups and among ASEAN states grew rapidly amid burgeoning intra-Asian trade and investment networks involving China in a central role, and in response to attentive and innovative Chinese diplomacy. China's increasing prominence was seen by many to steer the region in directions that reduced U.S. influence and worked against U.S. interests.[3] On the other hand, the massive and effective U.S.-led relief effort in the wake of the tsunami disaster in South and Southeast Asia in December 2004 showed unsurpassed American power and influence and underlined the continuing importance of the United States for regional stability and well-being.[4]

Against this background, U.S. interest grew. The government of President Obama and his evolving rebalance initiatives saw U.S. policy give much higher priority to Southeast Asia and the nearby Pacific. The United States appointed an ambassador to ASEAN and established a representative office at the ASEAN headquarters in Jakarta. After many years of deliberation and delay, it signed the ASEAN Treaty of Amity and Cooperation (TAC), a necessary condition for the United States to join important regional groupings convened by ASEAN, notably the East Asia Summit. President Obama participated actively in the summit meetings and in American summit meetings with the leaders of the ASEAN nations. The American secretaries of state and defense were regular participants in regional security meetings of the ASEAN Regional Forum and the ASEAN Defense Ministers Meetings. The United States strengthened alliances and partnerships with several countries including the Philippines, Indonesia, Malaysia, and Singapore. It engaged in business and other economic initiatives of mutual benefit.[5]

In announcing the new Obama government policy, Secretary of State Hillary Clinton alerted the world to the changed American view of Southeast Asia as the "fulcrum" of Asia's strategic and economic relations. Straddling the sea lines of communication between the Indian Ocean and the Pacific, Southeast Asia loomed much larger in the new American calculus, which saw U.S. interests in substantially broader terms than in the recent past, ranging from India in the west to Guam in the east and from Japan in the north to New Zealand in the south. Subsequent American initiatives featured efforts to draw Southeast Asian nations, Australia, New Zealand, and others into closer economic cooperation arrangements of benefit to the United States, notably the Trans-Pacific Partnership (TPP) arrangement. Ever-closer security and intelligence cooperation with these nations saw arrangements that substantially expanded American options for deployment of U.S. forces in dispersed ways that would be harder for a potential adversary like China to deter with its more concentrated area denial and anti-access deployments in areas along China's rim.[6]

In carrying out its new approach, the United States built on strong security relations developed with allies and associated states for many years as well as on long-standing government and nongovernment economic, social, educational, and political relations with the countries in the region. American policy recognized that most of these countries had become economically closely integrated with China, which became the main trading partner of most of its neighbors, and that China demonstrated careful diplomatic attentiveness in bilateral relations and multilateral forums. The regional governments did not wish to face a choice between the United States and China; they preferred good relations with both and expected Washington and Beijing to manage their competition in ways that did not disrupt the regional order.[7]

As a result, a bottom line for the Obama rebalance policy has been that an appropriate American mix of advancing U.S. interests sometimes in competition with those of China and sustaining stable American engagement with China remains a must. The balance can alter with circumstances. Notably, China's recent assertiveness over the South China Sea has put many neighboring countries on alert. Nonetheless, they generally seek American reassurance against Chinese ambitions that avoids the instability which they fear would come with U.S. actions that directly confront the Chinese expansion. Other requirements for successful implementation of the rebalance among regional governments involve meshing together economic, diplomatic, and security initiatives in ways that avoid overemphasis on the military dimension that is sometimes unpopular with regional populations and is possibly disruptive of regional stability, and providing tangible evidence that the planned U.S. elements under the rebalance policy are sustainable and likely to be carried out.

In assessing American relations with the countries and organizations of this region, observers are advised to use the lens of realism in international relations theory to evaluate the power politics underway in this broad-ranging and increasingly important part of the world.[8] In particular, Sino-American competition for influence involves military and nonmilitary dimensions, and it has intensified in recent years. The regional governments are called upon to adjust to the implications of moves by one power or the other. Meanwhile, there is an ever-stronger desire of most regional governments to prosper and develop in the existing international economic order involving ever more economic openness to trade, investment, and related interchange. This trend drives the governments to adhere to tenets of the generally liberal international order. Thus liberalism in international relations theory seems to provide an appropriate lens for understanding this feature of regional dynamics.[9] Finally, the strong emphasis on community building in ASEAN and the increasingly important regional groups convened by AS-EAN cannot be fully understood without close reference to constructivist thinking in world politics. This part of Asia is more influenced by community building than any other; its leaders seek a strong sense of "we-ness." The great powers involved in the region have been compelled to adapt to the norms that flow from the so-called ASEAN way of gradualism and decision by consensus.[10]

PRIORITIES IN SOUTHEAST ASIA AND THE PACIFIC

Until recently, the priorities of the governments in these parts of the Asia-Pacific generally had less importance for Washington's relations with Asia than had the priorities of governments in China, Japan, and Korea. The United States continued to play a leadership role in Southeast Asia, and the war on terrorism saw an upswing in the importance of the United States for the governments of the region.

As elsewhere in the Asia-Pacific region, the government leaders in Southeast Asia and the Pacific have generally endeavored to meet growing popular demand for greater economic development and nationalistic respect through balanced nation-building strategies. They have placed a premium on encouraging economic growth beneficial to broad segments of their societies. Most governments have tended to eschew radical ideologies and to emphasize conventional nationalism. The latter has seen some regional leaders, such as Malaysia's former prime minister Mahathir Mohamad, seek greater international prominence in defending their national interests in the face of perceived outside pressures or threats. Military power has developed in line with economic power, but few administrations in Southeast Asia and the Pacific have emphasized military power at the expense of economic development. Myanmar's long-ruling military junta was an exception to this trend, but the newly liberalized government reforms since 2011 have seen an emphasis on development and popular well-being.[11]

The post–Cold War economic and security environment witnessed major changes that created fundamental challenges and uncertainties for most governments in the region. The Asian economic crisis of 1997–1998 undermined the prominence of the region's newly industrializing economies, especially Thailand and Indonesia. What followed was a long and slow process of economic recovery under often weak administrations.[12]

Regional security seemed less certain following the withdrawal of U.S. forces from bases in the Philippines as demanded by the Manila government in the early 1990s. U.S. security interests in the area revived strongly after the terrorist attacks on the World Trade Center and the Pentagon in 2001.

Some regional governments had strong differences with the coercive U.S. focus against terrorism in Southeast Asia, which the United States for a time emphasized was a "second front" in the global war on terrorism. The U.S.-led war in Iraq and other U.S. policies in the Middle East were widely criticized. At the same time, however, the United States managed to build upgraded military relations with most leading Southeast Asian governments, which quietly welcomed closer security ties with the United States in the uncertain regional security environment. [13]

China's growing economic and military advances were initially viewed with considerable alarm in Southeast Asia. Over time, Beijing's good neighbor policies and cooperative economic proposals went far toward reassuring area governments about Chinese policies and behavior. More recent Chinese assertiveness and expansion at others' expense in the South China Sea, however, have renewed regional angst over Chinese coercion and intimidation. Japan remained an important economic and political partner of Southeast Asian governments, as well, but Japan's prominence in the region declined with the stagnation of the Japanese economy throughout much of the post–Cold War period. India's expanding economy and growing military power on the whole were welcomed by Southeast Asian governments. The governments encouraged various powers—the United States, China, Japan, India, and others, such as the European Union, Russia, and Australia—to deepen their involvement in the region and thereby create a security environment where the danger of one outside power dominating the region would be reduced. [14]

The Asian economic crisis had its most serious impact in Indonesia, bringing down the authoritarian Suharto government, but it also provided a central challenge to the other leading states in ASEAN. The founding members of ASEAN in 1967 were Indonesia, the Philippines, Thailand, Malaysia, and Singapore. Five notably weaker Southeast Asian states—Brunei, Myanmar, Cambodia, Laos, and Vietnam—joined later. Only Singapore, with its modern and globally integrated economy and efficient civil service, was relatively well positioned to weather the economic crisis and pursue its interests forthrightly in regional and world affairs. However, even this technically successful city-state was increasingly unsettled by the massive difficulties in neighboring Indonesia and by a broader cycle of economic and political weakness throughout ASEAN. It sought assurance through closer ties with the United States, Australia, the European Union, Japan, and China. While continuing to give public emphasis to fostering ASEAN unity, it sought a diversified range of security and economic contacts and guarantees that would help to sustain and preserve Singapore's interests in the prevailing atmosphere of economic and political uncertainty. [15]

At the start of the twenty-first century, prevailing trends seemed to forecast an outlook for Southeast Asia of mixed recovery from the many consequences of the Asian economic crisis, along with continued political and economic uncertainty. This outlook posed challenges for democratic growth and interests in good governance, development, and regional cooperation. It reinforced the prevailing preoccupation of most regional governments with internal economic and political difficulties. [16]

ASEAN became more prominent as the venue and convener of a variety of emerging regional multilateral organizations that achieved greater prominence in this period. The organization was seriously weakened by the collapse of the Suharto administration, ASEAN's previous leader, and Indonesia's slow revival. There were also serious internal weaknesses and problems in Thailand and the Philippines. ASEAN's annually changed leadership meant that leadership by governments like Cambodia's and Laos's seemed less than optimal in promoting effective policy and practice in the organization. China's more assertive policy over the South China Sea saw Beijing manipulate the ASEAN chair, Cambodia, and thereby publicly split ASEAN leaders on this issue at meetings in 2012. [17]

In the face of Bush administration foreign policies seen as offensive in Southeast Asia, there was plenty of criticism of the United States and its policies, though the potential for region-wide anti-Western and anti-American activity remained low. For a time, contests for political power and terrorist threats in Indonesia and other Southeast Asian countries generated sporadic protests and occasional violent clashes that increased the threat environment for U.S., Australian, and other Western nationals. Radical Islamic groups and others opposed to the U.S. antiterrorism campaign also threatened U.S. personnel and interests in several Southeast Asian nations. [18]

Following are the key trends in the region during this period:

Leadership instability. Short-term presidencies in the Philippines and Indonesia early in the decade were followed by the onset of what would turn out to be protracted political instability in Thailand, begun after a military coup backed by the Thai king replaced the elected government in 2006 and running up to the most recent military coup in 2014. [19]

Fragile political liberalization. Democratic institutions and established political practices remained weak. The 2006 coup in Thailand and another coup in 2014 highlighted ongoing politically motivated disturbances that seriously undermined democratic governance. Democratic practices gradually took hold in Indonesia, and the military leadership in Myanmar gave way to a considerable degree to a more pluralistic political order. Nevertheless, authoritarian rule prevailed in Vietnam, Laos, and Cambodia. Long-standing ASEAN members Singapore, Malaysia, and the Philippines were ranked by Freedom House as partly free. In many states, traditions of authoritarianism were strong and prevented the development of cooperative legislative-executive relations. The region's legacy of military-led politics remained in play: civilian leaders often were wary of military intentions but sought to cultivate military support. Testing the limits of constitutional amendments, decentral-ization laws, and other newly created political mechanisms added to the atmosphere of unpredictability.[20]

Steadier economic growth. Economic recovery and reform after the 1997 Asian economic crisis were hampered by a negative cycle seen in such lead-ing regional states as Indonesia, the Philippines, and Thailand, where weak economic conditions fueled demands for political change, which then dis-tracted the region's leaders from effective economic policy, thus furthering public discontent. Regional economies eventually grew at an average rate of over 5.5 percent in 2000–2007. The downturn from the global economic crisis and recession beginning in 2008 was more limited in Southeast Asia than in the West. The economies had a 4.6 average growth rate in 2011 and were projected to grow by 5.5 percent in the 2013–2017 period. The Organ-isation for Economic Co-operation and Development (OECD) predicted in 2012 that Southeast Asian economies will show resilience through 2017, maintaining the same 5.5 percent annual level of growth momentum as dur-ing the precrisis period, although real gross domestic product (GDP) growth in the rest of so-called emerging Asia, in particular China, will begin to slow gradually. It concluded that the impact of global uncertainty has remained limited overall and that domestic demand growth, particularly private con-sumption and investment, will be the main driver of growth in most cases. Growth will be less reliant on net exports than in the past.[21]

Evidence of these trends and their mixed implications was prevalent among several of the leading governments in Southeast Asia over the past decade.

INDONESIA

Political and economic conditions appeared to be stabilizing in Indonesia after several years of upheaval following the demise of the Suharto regime in the late 1990s. Reforms continued to be implemented. The presidency of Susilo Bambang Yudhoyono (SBY), who was in power in 2004–2014, pro-vided the most stable and effective government administration in decades. Expanded civil society and a vigorous and open media have helped to sup-port and safeguard democratic governance. In addition to the direct election of the president, the military no longer has seats in Parliament, and the police have been separated from the military. Indonesia's parliamentary elections in April 2004, and the presidential elections of July and September 2004, were deemed by international observers to be free and fair; the parliamentary and presidential elections of 2009 and 2014 further consolidated democratic governance.[22]

Indonesia weathered the recent global economic downturn comparatively well. While gross national product (GNP) growth dipped from 6 percent in 2008 to 4.5 percent in 2009, it rose to around 6.1 percent in 2010, 6.46 percent in 2011, 6.23 percent in 2012, and 5.78 percent in 2013. Growth has been driven by private consumption and investment. Indonesia's comparative lack of exposure to export markets in the United States and Europe helped, as has its resource base and favorable demographics. Such growth is needed to keep pace with population growth. The number of Indonesians in poverty has declined significantly in recent years, though estimates in 2010 said close to 20 percent of the population was below a poverty income level of $1.25 a day (purchasing power parity, or PPP).[23]

The relatively good performance of the Indonesian economy was thought to be at least partially responsible for the electorate's support for President SBY and his Democrat Party in the 2009 elections. Poverty alleviation, social welfare, and jobs were central issues in those elections. For this reason, economic growth will likely continue to be a priority for government rulers. Nonetheless, Indonesia will continue to struggle with poverty, and corruption also remains a major problem.

Despite having long been a key oil exporter, Indonesia has in recent years become a net oil importer. A strong economy, population growth, and state subsidies for fuels have worked together to push domestic oil demand beyond supply. Fuel subsidies cost the government $18 billion in 2012, pressuring the government to reduce fuel subsidy spending. Indonesia's rising domestic demand and waning oil production in the past few years have led to increased import levels of both crude oil and petroleum products.[24]

Natural gas production has increased by almost 25 percent between 2002 and 2012. While Indonesia still exports about half of its natural gas, domestic consumption is increasing in tandem with production. Indonesia was the fourth-largest liquefied natural gas (LNG) exporter in 2013, following Qatar, Malaysia, and Australia. Expected growth in natural gas demand led the government to pursue policies that secure domestic natural gas supplies for the local market.[25]

Indonesia remains the world's largest exporter of coal by weight and exports about 75 percent of its production. Indonesia's coal production, mostly bituminous and subbituminous, has climbed sharply over the past decade. Indonesia's government encourages the use of coal in the power sector because of the relatively abundant domestic supply. Coal use also reduces the use of expensive diesel and fuel oil.[26]

A positive development was major progress in 2005–2006 in implementing a settlement of the protracted conflict with separatist forces in Aceh.[27] Discussion of Indonesia has shifted from speculation at the turn of the century about its possible breakup due to separatist sentiments in places such as Aceh, the Malukus, West Papua, and the now independent state of Timor-

Leste. More common are admiration of its democratic transformation, its relatively strong performance in the recent global economic crisis, its cooperation in efforts to combat terrorism, its growing role in regional diplomatic institutions and international efforts to combat climate change, and its membership in the G-20.[28]

Fear of terrorism fostered by radical Islamists and other promoters of intercommunal and other violence is on the wane. The vast majority of Indonesians practice a moderate form of Islam; a very small radical minority has sought to establish an Islamic state. Some extremists are hostile to the Christian minority, and an even smaller group would use violence to establish an Islamic Caliphate throughout the Muslim areas of Southeast Asia.

Representing only a very small percentage of the population, such groups for a time created much internal turmoil in Indonesia. They included groups such as the now disbanded Lashkar Jihad, which focused on Indonesian intercommunal conflict between Muslims and Christians in Maluku, and factions of Jemaah Islamiyah (JI), which used terrorist methods to promote an extreme Islamist agenda with linkages to al-Qaeda. There were allegations that Lashkar Jihad was a tool of hard-liners within the military that opposed the reform movement and enabled Lashkar Jihad activities that destabilized the nation, thereby highlighting the need for a strong military that could impose order. There has also been intergroup conflict elsewhere in Indonesia such as between Muslims and Christians in Sulawesi and the Maluku, and between local Dayaks and internal Madurese migrants in Kalimantan.[29]

Meanwhile, there have been challenges to the secular nature of the Indonesian state over cultural and moral issues. Not only the strictly fundamentalist Muslims but also more traditional Muslims protest the influence of Western cultural and moral values in Indonesian society.

Preoccupation with many internal issues made Indonesia's regional leadership weaker than in the past. The country's neighbors were also alienated by unregulated dry-season forest fires that sent clouds of choking smoke across the region. Because of such deforestation, Indonesia is the world's third-largest contributor to rising greenhouse gasses. Relations with Australia are negatively affected by Australian immigration and human rights issues but have witnessed greater cooperation in military and antiterrorism activities. Both the Bush and Obama governments gave high priority to improving relations with Indonesia, notably by increasing military contacts and exchanges, and China is endeavoring to improve relations as part of its politically reassuring and economically growing presence in Southeast Asia. Indonesia reportedly sided with Japan and Singapore in opposing a Chinese-supported effort to limit the 2005 East Asia Summit to ASEAN+3 countries, which allowed India, Australia, and New Zealand to participate and left the door open for U.S. participation.[30] Indonesia has reacted cautiously to China's coercion and expansion in the disputed South China Sea; it has stressed adherence to provisions of international law and ASEAN-China agreements seemingly at odds with Beijing's recent behavior.[31]

THE PHILIPPINES

The Philippines experienced considerable leadership and political turmoil prior to the election in 2010 of President Benigno Aquino. President Joseph Estrada's ouster in January 2001 came in part after active-duty and retired military officers shifted their support to then vice president Gloria Macapa-gal-Arroyo. Advised by former president and retired general Fidel Ramos, Arroyo was committed to tackling the country's economic problems. But she also needed to keep her disparate backers together as she faced continued opposition, including efforts by Estrada and his remaining supporters and other political rivals in the Philippine elites to undermine her.

By 2006, political instability had worsened as a wide range of groups endeavored to force Arroyo from power. They failed when Arroyo resorted to proclamations, restrictions, and bans on political activities and demonstrations and sought the support of the military. The president appeared to be alienated from the political elites in Manila and relied on military leaders and alliances with provincial political leaders. In this uncertain political situation, there was widespread dissatisfaction with the Philippines' dysfunctional democracy, but there was no consensus on how it should be reformed.[32]

The Arroyo administration added to the internal instability by launching an intensified conflict with the Communist Party of the Philippines and its armed wing, the New People's Army. The administration also carried out repression of leftist activists in various political and other organizations. This resulted in scores of "politically targeted extrajudicial executions," according to Amnesty International. At the same time, the government made progress in peace talks, brokered by Malaysia, to reach a settlement in the long-running conflict between the government and the Moro Liberation Front. That breakthrough came as the Philippine military, backed by U.S. troops deployed to the southern Philippines in recent years, continued efforts to suppress the small extremist Abu Sayyaf Group, which has been linked to abductions and terrorist attacks and to connections with broader Southeast Asian terrorist groups.[33]

President Arroyo faced low approval ratings throughout her presidency. There were important instances of political corruption. By contrast, Benigno Aquino built on the stature of his mother, a former president, and father, a revolutionary martyr. Aquino retained high public approval ratings four years into his presidency and a reputation for eschewing corruption. Elected president in 2010 by a large margin, Aquino's presidency has represented to many a political and cultural shift in the Philippines—a move toward cleaner government, greater sensitivity to political and economic grievances, and less emphasis on eradicating Muslim and communist insurgencies through military means. In May 2013, Aquino's Liberal Party performed strongly in midterm parliamentary and local elections, giving the president a strong political mandate until the end of his term in 2016.[34]

Arroyo's economic policies saw an annual growth of 6 percent in 2006. That year, foreign direct investment increased substantially from past years, and there was a rise in remittances by an estimated eight million Filipinos overseas to a level worth $12 billion. This good news was offset by continued gross inequities that saw massive poverty and unemployment, widespread child malnutrition, and poor access to education.[35]

Since then, the Philippines has experienced steady economic growth, averaging annual growth rates of about 5 percent. Though its long-term economic expansion has been slower than that of some of its Southeast Asian neighbors, growth has accelerated substantially over the past two to three years, with some observers describing the Philippines as one of the strongest-performing economies in the region. The economy is forecast to expand by 6.7 percent in 2014, slightly less than the estimated 6.9 percent growth of 2013. According to some analysts, GDP growth is expected to continue to be strong despite the costs of Typhoon Yolanda (Haiyan), which devastated the island nation in November 2013 with an estimated cost of $13 billion.

Foreign direct investment (FDI) has also improved. Although FDI in the Philippines remains low by regional standards, it has been growing at a faster rate than that in neighboring countries—185 percent in 2012, to $2.8 billion. Both Moody's and Standard & Poor's upgraded the country's credit rating to full investment grade in 2013. Last year, the World Bank's International Finance Corporation ranked the Philippines 108th out of 189 economies in the world for "ease of doing business," an improvement of 30 places compared to 2012. The Philippines is the world's fourth-largest recipient of remittances, after India, China, and Mexico. Remittances from over ten million overseas Filipino workers (OFW) totaled an estimated $26 billion in 2013, representing about 10 percent of GDP and the largest source of foreign exchange after exports.[36]

President Arroyo improved relations with China while sustaining close security and other ties with the United States. She used her position as the rotating chair of ASEAN in 2006–2007 to enhance her international profile as a means to build greater legitimacy abroad and at home.[37] Aquino saw relations with China deteriorate sharply as China moved more coercively but short of using military force to defend its claimed territory at Manila's expense in the South China Sea. Few in Southeast Asia took sides with the Philippines. As Chinese expansion continued, Japan, the United States, and Australia showed support and condemned Chinese tactics.

Against this background, the Philippines has played a key role in the Obama administration's rebalance to Asia, particularly as maritime territorial disputes between China and other claimants in the South China Sea have intensified. The U.S. government has pledged greater security assistance to the Philippines as joint military exercises reorient from a domestic focus to an outward one. In 2013, after attempting other means of resolving its disputes with China, the Philippines formally requested that an arbitral tribunal under the UN Convention on the Law of the Sea (UNCLOS) rule on whether China's claims and actions comply with the Law of the Sea. China objected strongly. The United States is not a party to UNCLOS and does not take a position on the territorial disputes between the Philippines and China, but the U.S. government supports the Philippine initiative and a peaceful resolution that is based upon international law and involves multilateral processes. In the face of strong pressure from Chinese expansion at the expense of Philippine claims in the South China Sea, the United States and the Philippines agreed in April 2014 to a ten-year Enhanced Defense Cooperation Agreement that will allow much greater American military rotations through various Philippine military installations and will enhance American efforts to build the country's defense capabilities and establish areas of closer cooperation with the United States. [38]

THAILAND

The military coup in 2014 represents the latest round of political turmoil in Thailand since the coup of 2006. Domestic politics continue to preoccupy Thai leaders. [39] The problems go back to the January 2001 elections in Thailand—overwhelmingly won by the Thai Rak Thai party of Thaksin Shinawatra—which were clouded by a corruption investigation. The courts eventually ruled in Thaksin's favor. Despite Thaksin's great popularity in rural areas, opposition politicians, academics, journalists, and middle-class residents of Bangkok showed growing concern that the prime minister's government was eroding the mechanisms and principles of democracy. Worries centered on developments such as the undermining of independent monitoring agencies that were supposed to be neutral, creating new emergency laws that overrode constitutional guarantees, and weakening the independence of the media. There were also widespread charges of extensive corruption involving the prime minister and his family and associates. [40]

The opposition boycotted the parliamentary election in April 2006 and triggered a constitutional crisis. Thaksin remained a caretaker prime minister. At the instigation of the king, the judiciary investigated the 2006 elections and found irregularities, and the Constitutional Court annulled the election. Fear of violence, along with perceptions of corruption and the undermining of democracy and royal authority, added to problems associated with an insurgency in the south and divisions within the military. These developments prompted military leaders to stage a coup in September and oust Thaksin before the expected elections on October 15.[41] It took over a year after the coup to agree on a new constitution and hold elections, which Thaksin's party won. Subsequently, the struggle between Thaksin (now in exile) and his opponents, a mix of conservative royalists and military figures, and other Bangkok elites has gone through stages. Despite his exile, pro-Thaksin political parties have repeatedly won nationwide elections since his ouster. The most recent elected government was led by Thaksin's younger sister, Prime Minister Yingluck Shinawatra (2011–2014). Recent years have seen mass movements both supporting and opposing Thaksin stage vigorous demonstrations, including protests in 2010 that caused riots in Bangkok and other cities, resulting in the worst street violence in Thailand in decades. Large-scale anti-Thaksin demonstrations in November and December 2013 forced Prime Minister Yingluck to dissolve Parliament. Thailand was without a fully functioning government prior to the military coup of May 2014.

Traditional Thai elites—particularly the military's top brass and many prominent royalist figures—remain deeply opposed to Thaksin and any indication that he might seek to return to a political role in Thailand. But Thaksin (and Yingluck) have support in poorer regions, stemming from populist programs Thaksin pursued during his rule. Thaksin's ouster has brought out divisions that had been emerging for years between the growing middle class and the poorer rural population. Risks are heightened by uncertainty about the health of Thailand's widely revered King Bhumiphol Adulyadej, who is eighty-seven and has been hospitalized for much of the past four years.[42]

Thailand's economy performed reasonably well during the nation's years of political turmoil, but the political turmoil of 2013, spilling over to 2014, has hurt tourism and manufacturing. Growth in 2014 is said to be likely to range around 2.5 percent, in contrast with such Southeast Asian counterparts as Malaysia which expects growth around 6 percent.[43]

Under the Obama administration, the United States has prioritized engagement with Southeast Asia and a broader strategic rebalance toward the Asia-Pacific, but initiatives with Thailand have been lacking. With its favorable geographic location and broad-based economy, Thailand has traditionally been considered among the most likely countries to play a major leadership role in the region. But growing U.S. engagement with other allies and partners such as the Philippines and Singapore and Thailand's domestic problems appear to have dimmed the prominence of the U.S.-Thai relationship in Southeast Asia. The Obama administration expressed disappointment with the May 2014 coup and promised cutbacks in military and other ties in accordance with U.S. law. Thailand maintains close relations with China and is considered to be a key arena of competition between Beijing and Washington for influence.[44]

MALAYSIA

Political stability and economic development have been more positive in Malaysia and Singapore, the two smaller Southeast Asian nations that were among the five states that founded ASEAN forty years ago. Dr. Mahathir Mohamad was the prime minister of Malaysia between 1981 and 2003, leading his parties to successive election victories. Mahathir emphasized economic development during his tenure, in particular the export sector, as well as large-scale infrastructure projects. He attributed the success of the Asian Tiger economies to the "Asian values" of its people, which he believed were superior to those of the West. The end of Mahathir's administration was marred by a falling-out with his deputy and presumed successor, Anwar Ibrahim. Mahathir stepped down as prime minister in October 2003.[45]

Despite a diverse ethnic and religious mix, Malaysia has enjoyed considerable political stability. Political coalitions led by the United Malays National Organization (UMNO), the country's dominant political party, have ruled Malaysia without interruption since independence. The Malaysian government has been criticized for its weak human rights protections, constraints on press freedom, and prosecution of opposition political leaders such as Anwar Ibrahim.[46]

Malaysia achieved high rates of GDP growth throughout the 1970s and into the 1990s. The Malaysian economy went into sharp recession in 1997–1998 during the Asian financial crisis. It narrowly avoided a return to recession in 2001 when the economy was negatively impacted by the bursting of the dot-com bubble (which hurt the information technology sector) and slow growth or recession in many of its important export markets. Malaysia was able to recover from the global recession and an economic downturn in 2009 comparatively quickly, and its economic performance in early 2014 was close to its precrisis level, with growth expected to be over 6 percent for that year.[47]

Regional cooperation is a cornerstone of Malaysia's foreign policy. A founding member of ASEAN, Malaysia served as the group's chair in 2005 and 2015. Malaysia has been a constructive diplomatic actor on numerous regional and global issues. Efforts to promote moderate Islam and marginalize religious extremism have been a major part of Malaysian diplomacy, including acting as a mediator in conflicts between Muslim separatist groups and the central government in both Thailand and the Philippines. Malaysia is one of several Southeast Asian countries with maritime and territorial claims in the South China Sea, although it has assumed a low profile in those disputes. President Obama solidified bilateral relations while visiting Malaysia in April 2014 on the basis of cooperative economic and security ties, including overlapping positions on how the South China Sea disputes should be handled and on working together to achieve the TPP agreement.[48]

SINGAPORE

Political stability in Singapore is underscored by the ruling People's Action Party, which has been in power since 1959.[49] With GDP per capita of over US$62,000 (PPP), the advanced economy grew over 4 percent in 2013. Manufacturing and services are the twin engines of the Singapore economy; the electronics and chemicals industries lead Singapore's manufacturing sector.[50]

To maintain its competitive position despite rising wages, the government has sought to promote higher-value-added activities in the manufacturing and services sectors. It has also opened, or is in the process of opening, the financial services, telecommunications, and power generation and retailing sectors to foreign service providers and greater competition. In addition, the government has pursued cost-cutting measures, including tax cuts and wage and rent reductions, in order to lower the cost of doing business in Singapore. It has negotiated free trade agreements (FTAs) with key trading partners including the United States. Singapore and the United States are among the twelve countries on both sides of the Pacific involved in the Trans-Pacific Partnership, which is the centerpiece of the Obama administration's economic rebalance to Asia.[51]

Singapore is nonaligned. It provided a training unit to assist in training Iraqi police and deployed naval ships, air force transport planes, and refueling tankers to the Persian Gulf to support the multinational coalition effort to bring stability and security to Iraq. The 2005 Strategic Framework Agreement formalizes the bilateral security and defense relations with the United States. The agreement, the first of its kind with a non-ally since the Cold War, builds on the U.S. strategy of "places-not-bases" in the region, a concept that allows the U.S. military access to facilities on a rotational basis without bringing up sensitive sovereignty issues. Sophisticated exercises and deployment of U.S. warships on rotation to Singapore highlight recent cooperation with the United States. Singapore relies primarily on its own defense forces, which are continuously being modernized. The defense budget accounts for approximately 5 percent of GDP.[52]

The city-state supports the concept of Southeast Asian regionalism and plays an active role in ASEAN and the Asia-Pacific Economic Cooperation (APEC) forum. Maintaining strong relations with both China and the United States is a keystone of Singapore's foreign policy. Singapore often portrays itself as a useful balancer and intermediary between major powers in the region. In the South China Sea dispute, for example, Singapore—a nonclaimant—has called on China to clarify its island claims, characterizing its stance on the issue as neutral, yet concerned because of the threat to maritime stability.[53]

VIETNAM

Vietnam's communist administration has pursued pragmatic economic policies that registered annual growth rates of better than an average of 7 percent from 1987 to 2007. Subsequent growth rates were lower, with an annual growth rate of 5.4 percent in 2013. Vietnam joined the World Trade Organization (WTO) in 2006. It participates with the United States and others in negotiations on the Trans-Pacific Partnership agreement.[54]

Vietnam's government has continued efforts in recent years to moderate border and other tensions with neighbors, notably China. It has integrated the country more closely into ASEAN and has played an active role in APEC and other regional groups. Relations with the United States have grown in importance. Vietnamese leaders have sought to upgrade relations with the United States in part due to the desire for continued access to the U.S. market and to worries about China's expanding influence in Southeast Asia. In 2010, the two countries mobilized a multinational response to China's perceived attempts to boost its claims to disputed waters and islands in the South China Sea, and they have continued to work closely on issues of maritime freedom and security. Vietnamese leaders strive to stay between Washington and Beijing; improved relations with one capital should not be perceived as a threat to the other. Also, some Vietnamese remain suspicious that the United States' long-term goal is to erode the Vietnamese Communist Party's (VCP's) monopoly of political power. Vietnam faced a much tougher challenge from China with the deployment of a large Chinese oil rig in disputed South China Sea waters in May 2014. The result was a face-off of Vietnamese and Chinese coast guard and civilian forces and mass demonstrations that led to violence and a few deaths directed against Chinese enterprises in Vietnam. The United States condemned the Chinese deployment of the oil rig and called for restraint by Vietnam. The United States seemed to please Vietnamese leaders in agreeing in October 2014 to sell weapons to Vietnam.[55]

MYANMAR

In power from 1988 to 2011, the military-dominated Myanmar government was an exception to the pattern of Asian governments seeking legitimacy through pragmatic nation building, closer integration with the world economy, and convergence with international norms. Instead, the Myanmar authorities were defiant in the face of intense and growing pressure from the United States and the West, as well as from some neighbors in Southeast Asia. Instead of seeking reconciliation and accommodation with the political opposition, it chose a path of remaining in power indefinitely by coercive means. This was the case until the start of reforms with a quasi-civilian government in March 2011.[56]

Since assuming power, Myanmar's quasi-civilian government, led by President Thein Sein, has undertaken several reforms. Hundreds of political prisoners have been released from detention, and a few of Myanmar's more oppressive laws have been repealed or amended by Myanmar's Union Parliament. In April 2012, Myanmar held parliamentary by-elections in which Nobel Peace Prize recipient Aung San Suu Kyi and her political party, the National League for Democracy (NLD), won forty-three of the forty-six seats. The U.S. government was encouraged by the changes, and first Secretary of State Clinton and then President Obama visited the capital to meet with ruling and opposition leaders.[57]

As relations with the United States and Western developed countries rose, relations with China, Myanmar's long-standing international supporter, seemed to be in at least relative decline. Popular opposition to a very large Chinese-backed dam project grew, and the project was halted by the Myanmar government. Both Myanmar and Chinese government officials endeavored to preserve important economic and other ties, but the days of China's role as the country's preferred international partner seemed over.[58]

AUSTRALIA

Australia is an increasingly active and influential power in the Asia-Pacific. A prosperous economy with an advanced military capable of sophisticated military cooperation with the United States and others throughout the region, Australia became a member of the select group of so-called middle powers in the G-20. Australia and the United States enjoy a very close alliance relationship. The relationship is as close as the American strategic relationships with Great Britain and Canada. The alliance enjoys broad bipartisan support on both sides of the Pacific.

In recent years, Australia has prospered greatly through exports of raw materials to China. Its international position rests to a considerable degree on its economic relationship with China and its strategic relationship with the United States. Despite sometimes serious frictions between Beijing and Washington, Australian politicians have a tendency to believe the government does not have to choose between the two and that it can seek to have a constructive trade relationship with China while maintaining its close strategic relationship with the United States.[59]

When differences between China and the United States emerged during the past two years over Chinese coercive and intimidating actions against disputants in the East and South China Seas, Australia supported the United States. The Australian government strongly backs the Obama government's rebalance policy and participates actively in its security measures and the TPP negotiations. At the same time, Australia is a participant in the large regional body negotiating a less stringent trade arrangement called the Regional Comprehensive Economic Partnership (RCEP), which China favors over the TPP. And it engages in defense cooperation as well as close economic and political relations with China.[60]

NEW ZEALAND

New Zealand is a well-established political democracy, a trade-dependent nation, and a strong advocate of free trade. New Zealand's principal exports are dairy products, meat, timber, fish, fruit, wool, and manufactured products. Its top trading and economic partners are China, Australia, Japan, and the United States.[61]

Because of differences with the United States over nuclear weapons, in the 1980s New Zealand imposed conditions on U.S. warships visiting New Zealand ports that led to the U.S. suspension of alliance relations with the country. In recent years, the New Zealand administration has endeavored to improve relations with the United States, to enhance its military preparations in ways supported by the United States and Australia, and to take on other international commitments welcomed by the United States. Acknowledging the need to improve its defense capabilities, the government in 2005 allocated an additional US$3.19 billion over ten years to modernize the country's defense equipment and infrastructure and increase its military personnel. The funding represented a 51 percent increase in defense spending.[62]

New Zealand is an active participant in multilateral peacekeeping. It has taken a leading role in trying to bring peace, reconciliation, and reconstruction to areas of the South Pacific disrupted by armed conflict or natural disasters. New Zealand participated along with the United States and allies in Operation Enduring Freedom and fielded a provincial reconstruction team in Afghanistan, as well as deploying a frigate to the Gulf of Oman. In support of the effort to reconstruct Iraq, New Zealand deployed an engineering team to the country.

New Zealand participates in sharing training facilities, personnel exchanges, and joint exercises with the Philippines, Thailand, Indonesia, Papua New Guinea, Brunei, Tonga, and South Pacific states. It also participates in exercises with its Five Power Defense Arrangement partners—Australia, the United Kingdom, Malaysia, and Singapore.[63]

As part of its strategy to rebalance toward Asia, the Obama administration has greatly expanded cooperation and reestablished close ties with New Zealand. Changes in the security realm have been particularly notable as the two sides have restored close defense cooperation, which was suspended in the mid-1980s due to differences over nuclear policy. The two nations are now working together increasingly closely in the area of defense and security cooperation while also seeking to coordinate efforts in the South Pacific. The United States and New Zealand are also working together to help shape emerging architectures in the Asia-Pacific such as the twelve-nation Trans-Pacific Partnership free trade agreement negotiations in which New Zealand has played a key role.

New Zealand's move in restoring bilateral ties with the United States is not without controversy. Some in New Zealand are concerned that the move could threaten New Zealand's trade interests with China, and others worry about New Zealand's independence in foreign policy.[64]

PACIFIC ISLANDS

Leading Pacific Island governments such as Fiji, Papua New Guinea, the Solomon Islands, and Vanuatu have faced major challenges from political instability, domestic violence and tensions, and poor economic performance. Outside powers led by Australia and New Zealand have repeatedly intervened in the affairs of these states, sometimes sending police and military forces, in order to calm violence, help to restore order, and promote good governance. Unlike their much smaller and aid-dependent Pacific Island neighbors, these larger Pacific states have more resources that seem sufficient to promote viable economic development. But progress is slow and encumbered by corruption, political and ethnic divisions, and a variety of other problems.

Many years of intense competition between China and Taiwan for diplomatic recognition by small Pacific Island countries saw transfers of assistance and other funds that are widely seen in Australia and New Zealand as fostering increased corruption, poor governance, and overall instability. The Taiwan-China diplomatic competition has subsided since 2008, but China in particular is advancing interests with offers of loans that regional analysts fear will be spent poorly by island governments, deepening their debts.[65] In 2012, Secretary of State Hillary Clinton's attendance at the Pacific Islands Forum (PIF) Post Forum Dialogue, the first ever by a U.S. secretary of state, demonstrated the United States' growing commitment to partnering with the Pacific Island countries to address local and global challenges, such as climate change, economic development, gender equality, education, and peace and security. The Obama administration has included the Pacific Islands among the enhanced engagement seen in its rebalance policy toward the Asia-Pacific.[66]

U.S. PRIORITIES IN SOUTHEAST ASIA AND THE PACIFIC

The evolution of ever-stronger American interest and activism in Southeast Asia and the Pacific in the twenty-first century first saw U.S. policy with scattered concerns focused on individual countries and their specific circumstances. U.S. policy making generally involved much smaller groups of U.S. policy makers and concerned American observers than those involved in debates and discussions over U.S. policies toward China, Korea, and Japan.

Heading the list of regional trouble spots was Indonesia, where the political transition from the authoritarian rule of President Suharto was uncertain and weak. A new order emerged slowly amid leadership maneuvering, mass demonstrations, persistent corruption, economic mismanagement, and an overall decline in governance. The government of President Joseph Estrada in the Philippines revived the cronyism of the Ferdinand Marcos era and seemed inattentive to fundamentals of good economic management. The successor government of Gloria Macapagal-Arroyo faced constant political challenge and charges of mass corruption. Prime Minister Thaksin's election in Thailand foreshadowed later political crises, while Prime Minister Mahathir's stepping down ended strongman rule in Malaysia.

For a time, the ten-member ASEAN appeared to decline. The loss of Indonesia's Suharto was a major blow to the association's leadership. Intra-ASEAN bickering increased as members pursued contradictory agendas.[67] Foreign investors, including U.S. businesses, shifted away from the region. China in 1999 captured 61 percent of foreign direct investment in emerging Asian economics, while ASEAN had 17 percent—a reversal of the shares ten years earlier. FDI in ASEAN declined 22 percent in 1999, after dropping 21 percent in 1998.[68]

Against this backdrop, U.S. policy concerns focused on particular issues in individual countries. The controversy over the Indonesian government's handling of East Timor dominated debate over U.S.-Indonesia relations. Democracy and human rights issues drove the U.S. discussion about policy toward Myanmar. Meanwhile, controversy and debate marked every step of the U.S. path toward normalizing relations with Vietnam.

THE WAR ON TERRORISM IN SOUTHEAST ASIA

There was little opposition in the United States to the increased U.S. military and other counterterrorism cooperation with Southeast Asian governments after the September 11, 2001, terrorist attack on America. Nonetheless, several years of strong antiterrorism efforts combined with the U.S.-led wars in Afghanistan and Iraq prompted Southeast Asian leaders to complain that the United States was conducting the war on terrorism in the wrong way. American actions were seen as radicalizing Asia's Muslims and strengthening domestic opposition to Southeast Asian governments friendly to the United States. Meanwhile, Southeast Asian leaders also complained that U.S. preoccupation with the war in Iraq and the broader war on terrorism made U.S. leaders inattentive to Southeast Asia and the priorities leaders there put on nation building, economic development, and cooperation in an emerging array of regional multilateral organizations. [69]

The U.S. actions against terrorism in Southeast Asia were primarily bilateral. Some attention focused on regional organizations such as the ASEAN Regional Forum (ARF), APEC, and ASEAN itself. With American encouragement, APEC members in particular undertook obligations to secure ports and airports, combat money laundering, secure shipping containers, and tighten border controls. Meanwhile, the Australian government of Prime Minister John Howard was a staunch U.S. ally in most aspects of the U.S.-led war on terrorism, including the conflict in Iraq. New Zealand also supported various U.S. initiatives and contributed forces to antiterrorism actions in Afghanistan. Both Australia and New Zealand received strong U.S. support for their military and other interventions designed to calm recurrent instability in several Pacific Island states during this period. [70]

The U.S. military presence in Southeast Asia declined markedly with the closing of U.S. bases in the Philippines in 1992 after the end of the Cold War. The U.S. military endeavored to gain temporary access for transit and training. Extensive U.S. exercises continued with Thailand, and a small but important permanent U.S. presence was arranged with Singapore. No Southeast Asian state agreed to provide locations for prepositioned U.S. supplies until the Philippines negotiated a new visiting forces agreement late in the 1990s. [71]

The U.S. military took the lead after 9/11 in arranging for close cooperation with Philippine security forces to deal with terrorists in the country. U.S. military supplies to the Philippines increased markedly. Joint and prolonged exercises allowed hundreds of U.S. forces to help train their Philippine counterparts to apprehend members of the terrorist Abu Sayyaf Group, which was active in the southwestern islands of the Philippines. Other U.S. military training activities helped to strengthen Philippine forces to deal with other terrorist and rebellious groups. These included members of Jemaah Islamiyah, which was reportedly training terrorists in the Philippines. The United States awarded the Philippines the status as a "major non-NATO ally," provided increased American military assistance, and welcomed the small contingent of Philippine troops in Iraq. The contingent was withdrawn in 2004 to save the life of a kidnapped Philippine hostage. [72]

The Bush administration also awarded increased military aid and major non-NATO ally status to Thailand, which sent nearly five hundred troops to Iraq. Thailand also reversed its refusals of the 1990s and offered sites for the forward positioning of U.S. military supplies. Cobra Gold, the annual U.S.-led military exercise in Thailand, attracted participation from other Asian countries. Meanwhile, Singapore developed a new security framework agreement with the United States, involving counterterrorism cooperation, efforts against the proliferation of WMD, and joint military exercises. [73]

The United States also supported a Southeast Asian antiterrorism center in Malaysia. U.S. support for Indonesia focused at first on the Indonesian Police Counter-Terrorism Task Force and broader education and other assistance designed to strengthen democratic governance in Indonesia in the face of terrorist threats. Restrictions on U.S. assistance to the Indonesian military were slowly eased, despite continued reservations in Congress over the military's long history of abuses. Popular sentiment in Malaysia and Indonesia was strongly against a perceived bias in the Bush administration's focus against radical Islam as a target in the war on terrorism. This added to the unpopularity of American policies toward Iraq and the Palestinian-Israeli dispute. Nonetheless, the Bush administration worked hard to improve relations with Malaysia and particularly Indonesia, the world's largest Muslim state, whose government emphasized moderation and democratic values. U.S. aid, military contacts, and high-level exchanges grew as the Indonesian democratic administration made progress toward more effective governance. [74]

ASIAN MULTILATERALISM AND THE RISE OF CHINA

As the intensity of the focus against terrorism in Southeast Asia waned, Bush administration policy makers and nongovernment specialists concerned with Asia actively debated approaches to the emerging challenges and opportunities for the United States posed by advances in Asian multilateralism and China's growing role in these organizations. U.S. allies and friends in Japan, Australia, Southeast Asia, and elsewhere urged Washington to adopt a more active stance toward Asian multilateralism. The focus of U.S. discussion and debate was on Southeast Asia and Asian multilateral groupings that gave prominence to ASEAN, and this focus was maintained even though key members of ASEAN—notably the three largest of the founding members,

Indonesia, the Philippines, and Thailand—were preoccupied with serious internal problems and unable to lead the organization effectively.[75]

Regional groupings involving Central Asia, particularly the Shanghai Cooperation Organization led by China and Russia, did not include the United States. The United States participated as an observer in the main South Asian regional group, the South Asia Association for Regional Cooperation. Northeast Asian cooperation in the six-party talks also had the potential to develop into a workable regional grouping in the future, but the talks remained focused on dealing with the protracted process of ending North Korea's nuclear weapons program.

Asian multilateralism based on ASEAN had two foundations. The first was economic cooperation, which was growing. It involved various free trade and regional monetary agreements. These arrangements reflected a quest for business profits, economic stability, and higher rates of growth, which were deemed very important to Asian entrepreneurs and to the Asian government leaders who depended on economic growth to shore up support for their continued political leadership. The Asian economies carried out a variety of free trade agreements. An ASEAN FTA in 1992 lowered, but did not eliminate, intraregional tariffs. Singapore set the pace in negotiating FTAs with various countries. Indonesia, Thailand, Malaysia, the Philippines, and Vietnam sought various such agreements, as did Japan, South Korea, and Taiwan. China took the initiative in 2002 by launching the process of establishing an FTA with ASEAN. Japan, India, South Korea, and others followed with FTAs or similar trade schemes for their respective relations with ASEAN.[76]

China and South Korea favored a plan that would develop a free trade agreement among the ten members of ASEAN plus China, South Korea, and Japan. This was part of efforts, especially by China, to strengthen and develop the ASEAN+3 grouping, begun in the late 1990s, into Asia's premier regional grouping. One proposal called for the creation of an East Asia Economic Community based on the ASEAN+3 members. Meanwhile, the ASEAN+3 members developed cooperative financial arrangements following the adverse effects of the 1997–1998 Asian economic crisis. Under the rubric of the Chiang Mai Initiative, they created a growing web of bilateral swap arrangements, by which short-term liquidity was available to support participating ASEAN+3 countries in need.[77]

Though supportive of ASEAN+3, Japan was wary of China's growing role in Asian regional groupings and sought to involve other powers in these groups. In 2006, Japan proposed a sixteen-nation Asian free trade area. The sixteen members would include the members of ASEAN+3 along with India, Australia, and New Zealand. The membership was identical to that of the East Asia Summit (EAS) regional grouping (discussed more below) that

began in 2005. This grouping indicated a willingness to accept the United
States and Russia as members in the future.

Japan said it planned to launch negotiations in 2008 for an Asia FTA
among the sixteen Asia-Pacific nations. The concept was welcomed by India
and ASEAN, but China and South Korea indicated that their first priority was
the ASEAN+3 FTA. Japan actively encouraged the United States to join the
EAS. Japan was not enthusiastic about U.S. support for APEC, seeing the
latter group as large and unwieldy and excluding India, an important Asian
power in recent Japanese calculations.[78]

For its part, the Bush administration gave priority to continued strong
U.S. support for APEC. Founded in 1989 as an international organization
focused on facilitating economic growth, cooperation, trade, and investment
in the Asia-Pacific region, APEC for a time included twenty-one members:
China, Japan, South Korea, seven members of ASEAN (Myanmar, Laos, and
Cambodia were not members), Taiwan, Hong Kong, Australia, New Zealand, Papua New Guinea, Russia, Canada, Mexico, Peru, Chile, and the
United States. The United States favored a broad pan-Pacific membership
that included the United States and that allowed Taiwan, a friend of the
United States, to participate despite China's broad efforts to isolate Taiwan
from formal international organizations and contacts. U.S. and other leaders
valued the annual APEC summit, begun by President Clinton in 1993, which
allowed for discussion of relevant international issues at the highest level.
President Bush used the APEC summit in October 2001 to pursue an agenda
fostering international efforts to combat terrorism. APEC efforts at trade and
investment liberalization, business facilitation, and economic and technical
cooperation tended to slow in following years, though Bush used the summit
in 2006 to propose an APEC-based pan-Pacific FTA.[79]

In recent years, large and seemingly competing regional trade arrangements are moving toward completion. The U.S.-backed Trans-Pacific Partnership involves twelve Asia-Pacific countries seeking an economic arrangement that would advance free trade, safeguard intellectual property, promote
free market access, and implement other measures of benefit to the United
States and other advanced economies. American officials and commentators
commonly view less stringent free trade arrangements as disadvantageous;
state-directed economies, notably China, are able to use them unfairly to
advance China's economy at the expense of more liberal economies. China
supports the Regional Comprehensive Economic Partnership, which excludes the United States, involves more lax standards, and includes the members of ASEAN+3 along with India, Australia, and New Zealand. At the
APEC summit meeting in Beijing in November 2014, China pushed a free
trade agreement based on APEC members known as the Free Trade Area of
the Asia-Pacific. The move was seen to run counter to the U.S.-backed TPP.
Meanwhile, China at this time launched the Asian Infrastructure Investment

Bank (AIIB) in a move widely seen as challenging existing U.S.-backed international financial institutions like the Asian Development Bank and the World Bank.[80]

The second foundation of Asian multilateralism was political and security cooperation. This foundation was decidedly weaker than the robust economic cooperation but has become stronger in recent years. Progress has been made in groups in which ASEAN plays the role of convener, notably the ASEAN Security Community, the ARF, the EAS, and ASEAN+3. The ASEAN Security Community involved the ten members of ASEAN. ASEAN also played a leading role in broader Asian groups. ASEAN was often able to take the lead in building multilateral institutions because it was viewed as more neutral and nonthreatening than China, Japan, the United States, or other major powers.[81]

The ASEAN Regional Forum was established in 1994 with the purpose of bringing non-ASEAN nations from the Asia-Pacific region together with ASEAN officials to discuss political and security matters and to build cooperative ties. The participants included all ten ASEAN members, China, Japan, the United States, the European Union, Russia, Australia, Canada, New Zealand, South Korea, North Korea, India, Pakistan, Bangladesh, Mongolia, Papua New Guinea, East Timor, and Sri Lanka. The Asian region had little experience with broad security cooperation. ARF was created to complement U.S. security guarantees that appeared to be weakening in the early 1990s, as evidenced by the U.S. withdrawal from bases in the Philippines. And it endeavored to deal with uncertainties caused by changing power relationships in Asia, particularly the ascent of China. Since the member states tended to be independent minded and wary of one another, ARF was characterized by minimal institutionalization and the "ASEAN way" of gradualism and decisions by consensus. The ARF process began with transparency (through the publication of military spending and deployment information), dialogue, and confidence-building measures; then moved to preventive diplomacy (discussion and mutual pledges to resolve specific disputes solely through peaceful means); and, in the long term, hoped to develop a conflict resolution capacity.[82]

Most of the ARF measures have focused on dialogue and confidence building. The annual ARF ministerial meeting provided an opportunity for foreign ministers to meet and discuss current issues. Significantly, defense ministers did not participate in the dialogue. This perceived gap was addressed in part by an informal group, the International Institute of Strategic Studies' Shangri-La Dialogue, meeting annually in Singapore. The dialogue attracted senior defense officials from most ARF members and elsewhere to discuss relevant security questions.[83] Further filling the gap, in 2010, the inaugural meeting of the ASEAN Defense Ministers Plus Forum (better known by the shorthand ADMM+) took place in Hanoi. It brought together for the first time in an official setting the defense ministers of the ten-strong ASEAN community and of eight other Asia-Pacific countries: Australia, China, India, Japan, New Zealand, the Republic of Korea, Russia, and the United States. ADMM+ mirrors the membership of the East Asia Summit.[84]

The East Asia Summit met first in Malaysia in December 2005. Attending were leaders of the ten ASEAN states, China, Japan, South Korea, India, Australia, and New Zealand. Russian president Vladimir Putin came as a guest. The meeting was timed to follow the 2005 ASEAN summit as well as bilateral meetings between ASEAN and Russia, Japan, South Korea, and India. China at first played a strong role in promoting the EAS and was reportedly motivated in part by a desire to use the grouping to offset U.S. influence in the Asia-Pacific. Japan, Singapore, and Indonesia reportedly pushed to have Australia and India included in order to avoid feared dominance by China. As the latter efforts succeeded, China reduced support for the EAS and focused positive attention instead on ASEAN+3, where China had a stronger position.

The EAS said it was open, inclusive, transparent, and outward looking, with ASEAN as the leading force in the group. Several members encouraged the United States to meet the initial requirements for membership; namely, signing the ASEAN Treaty of Amity and Cooperation, becoming a formal dialogue partner of ASEAN, and having substantive cooperative relations with ASEAN. During the Obama administration, the United States met the conditions and became an active member of the group.[85]

Meanwhile, ASEAN+3 had security as well as economic importance. It came about in 1997 as a result of a Japanese proposal to create a regular summit process between ASEAN and Japan with an economic, political, and security agenda. Concerned with possible negative reactions from other Asian nations, ASEAN subsequently broadened the proposed summit to include China and South Korea. The ASEAN+3 members met regularly after each ASEAN summit to discuss finances, economics, and security. As noted earlier, China reportedly favored this organization over the East Asia Summit because it was not open to U.S. membership and did not include India, though Beijing continues to support the EAS, APEC, and other groups.[86]

U.S. POLICY CHOICES AND RECENT ACTIONS

Bush Administration Actions

In the Southeast Asian–oriented groupings, the Bush administration debated on whether or not the U.S. government should take steps to further advance the American profile in regional groupings. Spurred on by the growing Chinese influence in Asian multilateral groups and by the strong encouragement of Japan, Australia, Singapore, and others that the United States play a more prominent role in the Asian groups, the Bush government increased its involvement in these organizations as it took a variety of steps to shore up U.S. relations with Southeast Asian governments.[87] As noted earlier, under the rubric of its broad-ranging rebalance policy, the Obama government's stronger emphasis on Southeast Asia, ASEAN, and ASEAN-centered regional groupings substantially advanced the Bush-era developments.

The Bush administration gradually developed U.S. initiatives to individual Southeast Asian nations and to the ASEAN regional organization and related regional multilateral groups. These initiatives were based on the American position as a leading trading partner, foreign investor, aid donor, and military partner. U.S. initiatives to ASEAN represented in part Bush administration efforts to catch up with ASEAN's free trade agreements and other formal arrangements with China, Japan, and other powers. Strong U.S. opposition to the military regime in Myanmar continued to complicate American relations with the ASEAN group. That regime's crackdown on large demonstrations led by Buddhist monks in 2007 saw the Bush administration take the lead in pressing the United Nations and individual states to initiate actions against the repressive government.[88]

In contrast to other powers seeking closer ties with ASEAN, the United States under President Bush did not agree to the ASEAN Treaty of Amity and Cooperation and remained ambivalent on participation in the annual ASEAN-led Asian Leadership Summit, which required agreement to the TAC as a condition for participation. U.S. officials also said they were not opposed to Asian regional organizations that excluded other involved powers such as the United States, but U.S. favor focused on regional groupings open to it and other concerned powers.

For one, the United States supported the ASEAN Regional Forum, the primary regional forum for security dialogue. Secretary of State Colin Powell duly attended ARF annual meetings. His successor, Condoleezza Rice, missed the annual ARF meeting twice during her four-year tenure. President Bush at the APEC summit meeting in November 2006 urged APEC members to consider forming an Asia-Pacific Free Trade Area. The U.S. initiative was seen to underline its interest in fostering trans-Pacific trade groupings in the face of Asian multilateral trade arrangements that excluded the United States.[89] At the APEC summit in 2007, President Bush proposed the formation of a democratic partnership among eight democratically elected members of APEC and India.[90]

Regarding Southeast Asia, President Bush in November 2005 began to use the annual APEC leaders' summit to engage in annual multilateral meetings with attending ASEAN leaders. At this meeting, he and seven ASEAN heads of state launched the ASEAN-U.S. Enhanced Partnership, involving a broad range of economic, political, and security cooperation. In July 2006, Secretary Rice and her ten ASEAN counterparts signed a five-year plan of action to implement the partnership. In the important area of trade and invest-ment, the ministers endorsed the Enterprise for ASEAN Initiative (EAI) launched by the U.S. government in 2002 that provided a road map to move from bilateral trade and investment framework agreements (TIFAs), which were consultative, to free trade agreements, which were more binding. The United States already had bilateral TIFAs with several ASEAN states. The Bush administration followed its FTAs with Singapore and Australia with FTA negotiations with Thailand and Malaysia, but those negotiations had stalled by 2007.[91]

The initiation in 2005 of the U.S. presidential mini-summits with ASEAN leaders attending the annual APEC leaders' meeting conveniently avoided the U.S.-ASEAN differences over Myanmar, which was not an APEC mem-ber.[92] The Bush administration for a time accepted a working engagement with Myanmar as an ASEAN member at lower protocol levels. Myanmar was represented in the ASEAN-U.S. Dialogue, and Secretary of State Rice shook hands with all ASEAN foreign ministers at the signing ceremony of the ASEAN-U.S. Enhanced Partnership in July 2006.[93]

Indonesia received notable U.S. attention, with Rice and Defense Secre-tary Donald Rumsfeld making separate trips during 2006 and President Bush making a visit in conjunction with the APEC summit in November. U.S. assistance to Indonesia in FY 2006 topped $500 million. Vietnam, the host of the November 2006 APEC leaders' meeting, also received notable U.S. at-tention. The United States took the lead in negotiations on Vietnam's suc-cessful entry into the WTO. The United States was a close second to China as Vietnam's leading trade partner, and it was the largest foreign investor in the country. Rumsfeld visited Vietnam in 2005, and Vietnam modestly strength-ened its defense ties with the United States.[94]

U.S. military activism in the region also included participation by Rums-feld and his successor Robert Gates at the annual Shangri-La defense forum in Singapore and by secretaries Powell and Rice at the ARF; a strong pro-gram of bilateral and multilateral exercises and exchanges between U.S. forces in the Pacific Command and friendly and allied Southeast Asian forces; an active U.S. International Military Education and Training program with regional governments; and the U.S. role as the top supplier of defense equipment to the leading ASEAN countries. The U.S. military maintained what was seen as a "semicontinuous" presence in the Philippines to assist in dealing with terrorist threats, and it resumed in November 2005 a "strategic dialogue" with Thailand. These moves added to progress made in U.S. secur-ity ties with Singapore (the largest regional purchaser of U.S. military equip-ment) and the upswing in U.S. military ties with Indonesia.

The pace and scope of U.S. military activism in the region reinforced the tendency of America's allies and associates to find reliance on the United States and its regional defense structures preferable to reliance on other nascent but rising Asian regional security arrangements. Australia and Japan in particular worked hard to provide support for a continued strong and prominent U.S. defense role in the region. They developed and engaged in a new ministerial trilateral strategic dialogue with the United States during the Bush administration. With U.S. support, they concluded in 2007 a bilateral security arrangement, the first by Japan with a non-U.S. partner. The three powers also engaged more in individual and collective security cooperation with India. Representatives of these four governments met for security consultations on the sidelines of the ARF ministerial meeting in May 2007.[95]

Numerous bilateral and multilateral U.S. military exercises were valued by Asian partners. The United States promoted maritime security cooperation in the area of the strategically important Strait of Malacca by working with the states bordering the strait—Singapore, Malaysia, and Indonesia—to develop a command, control, and communications infrastructure that will facilitate cooperation in maritime surveillance of the waterway.[96]

U.S. foreign assistance to Southeast Asian countries increased, along with substantial increases in U.S. foreign assistance budgets. In addition to Indonesia, which received the bulk of $400 million pledged by the U.S. government for relief from the December 2004 tsunami disaster in addition to a substantial U.S. aid program, other large recipients of U.S. assistance included the Philippines, Vietnam, Cambodia, and East Timor.[97]

Despite such progress, serious complications and uncertainties persisted. The ability and will of U.S. leaders to devote attention to regional bilateral and multilateral relations in Southeast Asia and the Pacific remained in question, especially given the overriding U.S. policy preoccupations with the Middle East and Southwest Asia. U.S. strategic cooperation with Japan was called into question with the election of a DPJ leadership intent on distancing Japan from the United States. The emerging U.S. security partnership with India was clouded by serious obstacles to the completion of the centerpiece of the new relationship, the U.S.-India nuclear cooperation agreement.

Obama Administration Highlights

As discussed in chapter 4 and earlier in this chapter, the Obama government built on Bush accomplishments and brought American relations with Southeast Asia and the Pacific to a much higher level. The evolving rebalance policy initiatives were highlighted by sustained high-level leadership diplomacy and activism calling attention to the growing sinews of American military, economic, and diplomatic influence. Secretary of State Clinton was in the international spotlight in her annual interactions at the ARF as well as visits advancing traditionally very strong relations with Australia. She also improved relations with New Zealand and the Pacific Island states, bringing them into the broad scope of the rebalance. Secretary of Defense Robert

Gates and his successors Leon Panetta and Chuck Hagel vigorously pursued the rebalance initiatives while calling on China to calm its assertiveness and conform to accepted international norms. Despite his diplomatic activism dealing with crises in Ukraine, Syria, and the Middle East peace process, Secretary of State John Kerry kept up a strong State Department role with Southeast Asia and the Pacific. President Obama was compelled to postpone participation in annual ASEAN-hosted meetings and related summits in Southeast Asia in late 2013, but he followed through with successful visits to Malaysia and the Philippines along with visits to Japan and South Korea in April 2014. He also carried out a major trip to China, Myanmar, and Australia for important international meetings during November 2014.

President Obama's visit to Australia on November 16 and 17, 2011, marked a significant expansion of an already strong tradition of military, economic, and diplomatic cooperation between the United States and Australia. President Obama's visit took place after the APEC meeting in Hawaii and immediately before the East Asia Summit meeting in Bali, Indonesia. Taken together, these events sent a clear signal under the rubric of the U.S. "pivot" or "rebalance" policy shift that underlined to Australia and the region that the United States had made a decision to shift strategic focus onto the Asia-Pacific region.

President Obama addressed a special sitting of Parliament on November 17 in Canberra, where he explained the new regional policy, before making a brief stop in Darwin, Australia, where some U.S. forces will be deployed on a rotating basis. His important speech clearly set out America's strategic commitment to the Asia-Pacific region and reaffirmed the bonds of solidarity between the United States and Australia.[98]

President Obama's much-anticipated November 2010 visit to Indonesia was seen as a success. The visit was postponed twice earlier in the year due to health-care legislation and the environmental disaster in the Gulf of Mexico. President Obama's efforts built on those of the Bush administration to advance the bilateral relationship between Indonesia and the United States. Indonesia is central to U.S. strategic interest to shape the evolving geostrategic environment in Asia relative to the rise of China. The Comprehensive Partnership Agreement signed during the visit facilitated a broadening of the relationship between the United States and Indonesia and supported continued collaboration with this leading moderate country in the struggle against Islamist extremists. Obama's initiative also offered the prospect of developing deeper trade and investment ties with Indonesia. The president returned to Indonesia in 2011 for the EAS and related meetings where he expanded on his speech in Australia to underline the U.S. government's commitment to sustained American engagement with Southeast Asia and the Pacific along with other parts of Asia.[99]

In April 2014, the U.S. profile rose further in Southeast Asia amid escalating U.S. public differences with China over Chinese coercive tactics in the South China Sea. That month, President Obama visited Malaysia and the Philippines, stops he had canceled the previous fall because of the U.S. government shutdown. The main deliverables of his trip—a comprehensive partnership with Malaysia and an enhanced defense agreement with the Philippines—shored up the administration's assertion that the U.S. "rebalancing" to Asia is real and that Southeast Asia is critical to that process.

On April 27, President Obama and Prime Minister Najib Razak announced the inauguration of the U.S.-Malaysia Comprehensive Partnership, the third such agreement forged between the United States and a Southeast Asian partner in recent years (the others being Indonesia in 2010 and Vietnam in 2013). As its title suggested, the comprehensive partnership is a policy umbrella, designed to bring together all aspects of the bilateral relationship: political and diplomatic cooperation; trade and investment; education and people-to-people ties; security and defense cooperation; and collaboration on the environment, science and technology, and energy. The driver of the partnership will be the U.S.-Malaysia Senior Officials Dialogue. [100]

President Obama's following visit to the Philippines, his first as president, centered on security and on strengthening the U.S.-Philippines alliance with careful respect for post–Cold War Southeast Asian sensitivities. The Enhanced Defense Cooperation Agreement (EDCA), signed in Manila on April 27 by Ambassador Philip Goldberg and Philippine defense secretary Voltaire Gazmin, is a ten-year pact that will give U.S. forces greater access to selected military bases on a temporary and rotational basis and permit prepositioning of some equipment. Precise numbers of U.S. troops and sites were still to be determined and were likely to be guided by joint military activities rather than unilateral U.S. moves. National Security Council Senior Director for Asia Evan Medeiros indicated that the U.S. government hoped Subic Bay will be one facility open to the United States under the EDCA. The agreement stated specifically that the United States would "not establish a permanent military presence or base in the Philippines"—a requirement for even the most U.S.-friendly Southeast Asian country—and that Philippine officials would have complete access to any areas to be shared with U.S. forces. As an executive agreement, the EDCA did not require ratification by either country's legislature. The EDCA is the logical next step in the Pentagon's incremental attempts to expand flexible basing in the Asia-Pacific region, following the agreement with Australia to rotate U.S. Marines through Darwin and the accord with Singapore to permit the U.S. Navy to rotate four littoral combat ships. [101]

Reinforcing the continued strong attention to Southeast Asia and the Pacific, Secretary of State John Kerry visited Indonesia in February 2014, delivering a speech on climate change that resonated in a region expecting a major impact from global warming and rising seas. In early April, Secretary of Defense Chuck Hagel underlined U.S. support for ASEAN and its regional groupings as he hosted the first-ever U.S.-ASEAN Defense Ministers Meeting in Hawaii. [102]

Meanwhile, in discussing how the United States is updating alliances to address new demands and "building new partnerships," Secretary of State Hillary Clinton cited in November 2011 the U.S. outreach effort to New Zealand, among other countries, as "part of a broader effort to ensure a more comprehensive approach to American strategy and engagement in the region." She added, "We are asking these emerging partners to join us in shaping and participating in a rules-based regional and global order." New Zealand, a nation that like Australia has fought alongside the United States in most of its wars, was now being reconceived as a "new" partner. And as noted earlier, Secretary of State Clinton's unprecedented visit to the annual Pacific Island Forum in 2012 similarly underlined the new emphasis in U.S. policy on this broad expanse of the Pacific. [103]

NOTES

1. Diane K. Mauzy and Brian L. Job, "U.S. Policy in Southeast Asia: Limited Re-engagement after Years of Benign Neglect," *Asian Survey* 47, no. 4 (July–August 2007): 622–41; Donald Weatherbee, "Strategic Dimensions of Economic Interdependence in Southeast Asia," in *Strategic Asia 2006–2007: Trade, Interdependence, and Security*, ed. Ashley J. Tellis and Michael Wills, 271–300 (Seattle, WA: National Bureau of Asian Research, 2006).

2. Evelyn Goh, "Southeast Asian Reactions to America's New Strategic Imperatives," in *Asia Eyes America: Regional Perspectives on U.S. Asia-Pacific Strategy in the 21st Century*, ed. Jonathan Pollack, 201–26 (Newport, RI: U.S. Naval War College, 2007).

3. Bruce Vaughn and Wayne Morrison, *China-Southeast Asia Relations: Trends, Issues, and Implications for the United States*, Report 32688 (Washington, DC: Library of Congress, Congressional Research Service, April 4, 2006); Dana R. Dillon and John J. Tkacik Jr., "China and ASEAN: Endangered American Primacy in Southeast Asia," Backgrounder 1886 (Washington, DC: Heritage Foundation, 2005).

4. Victor Cha, "Winning Asia: Washington's Untold Success Story," *Foreign Affairs* 86, no. 6 (November–December 2007): 98–113.

5. Mark E. Manyin, Stephen Daggett, Ben Dolven, Susan V. Lawrence, Michael F. Martin, Ronald O'Rourke, and Bruce Vaughn, *Pivot to the Pacific? The Obama Administration's "Rebalancing" toward Asia*, Report 42448 (Washington, DC: Library of Congress, Congressional Research Service, March 28, 2012); Robert Sutter, Michael Brown, and Timothy Adamson, *Balancing Acts: The U.S. Rebalance and Asia-Pacific Stability* (Washington, DC: George Washington University, Elliott School of International Affairs, 2013).

6. Philip Saunders, *The Rebalance to Asia: U.S.-China Relations and Regional Security* (Washington, DC: National Defense University, Institute for National Security Studies, 2012).

7. Sutter, Brown, and Adamson, *Balancing Acts*, 18.

8. Donald Weatherbee, *International Relations of Southeast Asia: The Struggle for Autonomy*, 3rd ed. (Lanham, MD: Rowman & Littlefield, 2014).

9. Evelyn Goh, *The Struggle for Order: Hegemony, Hierarchy and Transition in Post–Cold War East Asia* (New York: Oxford University Press, 2013).

10. Goh, *The Struggle for Order*; Amitav Acharya, *The Making of Southeast Asia* (Ithaca, NY: Cornell University Press, 2013).

11. Tin Maung Maung Than, "Myanmar in 2013," *Asian Survey* 54, no. 1 (January–February 2014): 22–29.

12. Robert Sutter, *The United States in East Asia* (Lanham, MD: Rowman & Littlefield, 2003), 169–96.

13. Sheldon Simon, "Southeast Asia's Defense Needs: Change or Continuity?," in *Strategic Asia 2005–2006: Military Modernization in an Era of Uncertainty*, ed. Ashley J. Tellis and Michael Wills, 269–304 (Seattle, WA: National Bureau of Asian Research, 2005).

14. Evelyn Goh, *Meeting the China Challenge: The U.S. in Southeast Asian Regional Security Strategies* (Washington, DC: East-West Center Washington, 2005).

15. Jorgen Ostrom Moller, "Realism and Interdependence in Singapore's Foreign Policy," *Contemporary Southeast Asia* 28, no. 1 (2006): 164–67.

16. Alan Collins, *Security and Southeast Asia* (Boulder, CO: Lynne Rienner, 2003).

17. "China-Southeast Asia Relations," *Comparative Connections* 14, no. 2 (August 2012): 61–65.

18. Stanley Foundation, "New Power Dynamics in Southeast Asia: Issues for U.S. Policymakers," *Policy Dialogue Brief*, October 2006, http://www.stanleyfdn.org/publications/pdb/spcpdb06.pdf.

19. "Thailand's Military Coup," *Economist*, June 6, 2014, http://www.economist.com/blogs/banyan/2014/06/thailands-military-coup.

20. Freedom House, *Freedom in the World 2013*, http://www.freedomhouse.org/report/freedom-world/2013.

21. Donald Weatherbee, "Strategic Dimensions of Economic Interdependence in Southeast Asia," in *Strategic Asia 2006–2007: Trade, Interdependence, and Security*, ed. Ashley J. Tellis and Michael Wills, 271–300 (Seattle, WA: National Bureau of Asian Research, 2006); Shamim Adam and Karl Lester M. Yap, "Southeast Asia Seen Resilient as Indonesia Outperforms," Bloomberg News, November 18, 2012, http://www.bloomberg.com/news/2012-11-19/southeast-asia-seen-resilient-as-indonesia-outperforms-economy.html.

22. For recent treatment of important Indonesian circumstances, see Ann Marie Murphy, "Indonesia's Partnership with the United States: Strategic Imperatives versus Domestic Obstacles," in *Strategic Asia 2014–2015: U.S. Alliances and Partnerships at the Center of Global Power*, ed. Ashley Tellis, Abraham Denmark, and Greg Chaffin, 197–226 (Seattle, WA: National Bureau of Asian Research, 2014).

23. "Indonesia Annual Growth Rate," *Economist*, http://www.tradingeconomics.com/indonesia/gdp-growth-annual (accessed June 25, 2014); *Index Mundi*, http://www.indexmundi.com/facts/indicators/SI.POV.DDAY/compare?country=id (accessed June 25, 2014).

24. Sophie Song, "Indonesia's Increasing Fuel Subsidy," *International Business Times*, March 14, 2014, http://www.ibtimes.com/indonesias-increasing-fuel-subsidy-continues-hurt-economy-reform-now-critical-1561299.

25. "Indonesia," U.S. Energy Information Agency, *Country Analysis*, March 5, 2014, http://www.eia.gov/countries/country-data.cfm?fips=id.

26. Ibid.

27. Damien Kingsbury, "Indonesia in 2006: Cautious Reform," *Asian Survey* 47, no. 1 (January–February 2007): 155–61.

28. Geoffrey Gunn, "Indonesia in 2013," *Asian Survey* 54, no. 1 (January–February 2014): 47–55.

29. Kate Lamb, "Indonesian Terror Mastermind Vows to Continue Jihad," *Voice of America*, January 22, 2014, http://www.voanews.com/content/indonesian-terror-mastermind-vows-to-continue-jihad/1835125.html.

30. Edward Cody, "East Asian Summit Marked by Discord," *Washington Post*, December 14, 2005, http://www.washingtonpost.com/wp-dyn/content/article/2005/12/13/AR2005121300753.html.

31. Tito Summa Siahaan, "Indonesia Disappointed with China over South China Sea Oil Rigs: Marty," *Jakarta Globe*, May 10, 2014, http://www.thejakartaglobe.com/news/indonesia-disappointed-china-south-china-sea-oil-rigs-marty.

32. Peter Wallace, "Philippines: Fragility and the Mixed Outlook," in *ISEAS Regional Outlook Forum*, 2007, 23–27.

33. Sheila S. Coronel, "The Philippines in 2006: Democracy and Its Discontents," *Asian Survey* 47, no. 1 (January–February 2007): 179–81.

34. John Sidel, "The Philippines in 2013," *Asian Survey* 54, no. 1 (January–February 2014): 64–70; for recent treatment of important Philippines circumstances, see Sheena Chestnut Greitens, "The U.S. Alliance with the Philippines: Opportunities and Challenges," in *Strategic Asia 2014–2015: U.S. Alliances and Partnerships at the Center of Global Power*, ed. Ashley Tellis, Abraham Denmark, and Greg Chaffin, 119–46 (Seattle, WA: National Bureau of Asian Research, 2014).

35. U.S. Department of State, "Background Note: Philippines," May 2007, http://www.state.gov/r/pa/ei/bgn/2794.htm.

36. World Bank, *Philippine Economic Update*, Report No. 83315-PH, March 2014; "Philippines Economy," *CIA World Factbook 2014*, https://www.cia.gov/library/publications/the-world-factbook/geos/rp.html.

37. See President Gloria Macapagal-Arroyo's speech during the opening ceremony of the Fortieth ASEAN Ministerial Meeting, Manila, July 30, 2007, at http://www.aseansec.org/20758.htm.

38. Greitens, "The U.S. Alliance with the Philippines"; White House Office of the Press Secretary, "Remarks by President Obama and President Benigno Aquino III of the Philippines in Joint Press Conference," April 28, 2014.

39. For recent treatment of Thailand circumstances, see Catharin Dalpino, "The U.S.-Thailand Alliance: Continuity and Change in the 21st Century," in *Strategic Asia 2014–2015: U.S. Alliances and Partnerships at the Center of Global Power*, ed. Ashley Tellis, Abraham Denmark, and Greg Chaffin, 147–64 (Seattle, WA: National Bureau of Asian Research, 2014).

40. "Opposition to Boycott Thai Vote on April 2," *International Herald Tribune Asia-Pacific*, February 27, 2006.

41. James Ockey, "Thailand in 2006: Retreat to Military Rule," *Asian Survey* 47, no. 1 (January–February 2007): 133–40.

42. "Thailand's Military Coup," *Economist*, June 6, 2014.

43. "Thailand Economy," *CIA World Factbook 2014*, https://www.cia.gov/library/publications/the-world-factbook/geos/th.html.

44. John Kerry, "Secretary of State Press Statement," May 22, 2014, http://www.state.gov/secretary/remarks/2014/05/226446.htm; James Ockey, "Thailand in 2013," *Asian Survey* 54, no. 1 (January–February 2014): 39–46.

45. N. Ganesan, "Malaysia in 2003," *Asian Survey* 44, no. 1 (January–February 2004): 70–77.

46. Freedom House, *Malaysia*, 2014, http://www.freedomhouse.org/country/malaysia#.U6slSpRdXxA (accessed June 25, 2014).

47. "Malaysia Economy," *CIA World Factbook 2014*, https://www.cia.gov/library/publications/the-world-factbook/geos/my.html.

48. White House Office of the Press Secretary, "Joint Statement by President Obama and Prime Minister Najib of Malaysia," April 27, 2014.

49. For recent treatment of Singapore circumstances, see Matthew Shannon Stumpf, "The Singapore-U.S. Strategic Partnership: The Global City and the Global Superpower," in , *Strategic Asia 2014–2015: U.S. Alliances and Partnerships at the Center of Global Power*, ed. Ashley Tellis, Abraham Denmark, and Greg Chaffin, 227–56 (Seattle, WA: National Bureau of Asian Research, 2014).

50. "Singapore Economy," *CIA World Factbook 2014*, https://www.cia.gov/library/publications/the-world-factbook/geos/sn.html.

51. Office of U.S. Trade Representative, *Fact Sheet Singapore*, 2014, http://www.ustr.gov/countries-regions/southeast-asia-pacific/singapore (accessed June 25, 2014).

52. Amitav Acharya, *Singapore's Foreign Policy: The Search for Regional Order* (Singapore: World Scientific, 2007); Stumpf, "The Singapore-U.S. Strategic Partnership."

53. Xenia Dormandy and Rory Kinane, *Asia-Pacific Security: A Changing Role for the United States* (London: Chatham House Report, April 2014), 11–12; "China-Southeast Asia Relations," *Comparative Connections* 16, no. 1 (May 2014): 68; "Singaporean Leader Calls for Resolution of South China Sea Disputes by International Law," Associated Press, June 24,

2014, http://www.coastreporter.net/photos-videos/singaporean-leader-calls-for-resolution-of-south-china-sea-disputes-by-international-law-1.1156037.

54. "Vietnam Economy," *CIA World Factbook 2014*; for recent treatment of Vietnam circumstances, see Nguyen Manh Hung, "U.S.-Vietnam Relations: Evolving Perceptions and Interests," in *Strategic Asia 2014–2015: U.S. Alliances and Partnerships at the Center of Global Power*, ed. Ashley Tellis, Abraham Denmark, and Greg Chaffin, 289–316 (Seattle, WA: National Bureau of Asian Research, 2014).

55. Hung, "U.S.-Vietnam Relations"; "Anti-China Riots Leave over 20 Dead," Reuters, May 15, 2014, http://www.newsweek.com/anti-china-riots-vietnam-leave-over-20-dead-251135; Carl Thayer, "The U.S. Lifts Arms Embargo," *The Diplomat*, October 6, 2014, http://thediplomat.com/2014/10/the-us-lifts-arms-embargo-the-ball-is-in-vietnams-court.

56. Sean Turnell, "Myanmar in 2011," *Asian Survey* 52, no. 1 (January–February 2012): 157–64.

57. Ian Holliday, "Myanmar in 2012," *Asian Survey* 53, no. 1 (January–February 2013): 93–100.

58. Yun Sen, "China Adapts to New Myanmar Reality," *Asia Times Online*, December 23, 2013, http://atimes.com/atimes/Southeast_Asia/SEA-04-231213.html; "China-Southeast Asia Relations," *Comparative Connections* 15, no. 2 (September 2013): 68–69.

59. Dormandy and Kinane, *Asia-Pacific Security*, 4–6; for recent treatment of Australia circumstances, see Bates Gill, "The U.S.-Australia Alliance: A Deepening Partnership in Emerging Asia," in *Strategic Asia 2014–2015: U.S. Alliances and Partnerships at the Center of Global Power*, ed. Ashley Tellis, Abraham Denmark, and Greg Chaffin, 87–118 (Seattle, WA: National Bureau of Asian Research, 2014).

60. Graeme Dobell, "Australia-East Asia/US Relations," *Comparative Connections* 15, no. 2 (September 2013): 145–59; Gill, "The U.S.-Australia Alliance."

61. "New Zealand Economy," *CIA World Factbook 2014*, https://www.cia.gov/library/publications/the-world-factbook/geos/nz.html.

62. Thomas Lum and Bruce Vaughn, *The Southwest Pacific: U.S. Interests and China's Growing Influence*, Report RL34086 (Washington, DC: Library of Congress, Congressional Research Service, July 6, 2007), 21–23.

63. "U.S. Relations with New Zealand," *Department of State Factsheet*, January 31, 2014, http://www.state.gov/r/pa/ei/bgn/35852.htm.

64. Jack Georgieff, "United States–New Zealand Relations: Where to in 2014?," *CSIS Cogint Asia*, December 9, 2013, http://cogitasia.com/united-states-new-zealand-relations-where-to-in-2014.

65. Lum and Vaughn, *Southwest Pacific*, 1–19.

66. Elke Larsen, "Our Ocean Offers a New Turn in U.S.-Pacific Relations," *Pacific Partners Outlook* (CSIS) 4, no. 4 (May 9, 2014), http://csis.org/publication/our-ocean-offers-new-turn-us-pacific-relations.

67. Sarah Eaton and Richard Stubbs, "Is ASEAN Powerful? Neo-realist versus Constructivist Approaches to Power in Southeast Asia," *Pacific Review* 19, no. 2 (June 2006): 135–56.

68. *Wrapup: ASEAN Ministerial Meetings, Regional Forum, and Post-Ministerial Conferences* (Washington, DC: U.S.-ASEAN Business Council, 2001).

69. Morton Abramowitz and Stephen Bosworth, *Chasing the Sun: Rethinking East Asian Policy* (New York: Century Foundation, 2006), 6; Stanley Foundation, "Economic Dimensions of New Power Dynamics in Southeast Asia," *Policy Memo*, July 12, 2007.

70. Mark Manyin, *Terrorism in Southeast Asia*, Report RL31672 (Washington, DC: Library of Congress, Congressional Research Service, August 13, 2004).

71. Bruce Vaughn, *U.S. Strategic and Defense Relationships in the Asia-Pacific Region*, Report RL33821 (Washington, DC: Library of Congress, Congressional Research Service, January 22, 2007), 22–23.

72. Temario C. Rivera, "The Philippines in 2004: New Mandate, Daunting Problems," *Asian Survey* 45, no. 1 (January–February 2005): 128–29.

73. Vaughn, *U.S. Strategic and Defense Relationships*, 23–25.

74. Donald Weatherbee, "Strategic Dimensions of Economic Interdependence in Southeast Asia," in *Strategic Asia 2006–2007*, ed. Ashley Tellis and Michael Wills, 271–302 (Seattle,

WA: National Bureau of Asian Research, 2006); Vaughn, *U.S. Strategic and Defense Relationships*, 26.

75. Joshua Kurlantzick, *Charm Offensive: How China's Soft Power Is Transforming the World* (New Haven, CT: Yale University Press, 2007); Bronson Percival, *The Dragon Looks South: China and Southeast Asia in the New Century* (Westport, CT: Praeger Security International, 2007). See also Hadi Soesastro, "East Asia: Many Clubs, Little Progress," *Far Eastern Economic Review* 169, no. 1 (January–February 2006).

76. Dick Nanto, *East Asian Regional Architecture: New Economic and Security Arrangements and U.S. Policy*, Report RL33653 (Washington, DC: Library of Congress, Congressional Research Service, September 18, 2006).

77. Richard Stubbs, "ASEAN Plus Three: Emerging East Asian Regionalism?," *Asian Survey* 42, no. 3 (May–June 2002): 440–55.

78. Nanto, *East Asian Regional Architecture*, 22.

79. White House, "The President's Trip to Southeast Asia," November 2006, http://www.whitehouse.gov/asia/2006.

80. Ralph Cossa and Brad Glosserman, "A Tale of Two Tales," *PacNet*, no. 84 (December 1, 2014), http://csis.org/files/publication/Pac1484.pdf.

81. Nanto, *East Asian Regional Architecture*, 18–26.

82. See the chairman's statements for the annual meetings of the ASEAN Regional Forum at the ASEAN website: http://www.aseansec.org.

83. The website for the Singapore dialogue is http://www.iiss.org/conferences/the-shangri-la-dialogue.

84. "Joint Declaration on the Second ASEAN Defense Ministers Meeting Plus," August 29, 2013, http://www.mindef.gov.sg/imindef/press_room/official_releases/nr/2013/aug/29aug13_nr/29aug13_fs.html#.U7kc3JRdXxA.

85. David Capie and Amitav Acharya, "The United States and the East Asia Summit: A New Beginning?," East Asia Forum, November 20, 2011, http://www.eastasiaforum.org/2011/11/20/the-united-states-and-the-east-asia-summit-a-new-beginning.

86. See chairman's statements on the annual ASEAN+3 ministerial and heads of government meetings on the ASEAN website.

87. Robert Sutter, "United States and Asia in 2006," *Asian Survey* 47, no. 1 (January–February 2007): 20–21.

88. Weatherbee, "Strategic Dimensions," 282–98; Peter Baker, "Bush Announces Sanctions against Burma," *Washington Post*, September 25, 2007, http://www.washingtonpost.com/wp-dyn/content/article/2007/09/25/AR2007092500136.html.

89. White House, "Press Briefing on the President's Trip to Southeast Asia," November 9, 2006, http://2001-2009.state.gov/p/eap/rls/rm/75954.htm.

90. Victor Cha, "Winning Asia," *Foreign Affairs*, November–December 2007, http://www.cfr.org/asia-and-pacific/winning-asia/p14649.

91. Weatherbee, "Strategic Dimensions," 292–300; Vaughn, *U.S. Strategic and Defense Relationships*, 14–26.

92. Sheldon W. Simon, "Burma Heats Up and the U.S. Blows Hot and Cold," *Comparative Connections* 9, no. 3 (October 2007): 61–70.

93. Sutter, "United States and Asia in 2006," 21.

94. Weatherbee, "Strategic Dimensions," 282–98.

95. Simon, "Burma Heats Up."

96. Vaughn, *U.S. Strategic and Defense Relationships*, 14–26.

97. Thomas Lum, *U.S. Foreign Aid to East and South Asia: Selected Recipients*, Report RL31362 (Washington, DC: Library of Congress, Congressional Research Service, Library of Congress, January 3, 2007), 11–25.

98. White House, Office of the Press Secretary, "Remarks of President Obama to the Australian Parliament," November 17, 2011, http://www.whitehouse.gov/the-press-office/2011/11/17/remarks-president-obama-australian-parliament.

99. "Full Transcripts of Speeches during U.S. President Barack Obama's State Visit to Indonesia, November 9–10," *Jakarta Post*, November 10, 2010, http://www.thejakartapost.

com/news/2010/11/10/full-transcripts-speeches-during-us-president-barack-obama039s-state-visit-indonesia.

100. Elina Noor, "President Obama in Malaysia: The Substance or Symbolism," *Asia Pacific Outlook*, no. 261 (May 8, 2014).

101. Carl Thayer, "Analyzing the U.S.-Philippines Enhanced Defense Cooperation Agreement," *The Diplomat*, May 2, 2014, http://thediplomat.com/2014/05/analyzing-the-us-philippines-enhanced-defense-cooperation-agreement; Aileen S. P. Baviera, "Implications of the U.S.-Philippines Enhanced Defense Cooperation Agreement," *Asia Pacific Outlook*, no. 262 (May 9, 2014).

102. Carl Baker and Brad Glosserman, "Regional Overview," *Comparative Connections* 16, no. 1 (May 2014): 6.

103. U.S. Department of State, "Secretary Clinton on America's Pacific Century at the East West Center," Honolulu, Hawaii, November 10, 2011, http://fpc.state.gov/176998.htm; Hillary Clinton, "America's Pacific Century," *Foreign Policy*, October 11, 2011, http://www.foreignpolicy.com/articles/2011/10/11/americas_pacific_century.

Chapter Nine

U.S. Relations with South Asia

The Obama administration rebalance policy has avowed sustained and enhanced engagement with a very broadly defined scope of Asian-Pacific countries anchored in the West by India. At the same time, it recognizes that this engagement comes with substantial American withdrawal from Afghanistan as prolonged U.S.-led military operations end there and security becomes the responsibility of Afghan government forces. The rebalance policy explicitly tries to reassure the broad range of Asia-Pacific countries that American military withdrawal from Afghanistan, following its earlier withdrawal from Iraq, will not result in a similar decline in American security and other involvement in the region from India in the West to the Pacific Islands in the East.

What the rebalance policy shows is an important difference in American policy priorities in South Asia. Afghanistan and the costly U.S. involvement in neighboring Pakistan related to the American military and other operations in Afghanistan will continue to decline in importance for the United States. Experienced observers in the region and the United States have seen this general pattern before. When the Soviet Union invaded and tried to militarily occupy Afghanistan in 1979, U.S. interest in the armed struggle against the Soviet forces became a focal point of U.S. foreign policy in the last decade of the Cold War. American ties with Pakistan focused on this anti-Soviet armed struggle became very close. In the end, the U.S.-backed efforts were successful. The Soviet forces withdrew from Afghanistan in 1989 as the Soviet Union weakened and ultimately ended in the last years of the Cold War. As a result, American policy interest in Afghanistan and its related close ties with Pakistan declined sharply.[1]

The terrorist attack on America on September 11, 2001, led directly to the U.S.-initiated war in Afghanistan that toppled the Taliban regime which harbored Osama bin Laden and other terrorist leaders responsible for the attack. The subsequent intense and protracted U.S.-led military struggle to pacify the country and support nation building in Afghanistan relied heavily on bases and operations in Pakistan. U.S. policy discussions commonly considered developments in the two countries together under the rubric on America's "Af-Pak" policy or strategy. The Obama government underlined the close connection between the two countries in its policy calculations; it appointed prominent officials to the position of U.S. special representative to Afghanistan and Pakistan.[2]

Against this background, the recent withdrawal of American military forces from Afghanistan and the reduction in related U.S. operations in Afghanistan and Pakistan foreshadows lower priority for these countries in U.S. foreign policy. Because the American stake in Afghanistan's security and nation building has been enormous over the past thirteen years, it's unlikely that the U.S. interest will decline as sharply as it did following the Soviet military withdrawal from Afghanistan in 1989. However, as noted above, the Obama government's avowed rebalance policy is premised on the pullback from Southwest Asia and juxtaposes that withdrawal with affirmations of stronger American involvement to the East.[3]

What the above circumstances mean for analysis of U.S. relations with the three countries treated in this chapter, India, Pakistan, and Afghanistan, strongly suggests that realist international relations theory is well suited to explain U.S. policy toward two of the three, Afghanistan and Pakistan. After over a decade of very costly involvement in combat and nation-building operations, the U.S. government has decided that the costs and benefits of the situation argue for military withdrawal, along with U.S. allies and associates. American concern regarding how the decision to withdraw affects the liberal world order or other considerations of the liberal perspective of international relations theory seems secondary. And assessing the U.S. withdrawal from a constructivist perspective also seems to miss the point of the change in U.S. policy and practice regarding Afghanistan and Pakistan that is signaled by the decision to withdraw.

Realism also explains closer and sustained U.S. engagement with India. India looms large in the power politics shaping Asia's future. U.S. leaders are working hard to advance ever-closer relations with this important rising power. American intent in India also relates to liberal aspects of world politics involving closer economic integration and common values regarding the rule of law, political pluralism, and democracy. Meanwhile, common experiences have involved the interchanges among large numbers of Indian migrants to the United States with their home country, creating bonds of identity across national boundaries appreciated by constructivists in the field of international relations. On balance, however, the realist perspective seems to explain best the U.S. approach to India in the past two decades.

RELATIONS WITH INDIA

Indian-American relations were also subject to a pattern of episodic American policy interest in close relations during the Cold War and its immediate aftermath. Despite the two countries' common democratic practices, the United States in the 1950s became frustrated with India's nonaligned posture as it complicated American coalition building against communist-backed expansion. Strong U.S. support for India in the face of Chinese expansion in the 1962 India-China border war did not last long. The Nixon administration's opening to China saw the United States tilt to China's side against Indian interests, as world powers adopted opposing positions regarding the brutal armed struggle that ultimately led to the breakup of Pakistan and the creation of Bangladesh in 1971. As India saw its interests better served with close relations with the Soviet Union, U.S. interest in and ability to make headway in relations with India declined. American efforts to build international support against the Soviet Union's military invasion of Afghanistan in 1979 saw India line up with Moscow, reducing prospects for closer relations.[4]

The end of Soviet support after the Cold War and India's recognition of reforms needed to open its economy in order to compete effectively in international globalization provided openings for closer relations with the United States. India's nuclear weapons program, along with that of Pakistan, was a major obstacle to closer relations with the United States. Ironically, the crisis caused by the Indian and Pakistani nuclear weapons tests in 1998 provided an opportunity for close official dialogue that resulted in a breakthrough in relations seen notably in President Clinton's 2000 visit to India.[5] The visit was seen as reorienting U.S. policy away from the Cold War alignment with Pakistan and toward a much closer strategic and economic relationship with India. The George W. Bush administration vigorously pursued this new relationship, which also received strong support from President Obama.[6]

The resulting strong and closer economic, security, diplomatic, and social ties between the two countries show that American interest in India, unlike Afghanistan and Pakistan, is in no danger of decline. The Obama government's rebalance and its avowed interest in closer Indian-American relations are well supported by prevailing realities.

The first reality results from the dramatic change in American immigration policies. Those policies were grossly discriminatory toward Asians, among others, for much of the late nineteenth and twentieth centuries. As a result of civil rights legislation in the mid-1960s, notably the Immigration and Nationality Act of 1965, related government practices opened the way to millions of Asian immigrants to the United States. Indian-Americans numbered 845,117 in the 1990 census and 1,678,765 in the 2000 census. The Indian-American community expanded by 69 percent between 2000 and

2010, numbering 3.2 million. The 2010 census of median household income of Indian-Americans reached almost $90,000, which was 80 percent of the U.S. average. Indian-Americans were deeply involved with the information technology industry, a national leader in both India and the United States, with the two countries' industries closely joined. [7]

Related developments included the advancing role of Indian-Americans in U.S. politics, with the nationally prominent governors of Louisiana and South Carolina being Indian-Americans. During the past decade, the Indian-American Congressional Caucus was the backbone of the India-U.S. bilateral relationship and played an important role in the passage of the historic U.S.-Indian civilian nuclear deal in 2005. In the 112th Congress, there were 135 congressional members in the caucus. The number subsequently dropped to 110, partly because there has been no fresh drive from the Indian-American community. [8]

The second reality is India's key position in the geopolitics of the region that extends from the Persian Gulf to the Pacific. [9] The end of the Cold War accelerated a shift toward Asia, including India, in U.S. geopolitical priorities. A series of polls carried out by the Chicago Council of Global Affairs shows a similar trend in public attitudes. In 2006, 43 percent of Americans believed that Asia was more important than Europe, up from 27 percent four years earlier. The trend toward increasing emphasis on what the Obama government and other commentators call the Indo-Pacific has continued up to the present. Even before the Obama government's rebalance policy, the U.S. Navy maritime strategy released in 2007 singled out the western Pacific and the Indian Ocean as the region where U.S. naval assets would be "continuously postured." The document illustrated the importance to U.S. security interests of both the Persian Gulf region as well as traditional U.S. engagement in East Asia and indicated that the Indian Ocean region—with India at the center—was no longer just an area of transit but was strategically important for its own sake. [10]

The mix of economics and security shows up in India's important role in shaping the order in this broad region of increasing interest to the United States. U.S. trade with the region from India to the Pacific is of ever-greater importance in American policy. U.S. trade with India is much less than that with China or Japan but is growing markedly, especially if services trade is included. India carries out growing strategic and economic engagement with neighbors to the East, especially Japan, Korea, and Southeast Asia, that seems to work in parallel with U.S. interests and with deepening U.S.-Indian security and economic ties. India now has an active security relationship with Japan and Australia and a regular security dialogue with the ASEAN countries, as well as a more cautious one with China. India has negotiated free trade areas with Japan, Korea, and ASEAN. India is sought after by Japan and other Asian countries seeking to counter possible Chinese dominance in regional multilateral groupings, and it is happy to participate as a powerful independent actor in these groups.[11]

Against this background comes the Obama administration's rebalance of U.S. policy and strategic assets toward Asia. The policy approach permits the United States, India, and arguably China to build a network of strong powers that can operate in creating a peaceful and prosperous Asia. India is linked to the larger Asian region in U.S. policy and strategic thinking. Such linkage is possible because U.S. and Indian interests are better aligned than in the past. In particular, the two countries view Asian security and economic issues in similar ways. Neither country wants to have a hostile relationship with China. At the same time, neither wants China to become the dominant power in East and Southeast Asia. Both are concerned about freedom of navigation. India is determined to expand its profile in Southeast Asia, and the United States is sympathetic to this goal. During several years of detailed bilateral dialogue on East Asia, the two countries found little to disagree over. Each maintains its own policies in the region, but these policies more often than not wind up being mutually supportive.[12]

The third reality that supports continued strong American interest in closer relations with India is India's economic surge following reforms begun in the 1990s. India has opened its economy much more to the private sector and to external trade and investment. Private investment was 24 percent of GDP in 2010, up from 17 percent in 2000. This compares with 7.8 percent for public sector investment, little changed since 2000. U.S. direct investment (FDI) in India was $28.4 billion in 2012, an increase of 15.3 percent from 2011.[13]

The share of India's economy accounted for by international trade was about 13 percent during much of the 1990s but rose to 50 percent by 2010. U.S. goods and private services trade with India totaled $93 billion in 2012. Exports totaled $34 billion; imports totaled $59 billion. The U.S. goods and services deficit with India was $25 billion in 2012.[14]

India's economy grew strongly for much of the past decade, though growth has slowed recently. The overall transformation of India's economic situation resulted in higher-level attention in U.S. policy and a tremendous increase in official engagement. There are thirty formal dialogues on subjects ranging from energy to education; security relations have grown to include highly sophisticated air, sea, and land force exercises. The two governments work in parallel on sensitive issues involving the Indian Ocean and East Asia. The U.S.-India civil nuclear agreement signed in 2008 and supplemented by agreement on the difficult issue of an Indian reprocessing facility remains a major achievement of the new partnership.[15]

INDIAN PRIORITIES

The democratically elected Indian government has emerged as one of Asia's rising powers despite a variety of complications in India's domestic and foreign policies. Political stability is repeatedly challenged by terrorist attacks and threats, extremist political movements, separatism supported by armed insurgents, and sometimes weak political coalitions leading the government. India's widely publicized economic growth sometimes hides major problems of poor infrastructure, continued government interference, excessive regulation, and corruption. Massive poverty involving hundreds of millions of Indians calls for government spending on health, education, and welfare that is well beyond the limited capability of the government. Improvements in relations with the United States, China, and Pakistan have markedly enhanced India's international position. The Indian military is dominant in South Asia, though Pakistan's armed forces, backed by nuclear weapons, pose a major continuing challenge. [16]

The Indian government switched in 2014 from a coalition of various parties led by the Congress Party to a Parliament dominated by the Hindu nationalist Bharatiya Janata Party (BJP), which won a historic mandate in the country's general election, emerging with 282 of 543 parliamentary seats, more than enough to form a government without having to broker a postelection coalition. The leaders of the Congress Party–led coalition had to consult with a variety of members in their coalition, including some Marxists, before pursuing economic reforms or other controversial policies. This slowed the economic reform process to some degree and complicated moves to establish closer relations with the United States, including Indian government approval of a landmark nuclear cooperation agreement with the U.S. [17]

India ranks among the world's top ten economies—and as the third largest in Asia behind China and Japan—with a total GDP of around $2 trillion. Although India has a good record of growth in the twenty-first century, its large population and relatively high income disparities have left much of India's population in poverty. India was struck by the secondary effects of the global financial crisis of 2008, but its impact was comparatively light. According to the IMF, real GDP growth decreased from 7.3 percent in 2008 to 5.7 percent in 2009. While its financial sectors were largely insulated from the collapse of selected financial markets, the ensuing economic slowdown (particularly in Europe and the United States) led to a drop in demand for India's leading exports. [18]

Recent reforms include liberalized foreign investment and exchange regimes, industrial decontrol, large reductions in tariffs and other trade barriers, reform and modernization of the financial sector, significant adjustments in government monetary and fiscal policies, and progress in safeguarding intellectual property rights. Obstacles to further economic development, including endemic poverty, poor infrastructure, corruption, market economy restrictions, inflationary pressures, and fluctuating rates of foreign investment, saw the economic growth rate decline in recent years. [19]

Features of growing goods trade and services trade along with growing U.S. investment include the following: U.S. direct investment in India is led by professional, scientific, and technical services; manufacturing finance/insurance; and the information sectors. India FDI in the United States was $5.2 billion in 2012, up 6.7 percent from 2011. India direct investment in the United States was primarily concentrated in professional, scientific, and technical services and the banking sector. Sales of services in India by majority U.S.-owned affiliates were $16.4 billion in 2011, while sales of services in the United States by majority India-owned firms were $9.3 billion. [20]

India's military is transforming, gaining greater global reach. India's is the world's third-largest military (after China and the United States), with more than 1.3 million active personnel. The defense budget was more than $38 billion for 2010, a nearly 12 percent increase over the previous year. Additional annual increases followed. New Delhi allocated just under $40.5 billion for defense expenditures in its FY 2012–13 budget. This represented a nominal increase of about 18 percent over the previous year's level. [21]

The army is more than one million strong and continues to account for half of the total budget. Army dominance has continued, along with the navy and air force becoming more important, as India seeks to project its power and protect an exclusive economic zone of more than two million square kilometers. Meanwhile, the 2008 Mumbai terrorist attacks elicited an increase in Indian security spending, including plans to enhance the navy's surveillance capabilities, across-the-board strengthening of the National Security Guard (NSG) counterterrorism force, and the raising of twenty-nine new Border Security Force battalions (elite NSG commandos now operate from four new regional hubs—in Chennai, Hyderabad, Kolkata, and Mumbai—to improve response time in emergencies). [22]

In recent years, China has increasingly been the central focus of Indian defense planners, a shift from their decades-long Pakistan focus. In May 2012, Defense Minister A. K. Antony informed the Indian Parliament that the government would seek an increase in the slated FY 2012–13 defense budget to respond to the "new ground realities and the changing security scenario." In India and the United States, expert commentators and media said that, in contrast to previous decades, India is now sufficiently confident in its military capabilities vis-à-vis Pakistan and is increasingly able to more substantively address other regional security issues beyond the traditional concerns about Pakistan. Foremost is the perceived need to pose a credible military deterrent to China. India prepares for the possibility of a multifront confrontation along both the disputed India-Pakistan and Sino-Indian borders and is expanding its naval presence in the Indian Ocean. More expansively defined national interests result in military planning and procurement to meet those needs.[23]

Though New Delhi and Washington share basic values and goals in foreign affairs, India's security objectives do not always mesh smoothly with those of the United States. As with other Asian-Pacific governments seeking greater development and nation building as the foundation of their leaderships' political standing and legitimacy, India's view of international security emphasizes the country's desire for a pacific external environment in which it can concentrate on economic development and improving popular well-being.[24]

There are four major security objectives[25]:

1. *India's periphery and regional security.* India's great power aspirations require an ability to manage relationships in India's own neighborhood. New Delhi seeks to establish and maintain predominant power in a stable region and thereby achieve a peaceful and predictable environment for economic development. Three major external factors appear to shape New Delhi's policies: the impact of regional dynamics on India's domestic security challenges, China's growing influence in the subcontinent, and the persistent threat posed to India by political instability among its neighbors. Instability in Afghanistan that spills over to nearby countries poses major concerns for India. It remains uncertain how India will deal with the implications of the U.S.-led NATO withdrawal from Afghanistan. Meanwhile, weaknesses and insecurity inside India add to the concerns about the security of the periphery. New Delhi's control of large swaths of Indian territory has been threatened by multiple secessionist movements and insurgencies. At present, conflicts in the Jammu and Kashmir and northeastern states, and in the Maoist or the so-called Red corridor in inland eastern India, constitute the most pressing domestic security challenges.[26]

2. *Asian power balances.* China's rapid economic and military rise changes the strategic balance in Asia in favor of Beijing. China's rise places on guard India, Japan, and the many other Asian countries that have historically difficult relations with Beijing. India also faces Beijing's greater presence in South Asia. As India expands its regional and global role, it repeatedly runs up against China. Constructive Indian engagement with China also grows, but with keen Indian awareness of the need to prepare for contingencies in case China were to become more assertive. Such Chinese assertiveness could be prompted by the disputed border, New Delhi's hosting of the Dalai Lama and his government in exile, ever-closer U.S.-Indian security ties, and other issues of great sensitivity in Sino-Indian relations. Part of India's con-

tingency planning involves closer security and other cooperation with the United States and with a range of China's neighbors in East Asia, Southeast Asia, and the Pacific that seek regional relations and ties with the United States deemed useful to hedge against possible Chinese intimidation and dominance. India has special concerns about growing Chinese naval capabilities that over time may emerge as a fundamental challenge to Indian strategic goals of control of maritime security in the nearby Indian Ocean.[27]

3. *Securing channels to West Asia*. Iran, Israel, and the Arab countries of the Persian Gulf are important for Indian economic and security interests. India's economic growth and its overall security depend on oil and gas imports from West Asia. The region supplies over 60 percent of India's crude oil. Saudi Arabia is the leading oil supplier but India is wary of depending on this country that has historically supported Pakistan. Thus India seeks energy from Iran. Iran also is a counterweight to Pakistan in Afghanistan, and it facilitates Indian access to Afghanistan and Central Asia through Iran's Chabahar port.[28]

   As NATO forces withdraw from Afghanistan, Iran's importance for India is likely to grow, despite New Delhi's moves to back U.S.-led sanctions against Tehran. Meanwhile, India receives over $30 billion annually from six million Indian laborers in the Persian Gulf states, underlining Indian interest in getting along with all concerned in the region. With the third-largest Muslim population in the world, India works diligently to cooperate with Muslim states in identifying and apprehending radical Islamic and other terrorists.

4. *Global security issues*. India seeks to build on its growing international profile through membership in the G-20 and other bodies. It wants a permanent seat on the UN Security Council. It seeks to be accepted as a legitimate nuclear power and thereby gain membership in the Nuclear Suppliers Group (NSG), the Wassenaar Arrangement, the Australia Group, and the Missile Technology Control Regime.

In foreign affairs, Indian calculations and maneuvers show some prevailing trends. Indian leaders view India as a more-or-less natural regional hegemon; they are focused on a relatively narrow set of Indian concerns and devote limited attention to global governance issues; they have a strong commitment to maintaining India's "strategic autonomy"; and they show a preference for hedging strategies that preserve Indian autonomy. Such hedging can involve balancing against a more aggressive China by welcoming a continued major U.S. presence in the region, or by working with China and Russia to preclude an excessively dominant American presence.[29]

Pakistan remains a major strategic concern for India. Three full-scale wars—in 1947–1948, 1965, and 1971—and a constant state of military preparedness on both sides of their mutual border have marked more than six decades of bitter rivalry between India and its western neighbor. U.S. and international interest focuses on the ability of the two recent nuclear powers to manage their differences despite competing territorial claims and cross-border terrorism in both Kashmir and major Indian cities. The Indian government suspended the bilateral peace process following the late 2008 terrorist attack on Mumbai that was traced to a Pakistan-based terrorist group.[30]

Indian-Pakistani rivalry has had a negative impact on U.S.-led efforts to stabilize Afghanistan.[31] Indian and Pakistani leaders often work to limit their rival's influence in a postwar Afghanistan. In Afghanistan, India takes an active role in assisting reconstruction efforts, having committed over $2 billion. It is the leading regional contributor to Afghan reconstruction. Using connections in and through Afghanistan, India seeks to bypass Pakistan when engaging West and Central Asia, to constrain the spread of Islamist militancy on its western flank, and also to dampen the influence of Islamist and other extremism domestically. Yet Indian efforts to project influence into Afghanistan are significantly hindered by geography and ethnicity (where Pakistan enjoys clear advantages). Islamabad also has undertaken provocative anti-India policies in Afghanistan.[32]

Elsewhere, India advances foreign relations with China, sustains cooperative relations with Russia, and improves relations with the United States. Despite suspicions over continuing boundary disputes, Tibet, and Pakistan, Sino-Indian efforts to improve relations continue. Both countries have sought to manage tensions and expand trade and cultural ties. Their bilateral trade was $65 billion in 2013. Bilateral trade reached a record $74 billion in 2011, when China became India's largest trading partner. Trade declined to $66.5 billion in 2012. Trade has been a source of friction with India as China ran a trade surplus with that country of over $30 billion in 2013. Both sides cooperate in finance, agriculture, water resources, energy, environment, tourism, and information technology, along with joint efforts in multilateral forums on international trade negotiations, energy security, and climate change. Both governments have repeatedly hailed their "strategic partnership."[33]

As discussed in chapters 7 and 8, India has been sought after by countries in Southeast Asia and by Japan as they seek to maneuver against possible Chinese dominance in regional groupings. India's role as a possible counterweight to China also looms large in U.S. calculations. India's long-standing close relations with both Iran and Russia work against U.S. interests when American-led efforts are underway to press Teheran to stop developing nuclear weapons and to deter Moscow from expansion at its neighbors' expense.[34]

U.S. POLICY CHOICES AND RECENT ACTIONS

The most dramatic advance in India's foreign relations since the turn of the century has come with the United States. Viewing India as important for strategic U.S. interests, the United States has sought to strengthen its relationship with New Delhi. The two countries repeatedly emphasize that they are the world's largest democracies, both committed to political freedom protected by representative government. India is also moving gradually toward greater economic freedom governed by market forces. The United States and India have a common interest in the free flow of commerce and resources, including through the vital sea lanes of the Indian Ocean. They also share an interest in fighting terrorism and creating a strategically stable Asia.[35]

Differences remain, however, including U.S. opposition to India's nuclear weapons program and dissatisfaction with the pace of India's economic reforms. In the past, these concerns might have dominated U.S. thinking about India, but today the United States views India as a growing world power with which it shares many common strategic interests.[36]

In late September 2001, President Bush lifted sanctions that had been imposed under the terms of the 1994 Nuclear Proliferation Prevention Act following India's nuclear tests in May 1998. A nonproliferation dialogue initiated after the 1998 nuclear tests bridged many of the gaps in understanding between the countries. In a meeting between President George W. Bush and Prime Minister Atal Vajpayee in November 2001, the two leaders expressed a strong interest in transforming the U.S.-India bilateral relationship. In January 2004, the United States and India launched the Next Steps in Strategic Partnership (NSSP), which was both a milestone in the transformation of the bilateral relationship and a blueprint for its further progress.[37]

In July 2005, President Bush hosted Prime Minister Manmohan Singh in Washington. The two leaders announced the successful completion of the NSSP, as well as other agreements to further enhance cooperation in the areas of civil nuclear, civil space, and high-technology commerce. Other initiatives announced at this meeting included a U.S.-India economic dialogue, the fight against HIV/AIDS, disaster relief, technology cooperation, a democracy initiative, an agricultural knowledge initiative, a trade policy forum, an energy dialogue, and a CEO forum. President Bush made a reciprocal visit to India in March 2006, during which the progress of these initiatives was reviewed and new initiatives were launched.

In December 2006, Congress passed the historic U.S.-India Peaceful Atomic Cooperation Act, which allowed direct civil nuclear commerce with India for the first time in thirty years. U.S. policy had opposed nuclear cooperation with India because the country had developed nuclear weapons in contravention of international conventions and never signed the Nuclear

Nonproliferation Treaty, but this legislation cleared the way for India to buy U.S. nuclear reactors and fuel for civil use. The agreement stalled in India beginning in 2007 due to political opposition to the accord. Nonetheless, the United States and India elevated the strategic partnership further in 2007 to include cooperation in counterterrorism, defense, education, and joint democracy promotion.[38]

In 2005, the United States and India signed a ten-year defense framework agreement in order to expand bilateral security cooperation. The two countries now engage in numerous and unprecedented combined military exercises, and major U.S. arms sales to India are underway. The value of bilateral trade tripled from 2004 to 2008 and, as noted earlier, continues to grow. In addition to the influence of a large, relatively wealthy, and increasingly influential Indian-American community, around one hundred thousand Indian students are attending American universities.[39]

President Barack Obama's administration has sought to build upon the deepened U.S. engagement with India begun by President Clinton and furthered under President Bush. This so-called U.S.-India 3.0 diplomacy was on display in July 2011 during the second U.S.-India Strategic Dialogue session in July 2011 where a large delegation of senior U.S. officials demonstrated that the U.S.-India relationship is among the world's most important, with forecasts of large benefits and convergent interests. Initiatives have continued in recent years, though media observers and some specialists argue that the partnership has lost momentum.[40]

Outstanding areas of bilateral friction include obstacles to bilateral trade and investment, including in the high-technology sector; outsourcing; the status of conflict in Afghanistan; climate change; and stalled efforts to initiate civil nuclear cooperation.

Experienced observers highlight significant differences and difficulties likely to complicate the relations[41]:

- *Differing "worldviews."* The United States usually seeks to lead in supporting an international order to its liking. India seeks what it calls strategic autonomy and is reluctant to be seen following the direction of other countries.
- *Economic differences focus on expectations.* The United States seeks an open economy with easy trade access and a friendly environment for investors. India seeks smooth movement of persons across the U.S. border and access to high technology, especially in defense. The United States and India have become more interdependent in the information technology (IT) sector, though outsourcing and the large Indian presence in the U.S. IT sector has led to some complaints.
- *Iran and Russia.* India will balance its interests in supporting U.S.-led pressures against both of these governments with very important interests

it has with each. The result will be less than fully satisfactory for the United States.

• *Multilateralism.* In the UN, the G-20, and forums dealing with free trade, climate change, energy, and other issues, India tends to align with developing countries. Its support for the United States in these instances is neither strong nor frequent. It will work with China in these circumstances in ways that may alienate the United States.

RELATIONS WITH PAKISTAN

The bipartisan American effort to improve relations with India since the 1990s and the important role India plays in the Obama government's recent emphasis on rebalance in the broad Indo-Asia-Pacific compares positively with the trials and tribulations of recent American relations with Pakistan. Despite Pakistan's position as an American security ally since 2004 and a "strategic partner" since 2006, U.S.-Pakistan relations remain unanchored and subject to abrupt change. The withdrawal of U.S.-led military forces from Afghanistan in 2014 represents the latest and one of the most serious tests for cooperative relations between the two countries.[42]

During the latest period of close U.S. relations with Pakistan in the post-9/11 period, the United States has sought and received Pakistan's support during the prolonged U.S.-led military operations in Afghanistan. In return, the United States has provided massive foreign assistance. Pakistan has received over $25 billion in assistance and military reimbursements since 2001.[43] The aid has faced obstacles and cutbacks based on sometimes tense U.S.-Pakistan relations, U.S. funding constraints, and demands for greater effectiveness. Legislated provisions set more rigorous restrictions and certification requirements on such aid. Pakistan reacts very negatively to such actions. Strong anti-American sentiments and xenophobic conspiracy theories prevail among ordinary Pakistanis, while government officials carry out policies at odds with American interests in a basically unstable domestic political, economic, and security environment.[44]

While the U.S. government seeks Pakistan's cooperation in support of operations in Afghanistan, it also provides aid to support Pakistan's role in the broader struggle against terrorism and to assist in the creation of a more stable, democratic, and prosperous Pakistan. U.S. interests also include Pakistan's handling of its nuclear weapons to avoid nuclear weapons proliferation; links between Pakistan and indigenous American terrorism; Pakistan-India tensions; democratization and human rights protection; and economic development. Pakistan is a haven for numerous Islamist extremist and terrorist groups and has been the world's most notable proliferator of nuclear weapons—both major concerns of the United States.[45]

   The U.S. military operation that killed Osama bin Laden in May 2011 revealed that the al-Qaeda founder had enjoyed apparently long and relatively comfortable refuge in a large house in a Pakistani city. Intensive U.S. government scrutiny and congressional questioning focused on the wisdom of providing significant U.S. foreign assistance to a government and nation that may not have the intention and/or capacity to be an effective U.S. partner. Meanwhile, the Pakistani military and intelligence services maintain links to Afghan insurgent and anti-India militant organizations operating from Pakistani territory as a means of forwarding Pakistan's perceived security interests.[46] Such actions undermine American interests in antiterrorism and regional stability. In 2011, Osama bin Laden was killed, and most bilateral security cooperation was suspended. There was also a spike in suspected Pakistan-backed Haqqani Network attacks in Afghanistan, continued controversy over U.S. drone strikes against suspected terrorists operating in Pakistan, and an incident in which two dozen Pakistani soldiers were inadvertently killed by NATO aircraft.[47]

   The withdrawal of U.S.-led forces from Afghanistan in 2014 is an obvious juncture for reassessment in both the United States and Pakistan. Discussed below is the argument by some specialists in favor of America's inclusion of Pakistan in the Obama government's rebalance to Asia. Gaining traction for such an effort seems difficult in a period of continued instability inside Pakistan amid declining U.S. interest in closer relations with Pakistan.

PAKISTAN'S CONDITIONS AND PRIORITIES

American and other international interest in India focuses on India's strengths and what they mean for U.S. and other partners. By contrast, American and other international interest focuses on Pakistan's weaknesses and the problems they can and do pose. The list of concerns includes a rapidly growing population of nearly two hundred million with poor education and poor economic prospects, an expanding nuclear arsenal, political turmoil with governance challenged both within and without, entrenched terrorist networks, and pervasive internal violence. As is widely known, the reason the United States will stay engaged with such a country following the withdrawal from Afghanistan rests a lot more on how Pakistan could negatively affect American interests than on how Pakistan could positively affect U.S. concerns.

   Daniel Markey of the Council on Foreign Relations argues that a hostile or destabilized Pakistan would upset U.S. plans in Asia simply by diverting Washington's attention and depleting U.S. resources.[48] A serious security crisis in nuclear-armed Pakistan would immediately come to the top of Washington's attention and upset other American policy initiatives. Pakistan has more than one hundred nuclear warheads; a war with India caused by Pakistan-harbored terrorists attacking India or other frictions could be an enormous disaster. Pakistan's poor governance and divided interests mean that nuclear technology and equipment may be passed to anti-American terrorists—a nightmare scenario for U.S. security. Pakistan-based terrorists and insurgents—including the remnants of al-Qaeda's core leadership and their sympathizers, and regional terrorist organizations like the Afghan Haqqani Network and Lashkar-e-Taiba (LeT) which targets India—threaten regional security and directly threaten forces in Pakistan and in the region that support good governance and development backed by the United States and other powers.

The achievements in Pakistan and its surroundings supported by U.S. foreign assistance, the war in Afghanistan, the U.S. drone campaign against suspected terrorists operating in Pakistani tribal areas, and a range of other regional counterterrorism activities are offset by adverse developments. Many of Pakistan's other militant and extremist organizations have grown more violent and sophisticated. The Pakistani Taliban (TTP) attacks Pakistan's state institutions and civilians in ways not seen before. Islamabad has low capacity to maintain basic law and order, let alone to attract trade and investment in ways that would grow the national economy. Meanwhile, other extremists such as LeT persist in targeting India, the subcontinent's nuclear-armed superpower.

The priorities Pakistan should follow in constructively dealing with prevailing problems are clear to various experts but thus far are not being well implemented. Pakistan's civilian and military leaders need to implement economic reforms and build better administrative institutions. Islamabad needs to take difficult steps to establish effective authority in curbing domestic organizations advocating and practicing violent extremism; senior military officers should be held accountable for implementing national security guidelines that prioritize the need to curb such internal security threats. A more stable and strong Pakistan would counter terrorist groups and their affiliates operating in Southeast Asia, China, Central Asia, and the Middle East. Meanwhile, Pakistani military operations in the tribal areas along its border with Afghanistan have benefited from U.S. equipment and training. Despite deep disagreements persisting between Washington and Islamabad over various aspects of these operations, the two sides have also achieved important military and counterterrorism successes, which provide the basis for stronger coordination and cooperation.[49]

It is plausible for Pakistan and India to overcome past animosity and build capacity to put down the armed groups that benefit from disrupting their trade and transit. Stability would allow Pakistan to offer a thoroughfare for Central Asian energy supplies—by way of pipelines or power lines—to feed the huge and increasing demand throughout South Asia. Years of negotiations on energy pipelines through Pakistan to India (from Turkmenistan and Iran) provide ample evidence of India's eagerness for such progress. Unfortunately, Pakistan security leaders remain skeptical of India's intentions and reluctant to crack down on anti-India militants in Pakistan. Border tensions with India remain high.[50]

Regarding economic conditions, internal political disputes and low levels of foreign investment have led to slow growth and underdevelopment in Pakistan. Agriculture accounts for more than one-fifth of output and two-fifths of employment. Textiles account for most of Pakistan's export earnings, and Pakistan's failure to expand a viable export base for other manufactures has left the country vulnerable to shifts in world demand. Official unemployment is under 6 percent, but much of the economy is informal and underemployment remains high. Over the past few years, low growth and high inflation, led by a rise in food prices, have increased the amount of poverty—the UN Human Development Report estimated poverty in 2011 at almost 50 percent of the population. Inflation has worsened the situation, climbing from 7.7 percent in 2007 to almost 12 percent in 2011, before declining to 10 percent in 2012. The Pakistani rupee has depreciated more than 40 percent since 2007.[51]

An International Monetary Fund Standby Arrangement was agreed to in November 2008 in response to a balance-of-payments crisis. Although the economy stabilized following the crisis, it failed to recover. Foreign investment is low on account of investor concerns related to governance, energy, security, and a slowdown in the global economy. Remittances from overseas workers have averaged about $1 billion a month. After registering a small current account surplus in FY 2011 (July 2010–June 2011), Pakistan's current account turned to deficit in FY 2012 because of higher prices for imported oil and lower prices for exported cotton. Pakistan is stuck in a low-income, low-growth situation; growth averaged about 3 percent per year from 2008 to 2012. Reforms are needed in dealing with government revenues and energy production in order to encourage the amount of economic growth that will be necessary to employ Pakistan's growing and rapidly urbanizing population; over half the population is under twenty-two. Also needed are more investment in education and health care, adaptation to the effects of climate change and natural disasters, and reduced dependence on foreign donors.[52]

In foreign affairs, Pakistan's priorities changed dramatically in 2001. After the World Trade Center and Pentagon were attacked on September 11, Pakistan came under intense pressure from the United States. Then president Pervez Musharraf pledged complete cooperation with the United States in the war on terror, which included locating and shutting down terrorist training camps within Pakistan's borders, cracking down on extremist groups, and withdrawing support for the Taliban regime in Afghanistan. The events of 9/

11 and Pakistan's agreement to support the United States led to a waiver of sanctions, and military assistance resumed. Large-scale U.S. foreign assistance followed. Presidents Bush and Musharraf affirmed the long-term, strategic partnership between their two countries. In 2004, the United States recognized closer bilateral ties with Pakistan by designating Pakistan as a major non-NATO ally. Bush visited Pakistan in March 2006, where he and Musharraf reaffirmed their shared commitment to a broad and lasting strategic partnership, agreeing to continue their cooperation on a number of issues, including the war on terror, security in the region, strengthening democratic institutions, trade and investment, education, and earthquake relief and reconstruction. [53]

When Musharraf visited Washington in September 2006, he held a bilateral meeting with President Bush and also participated in a trilateral meeting with Bush and President Hamid Karzai of Afghanistan. [54]

The tensions in U.S.-Pakistan relations following the killing of Osama bin Laden and other adverse developments beginning in 2011 which are noted above provided the backdrop of President Obama's meeting with Pakistan prime minister Nawaz Sharif at the White House in October 2013. The two leaders endeavored to deal constructively with various differences, with Sharif stressing Pakistan's public opposition to U.S. drone strikes against terrorists in Pakistan's territory, even though repeated media reports said the Pakistan authorities privately condoned the strikes. The two leaders sought cooperation in anticipation of the withdrawal of U.S.-led forces from Afghanistan. [55]

Pakistan's relations with Afghanistan remain complicated by the Taliban fighters finding havens along the poorly controlled Pakistan-Afghanistan border. Pakistani leaders have long sought access to Central Asia and "strategic depth" with regard to India through friendly relations with neighboring Afghanistan. American and Pakistani goals in Afghanistan are far from compatible; there is very little agreement beyond the shared interest in a negotiated settlement that leaves Afghanistan relatively stable and secure. Pakistan—and especially its military and intelligence services—is widely believed to be seeking a post-NATO Afghanistan that is deferential to and perhaps even dependent upon Islamabad, with Kabul setting foreign policies that do not run counter to Pakistani interests. To have its way, Pakistan can and reportedly does make use of the extremist groups Quetta Shura and the Haqqani Network as proxies in its dealings with Kabul. [56] In contrast, the U.S.-led coalition has endeavored to leave behind a capable and independent Afghanistan. Such a result would almost certainly see the Kabul government increase its cooperation with India, something at odds with Pakistan's objectives. [57]

Meanwhile, Pakistan may be unable to control Quetta Shura, the Haqqani Network, and other various Islamic militant groups within its borders. Islamist militant groups operating in and from Pakistani territory are of five broad types[58]:

- Globally oriented militants include al-Qaeda and its Uzbek and other affiliates that operate in the Federally Administered Tribal Areas (FATA) and in Karachi.
- Afghanistan-oriented militants involve the "Quetta Shura" of Afghan Taliban leader Mullah Omar; these militants are active in the city of Quetta as well as Karachi. They also involve the organization run by Jalaluddin Haqqani and his son Sirajuddin in the North Waziristan and Kurram tribal agencies; and the Hizb-e-Islami party led by Gulbuddin Hekmatyar (HIG), operating further north from the Bajaur tribal agency and Dir district.
- India- and Kashmir-oriented militants include the Lashkar-e-Taiba (LeT), Jaish-e-Mohammed (JeM), and Harakat ul-Mujahadeen (HuM), based in both the Punjab province and in Pakistan-held Kashmir.
- Sectarian militants involve the anti-Shia Sipah-e-Sahaba Pakistan (SSP) and its offshoot, Lashkar-e-Jhangvi (LeJ); the latter is closely associated with al-Qaeda, operating mainly in Punjab.
- Domestically oriented, largely Pashtun militants that in 2007 unified under the leadership of now-deceased Baitullah Mehsud. The unit formed the Tehrik-e-Taliban Pakistan (TTP), based in 2007 in the South Waziristan tribal agency, with representatives from each of Pakistan's seven FATA agencies. Later joiners incorporated into the group were the Tehreek-e-Nafaz-e-Shariat-e-Mohammadi (TNSM) led by Maulana Sufi Mohammed in the northwestern Malakand and Swat districts of the Khyber Pakhtunkhwa province.

Relations between Pakistan and India remain characterized by rivalry, suspicion, and armed conflict. The most sensitive issue since independence has been the status of Kashmir. The prospects for better relations between India and Pakistan improved in early January 2004 when a summit meeting of the South Asian Association for Regional Cooperation (SAARC) permitted India's Prime Minister Vajpayee to meet with President Musharraf. Both leaders agreed to establish a "Composite Dialogue" to resolve their disputes. The Composite Dialogue focused on several issues, notably confidence-building measures and Kashmir. Relations further improved when Musharraf met Indian prime minister Manmohan Singh in New York in October 2004. Additional steps aimed at improving relations were announced when Indian foreign minister Natwar Singh visited Islamabad in February 2005 and in April 2005 when Musharraf traveled to India.[59]

Forward movement came to a halt with the attack on Mumbai in 2008 carried out by Pakistani-based LeT militants. Subsequently, Pakistan has registered some halting progress in normalizing ties, notably trade relations, though border tensions and the ever-present danger of a terrorist attack on India from Pakistani territory continue. Newly elected Indian prime minister Narendra Modi was greeted warmly by Pakistan leaders in 2014, suggesting that further progress is possible.[60]

China has remained on friendly terms with Pakistan for decades. Indian officials have tended to see China using Pakistan as a means to hobble India's rising prominence in Asian affairs. Beijing provided Pakistan with important ingredients for its nuclear weapons and ballistic missile programs. It continues to supply Pakistan with significant military equipment. China has muted in recent years its past support for Pakistan against India over the Kashmir issue, and it generally has not attempted to compete with the United States and other major donors to Pakistan. Beijing prefers a posture of mutual benefit and "win-win" relations, which means that China will not supply aid that is unlikely to be paid back unless there is some other significant benefit for China.[61]

Pakistan's past support of the Taliban antagonized Iran, but relations have improved recently. Pakistan historically has provided military personnel to strengthen Persian Gulf state defenses and to reinforce its own security interests in the area.[62]

U.S. POLICIES AND PRIORITIES

U.S. relations with Pakistan have a checkered history reflecting periodically important but relatively narrow bases for U.S.-Pakistan relations. There remains considerable uncertainty and debate in the United States over the problems and prospects of U.S. ties with this South Asia power. In the twenty-first century, Pakistan has been the locus of U.S. foreign policy concerns regarding terrorism, the future of Afghanistan and overall regional stability, and weapons of mass destruction (WMD) proliferation. There also have been substantial issues over democratization and human rights, as well as trade and economic reform.[63]

The congressional role in dealing with Pakistan is substantial, particularly as Congress reviews and approves the large U.S. foreign assistance to Pakistan. In general, Congress joined with the administration in an often difficult balancing exercise. On the one hand has been an acute American interest in Pakistan's continued counterterrorism cooperation—especially in regard to the stabilization of Afghanistan and the capture or elimination of al-Qaeda and other terrorists. On the other hand have been concurrent concerns about weapons proliferation and the perceived need to encourage development of a more democratic and moderate Pakistani state administration that is genuinely committed to antiterrorism efforts at home and abroad.[64]

Antiterrorism Cooperation and the Future of Afghanistan

After the 9/11 terrorist attacks, Pakistan pledged and provided major support for the U.S.-led antiterrorist campaign. U.S. officials repeatedly praised Pakistan's unprecedented cooperation in allowing the U.S. military to use bases within the country, helping to identify and detain extremists, and tightening its border with Afghanistan. The Pakistani government also cracked down on militant groups involved in terrorist acts in Kashmir and India.[65]

As discussed above, some of the results of U.S.-Pakistan cooperation were mixed, and over time they prompted frustration and concern by U.S. officials regarding the Pakistani government's commitment to the antiterrorism effort. Al-Qaeda and Taliban leaders and forces were widely seen using Pakistani areas near Afghanistan to regroup and launch attacks against coalition forces in Afghanistan. While many observers acknowledged a decrease in Pakistan's support for militants targeting Indian-controlled Kashmir, India continued to complain that the Pakistani government was not doing enough to curb these terrorist groups. The bloody Mumbai attacks of 2008 seemed to support India's complaints. Meanwhile, the Pakistani administration faced a daunting challenge of dealing with a wide range of domestic militants who used bombings, assassinations, and other terrorist attacks in opposition to the government and its policies, especially its close alignment with the United States.[66]

Looking ahead, a key to stabilizing Afghanistan is to improve the long-standing animosity between Islamabad and Kabul. Afghan officials still openly accuse Pakistan of aiding and abetting terrorism inside Afghanistan. Pakistan's mixed record on battling Islamist extremism continues and includes an ongoing apparent tolerance of Afghan Taliban elements operating from its territory, notably the Quetta Shura Taliban (QST) of Mullah Omar and the Haqqani Network.[67]

Pakistan-U.S. Security Cooperation

After the breakthrough in U.S.-Pakistan cooperation against terrorism in 2001, the United States quickly waived sanctions that had been imposed on Pakistan as a result of Pakistan's 1998 nuclear tests and the military coup in Pakistan in 1999. In October 2001, large tranches of U.S. aid began flowing into Pakistan. Direct assistance programs included training and equipment for Pakistan's security forces. In 2002, the United States began allowing commercial sales, which enabled Pakistan to refurbish at least some of its American-made F-16 fighter aircraft. In March 2005, the United States announced that it would resume sales of F-16 fighters to Pakistan after a sixteen-year hiatus. There were many other major government-to-government arms sales and grants even though some in Congress and elsewhere held that

Pakistan might use the advanced jet fighters and other U.S.-supplied military equipment in a conflict with India.[68] As noted above, the security cooperation waned significantly following the 2011 killing of Osama bin Laden and struggled to recover in the face of strong hostility from many in Pakistan and rising skepticism in the United States. The U.S.-led NATO withdrawal from Afghanistan in 2014 seems likely to further narrow grounds for close American-Pakistani security cooperation.

Nuclear Weapons and Missile Proliferation

American policy makers have remained concerned with the arms race between India and Pakistan and the danger of nuclear war in South Asia. The May 1998 Indian and Pakistani nuclear tests were followed by continued development of weapons and delivery systems. Pakistan and India each have around one hundred nuclear warheads. Both countries have aircraft capable of delivering nuclear bombs (U.S.-supplied F-16s in Pakistan's air force reportedly have been refitted to carry nuclear bombs). Pakistan has acquired short- and medium-range ballistic missiles from China and North Korea, while India has developed its own short- and intermediate-range missiles. The missiles are assumed to be capable of delivering nuclear weapons.[69]

U.S. nonproliferation efforts in South Asia have been an issue of some controversy among U.S. policy makers in the administration and Congress, though the recent trend has been to give them lower priority than in the period following the 1998 nuclear tests. Congress and the president removed nuclear-related sanctions on India and Pakistan following 9/11 and the U.S. preparation for war in Afghanistan. The Clinton administration set forth nonproliferation "benchmarks" for Pakistan and India. The results were mixed, and the Bush administration set aside the benchmark framework.

U.S. policy makers remained concerned about Pakistan in particular, fearing onward proliferation from and internal instability in this nuclear weapons state.[70] Media reports in 2002 suggested that Pakistan was assisting North Korea's covert nuclear weapons program by providing uranium enrichment materials and technology beginning in the mid-1990s. Such assistance was seen to call for ending all U.S. nonhumanitarian assistance to Pakistan, but the Bush administration said in 2003 that the facts did not warrant imposition of sanctions under relevant U.S. laws. Libya's disclosure of its nuclear weapons program then showed Pakistani nuclear assistance. In 2004 a Pakistani government investigation of Abdul Qadeer Khan, the founder of Pakistan's nuclear weapons program, said that Khan had confessed to involvement in an illicit international nuclear smuggling network involving sales of nuclear weapons technology and uranium enrichment materials to North Korea, Iran, and Libya. The Pakistan government's assurance to the United States and other concerned powers that it had no knowledge of the illicit activities met with a skeptical international response, but the Bush administration did not alter support for the Pakistan government, a key ally in the war on terrorism.[71]

The security of Pakistan's nuclear arsenal, materials, and technologies continues to be a top-tier U.S. concern, especially as Islamist militants have expanded their geographic influence there. There is ongoing concern that Pakistan's nuclear know-how or technologies remain prone to leakage.

Pakistan-India Tensions over Kashmir

U.S. policy shows special concern with the likely flashpoint of a Pakistan-India war and possible nuclear conflict involving the intense dispute between the two countries over Kashmir. A separatist rebellion has been underway in the region since 1989. Tensions were very high in the wake of the so-called Kargil conflict of 1999 when an incursion of Pakistani soldiers led to a bloody six-week-long battle. In 2001, the bombing of the Jammu and Kashmir state assembly building in October was followed by a December assault on the Indian Parliament building in New Delhi. Both incidents were blamed on Pakistan-based terrorist groups. The Indian government mobilized seven hundred thousand troops along the frontier with Pakistan and threatened war unless Pakistan ended all cross-border infiltration of Islamic militants. Under strong pressure from the United States and others, Pakistan vowed to end the presence of terrorist entities in Pakistan and outlawed five militant groups. However, the implementation was only partial. There were further flare-ups amid continued infiltrations and terrorist attacks.[72] The 2008 Mumbai terrorist attacks discussed earlier were led by the Pakistani-based LeT; they killed 165 people and raised bilateral security tensions markedly.

Radical Islam and Anti-American Sentiment

American policy makers view with deep concern the prevalent anti-Americanism, xenophobia, and religious extremism in Pakistan fostered by politically active Islamic groups opposed to the Pakistan government. At times, those Islamic groups controlled the assemblies of territories bordering Afghanistan; they passed laws and took other actions in support of Islamic law that were at odds with the Pakistan central administration. They particularly criticized the Pakistan government's shift in policy in favor of the United States after September 2001. They deemed that the alliance with the United States represented a fundamental threat to their values and to the sovereignty of Pakistan. Meanwhile, broader gauges of public opinion showed a decided anti-American trend. Worldwide polls measuring opinion toward the United States showed Pakistan among those countries with the most negative view of the United States and its policies.[73]

Democratization and Human Rights

U.S. administration and congressional policy makers continue to register concerns over the lack of progress toward greater democracy and human rights practices in Pakistan. In 2014, the often-cited nongovernmental organization Freedom House rated Pakistan as overall "partly free" in the areas of political and economic freedom.[74] U.S. congressional committees periodically registered concerns about the slow pace of democratic development in Pakistan. The U.S. State Department's annual reports on human rights practices in countries abroad repeatedly registered a negative view of Pakistan's record, while the department's annual reports on religious freedom and trafficking in persons were similarly critical of Pakistan's performance.[75]

Economic Issues and U.S. Aid

Pakistan is a poor country that depends heavily on foreign aid. Since 2001, the United States has been the largest provider of aid to Pakistan. It is also the country's leading export market, taking in $3.7 billion worth of mainly cotton apparel and textiles in 2013. U.S. assistance provides an important indicator of U.S. policy concerns regarding Pakistan. On the whole, administration and congressional actions have shown strong but often grudging support for the Pakistan government despite the nuclear and missile proliferation, political, and human rights concerns. Added to the list of American issues are widespread corruption and ineffective governance. Assistance is in decline in tandem with the U.S. military withdrawal from Afghanistan.[76]

RELATIONS WITH AFGHANISTAN

In 2014, the beginning of the end came for the most important American involvement in Afghanistan. The U.S.-led coalition of military forces, the International Security Assistance Force (ISAF), proceeded rapidly with its withdrawal after over a decade of intense military operations. In June 2013, Afghan National Security Forces (ANSF) took over responsibility for the security of the country. Negotiations over a U.S.-Afghan Bilateral Security Agreement (BSA) dragged on without conclusion, raising questions about whether any international security forces would remain in Afghanistan. Growing U.S. frictions with the outgoing Afghan president Hamid Karzai accompanied the political campaigns in the 2014 presidential and provincial council elections in April. The run-off election of the leading vote getters in the presidential race took place in June. Unlike earlier polls under the U.S.-backed Karzai government that were accompanied by widespread fraud, the April elections were carried out without substantial corruption, though the run-off in June was subject to charges of corruption and fraud. Postelection power-sharing arrangements between the two rival candidates in the run-off elections proved difficult to establish, leading to divided governance in Kabul as government security forces faced intensified Taliban attacks. Though the new government quickly signed the U.S.-Afghan BSA, U.S. and coalition forces withdrew without much letup.[77]

Armed opposition to the Afghan regime by the Taliban insurgents intensified, seriously testing the strength of the ANSF and the central government.[78] Peace negotiations with the Taliban have remained stalled since 2012. Against this background, local power holders prepared for an uncertain future by building military and other forces in defense of local interests. The so-called return of the warlords involved an amalgam of indigenous forces with efforts by local power holders to control or influence central and local government security and police forces. Overall economic conditions remained weak amid an anticipated shrinkage in economic growth with the ISAF withdrawal.[79]

AFGHANISTAN DEVELOPMENTS

U.S. forces in Afghanistan peaked at about one hundred thousand in June 2011, declining to sixty-six thousand by September 2012 and thirty-four thousand in February 2014, with a target of twenty-two thousand by October. The so-called residual force that is planned to remain in Afghanistan for one year after 2014 will consist of about 9,800 U.S. troops. The U.S. force will be ended in 2016. President Obama announced the decisions on the residual force in May 2014 even though Afghan president Hamid Karzai continued to refuse to sign a required Bilateral Security Agreement as he prepared to leave office in 2014. The agreement was reached with the new government elected in 2014. The delay left little time for planning the roles and missions of the residual force. Adding to the complicated security mix, some ethnic and political faction leaders are reacting to the uncertain situation by reviving their militia forces in anticipation of needing to protect their interests if the international drawdown leads to a major Taliban push to retake power.[80]

The U.S.-led residual force and the elections in April and June 2014 have not substantially reduced angst over future developments. The main reasons include continued weak and corrupt Afghan governance and insurgent resiliency and attacks from safe havens in Pakistan. American and other international officials worked hard and with mixed results to avoid a repeat in the 2014 elections of the fraud that marked Afghanistan's elections in 2009 and 2010. Meanwhile, other U.S. and partner country anticorruption efforts in Afghanistan have yielded few concrete results. And as foreign workers retreat to Kabul with the more dire security conditions elsewhere in the country, international influence on local politics and behavior declines, foreshadowing a return to traditional politics and practices at odds with effective and progressive governance. [81]

The main insurgent force in Afghanistan is the Taliban movement, much of which remains at least nominally loyal to Mullah Muhammad Omar, leader of the Taliban regime during 1996–2001. He and subordinates reportedly still operate from Pakistan, probably areas near the border or near the Pakistani city of Quetta. Thus a term usually applied to Omar and his aides is "Quetta Shura Taliban." In recent years, Omar has lost some of his top aides and commanders to combat or Pakistan arrests. [82]

A former mujahedeen party leader Gulbuddin Hekmatyar leads Hizb-e-Islami Gulbuddin (HIG). The faction received extensive U.S. support against the Soviet Union but turned against its mujahedeen colleagues after the communist government fell in 1992. The Taliban displaced HIG as the main opposition to the 1992–1996 Afghan government. HIG currently is ideologically and politically allied with the Taliban insurgents, but HIG fighters sometimes clash with the Taliban over control of territory in HIG's main centers of activity in provinces to the north and east of Kabul. HIG has focused on suicide bombing and other high-profile attacks, including a suicide bombing in Kabul on May 16, 2013, that killed six Americans, two soldiers and four contractors. HIG is considered amenable to reconciliation with Kabul. In early January 2014, Hekmatyar reportedly told his partisans to vote in the April 5, 2014, Afghan elections—an instruction widely interpreted as an attempt to position HIG for a future political role.

The "Haqqani Network" is an insurgent group founded by Jalaluddin Haqqani, a mujahedeen commander and U.S. ally during the U.S.-backed war against the Soviet Union. Jalaluddin Haqqani served in the Taliban regime (1996–2001), and his network has since fought against the Karzai government. The Haqqani Network has targeted several Indian interests in Afghanistan, almost all of which have been located outside the Haqqani main base of operations in eastern Afghanistan. The attacks on Indian interests and the fact that it is at least tolerated in the North Waziristan area of Pakistan support the judgment that the network has ties to Pakistan's Inter-Services Intelligence Directorate (ISI).

The Pakistani Taliban (Tehrik-e-Taliban Pakistan) is an insurgent group that primarily challenges the government of Pakistan. It also supports the Afghan Taliban; some of its fighters reportedly operate from safe havens in Taliban-controlled areas on the Afghan side of the Afghan-Pakistan border.

The seriousness of the security challenges to the ANSF were apparent in the Taliban's campaign between April and October 2013. The campaign saw 6,604 attacks in thirty of thirty-four Afghan provinces. The ANSF suffered many casualties, which were reportedly not made public by military authorities in order not to undermine troop morale. The seriousness of the casualties was worsened by poor medical evacuation capacities. Foreign specialists judge the rate of attrition is unsustainable looking forward. [83]

Meanwhile, strong interest in possible peace talks between the government and the Taliban and other insurgents faded. Negotiations were sporadic, and U.S.-Taliban discussions that were expected when the Taliban opened a political office in Qatar in June 2013 failed to happen. [84]

Afghanistan's economy is recovering from decades of conflict. The economy has improved significantly since the fall of the Taliban regime in 2001, largely because of the infusion of international assistance, the recovery of the agricultural sector, and service sector growth. Despite the progress of the past few years, Afghanistan is extremely poor, landlocked, and highly dependent on foreign aid. Much of the population continues to suffer from shortages of housing, clean water, electricity, medical care, and jobs. Criminality, insecurity, weak governance, lack of infrastructure, and the Afghan government's difficulty in extending rule of law to all parts of the country pose challenges to future economic growth. [85]

Afghanistan's living standards are among the lowest in the world. The international community remains committed to Afghanistan's development, pledging over $67 billion at nine donors' conferences between 2003 and 2010. In July 2012, the donors at the Tokyo conference pledged an additional $16 billion in civilian aid through 2015. Despite this help, the government of Afghanistan will need to overcome a number of challenges, including low revenue collection, anemic job creation, high levels of corruption, weak government capacity, and poor public infrastructure. Afghanistan's growth rate slowed markedly in 2013, dropping to 3.1 percent after a rate of growth of over 14 percent in 2012. [86]

Given the unstable and insecure internal situation, foreign relations loom large in determining developments in Afghanistan. [87] Regional powers are playing an ever more important role with the withdrawal of U.S.-led NATO forces. The Obama administration has tried to influence Afghanistan's neighbors to support the country's stability and development and has asked them to provide Afghanistan with entry into regional security and economic organizations. The United States has used international meetings to seek formal pledges from Afghanistan's neighbors of noninterference in the country's affairs. Afghanistan has had some success in the past decade in participating in such groupings as the South Asian Association for Regional Cooperation (SAARC), the leading South Asian body, and the Shanghai Cooperation Organization (SCO), a security and economic coordination body that includes original members Russia, China, Uzbekistan, Tajikistan, Kazakhstan, and Kyrgyzstan, with Mongolia, India, Pakistan, and Iran also participating. [88]

Economically, the U.S. administration foresees sharp cutbacks in foreign assistance. One option is to emphasize a vision of the development of a

Central Asia-South Asia trading hub—part of a "New Silk Road" (NSR)—thereby promoting Afghan stability and economic development through such commercial means.[89]

The neighboring country most important to Afghanistan's future is Pakistan.[90] As discussed above, Afghan militants' safe haven in Pakistan is one of the most important threats to Afghan stability after 2014. Pakistan's goal is that Afghanistan, at a minimum, will not align with rival India, and, at best, will provide Pakistan with strategic depth against India. Consequently, Pakistan is seen by specialists to support developments that provide factions with interests compatible with Pakistan's (such as the Taliban) the ability to have a major influence in post-2014 Afghanistan. According to some specialists, Pakistan's goal in allowing some groups, such as the Haqqani Network, relative safe haven in Pakistan territory may be to develop leverage with Afghanistan to support Pakistan's policies.

Pakistan's strong interest in limiting India's influence in Afghanistan showed when Pakistani defense secretary Lieutenant General Asif Yasin announced in late January 2014 that Pakistan would not accept a robust role for India in Afghanistan after the international security mission ended in 2014. At a February 2013 meeting in Britain, Pakistan demanded that Afghanistan scale back relations with India and sign a strategic agreement with Pakistan that included Pakistani training for the ANSF.[91]

Afghanistan-Pakistan relations continue to fluctuate. Many Afghans came to oppose Pakistan as one of only three countries to formally recognize the pre-2001 Taliban regime as the legitimate government. Relations improved after military leader President Pervez Musharraf left office in 2008 and was replaced by a civilian president. However, President Karzai moved closer to India. Afghan-Pakistani border clashes in 2013 worsened tensions. Pakistan prime minister Nawaz Sharif worked to improve relations after entering office in June 2013.

The Afghan presidential run-off election in June 2014 between former foreign minister Abdullah Abdullah and ex–finance minister Ashraf Ghani Ahmadzai and the subsequent power-sharing arrangements means that Pakistan will now prefer President Ghani because he is a Pashtun and a potential friend of Pakistan. Dr. Abdullah, now chief executive officer, and his supporters in the Afghan organization known as the Northern Alliance are sharply critical of Pakistan and accuse it of directly and materially seeking a return to power of the Taliban in Afghanistan.[92]

India seeks to deny Pakistan "strategic depth" in Afghanistan, to deny Pakistan the ability to block India from trade and other connections to Central Asia and beyond, and to prevent militants in Afghanistan from attacking Indian targets in Afghanistan, India, and elsewhere. Afghanistan has sought close ties to India, in large part to access India's large and rapidly growing economy. In the past, it has usually tried to avoid alarming Pakistan. However, in May 2011, India and Afghanistan announced a "Strategic Partnership" agreement that demonstrated India's support for U.S. efforts to better integrate Afghanistan into regional political, economic, and security structures. On October 5, 2011, Karzai signed the pact in New Delhi that gave India a formal role as one of the guarantors of Afghan stability. Karzai's trip to India in November 2012 reportedly saw India agree to train up to six hundred ANSF personnel a year. After Afghanistan-Pakistan border clashes in early May 2013, Karzai visited India later that month, reportedly seeking sales of Indian artillery, aircraft, and other systems that would help it better defend its border with Pakistan. Karzai visited again in mid-December 2013 and reportedly sought Indian tanks, artillery, and helicopters.[93]

On the one hand, India reportedly does not want to be saddled with the burden of helping to secure Afghanistan as U.S.-led forces depart. It has resisted some of the Afghan requests in order not to become more directly involved in the conflict there. On the other hand, India seeks to offset potential preponderant Pakistani influence in post-2014 Afghanistan. India supported the Northern Alliance against the Taliban in the mid-1990s and has been in contact with them, preparing for possible future contingencies.[94]

Iran seeks to deny the United States the use of Afghanistan as a base from which to pressure or attack Iran. More broadly, Iran seeks to exert its historic influence over western Afghanistan, which was once part of the Persian Empire, and to protect Afghanistan's Shiite and other Persian-speaking minorities. Iran provides support for Taliban fighters, who are Pashtun, seemingly at odds with Iran's traditional support for Persian-speaking or Shiite factions in Afghanistan, many of whom have been oppressed by the Pashtuns. Iran's economic aid to Afghanistan does not conflict with U.S. efforts to develop Afghanistan. Iran has pledged about $1 billion in aid to Afghanistan, of which about $500 million has been provided to date, mainly for roads in western Afghanistan.[95]

Russia, Central Asian states, and China all have an interest in Afghanistan's stability. Radical Islamic movements targeting their countries received safe haven in Afghanistan during the Taliban regime. Russia and several Central Asian states also have been important in sustaining the so-called Northern Distribution Network supply route that U.S. and NATO suppliers used to support their military operations and other efforts in Afghanistan. China has sought to limit India's role in the Shanghai Cooperation Organization and other regional groups; Beijing may be sympathetic with Pakistani efforts to block suspected Indian efforts to expand ties with Afghanistan in order to weaken and encircle Pakistan. Russia for its part tends to support a stronger Indian role in the SCO and regional affairs.[96]

U.S. POLICIES AND PRIORITIES

The Obama administration remains committed to the U.S. military pullback from Afghanistan. NATO and other allied forces have been ahead of the United States in withdrawing troops from the country. As noted above, President Obama in May 2014 announced the U.S. plan for a temporary residual force in Afghanistan from 2014 to 2016, even though the United States had yet to reach agreement with the Afghan government on the proposed Bilateral Security Agreement governing the future U.S. military role in the country. Through the end of FY 2013, the United States had provided nearly $93 billion in assistance to Afghanistan since 2001: $56 billion has been to equip and train Afghan forces. The appropriated U.S. aid for FY 2014 is over $6.1 billion, including $4.7 billion to train and equip the ANSF, and the FY 2015 request is similar to the FY 2014–appropriated levels. Administration officials have pledged to Afghanistan that economic aid requests for Afghanistan are likely to continue roughly at recent levels through at least FY 2017.[97]

Afghanistan remains aid dependent. The United States and other donors continue to fund development projects, increasingly delegating project implementation to the Afghan government with results that remain to be seen. Other U.S. options involve promoting development of Afghanistan's mineral and agricultural resources and seeking greater Afghan integration into regional trade and investment patterns as part of a "New Silk Road." Persuading Afghanistan's neighbors, particularly Pakistan, to support Afghanistan's stability remains a U.S. priority.[98]

The level of U.S. commitment to many of these goals is uncertain. The strong American debate over the impact that the long military campaign and related developments have had on U.S. national interests arguably leans in the direction of further withdrawal. Because of the large requirements for military and economic assistance, the stakeholders in the U.S. policy debate range widely and involve Congress directly, along with the president and his subordinates.

Former Secretary of Defense Robert Gates worked against Obama administration leaders, including the president, seen seeking U.S. military withdrawal from Afghanistan. Since Gates's departure in 2011, developments have supported President Obama's efforts to remove U.S. forces and reduce the U.S. commitment to the country. The president's rebalance policy has shown that other issues in Asia have attracted the administration's attention. In a period of serious budget constraints, there are many in the U.S. policy community who argue that providing billions of dollars a year to Afghanistan, perhaps for another decade, is no longer feasible.[99]

Looking forward, a key U.S. objective is to continue efforts to prevent the return of the Taliban as a security threat and to ensure that Afghanistan does not once again become a base for Islamic terrorism. The United States continues to seek to project power in the region to counter significant terrorist threats. India and frontline Central Asia states, along with possibly Russia and even Iran, may work together or in parallel with the United States in such efforts. Pakistan, with its long-standing ties to the Taliban, and possibly Pakistan's supporters in China and Saudi Arabia, may oppose U.S. pressure on a terrorist-supporting Afghan regime.

The U.S. silk road and other development plans for Afghanistan seem visionary. More important will be how U.S. policy in Afghanistan plays into what is a complicated mix of interests in Afghanistan involving its most important neighbors—Pakistan, India, Iran, Russia, and China. The mix of interests evolves with changing circumstances, and as stressed above the U.S. military withdrawal marks the most important changed circumstance in the twenty-first century. It also signals that American stake in international maneuvering in the country is much less than in the recent past, and probably will diminish further.

More specific concerns in U.S. policy have been registered in provisions in legislation authorizing and appropriating funds for U.S. military operations and U.S. assistance in Afghanistan. The total cost of $93 billion for U.S. military, economic, and other assistance to Afghanistan during 2002–2013 does not include costs for U.S. combat operations. Those costs were about $90 billion in FY 2010, $104 billion in FY 2011, $93 billion in FY 2012, and $82 billion in FY 2013. When those costs are included, the United States has spent about $647 billion on the Afghanistan effort from 2002 to 2013.[100]

Some laws have required the withholding of U.S. aid subject to administration certification of Afghan compliance on a variety of issues, including counternarcotics efforts, anticorruption, vetting of the Afghan security forces, Afghan human rights practices and the protection of women's rights, and other issues. Prior to 2013, required certifications had been made, and virtually no U.S. funds had been withheld. In mid-2013, reports surfaced that the CIA had been giving cash payments to President Karzai's office and National Security Council to be used at their discretion. In response, Senator Bob Corker placed a hold on about $75 million in U.S. governance funds. Meanwhile, Afghanistan sought to charge the U.S. military to ship equipment out of the country. Legislation proposed in the 113th Congress would have reduced U.S. aid to Afghanistan by a multiple of the amount of funds Afghanistan sought to charge the U.S. military to ship equipment out of the country. The Afghan government dropped the levy in early August 2013.[101]

To support independent oversight of U.S. aid to Afghanistan, the conference report on the FY 2008 defense authorization bill (P.L. 110-181) established a special inspector general for Afghanistan reconstruction (SIGAR) modeled on a similar outside auditor for Iraq. The SIGAR issues quarterly reports and specific audits of aspects of Afghan governance and security, with particular attention to how U.S.-provided funds have been used. Some of the reports have been disputed by executive branch departments. [102]

NOTES

1. Xenia Dormandy and Michael Keating, "The United States and Afghanistan: A Diminishing Transactional Relationship," *Asia Policy*, no. 17 (January 2014): 6–7.

2. U.S. Department of State, Special Representative for Afghanistan and Pakistan, http://www.state.gov/s/special_rep_afghanistan_pakistan (accessed July 6, 2014); Richard Armitage and Samuel Berger, *U.S. Strategy for Pakistan and Afghanistan* (Washington, DC: Council on Foreign Relations, November 2010).

3. Michael Wills, "Afghanistan beyond 2014: The Search for Security in the Heart of Asia," *Asia Policy* 17 (January 2014): 2–3.

4. Stephen Cohen, *India: Emerging Power* (Washington, DC: Brookings Institution, 2001), 269–85.

5. Strobe Talbott, *Engaging India: Diplomacy, Democracy and the Bomb* (Washington, DC: Brookings Institution, 2004).

6. K. Alan Kronstadt and Sonia Pinto, *U.S.-India Security Relations: Strategic Issues*, Report R42948 (Washington, DC: Library of Congress, Congressional Research Service, January 24, 2013).

7. "Indian Americans Grow to 3.2 Mn., Top in Income," *Hindustan Times*, November 16, 2011, http://www.hindustantimes.com/business-news/indian-americans-grow-to-3-2-mn-top-in-income/article1-769858.aspx.

8. "Indian-Americans' Interest in Lobbying for Indo-U.S. Ties Wanes," *Times of India*, February 7, 2013, http://timesofindia.indiatimes.com/nri/us-canada-news/Indian-Americans-interest-in-lobbying-for-Indo-US-ties-wanes/articleshow/18381977.cms.

9. For recent treatment of important Indian circumstances and converging Indian-American interests, see Daniel Twining, "Building U.S. Partnerships for the 21st Century: The Case of (and for) India," in *Strategic Asia 2014–2015: U.S. Alliances and Partnerships at the Center of Global Power*, ed. Ashley Tellis, Abraham Denmark, and Greg Chaffin, 165–96 (Seattle, WA: National Bureau of Asian Research, 2014).

10. U.S. Navy, Marine Corps, Coast Guard, *A Cooperative Strategy for 21st-Century Sea Power*, October 2007, http://www.navy.mil/maritime/maritimestrategy.pdf.

11. Kronstadt and Pinto, *U.S.-India Security Relations*, 29–32.

12. K. Alan Kronstadt, coordinator, *India: Domestic Issues, Strategic Dynamics, and U.S. Relations*, Report RL33529 (Washington, DC: Library of Congress, Congressional Research Service, September 1, 2011), 82–84.

13. U.S. Trade Representative Office, *India Fact Sheet*, http://www.ustr.gov/countries-regions/south-central-asia/india (accessed July 6, 2014).

14. Ibid.

15. Kronstadt, *India*, 74–76, 79–81.

16. C. Raja Mohan, "Poised for Power: The Domestic Roots of India's Slow Rise," in *Strategic Asia 2007–2008: Domestic Political Change and Grand Strategy*, ed. Ashley J. Tellis and Michael Wills, 177–210 (Seattle, WA: National Bureau of Asian Research, 2007); Deepa Ollapally and Rajesh Rajagopalan, "The Pragmatic Challenge to Indian Foreign Policy," *Washington Quarterly* 34, no. 2 (Spring 2011): 145–62.

17. Ankit Panda, "BJP, Modi Win Landslide Victory in Indian Elections," *The Diplomat*, May 16, 2014, http://thediplomat.com/2014/05/bjp-modi-win-landslide-victory-in-indian-elections.

18. Kronstadt, *India*, 49–50.

19. Ibid., 50–55.

20. U.S. Trade Representative Office, *India Fact Sheet*.

21. Kronstadt and Pinto, *U.S.-India Security Relations*, 12.

22. Kronstadt, *India*, 58.

23. Eric Heginbotham and George Gilboy, *Chinese and Indian Strategic Behavior: Growing Power and Alarm* (New York: Cambridge University Press, 2012); Robert Kaplan, *Monsoon: The Indian Ocean and the Future of American Power* (New York: Random House, 2011).

24. Twining, "Building U.S. Partnerships."

25. Adapted from Kronstadt and Pinto, *U.S.-India Security Relations*, 21–27; see among others Vidya Nadkarni, *Strategic Partnerships in Asia: Balancing without Alliances* (London: Routledge, 2010); Teresita Schaffer, *India and the United States in the 21st Century* (Washington, DC: CSIS, 2009).

26. Stephen P. Cohen, *India's Military Modernization* (Washington, DC: Brookings Institution, 2010).

27. Kaplan, *Monsoon*; Van Jackson, "The Rise and Persistence of Strategic Hedging across Asia: A System-Level Analysis," in *Strategic Asia 2014–2015: U.S. Alliances and Partnerships at the Center of Global Power*, ed. Ashley Tellis, Abraham Denmark, and Greg Chaffin, 317–44 (Seattle, WA: National Bureau of Asian Research, 2014).

28. Shashank Joshi, "India's Role in a Changing Afghanistan," *Washington Quarterly* 37, no. 2 (Summer 2014): 87–102.

29. George Gilboy and Eric Heginbotham, "Double Trouble: A Realist View of Chinese and Indian Power," *Washington Quarterly* 36, no. 3 (Summer 2013): 125–42.

30. Stephanie Flamenbaum and Megan Neville, *Optimism and Obstacle in India-Pakistan Peace Talks*, Peace Brief 98 (Washington, DC: U.S. Institute of Peace, July 15, 2011).

31. C. Christine Fair, "Securing Indian Interests in Afghanistan beyond 2014," *Asia Policy*, no. 17 (January 2014): 27–33.

32. Sonia Luthra, "India-Pakistan Rivalry in Afghanistan," National Bureau of Asian Research, *2014 Asia-Pacific Watch List*, http://www.nbr.org/research/activity.aspx?id=387 (accessed July 6, 2014).

33. Gilboy and Heginbotham, "Double Trouble."

34. Tanvin Madan, "India's Reaction to the Situation in Ukraine," *Brookings Upfront*, March 14, 2014, http://www.brookings.edu/blogs/up-front/posts/2014/03/14-ukraine-india-madan; Twining, "Building U.S. Partnerships."

35. Robert Hathaway, "India and the U.S. Pivot to Asia," YaleGlobal Online, February 24, 2012, http://yaleglobal.yale.edu/content/india-and-us-pivot-asia.

36. S. Paul Kapur and Sumit Ganguly, "The Transformation of U.S.-India Relations: An Explanation for the Rapprochement and Prospects for the Future," *Asian Survey* 47, no. 4 (July–August 2007): 642–56; Twining, "Building U.S. Partnerships."

37. Ashley Tellis, *India as a New Global Power: An Action Agenda for the United States* (Washington, DC: Carnegie Endowment for International Peace, 2005).

38. Satu Limaye, "Consolidating Friendships and Nuclear Legitimacy," *Comparative Connections* 9, no. 4 (January 2008): 153.

39. U.S. Department of State, *U.S.-India Joint Fact Sheet: U.S.-India Cooperation in Higher Education*, June 24, 2013; Kronstadt, *India*, 1.

40. Andrew Wyatt, "India in 2013," *Asian Survey* 54, no. 1 (January–February 2014): 163.

41. Informed by Talking Points of Howard B. Schaffer and Teresita Schaffer at "The Asian Triangle: The United States and Rising India and China," University of Virginia, February 14, 2014.

42. Larry P. Goodson, "The New Great Game: Pakistan's Approach to Afghanistan after 2014," *Asia Policy*, no. 17 (January 2014): 33–40.

43. K. Alan Kronstadt, *Pakistan-U.S. Relations*, Report R41832 (Washington, DC: Library of Congress, Congressional Research Service, May 24, 2012), summary page.

44. Anas Malik, "Pakistan in 2013," *Asian Survey* 54, no. 1 (January–February 2014): 177–89.

45. Kronstadt, *Pakistan-U.S. Relations*, 2012, summary page.

46. C. Christine Fair, *Fighting to the End: The Pakistan Army's Way of War* (New York: Oxford University Press, 2014).

47. Salman Masood and Eric Schmitt, "Tensions Flare between U.S. and Pakistan after strike," *New York Times*, November 26, 2011, http://www.nytimes.com/2011/11/27/world/asia/pakistan-says-nato-helicopters-kill-dozens-of-soldiers.html?pagewanted=all.

48. Daniel Markey, *Reorienting U.S. Pakistan Strategy: From Af-Pak to Asia*, Council Special Report No. 68 (Washington, DC: Council on Foreign Relations, January 2014).

49. Kronstadt, *Pakistan-U.S. Relations*, 2012, 26–41.

50. Malik, "Pakistan in 2013," 183; Fair, *Fighting to the End*.

51. *CIA World Factbook 2014*, "Pakistan Economy," https://www.cia.gov/library/publications/the-world-factbook/geos/print/country/countrypdf_pk.pdf (accessed July 7, 2014).

52. Kronstadt, *Pakistan-U.S. Relations*, 2012, 46–50.

53. K. Alan Kronstadt, *Pakistan-U.S. Relations*, Report 33498 (Washington, DC: Library of Congress, Congressional Research Service, July 27, 2006), 4.

54. Sheryl Gay Stolberg, "Bush Plays Chaperon for Awkward Encounter," *New York Times*, September 28, 2006.

55. White House Office of the Press Secretary, "Joint Statement of President Obama and Prime Minister Nawaz Sharif," October 23, 2013, http://www.whitehouse.gov/the-press-office/2013/10/23/joint-statement-president-obama-and-prime-minister-nawaz-sharif.

56. Goodson, "The New Great Game"; Fair, *Fighting to the End*.

57. Sandra Destradi, "India: A Reluctant Partner for Afghanistan," *Washington Quarterly* 37, no. 2 (summer 2014): 103–17; Kronstadt, *U.S.-Pakistan Relations*, 2012, 26–33.

58. Adapted from Kronstadt, *U.S.-Pakistan Relations*, 2012, 36.

59. Kronstadt, *Pakistan-U.S. Relations*, 2006, 6.

60. Anjana Pasricha, "Indian, Pakistani Leaders Hold Landmark Talks," *Voice of America*, May 27, 2014, http://www.voanews.com/content/indian-pakistani-leaders-meet-in-new-delhi/1923254.html.

61. Raffaello Pantucci, *China in Pakistan: An Awkward Relationship beneath the Surface*, RUSI Newsbrief, January 15, 2014, https://www.rusi.org/publications/newsbrief/ref:A52D6767C1ECA7/#.U7roM5RdXxA.

62. Kayhari Barzegar, "Iran's Foreign Policy in Post-Taliban Afghanistan," *Washington Quarterly* 37, no. 2 (Summer 2014): 119–37; Sumitha Narayanari Kutty, "Iran's Continuing Interests in Afghanistan," *Washington Quarterly* 37, no. 2 (Summer 2014): 139–56; Kronstadt, *Pakistan-U.S. Relations*, 2006, 6–7; Kronstadt, *Pakistan-U.S. Relations*, 2012, 45.

63. Armitage and Berger, *U.S. Strategy for Pakistan and Afghanistan*.

64. Ashley Tellis, "U.S. Strategy: Assisting Pakistan's Transformation," *Washington Quarterly* 28, no. 1 (Winter 2004–2005): 97–116; Craig Cohen and Derek Chollet, "When $10 Billion Is Not Enough: Rethinking U.S. Strategy toward Pakistan," *Washington Quarterly* 30, no. 2 (Spring 2007): 7–19.

65. John Gill, "Pakistan: A State under Stress," in *Strategic Asia 2003–2004*, ed. Richard J. Ellings and Aaron L. Friedberg, 209–28 (Seattle, WA: National Bureau of Asian Research, 2003).

66. Malik, "Pakistan in 2013," 183–86.

67. Goodson, "The New Great Game."

68. Kronstadt, *Pakistan-U.S. Relations*, 2006, 7, 11–12.

69. Arms Control Association, *Nuclear Weapons: Who Has What at a Glance*, June 23, 2014, http://www.armscontrol.org/factsheets/Nuclearweaponswhohaswhat.

70. Paul Kerr and Mary Beth Nitkin, *Pakistan's Nuclear Weapons: Proliferation and Security Issues*, Report RL34248 (Washington, DC: Library of Congress, Congressional Research Service, March 19, 2013).

71. Charles H. Kennedy, "Pakistan in 2004: Running Very Fast to Stay in the Same Place," *Asian Survey* 45, no. 1 (January–February 2005): 107–9.

72. John Lancaster, "India, Pakistan End Talks Stalemated over Kashmir," *Washington Post*, September 7, 2004, A19.

73. "Pakistanis See U.S. as Enemy," Pew Research Center, 2010, http://www.pewresearch.org/daily-number/pakistanis-see-u-s-as-an-enemy; "Pakistani Public Opinion Ever More Critical of U.S.," Pew Research, June 27, 2012, http://www.pewglobal.org/2012/06/27/pakistani-public-opinion-ever-more-critical-of-u-s.

74. Freedom House, *Pakistan*, 2014, http://www.freedomhouse.org/country/pakistan#.U7sBd5RdXxA (accessed July 7, 2014).

75. Kronstadt, *Pakistan-U.S. Relations*, 2012, 53–54.

76. Susan Epstein and K. Alan Kronstadt, *Pakistan: U.S. Foreign Assistance*, Report R41856 (Washington, DC: Library of Congress, Congressional Research Service, July 1, 2013).

77. Vanda Felbab-Brown, "Afghanistan in 2013," *Asian Survey* 54, no. 1 (January–February 2014): 171–73; Mirwais Harooni and Maria Golovnina, "Afghanistan Abdullah Rejects Election Result," Reuters, July 7, 2014, http://www.reuters.com/article/2014/07/07/us-afghanistan-election-idUSKBN0FC0EN20140707; Missy Ryan, "Hagel Says U.S. to Leave 1,000 Extra Troops in Afghanistan," *Washington Post*, December 6, 2014, http://www.washingtonpost.com/world/hagel-pays-final-visit-to-afghanistan-as-pentagon-chief/2014/12/06/e6cf5c2c-7d17-11e4-9a27-6fdbc612bff8_story.html.

78. Stephen Biddle, "Afghan Legacy: Emerging Lessons of an Ongoing War," *Washington Quarterly* 37, no. 2 (Summer 2014): 73–86.

79. Felbab-Brown, "Afghanistan in 2013," 174–76.

80. Kenneth Katzman, *Afghanistan: Post-Taliban Governance, Security and U.S. Policy*, Report RL30588 (Washington, DC: Library of Congress, Congressional Research Service, April 9, 2014), summary page; Karen DeYoung, "Obama to Leave 9,800 Troops in Afghanistan," *Washington Post*, May 27, 2014, http://www.washingtonpost.com/world/national-security/obama-to-leave-9800-us-troops-in-afghanistan-senior-official-says/2014/05/27/57f37e72-e5b2-11e3-a86b-362fd5443d19_story.html.

81. Wills, "Afghanistan beyond 2014," 2–6.

82. This brief review of the main insurgent groups is taken from Katzman, *Afghanistan*, 2014, 13–16, and Kenneth Katzman, *Afghanistan: Post-Taliban Governance, Security and U.S. Policy*, Report RL30588 (Washington, DC: Library of Congress, Congressional Research Service, September 19, 2013), 13–16.

83. Felbab-Brown, "Afghanistan in 2013," 166–67.

84. Azam Ahmed and Matthew Rosenberg, "Karzai Arranged Secret Contacts with Taliban," *New York Times*, February 3, 2014, http://www.nytimes.com/2014/02/04/world/asia/karzai-has-held-secret-contacts-with-the-taliban.html?_r=0.

85. *CIA World Factbook 2014*, "Afghanistan Economy," https://www.cia.gov/library/publications/the-world-factbook/fields/2116.html.

86. Lalit K. Jha, "Afghanistan's Growth Rate Drops from 14.4 Percent to 3.1 Percent in a Year," *Rawa News*, January 15, 2014, http://www.rawa.org/temp/runews/2014/01/15/afghanistan-s-growth-rate-drops-from-14-4-to-3-1-percent-in-a-year.html; Katzman, *Afghanistan*, 2014, 56–60.

87. Wills, "Afghanistan beyond 2014," 2–6.

88. Katzman, *Afghanistan*, 2013, 44–45.

89. Kathleen Collins, "The Limits of Cooperation: Central Asia, Afghanistan and the New Silk Road," *Asia Policy*, no. 17 (January 2014): 18–27; U.S. Department of State, "U.S. Support for the New Silk Road," http://www.state.gov/p/sca/ci/af/newsilkroad (accessed July 7, 2014).

90. Goodson, "The New Great Game."

91. Ahmad Ramin, "Pakistan Warns U.S. on India's Role in Afghanistan," *Tolonews*, January 24, 2014, http://www.tolonews.com/en/afghanistan/13601-pakistan-to-not-accept-india-in-afghanistan; Katzman, *Afghanistan*, 2014, 44.

92. Ibid., 44.

93. Joshi, "India's Role in a Changing Afghanistan"; Destradi, "India: A Reluctant Partner for Afghanistan"; Government of India, Ministry of External Affairs, *Hamid Karzai's 14th Visit to Delhi: A "New Role" for India*, December 11, 2013, http://mea.gov.in/articles-in-indian-media.htm?dtl/22607/Hamid+Karzais+14th+visit+to+Delhi+A+new+role+for+India.

94. Ankit Panda, "Hamid Karzai Asks India for Defense Assistance," *The Diplomat*, December 14, 2013, http://thediplomat.com/2013/12/hamid-karzai-asks-india-for-defense-assistance.

95. Ellen Laipson, "Iran-Afghanistan Ties Enter a New Era," *Asia Times*, December 18, 2013, http://www.atimes.com/atimes/Middle_East/MID-01-181213.html.

96. Zhao Huasheng, "Chinese Views of Post-2014 Afghanistan," *Asia Policy*, no. 17 (January 2014): 54–59; Mark Katz, "Putin's Predicament: Russia and Afghanistan after 2014," *Asia Policy*, no. 17 (January 2014): 13–18; Katzman, *Afghanistan*, 2013, 52–56.

97. Amy Belasco, *The Cost of Iraq, Afghanistan and Other Global War on Terror Operations since 9/11*, Report RL33110 (Washington, DC: Library of Congress, Congressional Research Service, March 29, 2011); Katzman, *Afghanistan*, 2013, summary page.

98. Department of State, "U.S. Support for the New Silk Road."

99. Peter Baker and Matthew Rosenberg, "Old Tensions Resurface in Debate over U.S. Role in Post-2014 Afghanistan," *New York Times*, February 4, 2014, http://www.nytimes.com/2014/02/05/world/asia/old-tensions-resurface-in-debate-over-us-role-in-post-2014-afghanistan.html?_r=0; Dormandy and Keating, "The United States and Afghanistan."

100. Katzman, *Afghanistan*, 2014, 56–57.

101. Ibid., 57.

102. "Special Inspector General for Afghanistan Reconstruction" (SIGAR), http://www.sigar.mil (accessed July 8, 2014).

Chapter Ten

U.S. Relations with Central Asia, Mongolia, and Russia in Asia

U.S. interest and issues in relations with Central Asia have reflected chang-ing priorities in the post–Cold War period. The collapse of the USSR left some newly formed Central Asian countries with nuclear weapons of great concern to the United States. Central Asia also had significant energy re-sources of interest to U.S. and other international companies. Russia's prox-imity, military presence, and control of energy pipelines, railways, and other means of communication from the Central Asian countries abroad made it the dominant power in Central Asia. For many years, Russia exerted general-ly secondary influence in other parts of the Asia-Pacific. It appeared preoccu-pied with other pressing concerns and unable to conduct major diplomatic, economic, or military initiatives. U.S. issues with Russia generally focused on concerns apart from the Asia-Pacific region.

The 2001 terrorist attack on America and the U.S.-led war against the Taliban regime in Afghanistan had an important impact on U.S. interests and issues in Central Asia. Russia initially was supportive of a rapid increase in U.S. military and other interchange with Central Asian states that focused on the war against the Taliban and stabilizing the region from the terrorist threat. Over time, however, Moscow became much more ambivalent about the U.S. military presence, at times joining with China and some Central Asian states to limit and diminish the U.S. role in the region. Whatever replay of the nineteenth-century "great game" of international competition for influence in Central Asia emerged at this time also included Russian and Chinese compe-tition for energy resources and influence, even as the two powers periodically teamed up to criticize U.S. policy and U.S. military presence there. [1]

The withdrawal of U.S.-led NATO forces from Afghanistan in 2014 has reduced American interest in Central Asia. The importance of these countries and Russia for allowing overflight and transit to supply the allied forces diminishes with the withdrawal of those forces. American interest in competing for energy development also may decline as a result of substantial oil and gas development in the United States and forecasts of energy self-sufficiency in the country in twenty years.[2]

The important interests America developed in Central Asia in the post–Cold War period generally have not been explicitly included within the scope of the Obama government's rebalance policy. They focus on combating terrorism, proliferation, and transnational crime while supporting responsible governance and forging greater trade and transportation links for the landlocked countries that for many years saw most such links go through Russia.[3]

Meanwhile, Russia's greater activism in Asia has seen President Vladimir Putin, the driving force in Russian foreign policy for fifteen years, apply his brand of assertiveness to Asia. The levers of Russian influence heavily involve energy supplies for the strong and emerging regional economies. Russia's control of energy access to the Central Asian countries heretofore dependent on access through Russia for their energy exports has been reduced by pipelines from Kazakhstan, Turkmenistan, and other energy producers built by China and allowing direct access to the world's largest energy consumer.[4]

President Putin and Chinese leaders, in times of friction with the United States and the West, present a posture of unity at odds with U.S. goals. And they cooperate together in dealing with Central Asian issues as the leading powers in the most important regional multilateral body, the Shanghai Cooperation Organization (SCO). The SCO includes member states Kazakhstan, Kyrgyzstan, Tajikistan, and Uzbekistan in addition to China and Russia; observer states are Afghanistan, India, Iran, Mongolia, and Pakistan, and dialogue partners are Belarus, Sri Lanka, and Turkey. It excludes the United States and Japan. The Russia-China cooperation comes with tensions over China's growing influence in Central Asia at Russia's expense and differences over Russia's support and China's wariness of India's regional role. More broadly, Russia is an important arms supplier to India, Vietnam, and others around China's rim as they build military capacity as a hedge against China's rise. Russia also sometimes maneuvers seeking advantageous terms for improving relations with Japan, now that China has focused its foreign policy hostility against Tokyo.[5]

In sum, the fact that Central Asia is beyond the scope of the Obama rebalance policy underscores other signs of decline in U.S. interest in this part of Asia. The main driver of declining interest is the withdrawal of U.S. and NATO forces from Afghanistan and the resulting reduced American interest in bases and access in Central Asia and other nearby countries for use to supply U.S. and NATO forces in Afghanistan. As seen in chapter 9, U.S.

leaders have followed a realist pattern of examining costs and benefits of the withdrawal and deciding in its favor. A similar pattern seems evident for the U.S. role in Central Asia, where the United States has cut back its assistance and lowered costs in the interests of preserving resources in a period of budget constraints for use in higher-priority parts of the Asia-Pacific region or elsewhere.

CENTRAL ASIAN CONDITIONS AND PRIORITIES

Following the end of the Cold War and the breakup of the Soviet Union, the Central Asian governments of Kazakhstan, Kyrgyzstan, Tajikistan, Turkmenistan, and Uzbekistan have endeavored to stay in power and to achieve progress in economic development in the face of security challenges at home and abroad. The obstacles to development and stability involve regional tensions and conflicts. The legacies of comingled ethnic groups, convoluted borders, and emerging national identities have posed challenges to stability in all the Central Asian states. The legacies feature national identities that weaken national governance as they emphasize clan, family, regional, and Islamic self-identifications. Central Asia's borders do not accurately reflect ethnic distributions and are hard to secure, adding to regional tensions.

Another set of difficulties is posed by Islamic extremism and terrorism. Government based on Sharia (Islamic law) and the Koran is supported by small but increasing minorities in most of Central Asia. Most of Central Asia's Muslims appear to support secular government, but the influence of fundamentalist Salafist and extremist Islamic groups is growing. Central Asian leaders have pointed to the ongoing conflict against the Taliban in Afghanistan as justifying the constraints they impose on Islamic expression in their countries.

The Central Asian states repeatedly wrangle over water sharing, border delineation, trade, and transit issues. Tajikistan's relations with Uzbekistan have witnessed major disagreements about water sharing, Uzbek gas supplies, the mining of borders, border demarcation, and environmental pollution. Meanwhile, in February 2014, Uzbekistan sentenced four citizens to fifteen to eighteen years in prison on charges of spying for Turkmen intelligence on water supply, border security, and other issues. Uzbekistan and Kyrgyzstan repeatedly clash over charges that dissidents in Kyrgyzstan target Uzbekistan, and over conflicts between ethnic Uzbeks and ethnic Kyrgyz in Kyrgyzstan. The tensions have included exchanges of fire by border guards and the tightening of border controls, negatively affecting Kyrgyzstan.[6]

The smaller, mountainous, and economically less well-endowed states of Kyrgyzstan (population about 5.5 million) and Tajikistan (8 million) have been seriously undermined by ethnic and regional tensions. Because of ample energy resources, the outlook for Kazakhstan (population 18 million) and Turkmenistan (5 million) in economic development is good, but both countries have had widespread corruption and political tensions. Turkmenistan succeeded in making a sensitive leadership succession as the new government in Turkmenistan, begun in late 2006, has sustained internal stability while opening more to the rest of the world. Turkmenistan is characterized by ethnic homogeneity that also seems to assist its integrity.

Uzbekistan is led by a seventy-six-year-old authoritarian, President Islam Karimov, who has ruled Central Asia's most populous and powerful state for over two decades. Political succession remains a major issue as reports suggest Karimov seeks to pass leadership to his forty-one-year-old daughter. Kazakhstan also has been ruled for decades with a firm hand by seventy-three-year-old President Nursultan Nazarbayev. The lack of a clear succession plan in a country whose leader looms so large has constrained Kazakhstan's debt ratings for Standard & Poor's and Fitch Ratings by exacerbating political risks.

Uzbekistan appears to have the potential to become a regional power able to take the lead on policy issues common to Central Asian states and to resist undue influence from more powerful outside nations. However, tensions between Uzbekistan and other Central Asian states have thwarted regional cooperation.[7]

Economic conditions also highlight substantial differences among the states. The world's fifty-fourth largest economy with a population of eighteen million, Kazakhstan is geographically the largest of the former Soviet republics, excluding Russia. It has large fossil fuel reserves and plentiful supplies of other minerals and metals, such as uranium, copper, and zinc. It also has a large agricultural sector featuring livestock and grain. In 2002 Kazakhstan became the first country in the former Soviet Union to receive an investment-grade credit rating. Extractive industries have been and will continue to be the engine of Kazakhstan's growth. Landlocked Kazakhstan relies on its neighbors to export its products, especially oil and grain. Kazakhstan fell into recession as a result of the drop of oil and commodity prices in 2008. The economy, aided by prudent government measures, rebounded; rising commodity prices also helped the recovery. In 2010 Kazakhstan joined the Belarus-Kazakhstan-Russia Customs Union in an effort to boost foreign investment and improve trade relationships; it currently seeks membership in the World Trade Organization.[8]

Uzbekistan has thirty million people and ranks as the world's seventieth largest economy. The country is dry and landlocked; 11 percent of the land is intensely cultivated in irrigated river valleys. Export of hydrocarbons, primarily natural gas, provides a significant share of foreign exchange earnings. Uzbekistan is the world's fifth-largest cotton exporter and sixth-largest producer. Uzbekistan's growth has been driven primarily by state-led investments and a favorable export environment. In the past, Uzbekistani authorities have accused U.S. and other foreign companies operating in Uzbekistan of violating Uzbekistani laws and have frozen and even seized their assets. At the same time, the Uzbekistani government has actively courted several major U.S. and international corporations, offering financing and tax advantages. Diminished foreign investment and difficulties transporting goods across borders further challenge the economy.[9]

Having a population of five million and ranking as the world's ninety-fifth-largest economy, Turkmenistan is largely a desert country with intensive agriculture in irrigated oases and sizeable gas and oil resources. Agriculture accounts for roughly 7 percent of GDP; it employs nearly half of the country's workforce. Turkmenistan's authoritarian regime uses gas and other export revenues to sustain its inefficient and highly corrupt economy. From 1998 to 2005, Turkmenistan suffered from a continued lack of adequate export routes for natural gas. At the same time, however, total exports rose by an average of roughly 15 percent per year from 2003 to 2008, largely because of higher international oil and gas prices. Additional pipelines to China, which began operation in early 2010, and increased pipeline capacity to Iran have expanded Turkmenistan's export routes for its gas. Looking forward, major challenges include endemic corruption, a poor educational system, government misuse of oil and gas revenues, and a reluctance to adopt market-oriented reforms.[10]

Tajikistan (population eight million) ranks as the world's 137th-largest economy. Tajikistan has one of the lowest per capita GDPs among the fifteen former Soviet republics. A civil war in the country from 1992 to 1997 severely damaged an already weak economic infrastructure and caused a sharp decline in industrial and agricultural production. Because of a lack of employment opportunities in Tajikistan, more than one million Tajik citizens work abroad—roughly 90 percent in Russia—supporting families in Tajikistan through remittances. Less than 7 percent of the land area is arable, and cotton is the most important crop. Tajikistan imports approximately 60 percent of its food, most of which comes by rail. Uzbekistan closed one of the rail lines into Tajikistan in late 2011, hampering the transit of goods to and from the southern part of the country. As a result, food and fuel prices increased sharply.

Industry consists mainly of small obsolete factories in food processing and light industry, substantial hydropower facilities, and a large aluminum plant—currently operating below 25 percent of capacity. Electricity output expanded with the completion of the Sangtuda-1 hydropower dam—finished in 2009 with Russian investment. The smaller Sangtuda-2 hydropower dam, built with Iranian investment, began operating in 2012 at a limited capacity. The Tajik government is tens of millions of dollars in arrears for both Sangtuda dams, and Sangtuda-2 was closed for "maintenance" in January 2014.

The government is focusing on building the Roghun dam, which is scheduled for mid-2014. If built according to plan, Roghun will be the tallest dam in the world, will operate year around, and will significantly expand Tajikistan's electricity output. In 2013, the Tajik government finalized an agreement to import one million tons of fuel and oil products from Russia each year, at reduced prices. Tajikistan's economic situation remains fragile due to uneven implementation of structural reforms, corruption, weak governance, seasonal power shortages, and its large external debt burden. [11]

Kyrgyzstan ranks as the world's 145th-largest economy with a population of 5.6 million. A poor, mountainous country with a dominant agricultural sector, the economy depends heavily on gold exports and on remittances from Kyrgyzstani migrant workers primarily in Russia. Following independence, Kyrgyzstan was progressive in carrying out market reforms, such as an improved regulatory system and land reform. Kyrgyzstan was the first Commonwealth of Independent States (CIS) country to be accepted into the World Trade Organization. The overthrow of President Kurmanbek Bakiyev in April 2010 and subsequent ethnic clashes left hundreds dead and damaged infrastructure. Under President Almazbek Atambayev, Kyrgyzstan has developed a plan for economic development in coordination with international donors, and it has also expressed its intent to join the Customs Union of Russia, Belarus, and Kazakhstan. Major challenges to economic development include corruption, lack of transparency in licensing, business permits and taxations, poorly structured domestic industry, and needed foreign aid and investment. [12]

Among neighboring countries, the situation in Afghanistan has posed the most serious set of immediate problems for the Central Asian states. [13] The depth and scope of the concerns of the Central Asian governments seem certain to grow as U.S.-led military forces leave the country with an at best uncertain chance of the Afghanistan government's sustaining some degree of control over various violent and disruptive forces in the country.

Particular concerns focus on Islamic extremism and illicit drugs coming from Afghanistan. Central Asia's leaders do not want Islamic extremists to use bases in Afghanistan, as the militant opposition in Tajikistan did until recently. They objected to the refuge that the Taliban regime provided for the armed insurgents of the Islamic Movement of Uzbekistan (IMU) that threatened Uzbekistan and to its support for Osama bin Laden and his al-Qaeda operatives, who were thought to finance and train religious extremists determined to overthrow the existing governments throughout Central Asia.

Meanwhile, historical trade routes have facilitated the smuggling of drugs and other contraband through the region to Russian, European, and other markets. The problem posed by the drug trade has increased because the post-Taliban Afghan government has been weak and unable to enforce anti-drug production and trafficking measures. [14]

Central Asian governments have been concerned about Central Asian ethnic groups residing in northern Afghanistan, leading to a recent history of complicated interventions and alignments. During the rule of the Taliban, Uzbekistan's government was concerned with the 1.5 million ethnic Uzbeks in Afghanistan, and it supported an Uzbek paramilitary leader in Afghanistan. The leader was pushed out by Taliban forces in 1998 but returned to assist the Northern Alliance forces in defeating the Taliban in 2001.[15]

There are six million ethnic Tajiks in Afghanistan of concern to both Tajikistan and Iran. The comparatively weak administration in Tajikistan was strongly challenged by the Taliban's growing power, which added to concerns it had over neighboring Uzbekistan and Iran, who backed different sides in the long-running Tajik civil war. Tajikistan's instability and regional concerns caused the government there to rely more on Russia by granting it formal basing rights.[16]

China has substantially increased its regional financing and trade activities. China is the leading trading partner for four of the five Central Asian countries; it is the second-largest trading partner with Uzbekistan. The value of Chinese Central Asian trade was over $46 billion in 2013. Chinese purchases of oil and gas from Kazakhstan and Turkmenistan accounted for much of this expansion, but China works hard to balance the economic ledger with large sales of Chinese manufactured goods and valuable contracts for Chinese firms building infrastructure in the Central Asian countries.

China has emerged as Russia's ever-stronger leading partner in the Shanghai Cooperation Organization, the regional grouping formed in 2001 that includes Kazakhstan, Kyrgyzstan, Tajikistan, and Uzbekistan as full members. The SCO has focused on antiterrorist cooperation, mutual confidence building, and development issues. Beijing and Moscow periodically use SCO venues to voice opposition to U.S. policies. At the same time, they appear to compete in efforts to gain access to Central Asian energy resources and in other ways. An oil pipeline from Kazakhstan to China opened in 2006, providing Kazakhstan with access to international oil markets via routes not controlled by Russia. China has signed agreements for natural gas imports from Turkmenistan that have been implemented rapidly and taken together represent a major diversion from that Central Asian country's long-standing use of Russian supply lines.[17]

Of the other foreign countries with an interest in Central Asia, Iran was on the same side as Russia and most Central Asian states in backing the Northern Alliance against the Taliban regime in Afghanistan. Iran has good ties and rail and pipeline links with Turkmenistan. It also has improved relations with Kazakhstan, with whom it shares claims to the oil-rich Caspian Sea. Although the toppling of the Taliban benefited Iran, Tehran views the U.S. military presence and U.S. energy and pipeline activities in the region as contrary to its interests. The United States has supported pipelines between

Central Asia and Turkey that would bypass both Russia and Iran. Turkey's ability to play a leading role among Central Asia's mainly Turkic peoples has been hampered by its domestic preoccupations with economic, ethnic, and political problems.[18]

Adding to this complicated international mix, the Central Asian states were compelled to deal with the expansion of U.S. influence in the region, especially following the upsurge in U.S. activism and involvement in the war against the Taliban regime in Afghanistan. It is likely they will continue to deal with a decline in U.S. involvement from that high point, coincident with the withdrawal of U.S. forces from Afghanistan. The Central Asian states relied on U.S.- and NATO-led efforts against the Taliban insurgents in Afghanistan. Major differences arose between the United States and Uzbekistan over U.S. condemnation of the authoritarian government's violent crackdown on political dissent in 2005, which resulted in the expulsion of U.S. forces based in the country. Russia and China publicly supported Uzbekistan's position. The SCO also went on record in 2005 in calling for a deadline for U.S. and NATO forces to leave the region once the Afghan situation stabilized. Kyrgyzstan demanded higher U.S. payments for the continued use of a base in that country and announced in 2012 that the U.S. forces would leave the country in 2014.[19]

Energy-rich Kazakhstan welcomed unusual high-level Bush administration attention, including a very positive state visit by the Kazakh president to the United States and a visit by the U.S. vice president to Kazakhstan. However, the authoritarian government had strong reservations regarding the Bush administration's insistence that U.S. interests not only focus on security and energy development, which are compatible with Kazakh goals, but also stress fostering democratization and human rights that are at odds with the Central Asian administration's interests.[20] Meanwhile, the actual importance of such oil for the United States amid an upsurge of U.S. domestic oil production suggests that U.S. interest in Kazakhstan and other Central Asian energy producers may decline.[21]

MONGOLIA'S CONDITIONS AND PRIORITIES

Situated between Central and Northeast Asia, Mongolia is a large country with a small population (under three million). Following the demise of its main backer and controlling outside power, the USSR, the Mongolian government moved toward free market and democratic reforms. Since passing a democratic constitution in 1992, Mongolia has held several presidential elections and direct parliamentary elections. The State Department credited Mongolia's government with "generally" respecting freedoms of speech, press, assembly, and association. Mongolia's democracy has sometimes been chaotic, however. Parliamentary coalitions have collapsed, and prime ministers and cabinets have come and gone. Parliamentary elections in 2008 were marred by violence that claimed five lives, and the 1998 assassination of one of the charismatic leaders of the 1990 democratic revolution, Sanjaasuren Zorig, continues as a source of political division and controversy. Corruption has been an enduring problem.[22]

The world's 140th-largest economy, Mongolia has extensive mineral deposits. Growth in mining sector activities has transformed Mongolia's economy, which traditionally was dependent on herding and agriculture. Mongolia's copper, gold, coal, molybdenum, fluorspar, uranium, tin, and tungsten deposits, among others, have attracted foreign direct investment. Soviet assistance, at its height one-third of GDP, disappeared almost overnight in 1990 and 1991 at the time of the dismantlement of the USSR. The following decade led to deep recession because of political inaction and natural disasters, but there was also some economic growth because of reform-embracing, free-market economics and extensive privatization of the formerly state-run economy. The country opened a fledgling stock exchange in 1991. Mongolia joined the World Trade Organization in 1997 and continues to seek to expand its participation in regional economic and trade regimes. Growth averaged nearly 9 percent per year from 2004 to 2008, largely because of high copper prices globally and new gold production. Mongolia was hit hard by the global financial crisis in 2008. Slower global economic growth hurt the country's exports, notably copper, and cut government revenues. Mongolia's economy contracted 1.3 percent in 2009. In early 2009, the International Monetary Fund reached a $236 million standby arrangement with Mongolia; the country has largely emerged from the crisis with better regulations and closer supervision. The banking sector has strengthened, but weaknesses remain.[23]

In October 2009, Mongolia passed long-awaited legislation on an investment agreement to develop the Oyu Tolgoi mine, considered to be among the world's largest untapped copper-gold deposits. Mongolia's ongoing dispute with a foreign investor over Oyu Tolgoi, however, has called into question the attractiveness of Mongolia as a destination for foreign direct investment. Negotiations to develop the massive Tavan Tolgoi coalfield have also stalled.

The economy has grown more than 10 percent per year since 2010, largely on the strength of commodity exports to nearby countries and high government spending domestically. Mongolia's economy, however, faces near-term economic risks from the government's loose fiscal and monetary policies, which are contributing to high inflation, and from uncertainties in foreign demand for Mongolian exports. Foreign trade is dominated by China. China receives more than 90 percent of Mongolia's exports and is Mongolia's largest supplier. Mongolia has relied on Russia for energy supplies, leaving it vulnerable to price increases; in the first eleven months of 2013, Mongolia purchased 76 percent of its gasoline and diesel fuel and a substantial amount of electric power from Russia. A drop in foreign direct investment and a decrease in Chinese demand for Mongolia's mineral exports are putting pressure on Mongolia's balance of payments. Remittances from Mongolians working abroad, particularly in South Korea, are significant.

Mongolia has sought to maintain and develop good and mutually beneficial relations with its powerful neighbors Russia and China and with the newly independent republics of Central Asia. It has reached out to and gained support and assistance from the United States, Japan, South Korea, and other developed countries and international institutions. Mongolia endeavors to participate actively in Asian regional organizations. [24]

At the start of this decade, Mongolia updated its guiding foreign policy document, the Concept of Foreign Policy. Mongolia seeks foremost to maintain "a balanced relationship" with Russia and China, while not "adopt[ing] the line of either country." As noted above, Russia is Mongolia's largest source of energy products; China is its largest export market. And China is its largest foreign investor. Because Mongolia is landlocked, it is dependent on both countries for the transportation routes that allow its goods to access world markets.

Balancing Russia and China and attempting to ensure independence and sovereignty, Mongolia seeks strong relations with "highly developed countries of the West and East such as the United States of America, Japan and the Federal Republic of Germany," as well as with India, (South) Korea, Thailand, Singapore, Turkey, Denmark, the Netherlands, Finland, Austria, Sweden, and Switzerland (listed in that order). The priority countries are Mongolia's so-called "third neighbors," the United States, Japan, South Korea, Germany, and India. [25]

Seeking also to strengthen its position in Asia and to promote Mongolia's regional integration, the country's foreign policy calls for "initiating dialogues and negotiations" on regional security issues. The document identifies as a top priority securing membership for Mongolia in the Asia-Pacific Economic Cooperation (APEC) grouping. Mongolia also seeks to promote cooperation with the United Nations and with international financial and economic organizations such as the International Monetary Fund, World Bank, and Asian Development Bank. [26]

RUSSIA'S CONDITIONS AND PRIORITIES

Russia has remained the leading outside power in Central Asia. For Central Asian states, the challenge they face regarding Russia is to maintain useful ties with Moscow without allowing it undue influence.

During the 1990s, Russia's economic decline and demands by Central Asia caused it to reduce its security presence, a trend that Vladimir Putin since 2000 has appeared determined to reverse. In 1999, Russian border guards were largely phased out in Kyrgyzstan, the last Russian military advisers left Turkmenistan, and Uzbekistan withdrew from the Collective Security Treaty (CST) of the Russian-led Commonwealth of Independent States, in part because the treaty members failed to help Uzbekistan meet the growing Taliban threat in Afghanistan, according to Uzbek president Islam Karimov. Despite these moves, Russia appeared determined to maintain a military presence in Tajikistan. It has retained in the country the 201st Motorized Infantry Division of about five thousand troops. Russia's efforts to formalize a basing agreement with Tajikistan dragged on for years, as Tajikistan endeavored to charge rent and assert its sovereignty. In October 2004, a ten-year basing agreement was signed, formalizing Russia's largest military presence abroad, besides its Black Sea Fleet in then Ukraine's Crimea. After much delay caused by Tajikistan seeking Russian payment of rent for basing Russian soldiers, an agreement was ratified in 2013 to last until 2042 providing basing for seven thousand Russian soldiers in the country.[27]

The terrorist attacks of September 11, 2001, saw Russia acquiesce to increased U.S. and coalition presence in the region for operations against al-Qaeda and its supporters in Afghanistan. Russia was concerned about Islamic extremism in Afghanistan, Central Asia, and its own North Caucasus; it also was interested in boosting its economic and other ties to the West and regaining some influence in Afghanistan. In the later part of the 2000s, however, Russia appeared to step up efforts to counter U.S. influence in Central Asia and reassert its own status as an international and regional leader by advocating that the states increase economic and strategic ties with Russia and limit such ties with the United States. This stance included backing and encouragement for Uzbekistan and Kyrgyzstan to close their U.S. airbases.

Russia welcomed Kyrgyzstan's decision in 2012 not to renew arrangements allowing the United States to use a base in the country in connection with military operations in Afghanistan. President Putin visited Kyrgyzstan and met with President Almazbek Atambayev in September 2012. The two sides signed a fifteen-year extension to Russia's lease on military facilities in the country, including an airbase. Russia's rent payment for using the facilities—said to be $4.5 million per year—reportedly did not change. However, Russia agreed to cancel $190 million in Kyrgyz debt and to restructure another $300 million loan. Another agreement pledged assistance by Russian firms in building several hydropower projects in Kyrgyzstan. In a joint statement, Atambayev pledged to close the U.S. base in 2014, and Putin pledged to consider assistance to help convert the base to civilian use. Hailing agreements that further integrated the two countries militarily and economically,

President Atambayev stated at a press conference that "Russia is our main strategic partner. . . . We do not have a future separate from Russia."[28]

Following Uzbekistan's souring of relations with the United States and other Western countries as a result of a violent crackdown on dissidents in Uzbekistan in 2005, Russia signed a Treaty on Allied Relations with Uzbekistan in November 2005 that called for mutual defense consultations in the event of a threat to either party (similar to language in the Collective Security Treaty of the Russian-led Commonwealth of Independent States). Uzbekistan rejoined the CST Organization (CSTO) in June 2006. However, Uzbekistan declined to participate in Russian-sponsored regional rapid-reaction forces established in June 2009 because of concerns that the forces could become involved in disputes between member states. On June 20, 2012, Uzbekistan informed the CSTO that it was suspending its membership in the organization, partly because the CSTO was ignoring its concerns. However, Uzbek officials stated that the country would continue to participate in the CIS air defense system and other military affairs under the Allied Relations Treaty with Russia.[29]

Further maneuvering by Uzbekistan saw President Karimov visit China and meet President Hu Jintao in 2012; the two leaders signed a strategic partnership agreement. Uzbekistan strongly objected to the September 2012 Russia-Kyrgyz agreement on constructing the Kambarata-1 dam in Kyrgyzstan. It asserted that the project should involve talks including all countries along the watershed (the Naryn River, the proposed site of the dam, flows into the Syr Darya River which goes through Uzbekistan and Kazakhstan).

Kazakhstan has remained vulnerable to Russian influence because of its shared 4,200-mile border with Russia and its relatively large ethnic Russian population (about one-fourth of a total population of eighteen million). An important recent development in November 2013 saw visiting president Nazarbayev and President Putin sign a treaty on good neighborly relations and cooperation. As a prelude to the visit, Putin submitted a Kazakhstan-Russia agreement on joint air defenses, signed in January 2013, to the Russian Federal Assembly for approval. The air defense cooperation is reportedly more robust than that provided under the joint CIS air defense system shared by Russia, Kazakhstan, Armenia, Belarus, and Kyrgyzstan. Under the accord, a headquarters will be set up in Almaty. Kazakhstan nominally will still be in charge of its air defense system in peacetime, but the system will be jointly operated in case of war. Russian defense interests involving Kazakhstan also showed as Russia's Caspian Sea Flotilla has been bolstered by troops and equipment in recent years. A security cooperation agreement signed at a Caspian littoral state summit on November 2010 states that Caspian basin security is the exclusive preserve of the littoral states, thereby precluding involvement of the United States, China, or other powers.[30]

As Russia's economy improved in the 2000s with the increases in oil and gas prices, Russia reasserted its economic interests in Central Asia. Russia has countered Western businesses and gained substantial influence over energy resources through participation in joint ventures and by emphasizing that pipelines cross Russian territory. The numbers of migrant workers from Central Asia have increased, and worker remittances from Russia are significant to the economies of Kyrgyzstan, Tajikistan, and Uzbekistan and are a source of Russian leverage.

Russian economic interests in Central Asia face ever-growing competition from China. As Russia competes economically with China's surge, it has been seen to endeavor to constrict growing Chinese economic influence through a Russia-Belarus-Kazakhstan customs union that began operating in mid-2011. In an article in October 2011, then prime minister Putin called for boosting Russian influence over Soviet successor states through the creation of an economic, political, and military "Eurasian Union." In late October 2013, President Nazarbayev accused Russia of controlling the governing body of the Customs Union, even though the staffers were supposed to be international bureaucrats. He also complained that the Customs Union had resulted in an increase in imports into Kazakhstan and a decrease in exports, harming Kazakh businesses. During a November 2013 visit by Nazarbayev to Russia, President Putin reportedly refuted this assertion, arguing that Kazakhstan's exports to Russia were increasing.

At a meeting of the Eurasian Economic Commission (the governing body of the Customs Union and the larger Eurasian Economic Community) in early March 2014—after Russian forces had entered Ukraine's Crimea—Kazakhstan and Moldova indicated that they were ready to move forward with plans to form a Eurasian Union. However, Nazarbayev reportedly called for a secretariat to be formed before the rules and procedures of the Eurasian Union are worked out, perhaps indicating some concerns about protecting Kazakhstan's sovereignty within the Eurasian Union. Whatever their differences, Russia, Belarus, and Kazakhstan solidified their commercial arrangements in a Eurasian Economic Union signed in Kazakhstan in May 2014.[31]

Even before he was elected president of Kyrgyzstan, Almazbek Atambayev called for the country to join the Customs Union. In December 2013, however, President Atambayev rejected a road map promulgated by the Eurasian Economic Commission for Kyrgyzstan's admission to the Customs Union. Kyrgyz officials complained they had not been invited to participate in drawing up the plan and that their written proposals had been inadequately addressed. Atambayev said in May 2014 that his country intended to join the union by the end of the year.[32]

The Putin government also has used control of energy resources and transportation routes linking energy sources in Russia and Central Asia with markets in the West and the Pacific Rim. The Central Asian region's continued economic ties with Russia are encouraged by the existence of myriad Moscow-bound and Russian-controlled transportation routes, the difficulty of trade through war-torn Afghanistan, and U.S. opposition to ties with Iran. Also, there are still many inter-enterprise and equipment supply links between Russia and these states. The Uzbek and Kazakh governments have sometimes criticized Russian tendencies to treat Central Asia as an unequal partner, but in general the Central Asian states have had limited success in diversifying energy exports and developing alternative export routes apart from those involving Russia.[33] As noted above, recent and notable exceptions to this pattern have involved the opening of oil and gas pipelines to China from Kazakhstan and Turkmenistan.

In addition to efforts to sustain Russia's leading position in Central Asia, the administration of President Vladimir Putin pursues arms sales, energy deals, and sometimes active diplomacy to benefit Russian economic interests and exert greater influence in Asia, an area of generally secondary concern in Russian foreign policy. Unlike the weaker and less organized Russian government during the tenure of President Boris Yeltsin, the Putin administration's stronger control of the Russian state apparatus and of the important energy assets in the country has combined with improved conditions in the Russian economy to provide a somewhat improved basis for Russia's efforts to influence Asian affairs in line with Russian interests.[34]

What Russia is prepared to do in the wake of the U.S. military withdrawal from Afghanistan remains to be seen. The Shanghai Cooperation Organization provides a venue for regional discussion led by Russia and China. The group proved weak in the confrontation with Taliban-ruled Afghanistan. The members have strengthened resolve against terrorism, but they generally have avoided substantial commitments of military assets or other costs, which they have come to expect to be shouldered by the now departing Americans.[35]

China and India have received top priority among Russia's Asian partners. For many years, both received an average of more than $1 billion in advanced Russian arms annually, with India getting somewhat better access to them than China. Russia's trade with China has improved markedly from the low levels of only a few years ago. It amounts to over $80 billion a year and is forecast to grow rapidly. The trade focuses heavily on Russian oil sales to China. The oil was shipped by rail for many years as proposed pipelines had few concrete results. Russia vacillated on a proposed oil pipeline from Siberia to the east. In 2008 it appeared to have settled on a terminus on the Russian Pacific coast, favored by Japan, rather than in China as favored by Beijing. But Russia's need for markets given the decline in energy prices during the global economic slump and China's willingness to provide $25 billion in financing to be repaid in oil set the stage for a 2009 deal providing for the pipeline to terminate in China. Russia completed the part of the pipeline to the Pacific coast in 2012. The need to develop Siberian oil fields to obtain the oil to fill the pipelines to China and the Pacific coast resulted in a Sino-Russian joint venture deal in 2013 whereby a major Chinese oil company became directly involved in developing a very large but undeveloped Russian oil field. Meanwhile, a long-delayed deal to build a gas pipeline and sell thirty-eight billion cubic meters of Russian natural gas to China over thirty years was concluded during President Putin's visit to China in May 2014.[36]

Russia commonly takes international positions with China and India. It sometimes uses summit meetings with China to articulate criticisms of U.S. policies. Thus, President Putin's May 2014 visit to China for an international meeting soon after strong Western condemnation and sanctions prompted by Russia's annexation of Crimea was portrayed by Russia and to a degree by China as in opposition to U.S. interests and U.S.-led international practices. At the same time, Moscow, Beijing, and New Delhi have shown in various actions that they sometimes give higher priority to their respective relations with the United States than they do with one another. Russia demonstrates little concern about possible strategic differences with India, but it remains wary of China as a rapidly rising power along Russia's sparsely settled east and in Central Asia, an area of high security and economic concern for Russia. Russia supplies arms to India, Vietnam, and others around China's rim as they build military capacity as a hedge against China's rise.[37]

Putin's government gives lower priority to relations with Japan, though it was willing to accept for a time at least Japanese blandishments in deciding to end the proposed oil pipeline on the Pacific coast, as Japan wished. Putin remains uncompromising regarding the so-called Northern Territories, islands north of Hokkaido claimed by Japan but occupied by Russia. The Russian government joins with China and some others in criticizing Japanese defense advances and closer alignment with the United States. At the same time, Russia also maneuvers seeking possibly advantageous terms for improving relations with Japan, now that China has focused its foreign policy hostility against Tokyo.[38]

Russia probably was the least important participant in the six-party talks. The Russian representatives tended to adopt positions in line with China and at times South Korea, urging greater flexibility by the United States in dealing with North Korea. Russia plays an active diplomatic role in nascent Asian multilateral organizations. President Putin devoted great attention to the annual summit meeting of the APEC group that was hosted by Russia in its largest Asian city, Vladivostok, in 2012. However, Russia's ability and willingness to back up its diplomacy with substantive contributions remain low.[39]

U.S. POLICIES AND PRIORITIES REGARDING CENTRAL ASIA

Following the 9/11 terrorist attack on America and the U.S.-led war against the terrorist-harboring Taliban regime in Afghanistan, U.S. officials, backed by Congress, supported policies in Central Asia focused on three interrelated activities: the promotion of security, domestic reforms, and energy development. Contrary to a previous, less engaged U.S. policy approach toward Central Asia, after 2001 the U.S. government said it was an "enduring priority" for American foreign policy and national interests of the United States to enhance American relations with the five Central Asian countries (Kazakhstan, Kyrgyzstan, Tajikistan, Turkmenistan, and Uzbekistan) particularly to prevent them from becoming harbors of terrorism.[40]

Nevertheless, there remained considerable debate among U.S. specialists and policy makers regarding how deeply the United States should be involved with the countries in the region. There also were discussions and debates as U.S. policy makers endeavored to balance U.S. commitments to democracy and human rights with pragmatic needs to cooperate with authoritarian Central Asian states that are important for U.S. security and energy interests. U.S. security, energy, and political interests and involvement also ran up against occasional opposition from some regional governments, including Russia and China, leading some observers to speculate about a revival of the nineteenth-century "great game" of international competition for influence in Central Asia. However, the signs of rivalry between and among the concerned powers remained limited, and they are forecast to diminish as the United States withdraws forces from Afghanistan and reduces the importance of Central Asia for that prolonged but now ending American war.[41]

In general, American leaders have tailored U.S. policy in Central Asia to the varying characteristics of these states. U.S. interests in Kazakhstan have included securing and eliminating Soviet-era nuclear and biological weapons materials and facilities. U.S. energy firms have invested in oil and natural gas development in Kazakhstan and Turkmenistan, and successive administrations have backed diverse export routes to the West for these resources. U.S. policy toward Kyrgyzstan has long included support for its civil society. In Tajikistan, the United States focuses on developmental assistance to bolster the fragile economy and address high poverty rates. The United States and others have urged the regional states to cooperate in managing their water resources. U.S. relations with Uzbekistan—the most populous state in the heart of the region—were cool after 2005 but later improved. Congress was at the forefront in advocating increased U.S. ties with Central Asia and in providing backing for the region for the transit of U.S. and NATO equipment and supplies into and out of Afghanistan. Congress pursued these goals through hearings and legislation on humanitarian, economic, and democratization assistance; security issues; and human rights.

Annual U.S. foreign assistance figures indicate a rise and later a sharp fall in American commitment to Central Asia after September 11, 2001.[42] For much of the 1990s and until September 11, 2001, the United States provided much more aid each year to Russia and Ukraine than to Central Asia. Cumulative foreign aid budgeted to Central Asia for FY 1992 through FY 2010 amounted to $5.7 billion, about 14 percent of the amount budgeted to all the Eurasian states.

Budgeted spending for FY 2002 for Central Asia was greatly boosted in absolute amounts ($584 million) and as a share of total aid to Eurasia (about one-quarter of such aid). The Bush administration then requested smaller amounts of aid. Economic aid to Kazakhstan was phased out, and Congress imposed restrictions on aid to Uzbekistan. Other reasons offered by the administration included a more constrained U.S. budgetary situation.

The Obama administration boosted aid to Central Asia in FY 2009 to about $494.5 million (all agencies and programs), but aid declined to $436.3 million in FY 2010 and the decline accelerated in later years. The administration's FY 2015 budget request for aid to Central Asia was $113 million. A stark barometer of American interest, this figure was less than half of the amount of aid offered annually to the region in the years prior to September 11, 2001, and the U.S. war in Afghanistan.

Security Issues

U.S. security interests and involvement in Central Asia predated 2001. All the Central Asian states, except Tajikistan, had joined NATO's Partnership for Peace (PFP) program by 1994 (Tajikistan later joined in 2002). Central Asian troops thereafter participated in periodic PFP or PFP-related exercises in the United States, and U.S. troops participated in exercises in Central Asia beginning in 1997.[43]

A major U.S. concern after the breakup of the Soviet Union was to eliminate the nuclear weapons remaining in Kazakhstan and to control nuclear proliferation in the region. In December 1993, the United States and Kazakhstan signed the Cooperative Threat Reduction (CTR) umbrella agreement to allow for the "safe and secure" dismantling of 104 multiple-nuclear-warhead intercontinental ballistic missiles, the destruction of their silos, and related activities. In 1994, all bombers and their air-launched nuclear cruise missiles were removed, and in 1995 the last of more than a thousand nuclear warheads were transferred to Russia. Kazakhstan announced it was a nuclear-free state in 1995, but work in this area with the United States continued. In 1999, the United States announced that 147 missile silos were destroyed. The two governments set up a U.S.-Kazakh Nuclear Risk Reduction Center in Kazakhstan in order to facilitate verification and compliance with arms control agreements and to prevent the proliferation of WMD.[44]

Besides Kazakhstan's nuclear weapons, U.S. attention focused on research reactors, uranium mines, milling facilities, and nuclear waste dumps in Kazakhstan, Kyrgyzstan, Tajikistan, and Uzbekistan, endeavoring to guard against theft. Kazakhstan and Uzbekistan had also hosted major chemical and biological warfare facilities during the Soviet era. U.S. CTR aid was used to transport weapons-grade uranium and enriched nuclear fuel to safe-keeping in the United States, Russia, and elsewhere; to dismantle and secure anthrax and other biological warfare facilities; and to keep WMD weapons scientists employed in peaceful research.[45]

Soon after the terrorist attacks on the United States on September 11, 2001, all the Central Asian "frontline" states offered overflight and other support for coalition antiterrorism operations in Afghanistan. The U.S.-led war against the Taliban in Afghanistan saw U.S. military relationships with Central Asian countries grow rapidly. Kyrgyzstan provided basing for U.S. and coalition forces at a facility at Manas, where in 2005 there were reportedly fifteen hundred U.S. troops. Until the expulsion of U.S. forces ordered by the Uzbek government in 2005, there were around nine hundred American personnel at a base at Karshi-Khanabad. Uzbekistan also hosted several hundred German troops in Termez and provided a land corridor for humanitarian aid to Afghanistan. Tajikistan permitted use of its international airport in Dushanbe for refueling and hosted a small contingent of French forces until 2005. Kazakhstan and Turkmenistan provided other support in addition to overflight permission.[46]

In 2003, Kazakhstan and Uzbekistan also endorsed coalition military action in Iraq. About two dozen Kazakhstani troops served in Iraq until late 2008. In recent years, most of the regional states have also participated in the so-called Northern Distribution Network for the transport of U.S. and NATO supplies into and out of Afghanistan.

As noted above, the Uzbek government cracked down violently against demonstrators in the town of Andijon in May 2005. Dozens and perhaps hundreds of civilians were killed. The United States criticized the action and supported the airlifting of 439 people, who had fled to nearby Kyrgyzstan, from Kyrgyzstan to Romania, fearing that if they were forced to return to Uzbekistan they would be tortured. Uzbekistan's government then demanded the withdrawal of U.S. forces from the country, which was done in November 2005. Russia and China strongly supported Uzbekistan's decision. Meanwhile, the Kyrgyz government began vacillating over the U.S. military presence at their base at Manas. The United States came to pay higher rent for use of the facility. In 2012, the Kyrgyz leadership notified the United States that it would not extend the basing agreement. U.S. forces exited the "Manas Transit Center" in June 2014.[47]

U.S. security assistance to Central Asian countries grew after 2001. Security and law enforcement aid for the region was $188 million in FY 2002,

$101 million in FY 2003, $132 million in FY 2004, and $148 million in FY 2005. The aid involved equipment and training, as well as border security aid to counter trafficking in drugs, humans, and WMD. U.S. funding to support the basing in Manas in Kyrgyzstan and Karshi-Khanabad in Uzbekistan came from separate accounts. The U.S. Central Command, responsible for U.S. military engagement in Central Asia, also launched a program in 2003 to enhance security assistance on the oil-rich Caspian Sea involving Kazakhstan and Azerbaijan.[48]

Democratization and Human Rights

The falling out between the U.S. and Uzbek governments over U.S. criticism of and actions against the latter's crackdown on demonstrators in 2005 graphically illustrated the conflicts that frequently arose as U.S. policy makers tried to achieve goals of advancing democracy and human rights on the one hand while advancing security cooperation with the authoritarian Central Asian governments in the broad war on terrorism on the other. The Central Asian states were led by ex–Communist Party officials who generally had little stake in the kind of democracy and human rights practices sought by the United States. Throughout the post–Cold War period, U.S. officials solicited pledges from the region's leaders to support democracy, but in practice the leaders seemed more comfortable with the authoritarian practices they were more familiar with and which they judged posed less danger to their continued hold on power.[49]

Turkmenistan and Uzbekistan were generally viewed as having the most repressive governments. The death of Turkmenistan's despotic leader in late 2006 failed to lead to much greater freedom in the country. Given the large U.S. security stake in Uzbekistan after 2001, the government's authoritarian domestic practices repeatedly ran up against congressionally mandated restrictions on U.S. assistance. Kazakhstan, perhaps the most important Central Asian country for U.S. energy interests, also came under negative congressional scrutiny for its authoritarian practices.[50]

Economic and Energy Issues

U.S. trade with Central Asia accounts for less than 1 percent of U.S. foreign trade. U.S. private investment committed to Central Asian states seems more important and has exceeded that provided to Russia and most other Eurasian states. Much interest has focused on the Caspian Sea and its energy riches. U.S. government policy endeavors to support the sovereignty of the energy-rich Central Asian states and their ties with the West. It backs U.S. private investment, promotes Western energy security by obtaining supplies from the region, assists NATO ally Turkey as a terminal point for pipelines from the region, and opposes outlets to Iran. It remains to be seen how the importance of the distant energy fields in Central Asia for American investors will be affected by enhanced production in the United States and a growing level of American energy self-sufficiency.[51]

According to the U.S. Department of Energy, Kazakhstan possesses the Caspian region's largest proven oil reserves and significant gas deposits. U.S. policy encouraged Kazakhstan to export oil through a pipeline ending in Turkey. Russia currently controls most existing export pipelines, although as noted above Kazakhstan opened a new pipeline to China in 2006, and Turkmenistan opened a new pipeline to China in 2010; other pipelines to China followed.[52]

U.S. POLICIES AND PRIORITIES REGARDING MONGOLIA

Mongolia considers the United States to be the most important of its "third neighbors," countries that do not share a border with Mongolia but that Mongolia looks to for support of its independence and sovereignty and for balance against the influence of China and Russia. The United States established diplomatic relations with Mongolia in January 1987, after the rise of Mikhail Gorbachev in the Soviet Union produced a cautious warming in Soviet-U.S. relations. In that context, Moscow, which had previously objected to diplomatic relations between Mongolia and the United States, softened its position. The U.S. embassy in Mongolia opened in September 1988.[53]

U.S. relations with Mongolia in the post–Cold War period have been good and generally without major controversy in recent years. Top-level visits have occurred frequently. President Bush visited Mongolia in 2005, and Mongolian presidents visited Washington in 2007 and 2011.

The United States has assisted Mongolia's movement toward democracy and market-oriented reform and has expanded relations with Mongolia primarily in the cultural and economic fields. In 1989 and 1990, the two countries signed a cultural accord, a Peace Corps accord, a consular convention, and an Overseas Private Investment Corporation (OPIC) agreement. A trade agreement was signed in January 1991 and a bilateral investment treaty in 1994. Mongolia was granted permanent normal trade relations (PNTR) status and generalized system of preferences (GSP) eligibility in June 1999. In July 2004, the United States signed a trade and investment framework agreement with Mongolia to promote economic reform and more foreign investment.

The United States Agency for International Development (USAID) plays a lead role in providing bilateral American assistance to Mongolia. The program emphasizes two main themes: sustainable, private sector–led economic growth and more effective and accountable governance. Total USAID assistance to Mongolia from 1991 through 2007 was about $170 million, all in grant form. The United States provided $13.3 million in bilateral foreign assistance to Mongolia in FY 2010. For FY 2012, the State Department requested $10.55 million in bilateral foreign assistance, a $2.75 million reduction from FY 2010.[54]

The United States also supported defense reform and an increased capacity by Mongolia's armed forces to participate in international peacekeeping operations. Mongolia contributed small numbers of troops to U.S.-backed coalition operations in Iraq and Afghanistan. With U.S. Department of Defense assistance and cooperation, Mongolia and the United States jointly hosted the annual Khan Quest, the Asian region's premier peacekeeping exercise.[55]

U.S. ISSUES WITH RUSSIA IN ASIA

The Russian administration of President Vladimir Putin, in power since 2000, saw significant improvement in Russian-U.S. relations during the early period of the George W. Bush administration. Differences regarding the Putin administration's tighter control over Russian politics and Russian energy resources and enterprises, and differences over salient international issues such as Iran's suspected nuclear weapons program, NATO expansion, and U.S. ballistic missile defense programs, were among the issues that soured relations by the latter part of Bush's tenure.[56]

Putin's government endeavored to play a more important role in Asia-Pacific affairs than the previous administration of Boris Yeltsin. Russia was active in important multilateral groups like the six-party talks and the various multilateral meetings associated with the Association of Southeast Asian Nations (ASEAN), including the ASEAN Regional Forum. It was a leader along with China in the Shanghai Cooperation Organization, dealing with Central Asia. In contrast with Russian and Chinese cooperation with the United States and other powers in various Asian multilateral groups, Russia and China supported the SCO's stance that in effect precluded the United States from joining the regional body. This was widely seen as reflecting Russian and Chinese wariness of the U.S. presence in Central Asia and their respective interests in balancing the growth of U.S. power in Asia following the advent of the war on terror in 2001.

Russia exerts important diplomatic leverage by virtue of its position as a permanent member of the UN Security Council. As one of the world's leading oil and energy exporters, Russia influences the energy security considerations of the United States and leading Asia-Pacific powers. Militarily, as noted above, it remained for many years the largest supplier of advanced military equipment to Asia's two rising powers, China and India, as well as other recipients like Vietnam.

Putin's strong political control in Russia was seen in his reelection victory in 2004 and in later election victories, notably his return to the presidency in 2012 after a stint as prime minister. He has faced no serious competition. Pro-Putin political forces have had clear majority control over the Russian Duma parliament. Putin brought television and radio under tight state control and virtually eliminated effective political opposition. Putin used state power to gain control over the important energy sectors of the Russian economy. [57]

The Putin administration's key objectives of strengthening the state and reviving the economy had notable results:

- Federal forces suppressed large-scale military resistance in Chechnya and in 2006 succeeded in killing most of the remaining top Chechen rebel military and political leaders.
- The economic upturn that began in 1999 continued. GDP and domestic investment grew impressively after a long decline in the 1990s. They were fueled in large part by profits from oil and gas exports. Inflation was contained, the budget balanced, and the currency was stable. Major problems remained, though, including almost one-fifth of the population living below the poverty line, low foreign investment, and pervasive crime, corruption, capital flight, and unemployment.
- Russian defense spending began to increase after massive declines over many years.
- Russia projected greater international confidence as an "energy superpower." It had mixed results in efforts to reassert dominance in and integration of former Soviet states. [58] Russia's military conflict with Georgia in 2008 negatively affected relations with the West; after subsequent efforts to improve relations with the West, Russia had a major negative impact on Europe and broader relations with the United States and the West with its coercion of a recalcitrant Ukraine and annexation of Crimea in 2014. [59]

The U.S.-Russian "strategic partnership" of the early 1990s was replaced by increasing tension and mutual recrimination later in the decade. Key issues included NATO expansion, the U.S.-led war against Serbia, U.S. ballistic missile defense programs, and disagreements over Iraq, Iran, and other issues in the Middle East. In the first year of the George W. Bush administration, relations improved markedly. After a Bush-Putin summit, and particularly following the September 11, 2001, terrorist attacks on America, the two nations reshaped their relationship on the basis of cooperation against terrorism and Putin's goal of integrating Russia economically with the West. [60]

After 2003, however, tensions reemerged on a number of issues that again strained relations. Cooperation continued in some areas, and Bush and Putin strove to maintain the appearance of cordial personal relations, but there appeared to be more discord than harmony in U.S.-Russian relations.

Russia's construction of nuclear reactors in Iran and its role in missile technology transfers to that country were critical sources of tension with the United States. Facing strong U.S. and European Union pressure to move the Iran issue to the UN Security Council, Russia went along with Security Council efforts beginning in 2006 to impose modest sanctions on trade with Iran's nuclear infrastructure and other restrictions and pressures designed to curb Iran's suspected nuclear weapons program. Russia, along with China, generally opposed more stringent sanctions supported by the United States. [61]

The United States clashed repeatedly with Russia over Iraq. After 9/11, Russia moved away from full support of Iraq against the United States. Then, as the United States moved toward military action against the Saddam Hussein regime, the Putin administration tried to balance competing Russian interests: protecting Russian economic interests in Iraq, restraining U.S. unilateralism and global dominance, and maintaining friendly relations with the United States. In early 2003, Russia aligned with France and Germany in opposition to U.S. military action and threatened to veto a U.S.-backed UN resolution authorizing military force against Iraq. It continued criticism of U.S. behavior in the war in Iraq. [62]

Vigorous Russian criticism of U.S. ballistic defense efforts and expanding alliances with NATO and with Japan subsided in 2001 amid closer U.S.-Russian cooperation over terrorism and other issues. Putin revived the strong criticism in 2007, seriously complicating U.S.-Russian summit meetings. Meanwhile, U.S. leaders, including President Bush, were outspoken in criticizing the Putin administration's perceived restrictions and reversal of political rights and economic freedom in Russia. [63]

Russia's 2008 conflict with Georgia seriously threatened cooperation with the United States. The Obama administration worked to "reset" relations with Russia. It hailed such steps as the signing of a new Strategic Arms Reduction Treaty in April 2010, the approval of new sanctions against Iran by Russia and other members of the UN Security Council in June 2010, the accession of Russia to the World Trade Organization in August 2012, and the cooperation of Russia in Afghanistan. On the negative side of the ledger, however, in late 2012, Russia ousted the U.S. Agency for International Development from the country and criticized the help that USAID had provided over the years as unnecessary and intrusive. Russia also declined to renew a longtime bilateral accord on nonproliferation assistance (although a new more limited agreement was concluded in June 2013). The U.S. bill authorizing permanent normal trade relations for Russia was signed into law on December 14, 2012 (P.L. 112-208). The bill includes provisions sanctioning those responsible for the detention and death of lawyer Sergey Magnitsky and for other gross human rights abuses in Russia. A Russian bill ending U.S.

adoptions of Russian children appeared to be a reaction to the Magnitsky provision. President Obama canceled a U.S.-Russia summit meeting planned for early September 2013 on the grounds of lack of progress by Russia on bilateral cooperation, and the administration announced in December 2013 that lower-level delegations would attend the opening and closing of the Olympic Winter Games in Sochi, Russia, in February 2014.[64]

The Russian deployment of military forces to Ukraine's Crimea region at the end of February 2014 brought Russian-American relations to the lowest level since the Cold War. President Obama led efforts to isolate and sanction Russian leaders, strongly condemning Moscow's expansion. He canceled plans to attend a G-8 (Group of Eight industrialized nations) meeting to be hosted by Russia in Sochi in June 2014, some bilateral trade talks were halted, the Defense Department suspended planned military-to-military contacts, a visa ban and asset freeze were imposed, and the administration and Congress crafted a variety of sanctions against Russia. After pro-Russian Crimean elements staged a referendum on March 16, 2014, that approved joining Russia, the Russian legislature and President Putin quickly approved formal annexation. Russia's military forces also massed on its borders with the rest of Ukraine, threatening further incursions. As Russia moved to annex Crimea, President Obama issued further executive orders sanctioning individuals and one Russian bank. A revised G-7 meeting on March 24, 2014, announced that Russia was suspended from further proceedings. More sanctions and mutual recriminations followed.[65]

Specific U.S. Issues Involving Russia in Asia

The wide range of important domestic and international actions of the Putin government noted above posed significant issues for U.S. policy. However, they generally did not spill over directly to affect U.S. issues specifically involving Russian policy in the Asia-Pacific. Highlights of U.S. issues and concerns with Russian actions in the Asia-Pacific included the following:

- Russian leaders were often outspoken in criticizing U.S. policies in Asia. They criticized the hard-line U.S. approach toward North Korea in the six-party talks, and they welcomed the moderation the United States showed in reaching agreements at the end of the Bush administration. Russia worked with China in softening the U.S.-backed UN Security Council resolutions dealing with North Korea's missile and nuclear tests.
- Russia sided with Uzbekistan as it resisted U.S. pressure on human rights issues and democracy in 2005 and expelled American forces from the country. It worked with China in the SCO to call for a deadline for the withdrawal of U.S. and Western military forces from Central Asia.

- Russia periodically joined with China in declaring strong opposition to U.S. "hegemonism" in Asia-Pacific and world affairs.
- In 2005, Russia carried out a large military exercise with China under the auspices of the SCO that seemed targeted against U.S. security interests in the Asia-Pacific. Such exercises were conducted periodically. The exercise in May 2014 received widespread media attention as an alleged demonstration of China and Russia standing together against the United States and its allies in Asia in reaction to Western efforts to pressure and sanction Russia following the annexation of Crimea.[66]
- Russian sales of sophisticated arms to China amounted to over $1 billion annually in the recent past and severely complicated U.S. defense planning in the event of a military conflict with China over Taiwan. Of course, Russia sold even more weapons to India; it also made sales to regional states, notably Vietnam, which had a strong interest in building capacity to protect their interests against possible dominance from China.[67]

NOTES

1. Marlène Laruelle and Sébastien Peyrouse, *The Chinese Question in Central Asia: Domestic Order, Social Change, and the Chinese Factor* (London: Hurst and Co., 2012); Sally Cummings, *Understanding Central Asia* (New York: Routledge, 2012); Peter Golden, *Central Asia in World History* (New York: Oxford University Press, 2011); Dilip Hero, *Inside Central Asia* (New York: Overlook Duckworth, 2011); Martha Brill Olcott, *Central Asia's Second Chance* (Washington, DC: Carnegie Endowment for International Peace, 2005); Daniel Burghart and Theresa Sabonis-Helf, eds., *In the Tracks of Tamerlane: Central Asia's Path to the 21st Century* (Washington, DC: National Defense University Press, 2006); Boris Rumer, *Central Asia at the End of the Transition* (Armonk, NY: M. E. Sharpe, 2005); Celeste Wallander, "Russia: The Domestic Sources of a Less-than-Grand Strategy," in *Strategic Asia 2007–2008*, ed. Ashley Tellis and Michael Wills, 139–76 (Seattle, WA: National Bureau of Asian Research, 2007); Elizabeth Wishnick, "Russia and the CIS in 2005: Promoting East Asian Oil Diplomacy, Containing Change in Central Asia," *Asian Survey* 46, no. 1 (January–February 2006): 69–78.

2. Robert Blackwill and Meghan O'Sullivan, "America's Energy Edge," *Foreign Affairs*, March–April 2014, http://www.foreignaffairs.com/articles/140750/robert-d-blackwill-and-meghan-l-osullivan/americas-energy-edge; Brian Swint, "U.S. Will Be Energy Self Sufficient by 2035 by Shale, BP Says," Bloomberg News, January 15, 2014, http://www.bloomberg.com/news/2014-01-15/u-s-will-be-energy-self-sufficient-by-2035-on-shale-bp-says.html; National Committee on American Foreign Policy, *Central Asia/Caspian Sea Basin Region: After the Withdrawal of U.S. and NATO Troops from Afghanistan* (Washington, DC, November 2013).

3. Jim Nichol, *Central Asia: Regional Developments and Implications for U.S. Interests*, Report RL33458 (Washington, DC: Library of Congress, Congressional Research Service, March 21, 2014), summary page.

4. Lauren Dickey, "What China's Latest Deals Say about Its Grand Strategy," CNN, May 29, 2014, http://globalpublicsquare.blogs.cnn.com/2014/05/29/what-chinas-latest-deals-say-about-its-grand-strategy.

5. Chris Rickleton, "Russia and China Talk Past Each Other at SCO Pow-Wow," Eurasianet.org, June 25, 2014, http://www.eurasianet.org/node/68756; Yu Bin, "China-Russia Relations," *Comparative Connections* 16, no. 1 (May 2014): 141–52; Stephen Blank, *Toward a New Chinese Order in Asia: Russia's Failure* (Seattle, WA: National Bureau of Asian Research, March 2011).

6. Nichol, *Central Asia*, 2014, 17–19.

7. Laruelle and Peyrouse, *The Chinese Question in Central Asia*; Cummings, *Understanding Central Asia*; Olcott, *Central Asia's Second Chance*; Burghart and Sabonis-Helf, *In the Tracks of Tamerlane*; Rumer, *Central Asia at the End of the Transition*. This assessment also draws from Jim Nichol, *Central Asia's Security: Issues and Implications for U.S. Interests*, Report RL30294 (Washington, DC: Library of Congress, Congressional Research Service, January 7, 2005), and Nichol, *Central Asia*, 2014.

8. *CIA World Factbook 2014*, "Kazakhstan Economy," https://www.cia.gov/library/publications/the-world-factbook/geos/print/country/countrypdf_kz.pdf.

9. *CIA World Factbook 2014*, "Uzbekistan Economy," https://www.cia.gov/library/publications/the-world-factbook/geos/uz.html.

10. *CIA World Factbook 2014*, "Turkmenistan Economy," https://www.cia.gov/library/publications/the-world-factbook/geos/tx.html.

11. *CIA World Factbook 2014*, "Tajikistan Economy," https://www.cia.gov/library/publications/the-world-factbook/geos/ti.html.

12. *CIA World Factbook 2014*, "Kyrgyzstan Economy," https://www.cia.gov/library/publications/the-world-factbook/geos/kg.html.

13. Kathleen Collins, "The Limits of Cooperation: Central Asia, Afghanistan and the New Silk Road," *Asia Policy*, no. 17 (January 2014): 18–27; National Committee on American Foreign Policy, *Central Asia/Caspian Sea Basin*.

14. Olcott, *Central Asia's Second Chance*, 212–15.

15. International Crisis Group, *Uzbekistan: In for the Long Haul*, Asia Briefing No. 45 (Brussels: International Crisis Group, 2006).

16. International Crisis Group, *Tajikistan's Politics: Confrontation or Consolidation?*, Asia Briefing No. 33 (Brussels: International Crisis Group, 2004).

17. Robert Sutter, *Chinese Foreign Relations* (Lanham, MD: Rowman & Littlefield, 2012), 250–65.

18. Rollie Lal, *Central Asia and Its Neighbors: Security and Commerce at the Crossroads* (Santa Monica, CA: RAND Corporation, 2006); Sumitha Narayanan Kutty, "Iran and Afghanistan: The Urgent Need for Inclusive Regional Diplomacy," *Asia Policy*, no. 17 (January 2014): 40–47.

19. Nichol, *Central Asia*, 2014, 68–71.

20. Olga Oliker and David Shlapak, *U.S. Interests in Central Asia: Policy Priorities and Military Roles* (Santa Monica, CA: RAND, 2005); Robert Sutter, "The United States and Asia in 2006: Crisis Management, Holding Patterns, and Secondary Initiatives," *Asian Survey* 47, no. 1 (January–February 2007): 19–20.

21. Blackwill and O'Sullivan, "America's Energy Edge."

22. Susan Lawrence, *Mongolia: Issues for Congress*, Report R41867 (Washington, DC: Library of Congress, Congressional Research Service, June 14, 2011), summary page.

23. This discussion of Mongolia's economy is taken from *CIA World Factbook 2014*, "Mongolia Economy," https://www.cia.gov/library/publications/the-world-factbook/geos/mg.html; see also Lawrence, *Mongolia*, 5–10.

24. U.S. Department of State, "Background Note: Mongolia," July 2007, http://www.state.gov/r/pa/ei/bgn/2779.htm; Lawrence, *Mongolia*, 10–21.

25. Discussed in Lawrence, *Mongolia*, 10.

26. Ibid.

27. Roman Kozhevnikov, "Afghan Neighbor Tajikistan Ratifies Base Deal with Russia," *Reuters*, October 1, 2013, http://www.reuters.com/article/2013/10/01/us-tajikistan-russia-idUSBRE9900CZ20131001; Mark Vinson, "Russo-Tajik Relations Cool over Failure to Ratify Basing Agreements," Jamestown Foundation, *Eurasia Daily Monitor* 10, no. 85 (May 6, 2013).

28. Nichol, *Central Asia*, 2014, 13.

29. Ibid., 14.

30. Margarita Assenova, "Kazakhstan Expands Economic Cooperation with Russia, but Guards Own Interests," Jamestown Foundation, *Eurasia Daily Monitor* 10, no. 207 (November 18, 2013); Sergei Blagov, "Littoral States Struggle to Agree on the Caspian Settlement," Jamestown Foundation, *Eurasia Daily Monitor* 8, no. 88 (May 6, 2011).

31. Pavel Feigenhauer, "Russia, Kazakhstan and Belarus Sign Eurasian Economic Union," Jamestown Foundation, *Eurasia Daily Monitor* 11, no. 100 (May 29, 2014).

32. "Kyrgyzstan Aims to Join Eurasian Economic Union by Year-End—President," *Sputnik International*, May 29, 2014, http://en.ria.ru/world/20140529/190215559/Kyrgyzstan-Aims-to-Join-Eurasian-Economic-Union-by-Year-End-.html.

33. Peter Rutland, "Russia's Economic Role in Asia: Toward Deeper Integration," in *Strategic Asia 2006–2007*, ed. Ashley Tellis and Michael Wills, 173–204 (Seattle, WA: National Bureau of Asian Research, 2006).

34. Jim Nichol, coordinator, *Russian Political, Economic and Security Issues and U.S. Interests*, Report RL33407 (Washington, DC: Library of Congress, Congressional Research Service, March 31, 2014); Wallander, "Russia: The Domestic Sources of a Less-than-Grand Strategy"; Wishnick, "Russia and the CIS in 2005."

35. Joshua Kucera, "As 2014 Approaches, SCO Role in Afghanistan Remains Unclear," Eurasianet.org, September 13, 2013, http://www.eurasianet.org/node/67505; Mark Katz, "Putin's Predicament: Russia and Afghanistan after 2014," *Asia Policy*, no. 17 (January 2014): 13–18; Collins, "The Limits of Cooperation"; Zhao Huasheng, "Chinese Views of Post-2014 Afghanistan," *Asia Policy*, no. 17 (January 2014): 54–59.

36. Iacob Koch-Weser and Craig Murray, "The Russia-China Gas Deal: Background and Implications for the Broader Relationship," Staff Research Backgrounder (Washington, DC: U.S.-China Economic and Security Review Commission, June 9, 2014), http://origin.www.uscc.gov/sites/default/files/Research/China%20Russia%20gas%20deal_Staffbackgrounder.pdf.

37. Stephen Blank, "Russia and Vietnam Team Up to Balance China," *National Interest*, April 7, 2014, http://nationalinterest.org/commentary/russia-vietnam-team-balance-china-10195; Blank, *Toward a New Chinese Order in Asia*.

38. "Vladimir Putin and Shinzo Abe Hail Cordial Japan-Russia Relations," *South China Morning Post*, February 10, 2014, http://www.scmp.com/news/asia/article/1424843/vladimir-putin-and-shinzo-abe-hail-cordial-japan-russia-relations.

39. Sergei Radchenko, "Russia Elusive Quest for Influence in Asia," *The Diplomat*, May 20, 2014, http://thediplomat.com/2014/05/russias-elusive-quest-for-influence-in-asia.

40. The White House, "National Security Strategy of the United States," March 16, 2006, http://www.presidentialrhetoric.com/speeches/03.16.06.html.

41. Kathleen Collins and William Wohlforth, "Central Asia: Defying 'Great Game' Expectations," in *Strategic Asia 2003–2004*, ed. Richard Ellings and Aaron Friedberg, 291–320 (Seattle, WA: National Bureau of Asian Research, 2003); Michael Milhaka, "Not Much of a Game: Security Dynamics in Central Asia," *China and Eurasia Forum Quarterly* 5, no. 2 (2007): 21–39; Alexander Cooley, "After Afghanistan, a New Great Game," *New York Times*, August 21, 2014, http://www.nytimes.com/2012/08/22/opinion/after-afghanistan-a-new-great-game.html?.

42. This assessment of U.S. assistance is based on Nichol, *Central Asia*, 2014, 57.

43. Nichol, *Central Asia*, 2006, 14.

44. Ibid., 15.

45. Kenley Butler, "Weapons of Mass Destruction in Central Asia" (issue brief, Nuclear Threat Initiative [NTI], Washington, DC, October 2002), http://www.nti.org/e_research/e3_19a.html.

46. Lionel Beehner, "U.S. Military Bases in Central Asia" (backgrounder, Council on Foreign Relations, Washington, DC, July 26, 2005), http://www.cfr.org/publication/8440.

47. Jim Nichol, *Uzbekistan's Closure of the Airbase at Karshi-Khanabad: Context and Implications*, Report RS22295 (Washington, DC: Library of Congress, Congressional Research Service, October 7, 2005); Lt. Col. Max Despain, "Transit Center at Manas Hosts Transfer Ceremony," Transit Center at Manas, June 3, 2014, http://www.manas.afcent.af.mil/news/story.asp?id=123413098; Nichol, *Central Asia*, 2014, 67–71.

48. Nichol, *Central Asia*, 2006, 18.

49. Jim Nichol, *Unrest in Uzbekistan: Context and Implications*, Report RS22161 (Washington, DC: Library of Congress, Congressional Research Service, June 8, 2005).

50. Steven Lee Myers and Ilan Greenberg, "For Kazakh Leader's Visit, U.S. Seeks a Balance," *New York Times*, September 28, 2006; C. J. Chivers, "U.S. Courting a Somewhat Skittish Friend in Central Asia," *New York Times*, June 21, 2007; both cited in Robert Sutter, *The United States in Asia* (Lanham, MD: Rowman & Littlefield, 2009), 140.

51. Bernard Gelb, *Caspian Oil and Gas: Production and Prospects*, Report RS21190 (Washington, DC: Library of Congress, Congressional Research Service, March 4, 2006).

52. Roger McDermott, "Kazakhstan's Partnership with NATO: Strengths, Limits and Prognosis," *China and Eurasia Forum Quarterly* 5, no. 1 (2007): 7–20.

53. Information in this section comes from Lawrence, *Mongolia*; Sutter, *The United States in Asia*, 141–42; U.S. Department of State, "Background Note: Mongolia," February 2008, http://www.state.gov/r/pa/ei/bgn/2779.htm.

54. Lawrence, *Mongolia*, 15.

55. "The Khaan Quest 2014 Is Set to Take Place," Infomongolia.com, http://www.infomongolia.com/ct/ci/7035 (accessed July 9, 2014).

56. Sutter, *The United States in Asia*, 142–45; Stuart Goldman, *Russian Political, Economic, and Security Issues and U.S. Interests*, Report 33407 (Washington, DC: Library of Congress, Congressional Research Service, January 18, 2007); Stephen Hanson, "Russia: Strategic Partner or Evil Empire?," in *Strategic Asia 2004–2005*, ed. Ashley Tellis and Michael Wills, 163–99 (Seattle, WA: National Bureau of Asian Research, 2004).

57. U.S. Department of State, *Russia: Country Report on Human Rights Practices, 2006* (Washington, DC: Government Printing Office, 2007); U.S. Department of State, *Russia: Country Report on Human Rights Practices, 2006* (Washington, DC: Government Printing Office, 2013); both available at http://www.state.gov/j/drl/rls/hrrpt.

58. Wallander, "Russia: The Domestic Sources of a Less-than-Grand Strategy."

59. Nichol, *Russian Security, Economic and Political Issues*, summary pages.

60. William Wohlforth, "Russia," in *Strategic Asia 2002–2003: Asian Aftershocks*, ed. Richard J. Ellings and Aaron L. Friedberg, 183–222 (Seattle, WA: National Bureau of Asian Research, 2002).

61. Goldman, *Russian Political, Economic, and Security Issues*, 16.

62. Stephen Hanson, "Russia: Strategic Partner or Evil Empire?," in *Strategic Asia 2004–2005*, ed. Ashley Tellis and Michael Wills, 175–76 (Seattle, WA: National Bureau of Asian Research, 2004).

63. Joseph Ferguson, "Putin Picks a Successor," *Comparative Connections* 9, no. 4 (January 2008), 48–50.

64. Nichol, *Russian Political, Economic and Security Issues*, summary pages.

65. Steven Pifer, "Ukraine, Russia and the U.S. Policy Response" (Washington, DC: Brookings Institution, June 5, 2014), http://www.brookings.edu/research/testimony/2014/06/05-ukraine-russia-us-policy-response-pifer.

66. "China to Conduct Naval Drills with Russia in East China Sea," Reuters, April 30, 2014, http://www.reuters.com/article/2014/04/30/us-china-russia-idUSBREA3T0WK20140430.

67. Loro Horta, "From Russia without Love: Russia Resumes Weapons Sales to China," CSIS Pacific Forum, *PacNet*, no. 89 (December 12, 2013), http://csis.org/publication/pacnet-89-russia-without-love-russia-resumes-weapons-sales-china.

Chapter Eleven

The Future of U.S.-Asian Relations

Looking out in late 2014, a serious problem for effective U.S. policy and relations in the Asia-Pacific involves American sustainability and will. U.S. elite and public opinion and the elites and publics among friends and foes in the Asia-Pacific no longer see the proud and confident America that freely provided common goods of broad regional benefit while pursuing at times assertive, disruptive, and self-interested policies at odds with regional priorities in the post–Cold War period. President Obama ends his sixth year in office facing a divided government with adversaries in the Republican Party determined to limit significant accomplishments of his administration, foreign and domestic. Partisanship and acute disagreements over government spending block presidential initiatives and thwart effective policy. They preoccupy the president and his senior staff, sometimes to the point of disrupting plans for presidential visits and involvement with important foreign policy matters, including those in the Asia-Pacific.[1]

Continued wrangling over domestic issues comes amid perilous international developments that the United States and its partners find very difficult to resolve. The hope of progress as a result of the so-called Arab Spring in the Middle East has been dashed by the prolonged bloody civil conflict in Syria, continued armed combat in Libya, the return of military-led authoritarianism in Egypt, and the collapse of Iraqi governance in large parts of the country now under control of heavily armed Islamic extremists. Tense Israeli-Palestinian relations have worsened. Russian military coercion of Ukraine continues after Moscow's blatant grab of Crimea following disagreements with the West-leaning government in Kiev.

Against this background, President Obama at the commencement exercises at West Point on May 28, 2014, followed his decision to withdraw U.S. forces from their thirteen-year commitment to help stabilize Afghanistan and his earlier decision to withdraw U.S. forces from their protracted involvement in Iraq with a new national security doctrine that distances his administration from George W. Bush's policy of preemptive war. While reassuring to Americans who have become war weary with costly and inconclusive military commitments, the speech foreshadowed to many at home and abroad a new reluctance on the part of the United States to lead strongly in the resolution of important international security problems.[2]

The recent American posture adds to uncertainty about U.S. leadership amid the continued changes in the Asia-Pacific examined in this book. As noted in chapter 1, post–Cold War dynamics in the region are seen as determined by five sets of factors:

1. the changing power relationships among Asia's leading countries (e.g., the rise of China and India, change in Japan, rising or reviving middle powers—South Korea, Indonesia, Australia);
2. the growing impact of economic globalization and related international information interchange;
3. the ebb and flow of tensions in the Korean Peninsula and southwestern Asia, and the broader U.S.-backed efforts against terrorism and the proliferation of weapons of mass destruction;
4. the rise of Asian multilateralism; and
5. the changing extent of U.S. engagement with and withdrawal from involvement with Asian matters.

Adherents to the realist school of international affairs have been active in discussing U.S. policy and relations in Asia. As noted in chapter 5, many foresee serious trouble ahead on account of China's rise and the challenge it poses for U.S. leadership in Asia. On one side are those who urge the United States to prepare resolutely for a protracted struggle that might lead to war. On the other side are those who judge that China's rise has reached a point where the United States needs to come to terms with China now before it is too late to avoid full American retreat in the face of Chinese power.[3] Neither scenario—conflict or appeasement—is attractive to Americans.

Other proponents of the realist school of international relations,[4] including this writer, judge that the above assessments have an exaggerated view of China's strengths and an exaggerated view of American weaknesses. The assessment in chapter 5 examines in some detail Chinese and U.S. strengths and weaknesses in the prevailing dynamics of the Asia-Pacific. It finds that the Obama government's rebalance policy fits well with the interests of regional leaders who tend to incline toward realist perspectives in international affairs, but also meshes well with the priorities of those regional leaders reflecting liberal or constructivist views of international affairs. The strengths of the U.S. policy look even stronger when compared with China's recent approaches.

THE REBALANCE POLICY AND ASIAN PRIORITIES

The rebalance policy and relations have a broad scope—involving eastern Asia and the Indo-Pacific. Nonetheless, its priorities seem realistic even with recent U.S. government constraints. The United States is ending its very costly involvement in Afghanistan, a development likely to lead to reduction in the costly American involvement in Pakistan and reduction in the already declining American involvement in Central Asia. These areas are beyond the scope of the rebalance.

The Obama government's emphasis on the rest of the Asia-Pacific builds on a long record of deep American government and nongovernment engagement strengthened notably by pervasive and deeply rooted security and economic ties and large-scale Asian immigration to the United States that changes American society for the better while deepening positive U.S. ties to the region. While the Asia-Pacific has some authoritarian regimes, the vast majority of these governments seek legitimacy through economic development and good governance, methods generally in line with American values.

With such important world powers as China, India, and Japan, the Asia-Pacific warrants top American foreign policy attention in the years ahead to ensure that the United States has constructive and realistic policies with what is emerging as the most important region for American national security. The overall U.S. security effort has remained focused for many years on sustaining regional stability, a key requirement for Asia-Pacific governments pursuing economic development strategies.

The economic importance of Asia for the United States has become greater than any other region and continues to grow rapidly. As Secretary of Commerce Penny Pritzker said, "Home to nearly 60 percent of global GDP, the world's fastest growing economies, half of the world's population, and an emerging middle class that is eager for American products and services, the Asia-Pacific is a region of tremendous opportunity for United States businesses and workers."[5] As the United States pursues these opportunities, it does so in line with the liberal view of economic globalization emphasizing free flows of trade, investment, and other economic interchange that the vast majority of Asian leaders see in their interests.

The United States has a unique, long-tested record of bearing the costs and risks of sustaining regional stability and prosperity that is essential for the development and nation building sought by government leaders in the Asia-Pacific region. The United States is absolutely matchless in its willingness to bear the costs of its large military presence in the region and the risks of casualties if necessary to preserve regional stability. In reference to this reality, Australian National University specialist William Tow concluded an assessment warning of possible U.S. marginalization in Asia-Pacific politics with the following reminder: "There is still no substitute for Washington to deterring war on the Korean Peninsula, constraining both Chinese and Japanese nationalistic tendencies from intensifying security dilemmas in Northeast Asia, and providing an Asia-Pacific offshore balancing mechanism to prevent regional great power confrontations."[6] Meanwhile, America's open markets and active investment involve major costs in the form notably of a massive American trade deficit with the Asia-Pacific, which the United States bears without resorting to substantial protectionist measures.

At various times in the recent past, the United States pursued its policies in disruptive and unilateral ways; it carried out its objectives without enough attention to regional concerns. Against that sometimes troubled background, the Obama government has advanced other U.S. efforts to adapt American policies and relations to accord with Asian priorities; this recent U.S. effort is seen in ever-closer American cooperation with regional multilateralism and in strong American support for the constructivist goals of community building and national identity valued by Asian governments. Also, given the very recent sobering constraints in U.S. strategy noted above, there is little perceived danger in Asia of offensive, disruptive, or unilateral U.S. military, economic, or other policy actions contrary to the repeated stress by American leaders against one-sided change in the status quo.[7]

Fundamentally, the growing U.S. security, economic, and political relationships with the wide range of Asian-Pacific governments under terms of the Obama government rebalance has the effect of strengthening these governments and countries, reinforcing their independence and identity. While many of these governments disagree with U.S. policies regarding the Middle East peace process, electronic spying, and other issues, American interest in preserving a favorable balance of power and free economic and other access to the various states in the region is supported by the prevalence of such stronger independent actors.

The American interface with Asia-Pacific regional dynamics is not uniformly positive, however. Most notably, the U.S. military withdrawal from Southwest Asia leaves a power vacuum that provides an opportunity for radical insurgents and terrorists in Afghanistan and Pakistan to threaten nearby countries and others, perhaps even the United States. At minimum, the new situation in Afghanistan puts pressure on Russia, India, China, and Central Asian states to bear more of the burden of offsetting the threat of Islamic extremists in the area.

The prevailing Asian dynamics show only one possible challenger to U.S. leadership: China. Beijing's recent advances in efforts to take control of disputed territory in the East and South China Seas have come at the expense of American allies and have disrupted regional stability. The Chinese actions provide the focus of the arguments of some realists that China's rising power has reached a point where Beijing is prepared to confront the United States in competition for regional leadership. The Obama rebalance thus far has not shown clearly how the United States is prepared to deal with this rising Chinese challenge to the long-standing American role of security guarantor in the Asia-Pacific.

One major difficulty the United States faces in trying to dissuade and deter Chinese assertiveness is the fact that most Asian-Pacific governments expect the Obama government to carry out its improvement of relations in the region and its deterrence of Chinese assertiveness in ways that do not exacerbate China-U.S. tensions and thereby disrupt the Asia-Pacific region. Responding to these regional concerns, the Obama administration has at times made adjustments in its rebalance initiatives in ways that have given less public emphasis to sensitive military dimensions and competition with China, while stressing and carrying out an extraordinary series of top-level engagement efforts with China in order to manage tensions in line with regional concerns. The July 2013 Sino-U.S. presidential summit in California and the November 2014 summit in Beijing stressed positive engagement in order to manage serious differences and avoid conflict.

CHINA'S PRIORITIES IN ASIA: A MIXED PICTURE

China has accompanied its rise in regional prominence with a conflicted message of closer economic cooperation on a mutually beneficial (win-win) basis and often strident Chinese threats and coercive actions backed by civilian and military government power against neighbors that disagree with China, especially on issues of sovereignty and security. As China's stridency on these latter matters has grown with the expansion of Chinese coercive civilian and military power, Beijing signals Asian neighbors that China seeks to have its way at their expense ultimately through the use of hard power. Such practices mesh poorly with strong identity among regional states seeking to preserve their sovereignty, security, independence, and freedom of action. They fly in the face of the community-building priority of Asian multilateralism that is important to Southeast Asian governments in particular. China's cynical manipulation of ASEAN politics in using Cambodia, the ASEAN chair in 2012, to keep South China Sea disputes off the agenda of the group's meetings that year resulted in the most serious division in the group's history. It provided a graphic lesson on Chinese self-centered priorities coming at others' expense. [8]

As discussed in chapter 5, even though most Asian governments seek to get along with and benefit from relations with China and only a few governments in the region are prepared to confront China, many engage in active contingency planning to prepare for possible Chinese pressure and domination. In this context, many actively seek reassurance from closer relations with the United States in a variety of forms, notably in military, intelligence, and other security cooperation, thereby deepening and strengthening the already formidable American strategic integration with the region.

Meanwhile, Chinese leaders continue to focus on a narrow win-set of Chinese interests. They tend to avoid the kinds of costs and risks borne by the United States in support of perceived American interests in the broader regional order that are well recognized by regional governments, reinforcing the regional governments' support for closer American involvement in regional affairs. Given the U.S. military withdrawals from Iraq and Afghanistan and the gridlock seen in Washington politics, Asian leaders watch closely for signs of U.S. military withdrawal or flagging American interest in sustaining regional stability. The Obama government has affirmed its commitment to sustain the robust American security presence involving close military cooperation with the vast majority of Asian-Pacific governments built during the post–Cold War period. Thus far, it has been following these commitments.

Because of its economic growth and massive foreign exchange reserves, China looms much larger in Asia, notably in economic competition with the United States and with U.S.-backed financial institutions. China is Asia's and the world's largest trader. It is the second-largest site for foreign investment and an increasingly important foreign investor. It has a great deal of money that could be used to the benefit of its neighbors; neighboring governments see their interests well served by interchange with Chinese counterparts in the often protracted process of finding possible ways that such resources could be used in ways of mutual benefit according to China's win-win formula. China's location and advancing infrastructure connecting China to its neighbors are major positive attributes supporting closer Chinese relations with nearby states.

In 2014, China inaugurated the Asian Infrastructure Investment Bank (AIIB), and it pushed forward a new APEC-centered free trade area, the Free Trade Area of the Asia-Pacific. The moves were widely seen as challenging existing U.S.-backed international financial institutions like the Asian Development Bank and the World Bank, as well as the more rigorous U.S.-backed regional free trade pact, the Trans-Pacific Partnership (TPP).[9] What these Chinese initiatives actually amount to in practice remains to be seen. China already has a recent and reportedly mixed record of providing investment and loans to build infrastructure often constructed by Chinese firms with an eye toward easing Chinese access to resources and markets in Africa, Central Asia, and elsewhere in the developing world.[10] Because of Myanmar's long isolation from the West, China has long been the main provider of investment and infrastructure in that country. The Myanmar government showed clear dissatisfaction with Chinese practices as it halted a several-billion-dollar project and shifted toward greater economic and other interaction with the West in 2011.[11]

Meanwhile, it was explained earlier that much of the intra-Asian trade is dependent on foreign investment and access to foreign markets, the United States in particular. The United States sustains a very large trade deficit that undergirds the export-oriented economies of the region. Asian leaders are watchful for signs of American protectionism, but the Obama government's rebalance features strong emphasis on ever-greater American commitment to openness and free trade. By contrast, China's commitment to free trade is more selective and narrow. Beijing is prone to go well beyond international norms in retaliating against others over trade and other issues. China's cyber-theft of trade and economic information and property, currency manipulation, and other neomercantilist practices disadvantage neighboring economies.[12] China's disruption of Asian stability, notably by confronting Japan over territorial disputes, risks serious consequences for regional economic growth.

China argues against the growing U.S. security, economic, and political relationships with the wide range of Asian-Pacific governments under terms of the Obama government rebalance, which has strengthened these governments and countries, reinforcing their independence and identity. China's assertiveness shows its neighbors that Beijing expects them to put aside their independence and identity and accommodate a growing range of Chinese concerns, even to the point of sacrificing territory. U.S. strengthening of those in the region that resist China's pressure is seen in Beijing as a hostile act.

As noted above, the Obama government has also advanced markedly U.S. relations with the various regional organizations valued by Asian governments as part of what international relations scholars see as constructivist efforts to create and build institutions to ease interstate rivalries and promote cooperative relations.[13] The Obama government seems sincere in pursuing interchange that is respectful of the regional bodies. China also depicts close alignment with these groups, though China's more assertive ambitions regarding disputed territories have seen Chinese leaders grossly manipulate these bodies or resort to coercion and intimidation.

KEY VARIABLES

The uncertainty and debate surrounding the Obama rebalance initiatives and the future role of the United States in the Asia-Pacific noted at the outset of this book will continue in the years ahead. Despite the argument made here that current U.S. policy and relations much better fit the priorities of regional governments than do China's policy and practices, the fact remains that key variables can change, and with those changes could come shifts in Asian dynamics much less favorable to the United States.

In particular, the analysis in chapter 5 stresses the importance of the American willingness to bear the costs, risks, and commitments of regional security leadership. No other regional power or coalition of powers is willing to undertake even a fraction of these obligations. Nevertheless, the recent American withdrawals from Southwest Asia and the seeming American reluctance to take strong action against very recent international aggressors elsewhere raises questions about how reliable and sustainable the United States will prove to be in supporting regional stability in the Asia-Pacific. The Obama rebalance asserts that those requirements will be met, but prudence mandates that regional leaders watch carefully for American failures to meet security commitments. Such failures could result in recalibration of regional states' security calculus with a more marginal role for the United States.

Another important dimension of American regional leadership discussed in chapter 5 involves the willingness and ability of the United States to absorb the cost of a massive annual trade deficit with Asia without resorting to serious protectionist practices. Despite the Obama government's commitment to the freer trade standards in the proposed Trans-Pacific Partnership, such American economic openness could change. If the United States were to become protectionist, the majority of regional states that depend on exports for growth would presumably need to recalibrate their policies, giving less importance to the United States.

A third variable has to do with China and its relations with Asian countries. The assessment in chapter 5 shows that China has made mediocre progress in advancing Chinese influence in the region in the twenty-five years since the end of the Cold War. That second-rate record could change if China were to adopt less conflicted and more accommodating policies toward its neighbors, or if Chinese neighbors were to see their interests best served by accommodating Chinese interests even at the expense of their independence and key interests, or if some combination of these two reasons were to develop.

A final variable involves the dynamic in China-U.S. relations. Will the Obama government be able to come up with an effective mix of positive and negative incentives that can dissuade and deter China from its assertive advances in control of disputed territory in the East and South China Seas? And will the mix of American incentives avoid a serious disruption or confrontation in U.S.-China relations that would significantly upset the Asian stability sought by most regional governments? U.S. failure in this effort could undermine regional interest in continued American leadership and could also lead to recalibration upward of the priority of accommodating a demanding but powerful China.

RECOMMENDATIONS FOR U.S. POLICY

While the United States faces numerous difficulties at home and abroad, the assessment of this book shows that the Obama government's rebalance efforts reinforce the long-standing sinews of American influence and power in the region. The efforts fit well with regional dynamics in the Asia-Pacific and should be pursued. They provide a good framework for deepening constructive American security, economic, and political relations with what is emerging as the most important world region.

Some of the proposed U.S. policy advances seen in the rebalance, such as the Trans-Pacific Partnership multilateral economic arrangement, may be difficult to achieve. Notably, partisanship in the United States makes it difficult for President Obama to obtain from Congress the trade promotion authority he needs in order to convince Asia-Pacific economic partners of the seriousness of American support for the TPP. The assessment of this book shows that such advances as the successful conclusion of the TPP are important for closer U.S.-Asia-Pacific economic relations, but even more important in the economic area is the sustained openness of the United States to economic interchange with Asia. The Obama government's commitment to even greater economic openness under the TPP reassures Asia-Pacific traders that the United States, despite the costs of a very large trade deficit, sees its interests best served in avoiding protectionism and in working cooperatively with its Asia-Pacific economic partners.

A different kind of economic challenge could arise from the yet-to-be-determined results of China's recent widely publicized efforts to promote Chinese investment, trade, infrastructure development, and related Chinese-backed financial institutions like the Asian Infrastructure Investment Bank and wide-ranging free trade plans like the Free Trade Area of the Asia-Pacific (FTAAP). On the one hand, some projections forecast clear Chinese ascendance and U.S. decline.[14] On the other hand, despite China's long-standing position as the region's leading trader, continuing Chinese self-serving economic practices in line with a narrowly defined Chinese win-set under Beijing's ubiquitous "win-win" formula in international affairs have had mixed success in advancing Chinese influence in the Asia-Pacific and elsewhere.

In the security area, the rebalance promises to sustain the American security commitment to the region, despite the very large budget outlays and the risks of confrontation and conflict leading to casualties of American military personnel. Experienced officials in the region understand the uniquely influential depth and breadth of American military, intelligence, and other security involvement with almost all Asia-Pacific countries. Most regional governments welcome increased U.S. attention to this involvement and the various generally modest advances seen under the rubric of the rebalance policy. The major exception is China. As noted above, most Asian governments want the United States to sustain and advance its security involvement without major disruption in the region on account of confrontation between China and the United States. Thus far, the Obama government has succeeded in this delicate balancing act by actions within the framework of the rebalance. It has met with regional approval while deepening strategic involvement throughout China's rim among Chinese neighbors wary of recent Chinese assertiveness and while sustaining close businesslike engagement with China.

Whatever impact the various domestic and foreign difficulties faced by U.S. leaders will have on these basic economic and security requirements of the rebalance remains to be seen. This book emphasizes the deep roots and well-established patterns of interchange in American cooperation with the region along with ever-growing nongovernmental American interaction with the Asia-Pacific. Despite acute partisanship in Washington, there are few opponents in Congress of the rebalance policy, and there are several who want a more robust American commitment to the region. [15] A bottom line for U.S. policy makers is to continue to pursue the course and recognize that setbacks in one specific initiative or another need not upset the overall positive trajectory, provided the United States sustains its support for the common goods of regional stability and prosperity.

Nevertheless, the fact remains that the rebalance does have gaps and shortcomings that need careful management.

- It remains unclear how the United States will address the threat of extremist and terrorist insurgents in Afghanistan and nearby countries following the pullback of American forces from Afghanistan. The decline in the U.S. commitment to this effort will affect relations with many concerned countries in the broader Asia-Pacific region. How the United States will deal with these consequences should be clarified, hopefully in ways that do not detract from overall U.S. objectives in the Asia-Pacific.
- North Korea remains an egregious exception among Asia-Pacific governments seeking legitimacy through effective development and nation building. Its nuclear weapons development and related ballistic missile development continues. The rebalance policies seem to provide no clear path forward to ease these ongoing problems. The United States continues to play the key role in deterring North Korean aggression, but what else should be done and why needs better clarification.

DEALING WITH CHINA'S ASSERTIVENESS

It became clear to American leaders in 2014 that the rebalance as currently implemented was insufficient to dissuade China from its incremental advances at its neighbors' expense in disputed territories in the East and South China Seas using coercion and intimidation short of military force. American leaders escalated public criticism of Chinese assertiveness, deepened strategic support for Japan and the Philippines in the face of Chinese coercion, and took China to task in various regional meetings.

Nevertheless, China's commitment to pursue its coercive and intimidating advances at others' expense remained strong despite international disapproval and criticism. The resulting increase in Chinese neighbors' deepening strategic cooperation with the United States seemed not to alter Chinese determination to have their way in the East and South China Seas. It was widely judged that more needed to be done.[16]

Options reportedly under consideration by the U.S. Pacific Command[17] included the following:

- More extensive use of surveillance aircraft in the region coupled with a greater willingness to publicize images or videos of Chinese maritime activity. Some U.S. officials believe the Chinese might be given pause if images of their vessels harassing Vietnamese or Filipino fishermen were publicized.
- The Pacific Command has also been asked to coordinate the development of a regional system of maritime information, which would allow governments in the western Pacific detailed information about the location of vessels—notably threatening Chinese vessels—in the region.
- The United States has supplied the Philippines, Japan, and other countries in the region with improved radar equipment and other monitoring systems and is now looking for ways to build this information into a broader regional network that shares the data in common efforts to offset Chinese probes.
- The Pentagon has also been working on plans for calculated shows of force, such as the flight of B-52s over the East China Sea last year after China declared an air defense information zone over the area. Options include sending U.S. naval vessels close to disputed areas.
- Other possibly more confrontational options include deploying the U.S. coast guard to the South China Sea to counter the activities of Chinese coast guard vessels and using U.S.-led convoys to escort fishermen from the Philippines and other nations into areas where they have been expelled by the Chinese.

Recent hearings in Congress, media accounts, and think tank assessments have shown American debate over the seriousness of China's challenge to the United States and what should be done.[18] The Chinese challenge has sharpened American focus on U.S. interests in the Asia-Pacific. The Chinese challenge has also reinforced a recent tendency among American foreign policy elites to view long-standing efforts by the Obama government to reassure China of American intentions regarding various security, economic, and other issues as counterproductive, with arguments for a tougher American stance gaining more support. For example, the decline in American interest in reassuring China seems to be illustrated by the following development. The thaw in the Taiwan Strait following the advent of the Ma Ying-jeou government elicited full support from the U.S. government, while prominent security and foreign policy practitioners and specialists and even some leaders in Congress argued during 2009–2011 for a pullback of American support for Taiwan in order to reassure China and ease U.S.-China tensions over the Taiwan issue. More recently, those calls for such American reassurance toward China over Taiwan have stopped amid calls by some for an upgrading of U.S.-Taiwan security and other ties in the face of China's growing assertiveness and expansionism.[19]

Meanwhile, American views of Chinese intentions in their economic engagement with America have tended to echo the sentiment of President Obama when he advised a couple of years ago that China was deliberately "gaming" the international economic system to the detriment of the United States. The U.S. reluctance to support the Chinese AIIB and FTAAP noted above underline deep suspicion of Chinese economic initiatives. And the president's more recent portrayal of China as a free rider as far as costs and obligations in dealing with international trouble spots registered little disapproval in the United States.[20]

Against this background of greater wariness and lower American expectations in dealing with China, Americans have come to view more seriously China's challenge in the Asia-Pacific region and have viewed American interests challenged by China as more important than previously acknowledged. On one side there remain advocates anxious to avoid a deepening security dilemma with China or who for other reasons argue that American interests in the disputed territories are limited to the territories themselves, which are of low value, and freedom of navigation, which has not been significantly affected by the Chinese expansion. In contrast, the Obama government views the challenges more seriously, as they have an impact on U.S. relations with allies and they are carried out by coercive means beyond the bounds of international norms. The sometimes strident rhetoric coming from U.S. officials portrays the Chinese moves as a fundamental challenge to the prevailing U.S.-backed order in Asia.[21]

Of course, given the major American foreign policy preoccupations else-where, the Obama government devotes comparatively less attention and concern to Chinese expansion in disputed nearby areas. American actions show that the disagreements with China in Asia are of lower priority than issues relating to Iraq, Syria, Russia, Ukraine, Afghanistan, and probably others. The U.S. government posture has been reactive, vacillating between periodic harsh statements against Chinese coercive behavior and muting disputes, notably in the lead-up to U.S.-China summits in 2013 and 2014. The Obama rebalance policy includes improved surveillance capabilities for allies and partners and proposals dealing with territorial issues according to the rule of law that are criticized by China. The U.S. government waits to see if U.S. rhetorical opposition and resistance to Chinese expansionism from Japan, Vietnam, and the Philippines will dissuade Beijing from further advance.

On the other side is a growing contingent of congressional security officials, think tank representatives, academics, and other specialists who argue that the stakes are actually very high for America in the dispute with China over the Asia-Pacific.[22] One school of thought views the current situation with some alarm, arguing for much stronger American defense buildup along with military actions in direct support of allies facing Chinese coercion in disputed regions. They see Chinese intentions as malevolent, seeking to undermine the American alliance system and push the United States away from China's periphery. The outcome could lead to an Asia dominated by a Chinese government hostile to the United States and its international interests, thereby posing a grave threat to America.[23]

Another school of thought in this contingent—including this author—tends to view the current situation with less alarm, although the challenge to American interests is seen as serious. The rebalance policy captures a conventional view of American interests, but this school highlights that the policy depends on Asian countries having faith in American dependability. Chinese expansionism tests U.S. resolve. American friends and adversaries watch closely to see if the United States can come up with means to stop the Chinese expansion. If the United States does not come up with suitable means, the pragmatic Asian governments will understand better what they can and can't count on America to do. They will adjust toward Washington and Beijing, foreseeing an Asian order more influenced by China.

Perhaps of more importance to this school and this author is what a strong American position in support of its interests in Asia means for U.S. ability to deal with a China that cannot be reassured and thereby persuaded to cooperate with America; an alternative is that China must be shown by American leverage that the costs of challenging and undermining important American interests will result in negative consequences for China. The United States used to have more leverage in dealing with China on international economic issues when China needed American support for assistance from world insti-

tutions and access to technology, investment, and markets. The United States
used to have more leverage in dealing with China militarily over Taiwan, but
the power balance has eroded with China's massive military buildup opposite
Taiwan.

Despite such trends, this group judges that the situation in Asia shows
significant Chinese vulnerabilities and U.S. strengths that allow U.S. leverage to influence Beijing's cost-benefit calculations to avoid Chinese practices offensive to the United States. The balance of American and Chinese
power in Asia arguably represents the most important nexus of factors influencing even hard-line Chinese decision makers to avoid confrontation with
America. Shoring up American strengths and using them effectively against
Chinese vulnerabilities should have a higher priority in U.S. policy; it should
supersede the existing reactive American stance witnessing erosion of
American regional influence and Chinese expansionism. [24]

Chinese vulnerabilities in Asia are remarkable given that the region is by
far the arena of top-priority Chinese foreign policy attention. Yet, as noted
earlier, Chinese efforts since the Cold War to advance Chinese influence
have had mediocre results. Meanwhile, the United States enjoys good relations and broad support as it deepens security, economic, and diplomatic
relations with governments ranging from India to Japan and from Korea to
the Pacific Islands. Among other things, China today faces in Asia three hot
spots (North Korea, Japan, and the South China Sea) and two uncertainties
(Taiwan and Hong Kong)—none appear near resolution. [25]

As the United States government did successfully in 1982–1989 and
again in 2001–2002, [26] the Obama government is urged to assess carefully
current Chinese vulnerabilities. China is widely seen exploiting U.S. vulnerabilities in Asia. In particular, it does so by advancing territorial control at
neighbors' expense using civilian and not military power projection that
would prompt a response by the strong U.S. armed forces. The United States
remains in an advantageous position to do the same to China, with an eye
toward using proposals for such actions as leverage and warnings to China to
stop its efforts to undermine U.S. interests in Asia. The point is not that the
United States should actually exploit these vulnerabilities in all cases, but
rather that the United States should signal to China that it has the ability to do
so and might do so if China continues undermining U.S. interests in Asia. At
bottom, such positioning by the United States would advance U.S. leverage
on Chinese decision making that has an impact on the United States and its
interests in Asia.

Engagement should continue, but the United States should signal without
attribution disappointment with the meager results while China challenges
U.S. interests. American leaders should sidestep engagement used by China
in self-serving ways, suggesting in actions and not words that American
interests are better served with more attention to American power projection,

economic well-being, and working with various regional friends and multi-lateral groups. Meanwhile, American leverage over China can be made obvious in key areas, showing China the wisdom of cooperating with and not working against the United States. Of course, using U.S. leverage regarding Chinese weaknesses and vulnerabilities needs to be done with careful consideration of American and Chinese strengths and weaknesses, likely reactions in Asia, and other factors. In the United States, only the executive branch has the ability to understand and use these various elements fully. What are noted below are suggestions for consideration in that executive branch–led process. [27]

Regarding Taiwan, China faces great uncertainty as the ruling Nationalist Party, the Kuomintang (KMT), faces declining popularity and the opposition Democratic Progressive Party (DPP) rises to new prominence. The United States has the option to move away from its past indirect but important support for the KMT to a neutral stance in the 2016 presidential elections more consistent with general American practice. The move would seriously complicate Chinese interests, especially if the DPP were to win the 2016 elections. Yet such a step might seem warranted by the United States as a warning to Beijing that China's continued erosion of American interests in Asia will result in serious costs for China.

Meanwhile, American resolve vis-à-vis China requires a viable defense posture, which many strategists see requiring closer collaboration with Japan and the Philippines in a geographic ring along China's rim, with Taiwan in the middle. In this situation, the United States needs to be sure that Taiwan will play a role—probably a defensive role—compatible with American interests in the event of a crisis with China. Such close collaboration by the United States and Taiwan militaries would be done in secret but undoubtedly would be detected by Beijing; it would underline the costs to China that are resulting from U.S.-backed defense preparations prompted by Beijing's expansionism and intimidation and other efforts to undermine American interests.

Of course, Taiwan's current KMT government may prove to be wary of cooperating with America in this regard. More U.S. arms sales might help to persuade the government as well as to signal Beijing of U.S. resolve regarding Taiwan's defense. And the DPP leadership probably would be more open to such defense cooperation with the United States against China, thus adding to reasons for the U.S. government to alter existing favoritism toward the KMT.

China has ballistic missiles aimed at U.S. forces in bases in Asia that threaten Americans and undermine U.S. extended deterrence involving Japan in particular. The United States could and perhaps should begin deliberations to consider deploying conventionally armed ballistic missiles aimed at China for use in retaliation against any Chinese missile strikes against U.S. forces.

Other measures under America's so-called conventional "prompt global strike" could be considered in this regard. The consideration of such deployment would pose a clear cost as China would be compelled to divert resources to strengthen its weak ballistic missile defenses to protect sensitive Chinese sites at risk of conventional ballistic missile attack. Whether or not the United States goes beyond consideration to deployment of such weapons could be used as leverage in influencing China to avoid actions undermining American interests in Asia, for example, through its coercive expansionist practices in disputed territories at the expense of U.S. allies Japan and the Philippines and other neighbors.

Regarding undersea warfare, the United States should increase recent U.S. demonstrations of conventional missile and attack submarines that avoid detection by China and hold at risk of surprise attack and annihilation Chinese installations and force projections in disputed seas. China faces large costs in closing its serious defense gap in this area that can be highlighted or otherwise used by the United States in dissuading China from actions undermining American interests.

Regarding North Korea, China's continued support for that country is a vulnerability that can be highlighted by Congress and perhaps the administration, undercutting Beijing's Asian posture and reputation. The United States can respond to the nuclear threat posed by the North Korean regime (still supported by China) with discussions with Japan and South Korea involving possible transfers of offensive weapons and perhaps even deploying nuclear weapons to the region that would shore up the American extended deterrence with both allies in ways that would seriously complicate Chinese interests and policies. Each of these measures would seriously affect Chinese security interests in Northeast Asia, a cost China might not have to bear if it were more cooperative with the United States and less prone to undermining American Asian interests.

Regarding Asian economic interests, the United States could actively pursue constructive high-standard economic exchange measures with Asian-Pacific and European partners (e.g., the TPP) and with U.S.-backed international financial institutions while signaling indirectly its disappointment with the meager results of close economic dialogues with China and a clear American unwillingness to pursue measures favored by Beijing at odds with American trade and economic interests. The administration could articulate in congressional testimony or other suitable venues the meager results of economic dialogues with China and the reasons for American reservations about such Chinese initiatives as the Asian Infrastructure Investment Bank. In this process, discussion could highlight self-serving Chinese practices seen, for example, in China's long dominant and poor record in economic relations with Myanmar, and allies and associates could be warned of the downsides of a Chinese-led economic order. Chinese leaders seem to seek

American reassurance that the United States will not fundamentally challenge Chinese economic practices; the above will signal that the United States cannot be taken for granted in this regard, putting Chinese leaders on alert for shifts in U.S. policy costly to Chinese interests unless China proves to be more cooperative with Washington and less inclined to erode U.S. interests.

Regarding political interests, U.S. options include raising costs for China in Asia by showing greater support for popular sovereignty in Hong Kong (the so-called umbrella revolution) and also in Taiwan (the so-called sunflower movement)—areas of acute sensitivity and uncertainty in recent Chinese calculations. The United States can make clear that American interest in such steps is influenced in part by China's behavior at odds with U.S. Asian interests.

OUTLOOK: NEAR-TERM INDICATORS

As noted above, the Obama government under existing circumstances seems less than likely to undertake a much tougher approach to China or to give a much higher priority to dealing with the Chinese challenge to American interests in Asia. If China continues its incrementally expansionist tactics or escalates coercive expansion, the pressure for a harder U.S. response will probably rise. On the other hand, if China halts the expansion, the pressure for a harder U.S. response will probably decline.

The House of Representatives Armed Services and Intelligence Committees' leaders have recently come out for a more robust American posture focused on supporting important U.S. interests in Asia in the face of challenges from China. They will surely be joined by the incoming Senate Armed Services Committee chair Senator John McCain. How much influence this increase in congressional pressure will have on existing Obama government policy remains to be seen.

What does seem likely if the Chinese continue coercive expansion is that the issue of the U.S. posture in Asia in opposition to China will be important in the 2016 U.S. presidential campaign. Republican political strategists effectively used criticism of alleged naïveté and softness regarding China against the outgoing Democratic government in the 2000 election. Mitt Romney, the 2012 presidential challenger, used such charges especially regarding economic issues with China. If Chinese expansion continues in disputed regions along China's rim, the need to reevaluate existing American policy and to highlight the importance of American interests there seems likely and probably will favor a tougher U.S. approach to China.

Meanwhile, perhaps the greatest immediate consequence of Chinese expansionist moves and their impact on U.S. perceived interests and policy in

Asia is the negative impact it has on those leading Americans seeking cooperation with China.

The annual report of the U.S. China Economic and Security Review Commission (USCC) is not known for moderation about China. Yet every year the most moderate Commissioner William Reinsch issues a separate statement in the report providing corrections for what he sees as the many exaggerations in the report backed by his more hard-line colleagues.

His statement in the report issued in November 2014 is quite different because of China's assertive and coercive behavior. Two passages are excerpted from his statement (with some words italicized by me)[28]:

> It is a real disappointment for me to write these things. I have spent a good part of my professional life, beginning in graduate school, studying China, and arguing for greater efforts at mutual understanding that focus on the benefits of cooperation rather than give in to the mutual suspicion that is rapidly enveloping both of us. *I have always been an optimist about the relationship, but that view is becoming increasingly untenable, as China asserts itself in ways that are inevitably going to bump up against our interests in the region and in multilateral fora.* It is common knowledge that there is no shortage of people in each country who believe the other is an existential threat, and I have thought for some time the fundamental policy goal for each country should be to keep those people out of power. I have not changed my view about that, but it does not appear to be happening in China, which will only make it harder to prevent it from happening here. . . .
>
> Finally, close readers of this year's report will notice that it is less nuanced and less temperate with respect to China's military activities. That is deliberate, and while it is not my style, I did not object to it. *It appears the Chinese have embarked on a path intended to push the U.S. to choose between confronting them militarily or abandoning our friends and allies in the region, gambling that we will choose the latter. That is a dangerous path,* and the Commission is right to note it. Hopefully, adroit diplomacy, with both China and others in the region, will prevent us from having to make that choice.

CONCLUSION

The assessment of this book shows that China's recent assertiveness in disputed territory is a problem for the United States but not (at least not yet) a fundamental challenge to continued American leadership in the Asia-Pacific. Thus, the options listed above should be used carefully and in proportion to the threat to American interests posed by Chinese actions. Ideally, quiet demonstration of American willingness and ability to pursue some of these options may be enough to dissuade further expansion by China at the expense of its neighbors.

In the meantime, U.S. policy makers are urged to pursue the broad range of American interests in the Asia-Pacific within the framework of the Obama government's rebalance initiatives. The foundation for U.S. leadership at the level of government and at the level of the nongovernment sector is very strong. The incentives for developing closer U.S. relations in this ever more important world area are widely recognized and growing. China may be standing in the way in some respects, but Beijing's obnoxious and coercive behavior has the effect of opening even wider the doors of opportunity for American advancement in relations with most regional governments. In this context, well-thought-out U.S. responses promise fruitful results.

NOTES

1. William Tow, "The United States and Asia in 2013," *Asian Survey* 54, no. 1 (January–February 2014): 12–21; David Rothkopf, *National Insecurity: American Leadership in an Age of Fear* (New York: Public Affairs, 2014).

2. White House Office of the Press Secretary, "Remarks of the President at the United States Military Academy Commencement Ceremony," May 28, 2014, http://www.whitehouse.gov/the-press-office/2014/05/28/remarks-president-united-states-military-academy-commencement-ceremony; Paul Saunders, "A New Obama Doctrine at West Point?," *Tokyo Foundation Washington Update*, June 4, 2014, http://www.tokyofoundation.org/en/articles/2014/new-obama-doctrine.

3. Aaron L. Friedberg, *A Contest for Supremacy: China, America and the Struggle for Mastery in Asia* (New York: Norton, 2011); Hugh White, "The China Choice," book review by Andrew Nathan, *Foreign Affairs*, January–February 2013, http://www.foreignaffairs.com/articles/138661/hugh-white/the-china-choice-why-america-should-share-power.

4. Andrew J. Nathan and Andrew Scobell, *China's Search for Security* (New York: Columbia University Press, 2012).

5. "Secretary of Commerce Penny Pritzker Highlights Administration's Commitment to Asia-Pacific Region," Commerce.com, April 17, 2014, http://www.commerce.gov/news/secretary-speeches/2014/04/17/secretary-commerce-penny-pritzker-highlights-administration%E2%80%99s-com.

6. Tow, "The United States and Asia in 2013," 21.

7. "Secretary of State John Kerry Says U.S. Opposes Unilateral or Coercive Action to Change the Status Quo in the Senkaku Islands," Reuters, April 13, 2013, http://www.breakingnews.com/item/2013/04/14/secretary-of-state-john-kerry-says-us-opposes-any-unilateral-or-coerci.

8. "China Trumps ASEAN in the South China Sea," *Atlantic Sentinel* Asia briefing, July 19, 2012, http://atlanticsentinel.com/2012/07/china-trumps-asean-in-the-south-china-sea.

9. Ralph Cossa and Brad Glosserman, "A Tale of Two Tales," *PacNet*, no. 84 (December 1, 2014), http://csis.org/files/publication/Pac1484.pdf.

10. Howard French, *China's Second Continent* (New York: Random House, 2014); Marlène Laruelle and Sébastien Peyrouse, *The Chinese Question in Central Asia: Domestic Order, Social Change, and the Chinese Factor* (London: Hurst and Co., 2012).

11. Yun Sen, "China Adapts to New Myanmar Reality," *Asia Times Online*, December 23, 2013, http://atimes.com/atimes/Southeast_Asia/SEA-04-231213.html.

12. Wayne Morrison, *China-U.S. Trade Issues*, Report RL33536 (Washington, DC: Library of Congress, Congressional Research Service, December 16, 2013).

13. Evelyn Goh, *The Struggle for Order: Hegemony, Hierarchy and Transition in Post–Cold War East Asia* (New York: Oxford University Press, 2013).

14. "Will Asia Bank on China," Asia Society China File, October 14, 2014, http://www.chinafile.com/conversation/will-asia-bank-china.

15. "Oversight of the Military's Asia-Pacific Rebalance," U.S. Congress House Armed Services Committee, http://armedservices.house.gov/index.cfm/oversight-asia-pacific-rebalance (accessed July 11, 2014).

16. Geoff Dyer and Demetri Sevastopulo, "U.S. Strategists Face Dilemma over Beijing Claim in South China Sea," *Financial Times*, July 9, 2014, http://www.ft.com/intl/cms/s/0/b2176dea-0732-11e4-81c6-00144feab7de.html#axzz3MG7W1Fyo.

17. Geoff Dyer, Richard MacGregor, and Demetri Sevastopulo, "Pentagon Plans New Tactics to Deter China in South China Sea," *Financial Times*, July 10, 2014, http://www.ft.com/intl/cms/s/0/83c0b88e-0732-11e4-81c6-00144feab7de.html#axzz3MG7W1Fyo.

18. U.S.-China Economic and Security Review Commission, Hearing, "China and the Evolving Security Dynamics in East Asia," March 13, 2014, http://origin.www.uscc.gov/sites/default/files/transcripts/Hearing%20Transcript_March%2013%2C2014_0.pdf; Patrick Cronin, "How to Deal with China's Assertiveness: It's Time to Impose Costs," *National Interest*, December 4, 2014, http://nationalinterest.org/feature/how-deal-chinese-assertiveness-its-time-impose-costs-11785; Robert Sutter, "Asia's Importance, China's Expansion and U.S. Strategy," *Asia Pacific Bulletin*, October 28, 2014, http://www.eastwestcenter.org/publications/asia%E2%80%99s-importance-china%E2%80%99s-expansion-and-us-strategy-what-should-be-done.

19. Robert Sutter, "Hardening Competition with China: Implications for U.S. Taiwan Policy," *China-U.S. Focus*, September 5, 2014, http://www.chinausfocus.com/foreign-policy/hardening-competition-with-china-implications-for-us-taiwan-policy.

20. Doug Palmer and Matt Spetalnick, "Obama Hits China on Trade; Cautious on Currency Bill," Reuters, October 7, 2011, http://www.reuters.com/article/2011/10/07/us-usa-china-idUSN1E7950FF20111007; "Obama Labeling China as a 'Free Rider,'" *China Daily*, September 4, 2014, http://www.chinadaily.com.cn/world/2014-09/04/content_18543889.htm.

21. Simon Denyer, "China's Rise and Asian Tensions Send U.S. Relations into Downward Spiral," *Washington Post*, July 7, 2014, http://www.washingtonpost.com/world/asia_pacific/chinas-rise-and-asian-tensions-send-us-relations-into-downward-spiral/2014/07/07/f371cfaa-d5cd-4dd2-925c-246c099f04ed_story.html.

22. See source note 18.

23. Thomas Mahnken, *Asia in the Balance* (Washington, DC: American Enterprise Institute, 2012).

24. Sutter, "Asia's Importance, China's Expansion and U.S. Strategy."

25. Robert Sutter, "Dealing with America's China Problem in Asia: Targeting Chinese Vulnerabilities," *PacNet*, no. 58 (July 21, 2014), http://csis.org/publication/pacnet-58-dealing-americas-china-problem-asia-targeting-chinas-vulnerabilities.

26. Reviewed in Robert Sutter, *U.S.-Chinese Relations: Perilous Past, Pragmatic Present*, 2nd ed. (Lanham, MD: Rowman & Littlefield, 2013), 81–94, 123–28.

27. The options are discussed in Cronin, "How to Deal with China's Assertiveness"; U.S.-China Economic and Security Review Commission, Hearing, "China and the Evolving Security Dynamics in East Asia"; Sutter, "Asia's Importance, China's Expansion and U.S. Strategy"; CNAS-CSIS Workshop, "Imposing Costs on Coercion in the South China Sea," November 19, 2014, http://www.cna.org/news/events/2014-11-19-0.

28. USCC 2014 Annual Report, http://origin.www.uscc.gov/sites/default/files/annual_reports/Complete%20Report.PDF, 556–57.

Selected Bibliography

As noted in citations throughout this study, readers with an interest in contemporary U.S.-Asia relations are urged to consult, among others, the annual volume *Strategic Asia*, published by the National Bureau of Asian Research; the quarterly or tri-annual reviews of regional developments in the e-journal *Comparative Connections*; the wide range of very valuable reports published by the Congressional Research Service; the annual survey of Asia in the January–February edition of the journal *Asian Survey*; and the very useful reports published by the International Crisis Group.

Abramowitz, Morton, and Stephen Bosworth. *Chasing the Sun: Rethinking East Asian Policy*. New York: Century Foundation, 2006.
Acharya, Amitav. *The Making of Southeast Asia*. Ithaca, NY: Cornell University Press, 2013.
———. "Power Shift or Paradigm Shift? China's Rise and Asia's Emerging Security Order." *International Studies Quarterly* 58, no. 1 (March 2014): 158–73.
Acharya, Amitav, and Arabinda Acharya. "The Myth of the Second Front: Localizing the 'War on Terror' in Southeast Asia." *Washington Quarterly* 30, no. 4 (Autumn 2007): 75–90.
Alagappa, Muthiah, ed. *Asian Security Order*. Stanford, CA: Stanford University Press, 2003.
Armitage, Richard, and Samuel Berger. *U.S. Strategy for Pakistan and Afghanistan*. Washington, DC: Council on Foreign Relations, November 2010.
Armitage, Richard, and Joseph Nye. *CSIS Commission on Smart Power: A Smarter More Secure America*. Washington, DC: Center for Strategic and International Studies, 2007.
———. *U.S.-Japan Alliance: Getting Asia Right through 2020*. Washington, DC: Center for Strategic and International Studies, 2007.
Atanassova Cornelius, Elena, and Frans-Paul van der Putten, eds. *Changing Security Dynamics in East Asia: A Post U.S. Regional Order in the Making*. London: Palgrave Macmillan, 2014.
Bader, Jeffrey. *Obama and China's Rise*. Washington, DC: Brookings Institution, 2012.
Beckley, Michael. "China's Century? Why America's Edge Will Endure." *International Security* 36, no. 3 (Winter 2011/2012): 41–78.
Bell, Coral. "The Twilight of the Unipolar World." *American Interest* 1, no. 2 (Winter 2005): 18–29.
Berger, Thomas, ed. *Japan in International Politics: The Foreign Policies of an Adaptive State*. Boulder, CO: Lynne Rienner, 2006.

Biddle, Stephen. "Afghan Legacy: Emerging Lessons of an Ongoing War." *Washington Quarterly* 37, no. 2 (Summer 2014): 73–86.

Blair, Dennis C., and John T. Hanley Jr. "From Wheels to Webs: Reconstructing Asia-Pacific Security Arrangements." *Washington Quarterly* 24, no. 1 (Winter 2001): 7–17.

Borthwick, Mark. *Pacific Century: The Emergence of Modern Pacific Asia*. Boulder, CO: Westview Press, 2013.

Bush, Richard. *The Perils of Proximity: China-Japan Security Relations*. Washington, DC: Brookings Institution, 2010.

———. *Unchartered Strait*. Washington, DC: Brookings Institution, 2013.

———. *Untying the Knot*. Washington, DC: Brookings Institution, 2005.

Bush, Richard, and Michael O'Hanlon. *A War Like No Other*. Hoboken, NJ: Wiley, 2007.

Calder, Kent. *Pacific Alliance: Reviving U.S.-Japan Relations*. New Haven, CT: Yale University Press, 2009.

Carlin, Robert, and Joel Wit. *North Korean Reform*. Adelphi Paper 382. London: Routledge and International Institute for Strategic Studies, 2006.

Cha, Victor. *The Impossible State: North Korea Past and Future*. New York: HarperCollins, 2012.

———. "Powerplay: Origins of the U.S. Alliance System in East Asia." *International Security* 34, no. 3 (Winter 2009/2010): 158–96.

———. "Winning Asia: Washington's Untold Success Story." *Foreign Affairs* 86, no. 6 (November/December 2007): 98–113.

Christensen, Thomas. "Fostering Stability or Creating a Monster? The Rise of China and US Policy toward East Asia." *International Security* 31, no. 1 (Summer 2006): 81–126.

Chu, Yun-han, and Andrew Nathan. "Seizing the Opportunity for Change in the Taiwan Strait." *Washington Quarterly* 31, no. 1 (Winter 2007/2008): 77–91.

Chung, Jae Ho. *Between Ally and Partner: Korea-China Relations and the United States*. New York: Columbia University Press, 2006.

Cohen, Stephen. *The Idea of Pakistan*. Washington, DC: Brookings Institution, 2004.

———. *India: Emerging Power*. Washington, DC: Brookings Institution, 2001.

Crosston, Matthew. *Fostering Fundamentalism: Terrorism, Democracy and American Engagement in Central Asia*. Burlington, VT: Ashgate, 2006.

Davis, Elizabeth Van Wie, and Rouben Azizian. *Islam, Oil, and Geopolitics: Central Asia after September 11*. Lanham, MD: Rowman & Littlefield, 2006.

Foot, Rosemary. "Chinese Strategies in a U.S.-Hegemonic Global Order: Accommodating and Hedging." *International Affairs* 82, no. 1 (2006): 77–94.

Fravel, M. Taylor. *Strong Borders, Secure Nation: Cooperation and Conflict in China's Territorial Disputes*. Princeton, NJ: Princeton University Press, 2008.

Friedberg, Aaron. *Beyond Air-Sea Battle: The Debate over US Military Strategy in Asia*. Adelphi Paper 444. London: International Institute for Strategic Studies, 2014.

———. *A Contest for Supremacy: China, America, and the Struggle for Mastery in Asia*. New York: Norton, 2011.

———. "The Future of U.S.-China Relations: Is Conflict Inevitable?" *International Security* 30, no. 2 (2005): 7–45.

Glaser, Charles. "Will China's Rise Lead to War?" *Foreign Affairs* 90, no. 2 (March/April 2011): 80–91.

Green, Michael J. *Japan's Reluctant Realism*. New York: Palgrave, 2001.

Goh, Evelyn. *The Struggle for Order: Hegemony, Hierarchy and Transition in Post–Cold War East Asia*. Oxford: Oxford University Press, 2013.

Goldstein, Avery, and Edward Mansfield. *The Nexus of Economics, Security and International Relations in East Asia*. Stanford, CA: Stanford University Press, 2012.

Heginbotham, Eric, and George Gilboy. *Chinese and Indian Strategic Behavior: Growing Power and Alarm*. New York: Cambridge University Press, 2012.

Hughes, Christopher. *Japan's Re-emergence as a Normal Military Power*. Adelphi Paper 368–69. London: International Institute for Strategic Studies, 2004.

Ikenberry, G. John, and Michael Mastanduno, eds. *International Relations Theory and the Asia-Pacific*. New York: Columbia University Press, 2003.

Johnston, Alistair Iain. "How New and Assertive Is China's New Assertiveness?" *International Security* 37, no. 4 (Spring 2013): 7–48.

———. "Is China a Status Quo Power?" *International Security* 27, no. 4 (Spring 2003): 5–56.

Kang, David. *China Rising: Peace, Power, and Order in East Asia*. New York: Columbia University Press, 2007.

———. "Getting Asia Wrong: The Need for New Analytical Frameworks." *International Security* 27, no. 4 (Spring 2003): 57–85.

Kaplan, Robert. *Monsoon: The Indian Ocean and the Future of American Power*. New York: Random House, 2011.

Kapur, S. Paul, and Sumit Ganguly. "The Transformation of US-India Relations: An Explanation for the Rapprochement and Prospects for the Future." *Asian Survey* 47, no. 4 (2007): 642–56.

Kim, Samuel. *The Two Koreas and the Great Powers*. New York: Cambridge University Press, 2006.

Krauss, Ellis, and T. J. Pempel, eds. *The U.S.-Japan Relationship in the New Asia-Pacific*. Stanford, CA: Stanford University Press, 2004.

Kurlantzick, Joshua. *Charm Offensive: How China's Soft Power Is Transforming the World*. New Haven, CT: Yale University Press, 2007.

———. "Pax Asia-Pacifica? East Asian Integration and Its Implications for the United States." *Washington Quarterly* 30, no. 3 (Summer 2007): 67–77.

Lampton, David M. *The Three Faces of Chinese Power: Might, Money, and Minds*. Berkeley: University of California Press, 2008.

Laruelle, Marlène, and Sébastien Peyrouse. *The Chinese Question in Central Asia: Domestic Order, Social Change, and the Chinese Factor*. London: Hurst and Co., 2012.

Lieberthal, Kenneth, and Wang Jisi. *Addressing U.S.-China Strategic Distrust*. Washington, DC: Brookings Institution, March 2012.

Lincoln, Edward. *East Asian Economic Regionalism*. Washington, DC: Brookings Institution, 2004.

Mahbubani, Kishore. *The Great Convergence: Asia, the West, and the Logic of One World*. New York: Public Affairs, 2013.

Markey, Daniel. *Reorienting U.S. Pakistan Strategy: From Af-Pak to Asia*. Council Special Report No. 68. Washington, DC: Council on Foreign Relations, January 2014.

Medeiros, Evan. "Strategic Hedging and the Future of Asia-Pacific Stability." *Washington Quarterly* 29, no. 1 (Winter 2005/2006): 145–67.

Meijer, Hugo, ed. *Origins and Evolution of the US Rebalance toward Asia: Diplomatic, Military and Economic Dimensions*. London: Palgrave Macmillan, 2015.

Midford, Paul. *Rethinking Japanese Public Opinion and Security: From Pacifism to Realism?* Stanford, CA: Stanford University Press, 2011.

Miller, Alice Lyman, and Richard Wich. *Becoming Asia: Change and Continuity in Asian International Relations since World War II*. Stanford, CA: Stanford University Press, 2011.

Munakata, Naoko. *Transforming East Asia: The Evolution of Regional Economic Integration*. Washington, DC: Brookings Institution, 2006.

Nathan, Andrew, and Andrew Scobell. *China's Search for Security*. New York: Columbia University Press, 2012.

Olcott, Martha Brill. *Central Asia's Second Chance*. Washington, DC: Carnegie Endowment for International Peace, 2005.

Percival, Bronson. *The Dragon Looks South: China and Southeast Asia in the New Century*. Westport, CT: Praeger Security International, 2007.

Pollack, Jonathan, ed. *Asia Eyes America: Regional Perspectives on U.S. Asia-Pacific Strategy in the 21st Century*. Newport, RI: U.S. Naval War College, 2007.

———. *No Exit: North Korea, Nuclear Weapons and International Security*. London: Routledge and International Institute for Strategic Studies, 2011.

Pritchard, Charles. *Failed Diplomacy: The Tragic Story of How North Korea Got the Bomb*. Washington, DC: Brookings Institution, 2007.

Pyle, Kenneth. *Japan Rising: The Resurgence of Japanese Power and Purpose*. New York: Public Affairs, 2007.

Ross, Robert. "The Geography of Peace: East Asia in the Twenty-First Century." *International Security* 23, no. 4 (Spring 1999): 81–118.

Roy, Denny. *The Pacific War and Its Political Legacies*. Westport, CT: Greenwood Press, 2009.

———. *Return of the Dragon: Rising China and Regional Security*. New York: Columbia University Press, 2013.

Rozman, Gilbert. *Northeast Asia's Stunted Regionalism: Bilateral Distrust in the Shadow of Globalization*. New York: Cambridge University Press, 2004.

Rumer, Boris, *Central Asia at the End of the Transition*. Armonk, NY: M. E. Sharpe, 2005.

Rumer, Eugene. *China, Russia, and the Balance of Power in Central Asia*. Washington, DC: National Defense University Institute for National Security Studies, 2006.

Samuels, Richard. *Securing Japan: Tokyo's Grand Strategy and the Future of East Asia*. Ithaca, NY: Cornell University Press, 2007.

Saunders, Philip. *The Rebalance to Asia: U.S.-China Relations and Regional Security*. Washington, DC: National Defense University, Institute for National Security Studies, 2012.

Shambaugh, David. "China Engages Asia: Reshaping the Regional Order." *International Security* 29, no. 3 (Winter 2004/2005): 64–99.

———, ed. *Power Shift: China and Asia's New Dynamics*. Berkeley: University of California Press, 2005.

———, ed. *Tangled Titans: The United States and China*. Lanham, MD: Rowman & Littlefield, 2012.

Shambaugh, David, and Michael Yahuda, eds. *International Relations of Asia*. 2nd ed. Lanham, MD: Rowman & Littlefield, 2014.

Shirk, Susan. *China: Fragile Superpower*. New York: Oxford University Press, 2007.

Snyder, Scott. *The U.S.–South Korean Alliance: Meeting New Security Challenges*. Boulder, CO: Lynne Rienner, 2012.

The Stanley Foundation. *Economic Dimensions of New Power Dynamics in Southeast Asia*. Muscatine, IA: Stanley Foundation Policy Memo, July 12, 2007.

———. *New Power Dynamics in Southeast Asia: Issues for U.S. Policy Makers*. Muscatine, IA: Stanley Foundation, 2007.

Suh, J. J., Peter Katzenstein, and Allan Carlson, eds. *Rethinking Security in East Asia: Identity, Power, and Efficiency*. Stanford, CA: Stanford University Press, 2004.

Sutter, Robert. *U.S.-Chinese Relations: Perilous Past, Pragmatic Present*. 2nd ed. Lanham, MD: Rowman & Littlefield, 2013.

Swaine, Michael. *America's Challenge: Engaging a Rising China in the Twenty-First Century*. Washington, DC: Carnegie Endowment for International Peace, 2011.

Swaine, Michael, and Zhang Tuosheng. *Managing Sino-American Crises*. Washington, DC: Carnegie Endowment for International Peace, 2006.

Talbott, Strobe. *Engaging India: Diplomacy, Democracy and the Bomb*. Washington, DC: Brookings Institution, 2004.

Tellis, Ashley. *India as a New Global Power: An Action Agenda for the United States*. Washington, DC: Carnegie Endowment for International Peace, 2005.

———. "The Merits of Dehyphenation: Explaining U.S. Success in Engaging India and Pakistan." *Washington Quarterly* 31, no. 4 (Autumn 2008): 21–42.

Tow, William, ed. *Security Politics in the Asia-Pacific*. New York: Cambridge University Press, 2010.

Tucker, Nancy. *Strait Talk*. Cambridge, MA: Harvard University Press, 2009.

Vogel, Steven K. *U.S.-Japan Relations in a Changing World*. Washington, DC: Brookings Institution, 2002.

Wan, Ming. *Sino-Japanese Relations: Interaction, Logic, and Transformation*. Stanford, CA: Stanford University Press, 2006.

Weatherbee, Donald E. *International Relations in Southeast Asia: The Struggle for Autonomy*. 3rd ed. Lanham, MD: Rowman & Littlefield, 2014.

White, Hugh. *The China Choice*. Collingwood, Australia: Black Inc., 2012.

Yahuda, Michael. *The International Politics of the Asia-Pacific*. 3rd ed. London: Routledge, 2011.

Index